LOST FARMSTEADS
DESERTED RURAL SETTLEMENTS IN WALES

LOST FARMSTEADS
DESERTED RURAL SETTLEMENTS
IN WALES

edited by Kathryn Roberts

CBA Research Report 148
Council for British Archaeology
2006

Published in 2006 by the Council for British Archaeology
St Mary's House, 66 Bootham, York YO30 7BZ

British Library Cataloguing in Publication Data
A catalogue record for his book is available from the British Library

ISBN 1-902771-63-X

Text designed and typeset by Carnegie Publishing Ltd, Lancaster
Printed in the UK by The Alden Press, Oxford

The CBA acknowledges with gratitude a grant from Cadw towards the publication of this volume.

Front cover: Hafod Eidos, Ceredigion, (photograph by Mick Sharp for Cadw)

Back cover: (vertical strip) Fron Top in snow (Crown copyright: RCAHMW)
            (below) Platform at Hafod Eidos (photograph by Mick Sharp for Cadw)

CONTENTS

LIST OF ABBREVIATIONS

CCW	Countryside Council for Wales
CPAT	Clwyd-Powys Archaeological Trust
DAT	Dyfed Archaeological Trust (Cambria Archaeology)
GAT	Gwynedd Archaeological Trust
GGAT	Glamorgan-Gwent Archaeological Trust
ICOMOS	International Council on Monuments and Sites
NLW	National Library of Wales
NMR	National Monument Record for Wales
PRN	Primary Record Number (used for site identification within SMRs)
RCAHMW	Royal Commission on the Ancient and Historical Monuments of Wales
SAM	Scheduled Ancient Monument
SLA	Special Landscape Area
SMR	Sites and Monuments Records (held by the four regional archaeological trusts)
SSSI	Site of Special Scientific Interest

List of Figures

LIST OF TABLES

LIST OF CONTRIBUTORS

Judith Alfrey is an Inspector of Historic Buildings with Cadw. She is an historian whose research interests lie in the social history of building, in the field of vernacular architecture, especially small rural dwellings, farm buildings, and the stone-building traditions of the countryside.

David Austin holds the established Chair of Archaeology in the Department of Archaeology and Anthropology in the University of Wales, Lampeter. He is a landscape and settlement archaeologist, specialising particularly in the medieval and early modern periods in Britain and Western Europe. He has also conducted major excavation programmes on castles, villages, and farmsteads, including Carew Castle and its landscape in south Pembrokeshire. He is now working on the Cistercian monastery of Strata Florida and its landscape in central Ceredigion.

Astrid Caseldine is Cadw Environmental Archaeologist for Wales and a Research Fellow at the University of Wales, Lampeter. Astrid is currently responsible for environmental work on excavations in Wales funded by Cadw. Prior to this she was palaeoenvironmentalist to the Somerset Levels Project. She specialises in pollen analysis and the study of plant macrofossil remains. Her main research interests include the reconstruction of past environments, particularly the relationship between anthropogenic activity and environmental change, wetland archaeology and wetland environments, and the development of crop husbandry practices in Wales.

Martin Locock is Project Manager at the Archives Network Wales, National Library for Wales, Aberystwyth. Martin took part in this project when Projects Manager for the Glamorgan-Gwent Archaeological Trust. He read Archaeology and Anthropology at Fitzwilliam College, Cambridge, and worked on rescue and MSC excavations in the Midlands before moving to Wales in 1991. His main interests include post-medieval archaeology, garden archaeology, animal bone analysis, and theoretical approaches to historical archaeology. He has served on the Council of the IFA and the Society for Post-Medieval Archaeology.

David Longley is the Director of the Gwynedd Archaeological Trust.

Kathryn Roberts is an Inspector of Ancient Monuments with Cadw. Kathryn has worked for Cadw for seven years, initially as Assistant Inspector responsible for scheduling, and now as Inspector for south-west Wales. Kathryn studied archaeology at Cardiff and Cambridge Universities and before joining Cadw worked at the Royal Commission on the Historic Monuments of England and lectured at Trinity College, Carmarthen. Her interests include the archaeological application of geophysical survey techniques, heritage management and public presentation of historic sites.

Paul Sambrook is a Heritage consultant and partner of Trysor Heritage Consultancy, co-founded with Jenny Hall in 2004. Born in Neath, Glamorganshire in 1963, he is married, with three children and lives on a dairy farm in North Pembrokeshire. Paul graduated in Archaeology and Welsh (BA Joint Hons) from St Davids UC, Lampeter, 1986 and is a qualified teacher. He was previously employed from 1993 to 2004 as Project Manager with the Dyfed Archaeological Trust (Cambria Archaeology), where he increasingly concentrated on developing methodologies in outreach and community archaeology. His interests include following Neath-Swansea Ospreys rugby team, Welsh politics and collecting antiquarian books.

Robert Silvester is Deputy Director at Clwyd-Powys Archaeological Trust. After spells in Devon and Norfolk, Bob Silvester moved to Wales in 1989, where he now heads the field services section of the Clwyd-Powys Archaeological Trust. His main interests are in the medieval and post-medieval periods with an emphasis on settlement, churches and the historic landscape, as well as historic cartography.

George Smith is a Senior Archaeologist at Gwynedd Archaeological Trust. George has worked as senior archaeologist in Gywnedd for 13 years. Previously he excavated at Hadrian's Wall, Carlisle, at the Hospital of St Mary of Ospringe, Kent and at a variety of prehistoric sites in Wiltshire, Somerset, Devon and

Cornwall. Excavations in Wales include work at a prehistoric mountain-top burial cairn at Tre'r Ceiri, Llanaelhaearn, at the Bishop's Palace, Bangor and at a late medieval farmstead at Moelyci, Llandegai. He has carried out and published major surveys of prehistoric settlement, lithic scatters and funerary and ritual sites in north-west Wales, as well as surveys of coastal and intertidal areas and has authored publication of excavations of a multi-period site at Capel Eithin, Anglesey and of crop mark evaluations on the Lŷn Peninsula. He is currently working on a survey of prehistoric defended enclosures and carrying out research into Bronze Age upland funerary and settlement patterns.

David Thompson is Deputy Director at Gwynedd Archaeological Trust. David Thompson has lived and worked in north-west Wales for over 20 years, and now heads the Heritage Management and Landscape section of Gwynedd Archaeological Trust. His interests in recent years have concentrated on historic landscape characterisation, particularly in marginal areas.

ACKNOWLEDGEMENTS

The Deserted Rural Settlement Project was an ambitious undertaking, and the four Welsh Archaeological Trusts are to be applauded for their enthusiastic response to this demanding and time-consuming exercise. Many people were actively involved during the course of the project and unfortunately it is not possible to thank them individually for their valuable contributions.

The editor would like to congratulate the authors of the papers published in this volume for their most informative discussions. Thanks are also extended to those who contributed illustrative material, including Brian Williams for his excellent drawings, Nigel Jones who produced the computer distribution maps and also David Longley and Paul Jones. In addition, the editor is grateful to those individuals and organisations who made available photographic material; Toby Driver and Penny Icke of the Royal Commission on the Historical Monuments of Wales; and officers of the National Library of Wales and Welsh Archaeological Trusts for their valiant efforts in locating obscure requests.

Finally, sincere thanks must go to Dr Anthony Ward for his valuable comments on an early draft of this volume.

SUMMARIES

No traveller in Wales can fail to notice the abundance of abandoned houses and farmsteads which characterise much of its marginal and upland landscape. These often insubstantial remains are tangible evidence that for many hundreds of years successive communities occupied and exploited rural areas which today are largely depopulated.

The papers presented in this volume result from a five-year programme of field study of deserted rural settlements throughout Wales undertaken by Cadw and the four Welsh Archaeological Trusts. The project was set up to increase the level of understanding of rural settlement in Wales; it was also prompted by the sites' recognised vulnerability to destruction, and in order to create a basis upon which future management and protection strategies could be built. Work focused primarily (although not exclusively) on upland landscapes where field evidence is best preserved, and the site evaluations provide the most complete assessment of surviving remains in those areas to date. Following an introductory chapter, the main body of the volume is divided into three parts: *Regional examinations*, *General themes*, and *Conclusions and future developments*.

The regional examinations (while following broadly similar formats in terms of methodology and presentation of results) differ in terms of focus and analysis, reflecting regional variability in archaeological data and the extent of previous research. In Chapter 2 Robert Silvester produces a comprehensive synthesis of settlement morphology throughout central and north-eastern Wales, an area encompassing numerous diverse topographical units which, across time, have variable local historical contexts. In Chapter 3 Martin Locock presents a timely reconsideration of the nature of occupation on Gelligaer Common and discusses evidence for monastic upland exploitation. In Chapter 4 David Longley analyses and interprets in an explicitly comparative manner archaeological field evidence relative to historical evidence for medieval townships in Gwynedd, producing persuasive results which positively advance understanding of how settlement developed across the region in social and functional terms. In Chapter 5 Paul Sambrook draws extensively on supporting documentary and cartographic evidence to produce an informative review of the form and purpose of *lluestau* in 17th-century Ceredigion.

The second part of the volume addresses a range of general themes. In Chapter 6 George Smith and David Thompson outlines the challenges faced when excavating deserted settlement sites and demonstrates how limited but targeted intervention can produce positive outcomes. The excavations demonstrated the important role that environmental evidence can play in identifying the function and date of sites. In Chapter 7 Astrid Caseldine's cogent summary outlines both the potential and limitations of techniques employed in palaeo-environmental studies and demonstrates how they can be used to open up new avenues of investigation. In Chapter 8 Judith Alfrey presents an architectural historian's view, and argues a case for closer collaboration between archaeologists, historians and architectural historians, particularly in respect of exploring the origins of vernacular building traditions.

In the third section, Kathryn Roberts provides a digest of the principal findings of the regional and thematic studies and considers what has been accomplished (Chapter 9); and looks at the ways in which the data is now being used by organisations such as Cadw to manage and conserve both individual sites and the wider historic landscape (Chapter 10). However, as with all research, we are left with many unanswered questions and there remains considerable scope for further study. In Chapter 11 David Austin steps back from the project in order to place the findings within a broader context, and also puts forward a thought-provoking analysis of what archaeologists could and should be aiming to achieve in the future.

This volume may be the culmination of the Deserted Rural Settlement Project but is merely a staging point in our investigation. It is the sincere hope of all those who have contributed to the project that it will serve to inspire continued research into this most interesting of subjects.

Crynodeb

Ni all teithwyr yng Nghymru fethu â sylwi ar y tai a'r ffermydd anghyfannedd niferus sy'n nodweddu llawer o dirlun ymylol ac uwchdirol y wlad. Mae'r olion hyn, sydd yn aml yn ansylweddol, yn dystiolaeth ddiriaethol fod cymunedau olynol wedi meddiannu a defnyddio ardaloedd gwledig ers canrifoedd; ardaloedd sydd heddiw i raddau helaeth wedi'u diboblogi.

Canlyniad rhaglen bum mlynedd o astudiaethau maes o aneddiadau gwledig anghyfannedd ledled Cymru a gynhaliwyd gan Cadw a'r pedair Ymddiriedolaeth Archeolegol yng Nghymru yw'r papurau a gyflwynir yn y gyfrol hon. Sefydlwyd y prosiect i gynyddu'r lefel o ddealltwriaeth o anheddiad gwledig yng Nghymru; fe'i ysgogwyd hefyd gan y ffaith gydnabyddedig fod y safleoedd yn agored i ddifrod, ac er mwyn gosod sylfaen y gellid datblygu strategaethau rheoli a gwarchodaeth y dyfodol arno. Canolbwyntiodd y gwaith yn bennaf (er nad yn unig) ar dirluniau uwchdirol lle cedwir tystiolaeth faes orau, ac mae'r gwerthusiadau o'r safleoedd yn darparu'r asesiad mwyaf cyflawn o'r olion sy'n goroesi yn yr ardaloedd hynny hyd yma. Yn dilyn pennod gyflwyniadol, rhennir prif gorff y gwaith yn dair rhan: *Arch-wiliadau rhanbarthol*, *Themâu cyffredinol* a *Casgliadau a datblygiadau'r dyfodol*.

Mae'r archwiliadau rhanbarthol (tra'n dilyn fformat tebyg i raddau helaeth o ran methodoleg a chyflwyno'r canlyniadau) yn wahanol o ran ffocws a dadansoddiad, gan adlewyrchu amrywioldeb rhanbarthol data archeolegol a graddau'r ymchwil flaenorol. Ym Mhennod 2 darpara Robert Silvester synthesis cynhwysfawr o forffoleg anheddiad ledled canolbarth a gogledd ddwyrain Cymru, sef ardal sy'n cynnwys nifer o unedau topograffigol amrywiol sydd wedi cael cyd-destunau hanes lleol amrywiol dros y blynyddoedd. Ym Mhennod 3 cyflwyna Martin Locock ailystyriaeth amserol o natur anheddiad ar Gomin Gelligaer, a thrafodir tystiolaeth am ddefnydd mynachaidd o'r uwchdiroedd. Ym Mhennod 4 ceir dadansoddiad a dehongliad cymharol pendant gan David Longley o dystiolaeth faes archeolegol sy'n perthyn i dystiolaeth hanesyddol ar gyfer trefgorddau canoloesol yng Ngwynedd, sy'n cynhyrchu canlyniadau argyhoeddiadol sy'n cynnig datblygiad cadarn-

haol yn y ddealltwriaeth o sut y datblygodd anheddiad ar draws y rhanbarth yn nhermau cymdeithasol a swyddogaethol. Ym Mhennod 5 defnyddia Paul Sambrook y dystiolaeth ddogfennol a chartograffig sylweddol i gynhyrchu adolygiad llawn gwybodaeth o ffurf a phwrpas lluestau yng Ngheredigion yn y 17eg ganrif.

Mae ail ran y gyfrol yn mynd i'r afael ag ystod o themâu cyffredinol. Ym Mhennod 6 amlinella George Smith a David Thompson yr heriau a wynebir wrth gloddio annedd anghyfannedd, a dengys sut y gall ymyriad cyfyngedig a dargedwyd gynhyrchu canlyniadau cadarnhaol. Dangosodd y cloddiadau y rôl bwysig y gall tystiolaeth amgylcheddol chwarae yn y broses o nodi swyddogaeth a dyddiad safleoedd. Ym Mhennod 7 mae crynodeb argyhoeddiadol Astrid Caseldine yn amlinellu potential a chyfyngiadau'r technegau a ddefnyddir mewn astudiaethau palaeoamgylcheddol, ac arddangosir sut y gellir eu defnyddio i agor llwybrau ymchwil newydd. Ym Mhennod 8 cyflwyna Judith Alfrey farn hanesydd pensaerniol, gan ddadlau dros gydweithrediad agosach rhwng archeolegwyr, haneswyr a haneswyr pensaernïol, yn arbennig o ran archwilio tarddiad traddodiadau adeiladu brodorol.

Yn y drydedd adran, darpara Kathryn Roberts grynodeb o brif ganfyddiadau'r astudiaethau rhanbarthol a thematig, gan ystyried yr hyn a gyflawnwyd (Pennod 9); a chan ystyried y dulliau y defnyddir y data nawr gan sefydliadau fel Cadw i reoli a chadw safleoedd unigol a'r tirlun hanesyddol ehangach (Pennod 10). Fodd bynnag, fel gyda phob maes ymchwil, mae nifer o gwestiynau heb eu hateb a cheir cwmpas sylweddol ar gyfer astudiaeth bellach. Ym Mhennod 11 mae David Austin yn cymryd cam yn ôl o'r prosiect er mwyn gosod y canfyddiadau o fewn cyd-destun ehangach, gan hefyd gynnig dadansoddiad pryfoclyd o'r hyn y gallai ac y dylai archeolegwyr anelu at ei gyflawni yn y dyfodol.

Efallai mai'r gyfrol hon yw penllanw'r Prosiect Aneddiadau Gwledig Anghyfannedd, ond dim ond carreg sarn yw hi yn ein hymchwiliad. Mae pawb a gyfrannodd at y prosiect hwn yn gobeithio'n fawr y bydd yn ysbrydoli ymchwil parhaus yn y maes hynod ddiddorol hwn.

Résumé

Les gens qui voyagent au pays de Galles remarquent toujours compte qu'il y a énormément de maisons et de fermes abandonnées car c'est là une caractéristique d'une grande partie du paysage des hautes terres et des terres à faible rendement. Ces vestiges souvent peu importants sont une preuve tangible de l'occupation et de l'exploitation par des communautés successives, pendant des centaines d'années, de zones rurales qui sont largement dépeuplées à l'heure actuelle.

Les communications présentées dans ce volume sont le fruit d'un programme d'études sur le terrain de peuplements ruraux abandonnés dans tout le pays de Galles, programme qui a duré cinq ans et qui fut entrepris par Cadw et les quatre Trusts Archéologiques Gallois. Ce projet avait été mis en place dans le but d'améliorer le niveau de compréhension des peuplements ruraux au Pays de Galles ; le fait que ces sites sont vulnérables et peuvent être détruit avait également incité ce projet, afin de créer une base sur laquelle pourrait être édifiées de futures stratégies de gestion et de protection. Les travaux ont principalement (mais non pas exclusivement) porté sur les paysages des hautes terres où les indices sur le terrain sont le mieux préservés, et où les évaluations des sites fournissent l'estimation la plus complète jusqu'à présent des vestiges restant encore dans ces régions. A la suite d'un chapitre d'introduction, la partie principale du volume est divisée en trois parties : *Regional examinations [Études régionales]*, *General themes [Thèmes généraux]*, et *Conclusions and future developments [Conclusions et développement futurs]*.

Les études régionales (tout en se conformant à des formats largement similaires au niveau de la méthodologie et de la présentation des résultats) diffèrent au niveau de leur objectif et de l'analyse, reflétant les variables régionales dans le domaine des données archéologiques et dans l'étendue des recherches antérieures. Dans le chapitre 2, Robert Silvester fournit une synthèse complète de la morphologie du peuplement de tout le centre et le nord-est du pays de Galles, une région qui englobe de nombreuses unités topographiques diverses, lesquelles, au fil des ans, ont acquis divers contextes historiques locaux. Dans le chapitre 3, Martin Locock présente un nouvel examen fort opportun de la nature de l'occupation de Gelligaer Common et traite des indices portant à croire à une exploitation monastique des hautes terres. Dans le chapitre 4, David Longley analyse et interprète de manière comparativement explicite les indices archéologiques sur le terrain relatifs aux indices historiques sur les villes médiévales de Gwynedd, produisant des résultats persuasifs, lesquels font progresser de manière positive la compréhension du développement du peuplement dans toute la région au niveau social et fonctionnel. Dans le chapitre 5, Paul Sambrook fait largement appel à des indices documentaires et cartographiques à l'appui afin de produire une mise en revue informative sur la forme et le but de *lluestau* dans le Ceredigion du 17ème siècle.

La deuxième partie de ce volume aborde divers thèmes d'ordre général. Dans le chapitre 6, George Smith et David Thompson trace les grandes lignes des problèmes qui doivent être affrontés quand on fouille des sites de peuplements abandonnés et montre comment une intervention limitée mais ciblée peut donner des résultats positifs. Les fouilles ont montré le rôle important que peuvent jouer les indices environnementaux pour l'identification de la fonction et de la date des sites. Dans le chapitre 7, le résumé succinct fait par Astrid Caseldine trace les grandes lignes à la fois du potentiel et des limites des techniques employées dans les études paléo environnementales et montre comment ces techniques peuvent être utilisées pour ouvrir de nouvelles voies d'enquête. Dans le chapitre 8, Judith Alfrey présente les vues d'un historien de l'architecte et soutient une collaboration plus étroite entre archéologues, historiens et historiens de l'architecture, tout particulièrement en ce qui concerne l'exploration des origines des traditions de construction locales.

Dans la troisième section, Kathryn Roberts offre un résumé des principaux résultats des études régionales et thématiques et prend en considération ce qui a été réalisé (chapitre 9); et elle regarde les manières dont les organismes tels que Cadw utilisent ces données à l'heure actuelle dans le cadre de la gestion et de la préservation des sites individuels ainsi que du paysage historique plus large (chapitre 10). Toutefois, comme avec toutes les recherches, de nombreuses questions restent sans réponse et bien d'autres études sont encore à faire. Dans le chapitre 11, David Austin prend du recul afin de placer les résultats du projet dans un contexte plus large, et il avance également une analyse qui pousse à la réflexion sur ce pourraient, et devraient, essayer de faire les archéologues à l'avenir.

Bien que ce volume soit peut-être le point culminant du projet des peuplements ruraux abandonnés [Deserted Rural Settlement Project], il ne représente qu'une étape de notre enquête. Tous ceux qui ont contribué à ce projet espèrent sincèrement qu'il servira d'inspiration pour d'autres recherches sur ce sujet fort intéressant.

Zusammenfassung

Kein Reisender, der nach Wales kommt, kann die Fuelle leerstehender Haeuser und Bauerngehoefte uebersehen, die das Land mit ihren grenzwertigen Hochlandschaften praegt. Diese oft gebrechlichen Ueberreste sind der greifbare Beweis, dass fuer viele hundert Jahre das baeuerliche Land fortlaufend von Gemeinden besetzt und ausgebeutet worden ist und damit heutzutage stark entvoelkert ist.

Die in diesem Band veroefentlichen Seiten sind das Ergebnis eines fuenf Jahre andauernden Progammes, das auf Feldforschungen der verlassenen laendlichen Niederlassungen in ganz Wales beruht, die von Cadw und den vier Archaelogischen Trusts in Wales durchgefuehrt worden sind.

Das Projekt ist in die Wege gelaeutet worden, um das Verstaendis fuer baeuerliche Niederlassungen zu weiten; es zielt zudem auch auf die Verwundbarkeit an Zerstorung fuer diese Stellen und hat die Absicht in Zukunft Verwaltungs- und Schutzstrategien zu schaffen. Die Arbeit setzt in erster Linie (wenn auch nicht auschliesslich) auf Hochlandschaften, wo die Feldbeweise am besten erhalten sind und die Feldermittlungen die vollstaendigsten Bewertungen der Ueberlebensreste erlauben. Folgend ein Einleitungskapitel, der Hauptteil dieses Bandes ist in drei Teile gegliedert: Regional Examinations, General Themes, and Conclusions and Future Developments.

Die regionalen Untersuchungen (waehrend allgeimein aehnliche Ausfuehrungen in Methodik und Praesentation der Ergebnisse verfolgt warden) unterscheiden sich in Schwerpunkten und Analysen, wiederspiegeln die Schwankungen in archaeologischen Daten und dem Ausmass vorheriger Forschung.

Im zweiten Kapitel erstellt Robert Silvester eine umfassende morphologische Synthese fuer zentral und nord-ost Wales, ein Gebiet umgeben von zahlreichen diversen topographischen Einheiten, die mit der Zeit einen vielseitigen historischen Hintergrund bekamen. Im dritten Kapitel praesentiert Martin Locock eine zeitgerechte Nachpruefung der natuerlichen Beschaeftigung in Gelligaer Common und eroertert den Beweis fuer kloesterliche Ausbeutung des Hochlandes. Im vierten Kapitel analysiert und interpretiert David Longley auf vergleichende Art und Weise archaeologische Feldbeweise als historischer Beweis fuer mittelalterliche Gemeinden in Gwynedd und schafft ueberzeugende Ergebnisse, die das Verstaendnis fuer die Entwicklung der Niederlassungen in der Region in sozialen und zweckmaessigen Punkten positiv erleichtert. Im 5. Kapitel zielt Paul Sambrook ausgiebig auf die Unterstuetzung dokumentarischer und cartographischer Beweise, um eine informative Sicht ueber die Form und den Zweck von Lluestau "in 17 th Century Ceredigion" zu geben.

Der zweite Teil des Bandes zielt auf eine Vielzahl von allgeimeinen Themen. Im 6. Kapitel reisst George Smith und David Thompson die Herausforderungen an, mit denen man waehrend der Ausgrabungen konfrontiert wird und zeigt wie begrenzt, aber zielgerichtet ein Eingriff positive Ergebnisse bringen kann. Die Ausgrabungen demonstrieren die wichtige Rolle, die die Beweise in der Umwelt spielen koennen, beim identifizieren der Funktion und Daten der Plaetze. Im 7. Kapitel beschreibt Caseldines stichhaltige Zusammenfassung beides, das Potential und die Begraenzung der Methoden, die in palaeo-environmental Studien angewandt werden und demonstriert wie sie verwendet werden koennen um neue Zugaenge zu Forschungen zu oeffnen. Im 8. Kapitel presentiert Judith Alfrey eine historisch architektonische Sicht und traegt einen Fall vor fuer nahe Zusammenarbeit zwischen Archaeologen, Historikern und architektonischen Historikern, ins besondere bezueglich Forschungen traditioneller Gebaeude Urspruenge.

Im dritten Abschnitt versorgt Kate Roberts uns mit einem Auszug von ersten Funden der regionalen und thematischen Studien und betrachtet was bisher erreict worden ist (Kapitel 9); und schaut sich die Art und Weise an, in der die Daten von den Organisationen, wie z.B. Cadw genutzt werden um beides sowohl die Wohngegenden als auch die historische Landschaft zu erhalten (Kapitel 10). Jedoch, wie in jeder Forschung, haben wir noch viele unbeantwortete Fragen und es bleibt ein betraechtlicher Spielraum fuer weitere Studien. Im 11. Kapitel tritt David Austin von dem Projekt zurueck um die Funde in einen breiteren Kontext zu bringen und bringt eine zum Nachdenken anregende Analyse, worauf die Archaeologen in Zukunft setzen koennten und sollten um die Ziele zu erreichen.

Dieser Band mag der Hoehepunkt des "Deserted Rural Settlement Projects"(Verwuestetes laendliches Niederlassungs Projekt) sein, aber es ist nur ein Schritt in unseren Forschungen. Es ist die aufrichtige Hoffnung aller die in diesem Projekt mitgewirkt haben, das es eine Anregung fuer fortlaufende Forschungen ist, im interessantesten aller Themen.

1 THE DESERTED RURAL SETTLEMENT PROJECT: BACKGROUND AND METHODOLOGY

by Kathryn Roberts

The Deserted Rural Settlement Project was the first all-Wales field-based survey of evidence for medieval and post-medieval rural settlement. The project was set up in order to increase the level of understanding of rural settlement in Wales; it was also prompted by the recognised vulnerability of these sites to destruction. The work was funded by Cadw and carried out by the Welsh Archaeological Trusts.

Cadw is the Welsh Assembly Government's historic environment service. It is responsible for advising the Assembly on the scheduling of ancient monuments (under the Ancient Monuments and Archaeological Areas Act 1979), and the listing of historic buildings (under the Planning (Listed Buildings and Conservation Areas) Act 1990). It also plays a major role in the protection, preservation and presentation of the built heritage of Wales, largely through the provision of grants for practical conservation and archaeological investigation.

The four regional Welsh Archaeological Trusts (Clwyd-Powys, Dyfed (now known as Cambria Archaeology), Glamorgan-Gwent and Gwynedd) (Fig. 1.1) were set up in 1975 as independent charitable trusts. Their activities include maintenance of the regional Sites and Monuments Records, and carrying out work which is grant-aided by Cadw and the Royal Commission on the Ancient and Historical Monuments of Wales (RCAHMW). They also provide curatorial archaeological advice on planning applications to unitary authorities and advise government agencies and other bodies.

This volume presents the results of survey work undertaken between 1995 and 2001, although in Dyfed work continued until March 2004. The significant amount of new field data acquired during the course of the project provides an ideal opportunity to reassess the valuable contribution that these sites can make to our overall understanding of rural settlement in Wales.

Previous and current unitary authority boundaries within Wales are shown in Fig. 1.2; the upland topography of Wales is illustrated in Fig. 1.3.

1.1 General introduction

The study of deserted rural settlement of the medieval and post-medieval periods in Wales has been described by Thompson and Yates (1999) as 'marginal', both in the sense that the known resource is often best preserved around the periphery of more productive agricultural land, and that it has been the subject of only limited academic study. As observed by Edwards (1997, 5): 'medieval settlement archaeology in Wales has received surprisingly little attention when compared with the amount of research, survey and excavation which has been carried out on both rural and urban settlements of the same period in England over the last fifty years'.

This sad state of affairs has certainly not arisen due to a lack of surviving sites. Indeed, as will be shown in the various studies incorporated within this volume,

the remains of many hundreds of historic homesteads, settlements, and farms are evident throughout the Welsh uplands, quite apart from unidentified sites that are thought to survive to some degree within the more intensively farmed lowlands. One possible explanation for this apparent anomaly may be the practical challenge that this area of study presents to the archaeologist; the dearth of identifiable diagnostic chronological characteristics makes interpretation from field evidence alone problematic, and even excavation does not always prove productive.

The term 'deserted rural settlement' invokes a relatively clear image: an abandoned structure or group of structures in a rural context, elements of which have been used at some time for human habitation. It is, however, an indeterminate classification which provides no explicit identification of either period or function. Such sites often have many physical similarities – in particular, the original presence of one or more rectilinear buildings (stone or timber/earth built) – but they do not belong to any single period and have been occupied by a wide range of people including lone shepherds, families, collective kinships and, in later periods, groups of mineral workers.

Settlements investigated during the project range from small hamlets to isolated farmsteads and dwellings potentially dating from the immediate post-Roman period to the 19th century, although most of those studied here are believed to have experienced their principal use during the medieval and post-medieval periods, broadly between the 12th and the late 17th century. We know from historical records that the majority of the population of Wales lived and worked within a rural economy, but our perception of their day-to-day existence is limited. Although a considerable amount of academic research has been carried out by both archaeologists and historians, this has tended to focus on a limited number of specific themes – in particular, castles and fortification, urban settlements, and the houses and lifestyles of the wealthy elite. It is important, therefore, to correct this disproportionate balance of research if we are to achieve a more representative understanding of medieval and post-medieval settlement in Wales.

An aspect of Welsh social history that is inextricably linked with rural settlement is the significance of the transhumant pastoral regime, which is generally agreed to have existed throughout much of rural Wales from at least the early medieval period until the onset of industrialisation. Under the medieval system animals were moved from their winter pasture around the homestead (*hendref*) to the summer pasture (*hafod*); in later periods this predominantly communal activity appears to have been abandoned in favour of a more individual system, as illustrated in the small *lluestau* shepherding stations recorded in Ceredigion. It is probable that a substantial number of the sites investigated were associated with the summer seasonal pasturing of animals. The *hafod* (literally 'summer dwelling place') is first documented in the 13th century but the concept is likely to be ancient. This flexible combination of permanent and temporary settlements reflects similar transhumance systems which existed in other mountainous regions of Europe and would have been well suited to the Welsh landscape, ensuring that the lush summer grass grown on the upland pastures was fully utilised and thereby enabling the lower fertile areas to be rested and freed up for growing crops. Whereas the decline of large-scale transhumance resulted in the abandonment and ultimate decay of many of the upland *hafodydd*, the locations of the main *hendrefi* settlements often remained in use, with modern farms now occupying many of the earlier dwelling sites.

1.2 Summary of past survey and research

Although there are occasional antiquarian allusions to deserted settlement sites, such as the reference to Hen Ddinbych by Edward Lhwyd at the end of the 17th century (Lhwyd 1909, 151), in general it was not until production of the earliest large-scale Ordnance Survey maps during the second half of the 19th century that they began to be depicted, albeit infrequently. Examples include the Dyrysgol terrace (designated the site of a chapel) above the Wye Valley near Rhaeadr (C Fox 1939a) and the Llanwddyn *Hospitium* in the upper Vyrnwy Valley (Silvester 1997).

The Royal Commission on the Ancient and Historical Monuments of Wales (RCAHMW) continued this recording work, describing the platforms of the settlement of Beili Bedw in the Radnorshire Inventory (RCAHMW 1913), together with Fron Bellaf in Denbighshire, long huts above Llandrillo, and medieval farmsteads within the Iron Age fortifications at Dinas. However, it was not until the pioneering excavations of Aileen and Cyril Fox that archaeological techniques began to cast further light on these enigmatic features. Their work on Margam Mountain and Gelligaer Common in the Glamorganshire uplands (Fox and Fox 1934; Fox 1937; Fox 1939; Fox and Fox 1949) identified rectangular buildings set on earthen platforms, which they termed 'platform houses'. Excavation dated these buildings to the medieval period – a deduction which was adopted by subsequent fieldworkers (Butler 1971).

Following the work of Fox and Fox, survey was for a time polarised, being concentrated at the geographical extremes of Glamorgan and Gwynedd. In Glamorgan, surveys were carried out in Neath and Gower (Green 1954; Morris 1954). In Gwynedd, fieldwork by Colin Gresham in Meirionnydd (Gresham 1954) and the RCAHMW in Caernarvonshire (RCAHMW 1964) led to the discovery of numerous previously unrecorded sites, for which it was found necessary to

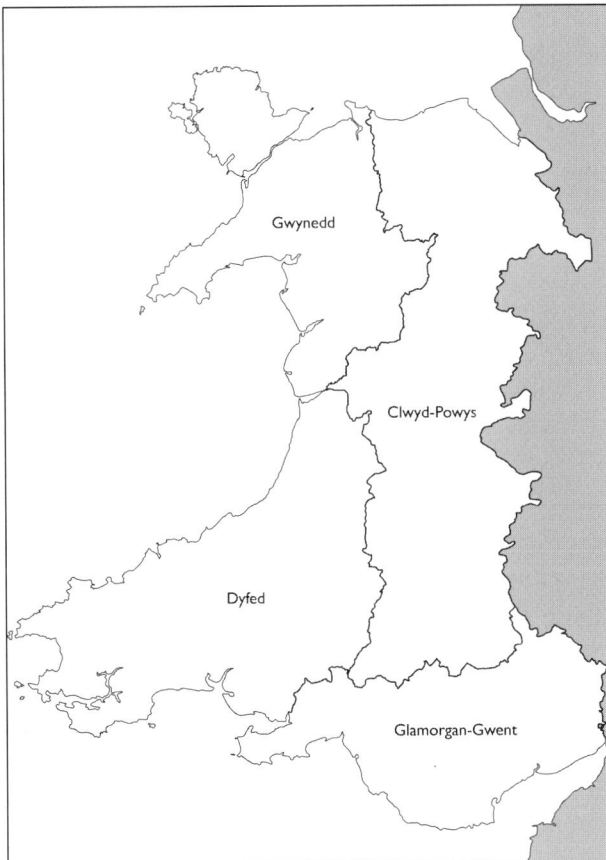

1.1 Regional organisation of Archaeological Trusts in Wales

introduce descriptive terminology. Typically the Gwynedd platforms were constructed by scooping soil from the back of the platform and piling it outwards at the front, occasionally with an additional bank set around the top of the fan which was presumably intended to deflect surface water around the building (Butler 1971, 257).

In 1971 Laurence Butler produced a useful summary of fieldwork and research which had been undertaken in Wales prior to 1968 to investigate medieval settlement. He noted that the body of evidence for rural settlement suggested a predominant pattern of dispersed single farmsteads, seasonally supplemented by summer dairy houses and occasionally interspersed with nucleated hamlets (Butler 1971, 257). However, accurate dating remained problematic and the modest number of excavations carried out on all three site types achieved only limited success. Following an auspicious start evinced by the Gelligaer and Dinas Noddfa excavations (Fox and Fox 1934; Fox 1937; A Fox 1939), subsequent studies proved less rewarding. Farmsteads at Bodafon Mountain (Griffiths 1955) and Bwlch-yr-hendre (Butler 1963) produced little datable material attributable to earlier than the 17th century. More productive were the studies of the

nucleated settlement of Hen Caerwys in Flintshire (Rogers 1979) and the work of Leslie Alcock at Beili Bedw (published by Courtney in 1991), where three excavated platforms revealed evidence of rectangular stone buildings, two of which yielded pottery belonging to the 15th–16th century (see Silvester, Chapter 2). In general, however, excavation of isolated farmsteads and suspected summer *hafod* sites has proved disappointing due to the limited number of datable material objects recovered.

In the three decades since Butler published his summary, a considerable amount of archaeological field survey work across Wales (particularly in the upland areas) has resulted in a significant increase in the number of recorded deserted rural settlement sites. On a national level, archaeological reconnaissance has been carried out by the RCAHMW, initially for preparation of inventories – of which the Glamorgan example is of particular note (RCAHMW 1982) and more recently as part of the Uplands Survey Initiative (Leighton 1997, Brown and Hughes 2003). The Cadw-funded Threat Related Surveys (whilst not specifically designed for reconnaissance purposes) have led to the discovery of many further sites. In addition, a number of regional studies have been conducted, including: (in Gwynedd) Peter Crew's studies of Cyfannedd (Crew 1984) and Richard Kelly's field survey of Ardudwy (Kelly 1982a; 1988); (in west Wales) the Blaencaron survey, Ceredigion (Williams and Muckle, 1992), the Preseli study (Drewitt 1983; 1984; 1985) and more recently Anthony Ward's work in the Black Mountain region of East Carmarthenshire (Ward 1991; 1995; 1997); and (in south Wales) Jonathon Kissock's studies on Cefn Drum (Kissock and Johnston 2000).

One of the more significant pieces of work is Richard Kelly's excavation and investigation of a 12th–13th-century lowland farmstead at Cefn Graenog, Clynnog, Caernarvonshire (Kelly 1982b). This complex site provided a considerable amount of information leading to the identification of two separate phases of occupation, the latter involving a series of buildings set side-by-side along a platform, each oriented at 90° to the prevailing slope. Although few artefacts were recovered, the site proved to be rich in environmental remains which, when combined with the structural evidence uncovered, enabled the buildings to be identified as a house, barn, byre, and stable.

Historians have made valuable contributions to the understanding of Welsh rural society, opening up considerable opportunities for subsequent confirma-

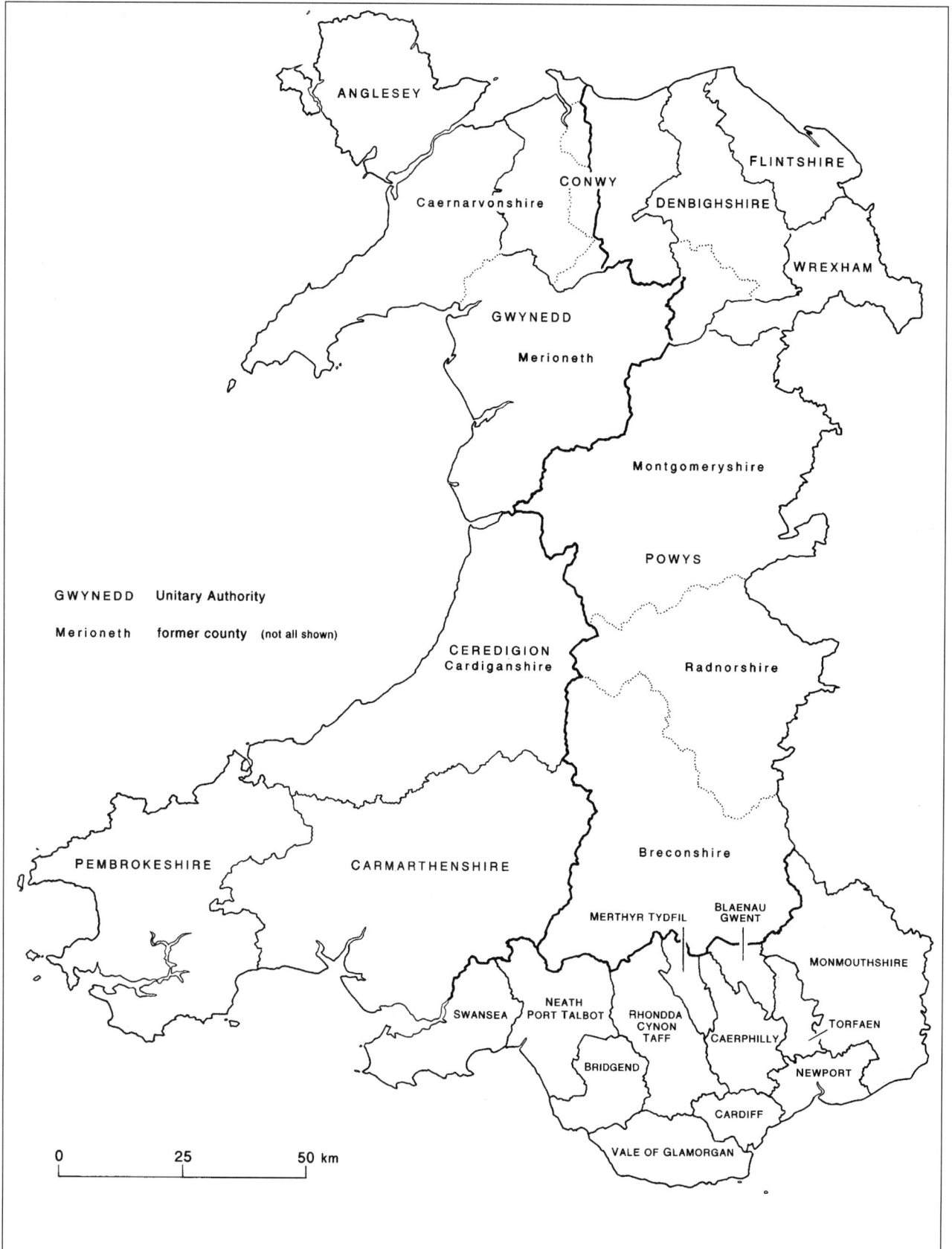

1.2 Unitary Authorities in Wales (current and historic)

tion by fieldwork. T Jones Pierce (1938; 1951; 1972a; 1972b) used native law books and Edwardian documents to investigate rural medieval society and tenu-

rial systems in Gwynedd and Ceredigion. Subsequently, Glanville Jones argued that some tenurial systems could be recognised by their resultant settlement patterns (Jones 1972; 1973; 1985). At Eifionydd, Gwynedd, he demonstrated that homesteads lying in girdle patterns could be equated with the *tir gwelyog* (hereditary land) of free (*gwelyau*) communities, whereas bonded (*taeogion*) communities farming *tir cyfrif* (reckoned land) could be identified from the presence of nucleated settlements (Jones 1985) (see Longley, Chapter 4). A comprehensive critique of the contribution made by historians to the study of medieval and later settlements is presented by David Austin in Chapter 11.

In 1994 a Welsh Archaeological Conference, the theme of which was 'Landscape and Settlement in Medieval Wales', was hosted by the University of Wales, Bangor. Presentations covered a broad spectrum of research, with many speakers highlighting the benefits of diverse fieldwork techniques and multi-disciplinary approaches. These included: Della Hooke's work on the use of place-names and vegetation history as an aid to understanding settlement in the Conwy Valley; Neil Johnstone and David Longley's documentary and archaeological investigation of Royal Courts in Gwynedd; and the aerial photographic study of the Great Orme, Llandudno, carried out by Mary Aris (all in Edwards 1997). Two of the authors who presented papers at that conference were subsequently involved with the Deserted Rural Settlement Project and produce chapters within this volume.

It is relevant at this point briefly to mention parallel studies of surviving standing buildings in the Welsh countryside. Since the publication of *The Old Cottages of Snowdonia* (Hughes and North 1908), the vernacular architectural traditions of Wales have become the subject of increasing academic interest. The most comprehensive reviews are *Houses of the Welsh Countryside* (Smith 1967; 1988) and the RCAHMW Inventories, such as the *Glamorgan Inventory of Farmhouses and Cottages* (RCAHMW 1988). Whereas the focus of the RCAHMW studies was primarily upon architectural development, Iorwerth Peate (1946) took an ethnographic approach, which was also adopted by Eurwyn Wiliam and colleagues at the Museum of Welsh Life, St Fagans, Cardiff (Wiliam 1982b; 1986; 1988; 1992; 1994). The foundation of this museum created the opportunity not only to preserve examples of regional vernacular buildings but also to present them for public appreciation. There are clearly benefits to be gained from combining investigation of surviving vernacular buildings with archaeological field evidence for earlier buildings, since they represent a long tradition of local styles and craftsmanship (see Alfrey, Chapter 8).

This brief summary of previous work is not comprehensive, and is intended merely to provide a background to the development of the Deserted Rural Settlement Project; it is supplemented in the following chapters by regional examples as appropriate.

1.3 Development of the project

The Deserted Rural Settlement Project was set up in order to increase the level of understanding of the numbers, range and condition of medieval and post-medieval rural settlement sites in Wales. It was also prompted by the recognised vulnerability of these sites to destruction, which in many cases occurred before they were adequately recorded.

As a result of recent national survey initiatives (including the English Heritage Monument Protection Programme and Cadw's Threat-Related Surveys), the threats facing archaeological sites and historic landscapes in rural situations are increasingly well-documented (Darvill 1988; Darvill 1998). These include the impact of afforestation, industrial development (particularly involving extractive and power industries) and natural erosion, but in rural Wales it is the changing nature of agricultural practices (in particular land improvement) that poses the greatest potential risk. It is impossible to quantify the extent and rate at which archaeological sites and historic features are being destroyed but field observations indicate significant ongoing loss.

There are various conservation mechanisms which can be employed by those organisations entrusted with heritage protection, including statutory designation, planning constraints and (increasingly) voluntary land management schemes. Perhaps the most obvious means of protecting archaeological sites is through the process of 'scheduling'. Under the Ancient Monuments and Archaeological Areas Act 1979, Cadw is responsible for discharging the Welsh Assembly Government's statutory duty to compile a Schedule of monuments which appear to be of national importance. This Schedule is intended to be representative of all periods and site types throughout Welsh history but inevitably reflects the current state of knowledge which, of necessity, dictates the selection process.

When the contents of the Schedule were reviewed

in 1997 a number of inconsistencies were identified and it was apparent that medieval and later rural settlement were under-represented. This problem was specific to Cadw, but taking a broader view it was acknowledged that statutory protection can only ever apply to the small number of sites which meet the strict criteria of 'national importance' necessary to merit scheduled status. This inevitably leaves a substantial number of sites which are unable to benefit from scheduled protection but which never-theless are of significant local or regional importance. Protection of these sites rests mainly with heritage organisations, such as the Welsh Archaeological Trusts.

The four Archaeological Trusts are responsible for the maintenance of the regional Sites and Monuments Records (SMR) databases. These, together with the National Monuments Record (NMR) maintained by the RCAHMW, comprise the current record of all known archaeological sites in Wales. SMR information is used extensively (by the Trusts and other organisations) for a wide range of purposes, including facilitating the provision of management advice, monument protection through the planning process, development of heritage management policy, research, and academic study. Obviously the efficacy of all these activities is totally dependent upon the adequacy of the original data. However, since SMR records were built up over a considerable period of time and from a broad range of sources, there were inevitably inconsistencies in the content, quality, and reliability of the infor-mation (Lang 1990; Fraser 1993; Baker 1999; Fernie and Gilman 2000). This was the case in respect of rural settlement site records where diverse methods of field assessment and analysis had resulted in

entries of uncertain quality. This situation was further exacerbated by the application of inconsistent terminology both within and between SMR regions (much of which could be traced back to the personal preference of individual fieldworkers) and use of non-standardised terms. By way of example, the term 'platform house', initially coined by Aileen and Cyril Fox to describe buildings excavated on Gelligaer Common, was subsequently adopted by the Royal Commission on the Ancient and Historical Monuments of Wales to describe similar structures in Caernarvonshire (RCAHMW 1964). However, by the time of the publication of the RCAHMW Glamorgan Inventory (1982) the term 'platform house' was being used solely to denote structures set across the contour of a hillside, and the term 'long hut' applied to those set along them (Ward 1997, 100). Consequently, the four Trusts found it increas-ingly difficult to make qualitative decisions in terms of planning, development and general management.

Since the early 1990s Cadw and the four Welsh Archaeological Trusts had engaged in a series of struc-tured surveys, the purpose of which was to validate records and generate up-to-date management infor-mation. Surveys included investigation of prehistoric/Romano-British hut settlement sites in Gwynedd, medieval motte and bailey monuments, and early metal-mining sites. It was against this background that in 1995 Cadw agreed to finance a pilot exercise during which the Gwynedd Archaeological Trust would investigate medieval and later rural settlement sites within a specified area of north-west Wales. In 1996, following successful completion of the pilot study, the project was developed as a pan-Wales study involving all four regional Trusts.

1.4 Project objectives

The defined objectives of the Deserted Rural Settlement Project were to:

1. examine and record the known deserted rural settlements in Wales;
2. quantify the resource and develop a working classification;
3. update and enhance the Sites and Monuments Records databases;
4. assess the condition of known sites and identify both local and more general threats;

5. develop criteria of national importance and identify sites which meet those criteria to be considered for scheduling;
6. make recommendations on the management and protection of deserted rural settlements in Wales.

In addition, each Trust developed its own academic objectives, which ultimately had an influence on the methodologies employed in each region.

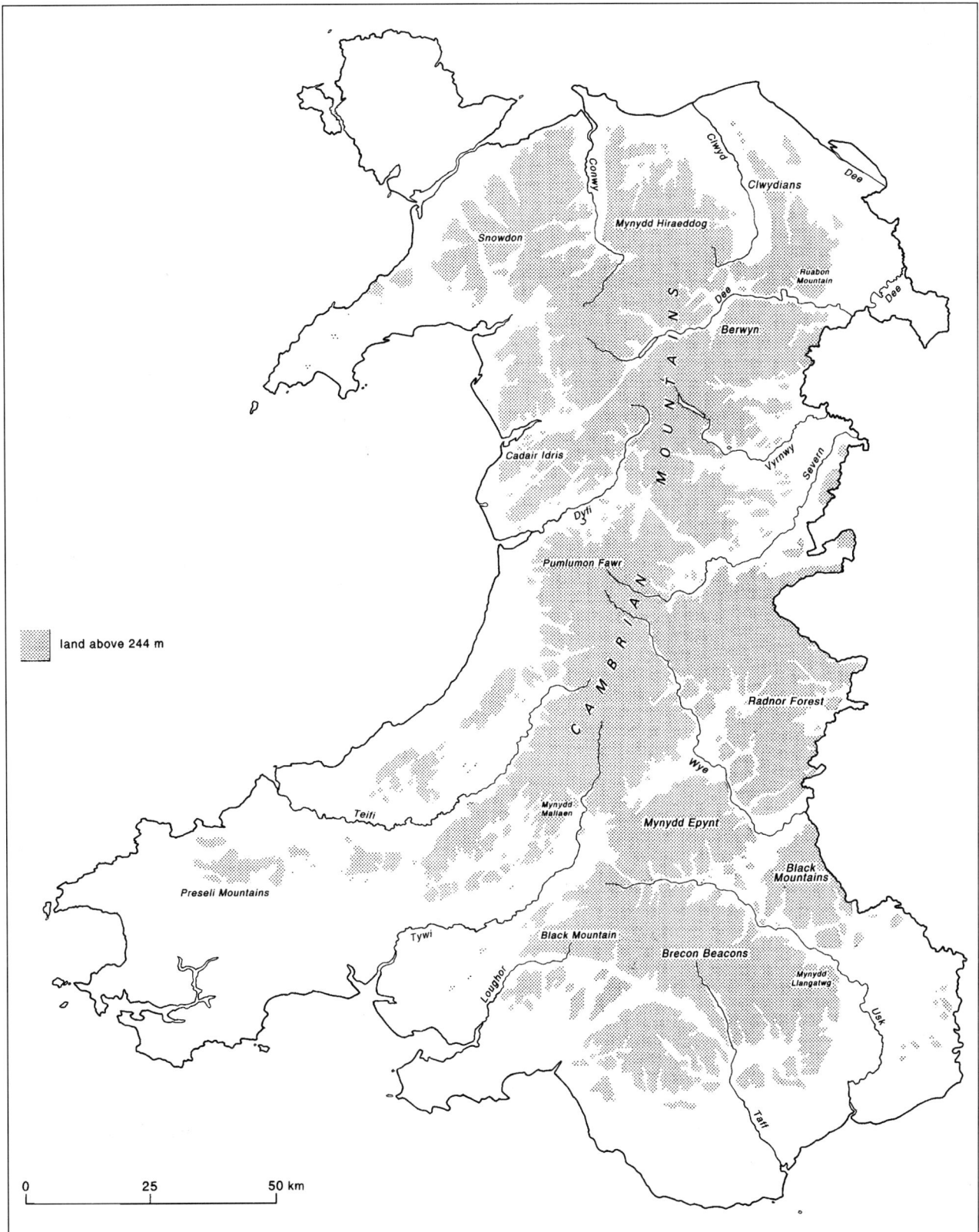

1.3 Upland topography of Wales

1.5 Methodology

The project comprised three inter-related elements: the
pan-Wales condition survey; rapid identification
surveys in selected areas; and small-scale excavations.

1.5.1 Condition survey
The condition survey was the main element of the
project. Each region created a working database of all

potentially relevant sites extracted from its existing SMR database; this was supplemented by additional information drawn from a wide range of other sources including Ordnance Survey maps, the National Monument Record, historic documentary records, early cartography (for example, the Badminton Manorial Survey; see Silvester, Chapter 2/Appendix III), and aerial reconnaissance surveys, where available.

In order to retain the project within manageable proportions, it was necessary to determine the chronological parameters within which sites would be selected for investigation. Three of the Trusts (Gwynedd, Clwyd-Powys, and Glamorgan-Gwent) investigated all sites thought to be of medieval/post-medieval date, thereby excluding those structures which could be shown to belong to the 18th century or later. However, the Dyfed Trust argued a case for extending these parameters in order to include sites known to post-date 1800, in the belief that this would open up additional avenues of research which could ultimately lead to better overall understanding. Since it was inevitable that adopting this latter approach greatly increased the number of potentially relevant sites in Dyfed, it was necessary to restrict the study sample to eighteen selected areas (see Chapter 5, Fig. 5.1). The selection process is discussed in greater detail in Chapter 9.

At that time Dyfed's approach was supported by Cadw on the basis that regional variations may well justify different approaches. As project work progressed, however, the benefits of adopting a uniform level of survey across Wales became increasingly apparent, not least following the introduction of a pan-Wales agri-environmental scheme (see Chapter 11). Dyfed therefore agreed to extend survey to those areas which had not previously been investigated; this work was carried out between 2001 and 2004, this time applying the same selection criteria which had been adopted by the other three regions.

Archaeologists visited and recorded to an agreed standard all known and probable deserted rural settlement sites. In order to ensure consistency, standard record forms were adopted: the first to record site description data, including location, dimensions and form (walls, doors, other features); the second to record management information, including condition, land use, and assessment of vulnerability/potential threats. Sketch plans and photographs were added where appropriate. Additional record sheets were used

in those cases where multiple associated structures were identified. The condition survey, although not specifically intended as a prospecting exercise, was responsible for the identification of a significant number of hitherto unrecorded sites, many of which were discovered coincidentally while on the way to inspect other known sites. The same level of recording was accorded to all newly discovered deserted rural settlement sites as that given to those previously known. In addition, a small number of sites were selected for more detailed recording, several of which are included for illustrative purposes in this volume.

Upon completion of the field survey each SMR entry was updated and reassessed, applying an agreed set of terms across all four regions (see Glossary at Appendix I). It was decided not to use any term that denoted specific functional or chronological interpretation unless validity could be established. The use of subjective designations was also to be avoided, for example: 'platform house' which implies use as a dwelling although in most cases this is not implicit from surface evidence alone; 'longhouse' which, as defined by Peate (1946), indicates shared use of a building by humans and animals; and 'hafod' which denotes seasonal occupation. The term 'hut' was used throughout the project, although even this may be misinterpreted due to its modern correspondence with the term 'hovel'.

1.5.2 Rapid identification surveys

It was appreciated from the outset that the results of the condition survey alone would not provide an accurate estimate of the total number of deserted rural settlement sites in Wales, since only previously recorded sites were investigated. It was, therefore, necessary to supplement the condition survey with a number of reconnaissance (or rapid identification) surveys in selected locations (Table 1.1), during which fieldworkers examined discrete areas defined by field boundaries or natural features. Survey areas were selected for a number of reasons including the availability of information from other sources such as contemporary documents and maps, and the wish to extend fieldwork into areas where there were few or no recorded sites (for example, lowland areas surrounding upland commons). These surveys provided an ideal opportunity both to explore the nature and extent of the 'unknown resource' and to test previous theories about location and setting (see Silvester, Chapter 2, and Locock, Chapter 3).

Table 1.1 Rapid identification survey areas

Trust (Region)	Survey area
North-east Wales (CPAT)	Aberedw Badminton Manorial survey
North-west Wales (GAT)	Castell (Rowen) Cwm Pennant Castell (Nanmor) Ystumgwern South-east Wales
(GGAT)	Neath Glyncorrwg Pontypridd Barry

1.5.3   Excavation

Cadw's funding brief was unable to accommodate an extensive programme of research excavation, but it was possible to identify a small number of sites at which small-scale selective excavation could be justified due to perceived active threat and/or other management considerations. Sites at Hafod Rug, Gesail Gyfarch, Llanberis Pass, and Ynys Etws in north-west Wales, and at Tro'r Derlwyn in Carmarthenshire, were all subjected to modest levels of excavation work, which included environmental sampling in order to provide some insight into prevailing climatic and environmental conditions. The excavation results are discussed by George Smith and David Thompson in Chapter 6.

1.6 Arrangement and content of the volume

This volume is presented in three sections. **Section One** outlines the regional studies carried out by each of the four individual Archaeological Trusts (Chapters 2–5). **Section Two** presents three thematic studies covering: the results of the project excavations (Chapter 6); the potential of palaeoenvironmental studies (Chapter 7); and architectural evidence (Chapter 8). **Section Three** draws together the survey results from a national perspective (Chapter 9); considers present and future means of providing protection within the overall framework of heritage management (Chapter 10); and discusses the academic implications of the project and puts forward suggestions for the direction of future research (Chapter 11).

Section One: Regional examinations

2 Deserted rural settlements in central and north-east Wales

by Robert Silvester

Abstract

Central and north-east Wales, the area considered in this chapter, extends for more than 180km from north to south and displays considerable topographical diversity. Known deserted rural settlements are commonplace in some parts of the region, rare in others, and a primary aim of the survey as it developed was to establish the range of settlement types attributable to the medieval and early post-medieval centuries, and detect whether they had any geographical cohesion. Platform sites represent the main settlement type in the medieval era, sometimes revealing the outline of buildings upon them, and in places grouped together and accompanied by enclosures or fields. In the late medieval period there is tenuous evidence for the emergence of more discrete farmholdings, particularly in central Wales. From the 16th to the 19th century, increasing expansion and encroachment onto the hills and commons is demonstrated by the presence of large numbers of long huts and farmsteads, some showing only as low foundations, others as abandoned buildings. In parallel with these permanently occupied settlements were the seasonally occupied sites or *hafodydd* that can also show only as platforms or as building foundations, and continued in some areas through to the 19th century.

2.1 General introduction

The region which here is termed central and north-east Wales spans the modern county of Powys and the former county of Clwyd (1974–96). Like their predecessors in central Wales, the historic counties of Brecknock (otherwise Breconshire), Radnorshire and Montgomeryshire (Fig. 2.1), which are used for descriptive purposes in this paper because of the extreme size of modern Powys, these modern counties are composites, lacking any internal cohesive geography. From a different perspective, however, the variations in the physiography have created a rich and varied range of environments which initiated very different settlement patterns in the historic era.

In the far south and running into Glamorgan lie the Brecon Beacons, rising precipitously to form the highest landscapes in southern Britain, with flat but steeply sided plateaux and deep valleys (Fig. 2.1 and Chapter 1: Fig. 1.3). Fforest Fawr (the Great Forest) extends over much of this area, but included, to the east, are Mynydd Llangynidr and Mynydd Llangatwg where sandstone gives way to limestone. The Black Mountains rise further to the east, divided from the Beacons by the River Usk and its tributary the Llynfi (and extending too into Herefordshire and Monmouthshire), their ridges and deeply incised valleys betraying their shared geology in the Old Red Sandstone. The fertile valleys of the Usk and Wye and their tributaries sever these mountain ranges – the central scarp of the Beacons reaches 886m above sea level on Pen y Fan while the Black Mountains also achieve heights of over 800m in one or two places – from the lower and more rounded hills further north. Mynydd Epynt, much of it given over to military training areas, is a bleak upland plateau broken only by the enclosures marking the valleys that run off it, while to the north-east are the hills of Radnorshire (central Powys), numerous blocks of unenclosed upland grazing intercalated with dendritic valleys that channel towards the major valleys of the Wye and the Lugg.

North of Epynt, the Cambrian Mountains, which define the high spine of Wales, project into the three constituent counties of modern Powys, remote and anonymous upland plateaux interrupted only by the reservoirs of the Elan Valley and the Clywedog, and the valley of the infant Severn further north. To the east of the Cambrians are the more fragmented foothills, some enclosed, some common, separated by small rivers, and littered with small villages and numerous farms.

The Berwyn Mountains, shared between Denbighshire and Montgomeryshire, rise to more than 820m above sea level, and are geographically, though not geologically, an extension of the Cambrians that spread eastwards towards the English border. The deep cleft of the Dee Valley divides the Berwyns from other uplands to the north, Llantysilio and Ruabon Mountains which themselves spread out from the base of that distinctive line of hills running almost north to south, the Clwydians. Sweeping tracts of flat and desolate upland plateaux, Clocaenog Forest and the Denbigh Moors, otherwise known as Mynydd Hiraethog, lie to the north-west. Lower hills edge the north coast and down the edge of the Dee Estuary, but even more distinctive is the broad span of the Vale of Clwyd, a great glacial valley running many miles inland from the coast, and in the extreme east the flatlands beyond Wrexham which see the last remnants of the Cheshire plain lapping up against the foothills of Wales.

2.2 Background history

The deserted rural settlements of medieval and later date in this region only occasionally attracted the attention of antiquaries. At the end of the 17th century, for instance, Edward Lhuyd's *Parochialia* contained a reference to Hen Ddinbych on the Denbigh Moors, (Lhwyd 1909, 151), but in terms that signalled it as a curiosity rather than as the site of an earlier settlement. It was only at the end of the 19th century that settlement sites first began to be identified as distinguishable entities. The earliest large-scale Ordnance Survey maps from the 1880s occasionally depicted settlement sites such as the Dyrysgol terrace above the Wye Valley near Rhaeadr (Rads), which at the time was claimed as the site of a chapel (C Fox 1939a), and the Llanwddyn *Hospitium* (Monts) above the upper Vyrnwy Valley (Silvester 1997b). Both, though, were exceptional, with local traditions attached to them. The earthworks were mapped reasonably accurately by the Ordnance Survey surveyors, but perhaps without any great comprehension.

While the *Hospitium* later made an appearance in the Royal Commission's volume on Montgomeryshire (RCAHMW 1911, 134), the companion volume for Radnorshire contained no reference to Dyrysgol. Yet the same volume did record the classic platform settlement at Beili Bedw as 'a confused mass of earthworks – mounds, banks and enclosures – ... which from superficial observation only, it is difficult to arrive at any conclusion concerning their origin. It seems evident that they were not thrown up for military purposes, and they may possibly be due to agricultural operations' (RCAHMW 1913, 143), a reflection of the then current state of awareness rather than on Beili Bedw itself. Other sites, too, though not many, emerged as the earliest Royal Commission investigators published their findings in the northern counties of Wales: Fron Bellaf in Denbighshire, the medieval farmsteads within the Iron Age fortifications at Dinas and Caer Drewyn (both then in Merioneth), one of the long huts above Llandrillo (Merioneth), and the earthwork in Lletty Field in Montgomeryshire were all reported in either the early Royal Commission inventories (RCAHMW 1911; 1914; 1921), or else in Ellis Davies' slightly later *Denbighshire* (1929). Yet the appearance of such sites in print was exceptional, and some certainly reflected no more than the association of longstanding local traditions with distinctive surface features, a luxury not afforded to more than a very small number of sites.

It was not until Cyril and Aileen Fox's pioneering investigations on platforms on Margam Mountain and Gelligaer Common in the Glamorgan uplands (Fox and Fox 1934; A Fox 1939; Fox 2000, 83) that the house platform emerged as a specific monument type, and it is clear that this was no gradual enlightenment, as Cyril Fox's puzzled description of Beili Bedw in his 1932 field notes reveals. As other, similar sites were drawn to Cyril Fox's attention, he followed the south Wales studies with an assessment of the Dyrysgol site (C Fox 1939a), and later of a series of platforms near Castell-y-Blaidd in northern Radnorshire (Fox and Fox 1949).

Hen Caerwys

Denbigh

Mold

Clwyd

Dee

Hafod y Nant Criafolen

Hen Ddinbych

Wrexham

Dee

Llandrillo
FFRIDD CAMEN
RHYD GETHIN

Ty Draw
Lake Vyrnwy Tyddyn Llwydion
TY-UCHAF
Llanwddyn

Vyrnwy

Severn

Welshpool
Pant-yr-alarch
Ty-mawr

Machynlleth

Carneddau

Newtown

Fron Top
MOELFRE HILL
Dyrysgol Cantreff Maelienydd
Beili Bedw

PENYBONT COMMON
Llandrindod Wells Cefnllys
Rhiwnant valley BANK HOUSE
UPPER HOUSE Garn Fawr

1

Builth Wells Little Hill Common

Aberedw

Gwenddwr
Gardiners Hill East
Carnau Bach TIR-CYD
PANT-Y-BLODIAU

Usk Llanddew
Brecon

3
Tre Graig
2 Patrishow Common
Y GYRN Bell Fountain Park
Nant Crew Nant Onneu valley

Wye

Unitary Authority — CONWY

Flintshire
Denbighshire FLINTSHIRE
DENBIGHSHIRE
WREXHAM

former county — Merioneth

Flint.
(det)

Montgomeryshire

POWYS

Radnorshire

Breconshire

0   25 km

0   50 km

study areas   1   Aberedw
              2 Badminton Manorial
                     Survey
              3   Brecon Beacons

land above 244m

illustrated site   MOELFRE HILL

0   5   10   15   20   25   50 km

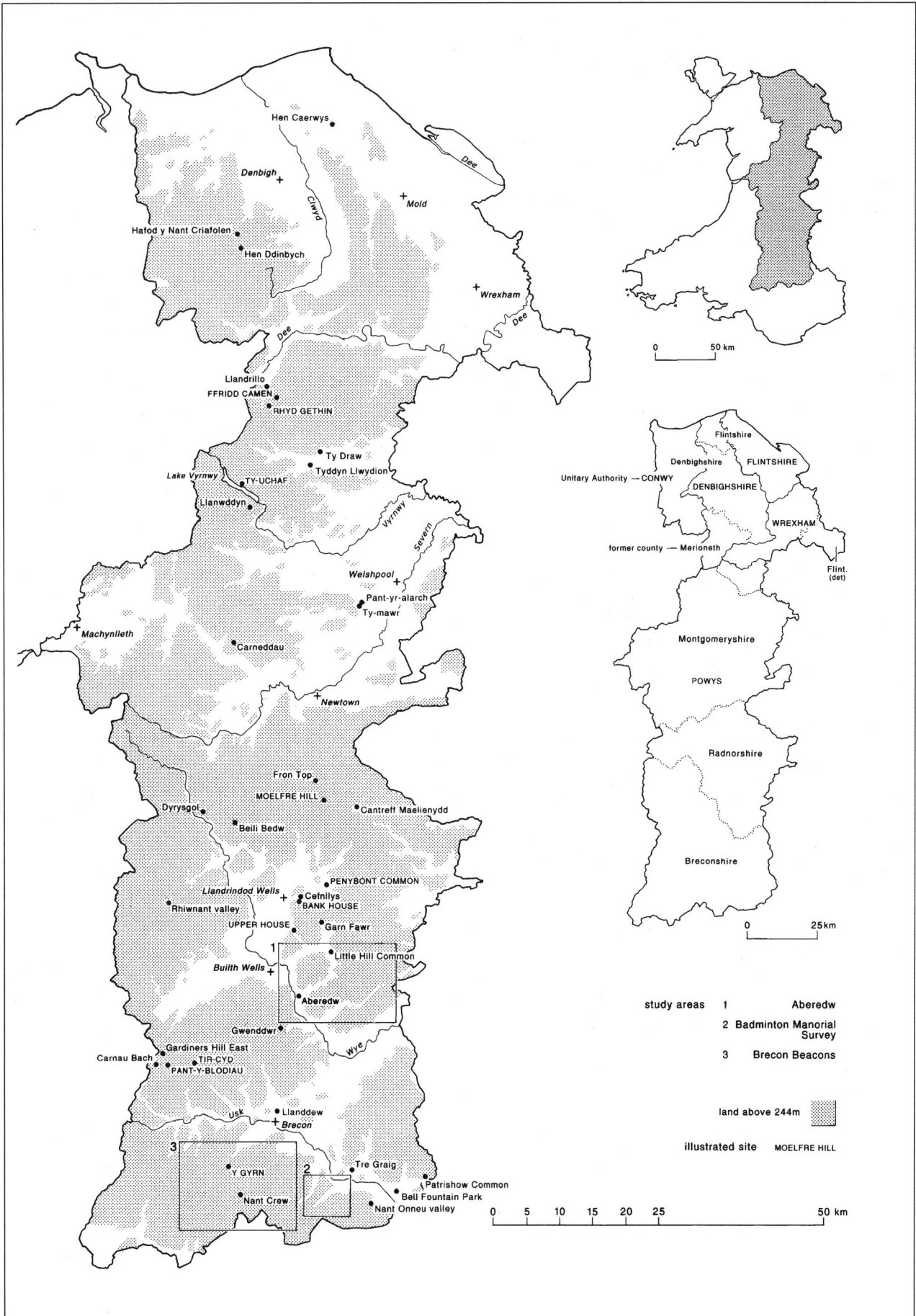

2.1 Map of central and north-east Wales showing principal sites and survey areas

Excavation, however, offered one means to enhance the understanding of these earthworks and an opportunity arose in 1960 when the site at Beili Bedw was damaged by ploughing. Leslie Alcock excavated three platforms in 1961–62, each revealing a rectangular stone building, and two yielding pottery of the 15th to 16th centuries (Courtney 1991). At much the same time a medieval house platform was examined at the nucleated settlement of Hen Caerwys in Flintshire (Rogers 1979), while a few years earlier F H Thompson had completed a trial excavation across the enclosure defences at Hen Ddinbych (Gresham *et al* 1959). Salvage work on the platform in Lletty Field near Llandinam in Montgomeryshire in 1973 and the late J Barfoot's unpublished excavations on a post-medieval settlement above Machynlleth virtually complete the very restricted picture of excavations in the region.

Since the time of those earlier excavations, work in central and north-east Wales has focused almost entirely on recognition and recording, initially by the Ordnance Survey and, in some areas, the RCAHMW, and more recently and sporadically by the Clwyd-Powys Archaeological Trust and others. At the same time the wider study of platforms has advanced, albeit only sporadically, and in 1982 the Royal Commission provided a useful framework including a valuable summary of earlier work, its merits having an impact beyond their study area of Glamorgan (RCAHMW 1982, 17). But the available information on the adjacent county of Brecknock was not collated in similar fashion, and as a consequence a geographical lacuna has opened up (at least in the literature) between the extreme south of Wales and north-west Wales in the understanding of both plat-

forms and long huts (see for instance Wiliam 1986, 63).

Research on seasonally occupied sites has also been limited. While there are clear parallels between the Welsh *hafod* and its Scottish equivalent, the shieling, the process of research in Wales as a whole and the eastern regions in particular has not kept pace with studies in northern Britain, and there are no obvious parallels to either Fenton's general paper (1999) or Bil's more detailed regional analysis of the central Scottish Highlands (1990). The early ethnographic studies of the Welshpool-based academic, R U Sayce, were concerned with the concepts of transhumance and *hafodydd* rather than the physical remains and their distribution (1956; 1957). Later, Elwyn Davies' research on place-names examined the distribution patterns and function in more topographically oriented analyses published in a series of papers (1973; 1977; 1980; 1984–85). But no excavation and relatively little focused fieldwork occurred in central Wales. C B Crampton briefly touched upon the subject with his study of hut sites in the Brecon Beacons (1966a), but in more recent years the study of seasonal settlement in the Brecon Beacons has been advanced significantly by the fieldwork of the RCAHMW (RCAHMW 1997; Leighton 1997). In addition, Anthony Ward's work in the Black Mountain region of eastern Carmarthenshire will be of considerable value when fully published, but has already led to several descriptive papers and one more analytical and in parts provocative assessment of the wider dynamics of upland settlement (Ward 1997). In the north, the creation of the Brenig reservoir allowed the excavation in 1973–74 of a group of seasonally occupied stone long huts on the Denbigh Moors (Allen 1979).

2.3 The condition survey

When the survey of deserted medieval and later rural settlement sites in central and north-east Wales commenced in 1996, a year after the initial pilot study in Gwynedd, a preliminary purpose of the fieldwork was to assess the current state of the known sites that fell within that broad, but rather poorly understood, class of monument, and to identify the best examples for statutory protection. An enhanced classification of the physical remains and the quantification of the resource were also proposed, the former an issue which would be resolved through the cooperation of all those involved in the pan-Wales study. Initially, there was no intention of visiting all the settlements. Rather a sampling procedure, based on the selection of the more promising examples, was implemented during the first

two years. Subsequently, a more all-embracing approach was adopted for the resource, including the revisiting of areas already sampled.

Underpinning the site database was the regional Sites and Monuments Record which provided the material for a primary index of sites, and this was amplified with data from the National Monument Record for Wales, administered by RCAHMW, particularly from its paper records of past fieldwork in Radnorshire and Brecknock.

Early cartography was considered a potentially useful if largely untested source of data, offering the potential of a *terminus ante quem* for a building depicted on a large-scale map. Regretably, however, as historians have pointed out (eg Thomas 1992, 3), the widespread mapping of estates in Wales was a late development by comparison with the situation in much of England, and the number of maps pre-dating the later 18th century is limited. One set of maps, the Badminton Manorial Survey of 1587, was assessed, and proved to be useful in establishing site survival rather than in identifying previously unrecognised settlement sites (see Appendix III).

Selective use of vertical aerial photography was rewarding for Radnorshire, but less so in other parts of the region (see Table 2.1). But the most productive source of new settlement sites was the fieldwork component of the survey, new sites being recognised regularly during visits to known sites, together with the several area-specific surveys completed during the lifetime of the project, such as that in Aberedw in Radnorshire. Such discoveries signal the ubiquity of abandoned farms and cottages in the Welsh landscape, whether showing as earthworks or masonry remains (Fig. 2.1).

Table 2.1 Deserted rural settlements visited in east and north-east Wales and the derivation of information on sites

	Brecknock	Montgomery	Radnor	Denbigh	Flint	Wrexham	Total
All field visits	595	412	517	172	12	23	1731
Total no. of proven sites	554	222	410	130	3	15	1334
No. of visits to proven sites	355	197	364	107	2	9	1034
Source: SMR	96	128	113	27	3	7	374
Source: NMR	233	0	32	0	0	0	265
Source: CPAT fieldwork	36	64	91	68	0	4	263
Source: Aerial photography	3	1	51	12	0	0	67
Source: project fieldwork	171	26	111	17	0	2	327
Source: other	15	3	12	6	0	2	38

In the end it proved impossible to visit all the known sites in the region. Some were simply too remote to justify the visit, a few others could not be examined because of uncooperative landowners, and the outbreak of foot and mouth disease early in 1992 terminated the fieldwork programme abruptly and unexpectedly, as it was nearing completion.

The recognition of new sites will inevitably continue and any future large-scale fieldwork programme will almost certainly generate its own set of new data. In this context Table 2.1 provides information on how many sites had been identified from the Trust's systematic fieldwork programmes, particularly in the uplands, in the seven years before the commencement of the project. And during the course of the project new sites were constantly coming to our attention, from RCAHMW, from other ground and aerial surveys, and from local fieldworkers. Brief details of these new sites were recorded in the project database (and are quantified in Table 2.1) because they help to inform the overall picture of past settlement, but the available resources would simply not allow more than a sample of these new examples to be assessed in the field.

It is necessary here to identify the parameters used for the inclusion of abandoned settlement sites in this study. Nominally, the chronological spread encapsulated the early medieval period through to about the 18th century. In practice there are so few known early medieval settlements that it is more legitimate to think in terms of the medieval period from about the 12th century as the real starting point. At the other end a positive decision was taken to restrict data collection on

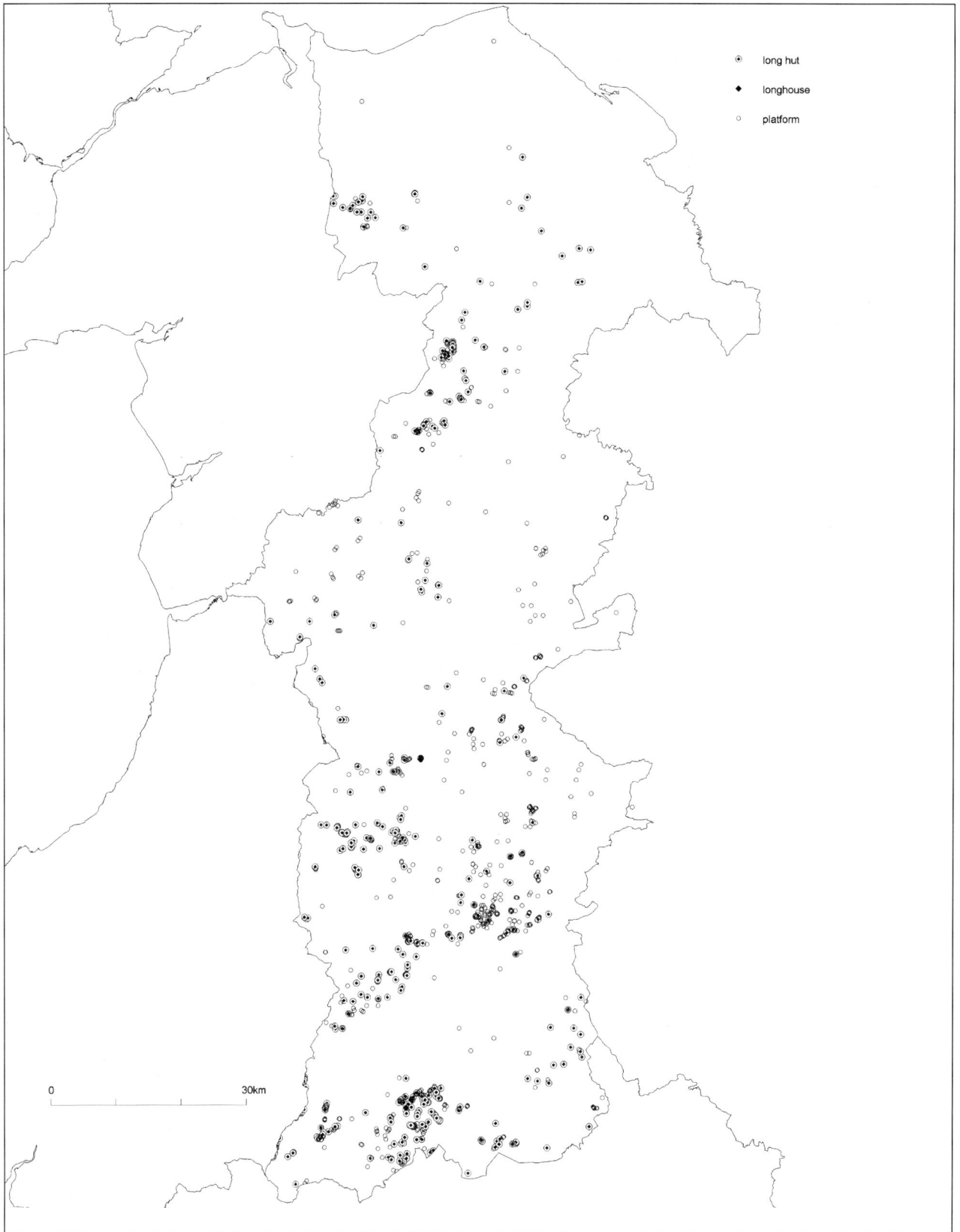

2.2 Distribution map of known sites

the extremely large number of now abandoned farms and cottages, often remaining as standing shells, that emerged on the commons and waste (and indeed on already enclosed land), particularly during the 18th and 19th centuries, although all such buildings could not be omitted from consideration. For one thing it is now clearly recognised that encroachments on common land commenced in the 16th century, if not earlier, and these

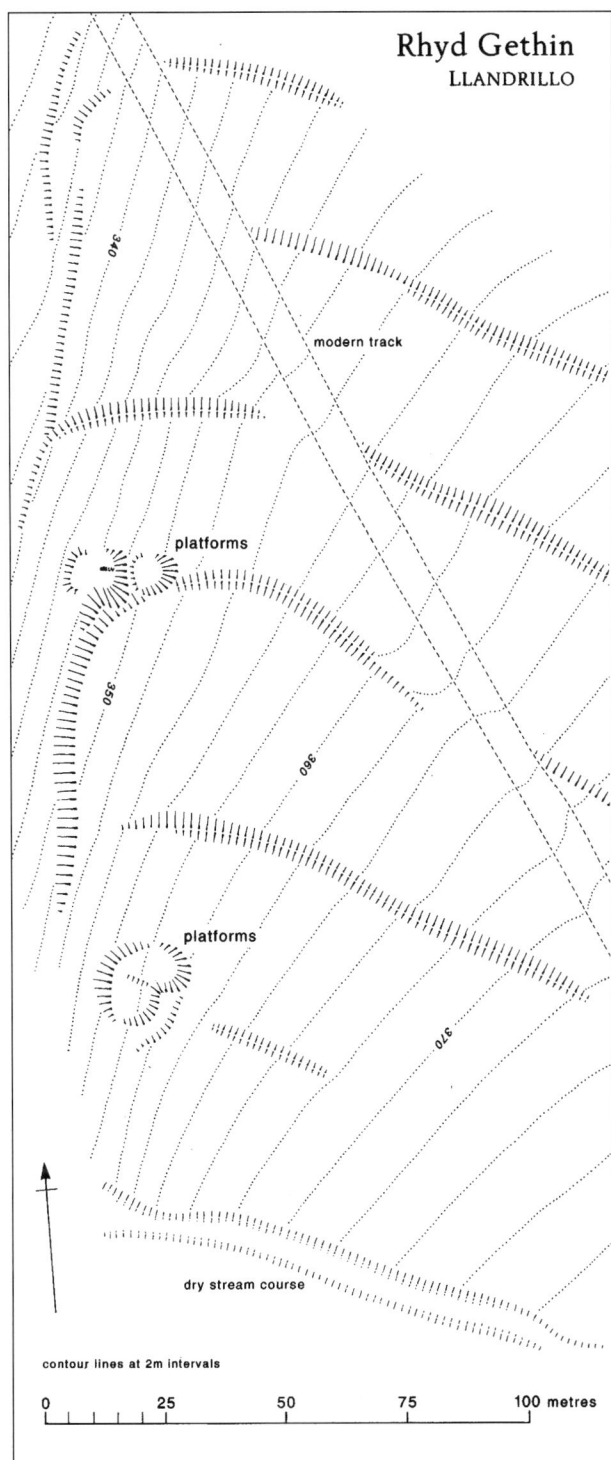

Rhyd Gethin
LLANDRILLO

modern track

platforms

platforms

dry stream course

contour lines at 2m intervals

0   25   50   75   100 metres

2.3 Rhyd Gethin, Llandrillo

A full description of the methodology used in collecting and collating the data is unnecessary: this information can be found in the yearly reports produced by CPAT. Suffice it to say that as a result of consulting the various sources mentioned above, over 1700 potential sites were visited in the field (Table 2.1). To facilitate the assessment and for the purposes of upgrading the SMR, each suspected habitation site was treated as a single unit. Thus paired platforms generated separate records, unless the second platform was considered as an ancillary feature. Similarly, a large nucleated site such as Beili Bedw (in Radnorshire: see below) with more than a dozen platforms has a record for each of them.

The collation of such a considerable quantity of survey data between 1996 and 2000, unevenly distributed though the sites are, offers an opportunity not previously available to consider some emerging patterns in the nature and form of medieval and later rural settlement. That there is little specific dating evidence for any but a handful of the numerous sites is a handicap, as unfortunate as it is inevitable, yet even with considerably more chronological data we would remain heavily dependent on comparison and analogy. What follows is an attempt, both provisional and also speculative, to detect chronological and morphological patterning in the remains identified through fieldwork. Particular settlement types are assessed within a broad chronological framework, in the belief that with the extensive data available it should be possible to make some progress in developing a sequence, even though the picture is complicated by the presence of both permanently occupied and seasonal settlements.

Two basic settlement forms can be distinguished in the field survey record, the platform and the long hut (Table 2.2). These cannot be treated as exclusive forms, for frequently a platform will display the foundations of a long hut upon it. No one would suggest that the two types represent anything other than a coarse division emerging from morphological characteristics, the terminology reflecting two different elements of a settlement site: the one the building itself, the other the levelled ground on which a building was erected. A further basic form, the shelter, has been identified as a result of work primarily in parts of north Wales where small, irregular and often roughly built structures have been identified in the uplands. Probably of relatively recent date, these are not considered further here.

centuries certainly fall within the ambit of the study (see below section 2.5). Also the regional SMR carries a great many records, especially for Montgomeryshire, where the details are so sparse that it was unclear whether a particular site was relevant to the study. It was felt that at least a sample of these sites should be visited, and this generated new records for a significant number of buildings which, strictly speaking, fell outside the purview of the project.

Table 2.2 Deserted rural settlements by site type in each old county in central and north-east Wales

Site type	Brecknock	Montgomery	Radnor	Denbigh	Flint	Wrexham	Total
Platform	162	108	275	33	1	4	583
Long hut	267	51	42	56	0	4	420
Platform with hut	53	22	48	10	1	2	136
Abandoned house	16	18	4	7	0	1	46
Shelter	26	8	2	10	0	2	48
Other	30	15	39	14	1	2	101
Total	554	222	410	130	3	15	1334

Absent from the site types are other more specific settlement forms including those defended or protected by a motte or a moat. Also absent, as a specific type, is the longhouse. Some long huts may well have been longhouses, but determining this from surface evidence alone can be difficult and the results potentially misleading. Approximately half the long huts located in the uplands of central and north-east Wales occupy level ground or lie along the contour (see Table 2.3), and consequently there is little variation in internal levels within the building, one of the key features in the definition of the longhouse. Even where there is evidence of changing levels within a building there can be no certainty that a byre was an integral part of that structure. Furthermore, as a building form the longhouse appears not to have been ubiquitous in Wales (Smith 1989, 103). It is essentially a product of architectural analysis and is best avoided in the context of this assessment.

Table 2.3 Location of deserted rural settlements by site type and topography

Site	Platform	Long hut	Platform hut	Abandoned house	Shelter	Other	Total
Ridge/hill top	3	5	2	3	2	0	15
Top valley/hill slope	78	39	16	5	3	9	150
Mid valley/hill slope	332	119	71	22	11	27	582
Base valley/hill slope	48	49	16	4	3	11	131
Spur	5	9	1	0	0	1	16
Valley floor	9	96	3	1	5	13	127
Others	10	20	3	0	2	5	40
Not established	76	79	23	11	21	35	245
Total	561	416	135	46	47	101	1306

2.4 Discussion of survey results

2.4.1 Platforms and their buildings: the evidence for medieval settlement

Distinctive though they appear, platform sites were not recognised for what they were until Cyril and Aileen Fox first identified significant numbers in the uplands of east Glamorgan in the mid-1930s. Since then there has been a gradual rather than a spectacular increase in new identifications across Wales but, as noted above, research has focused very much on Glamorgan (RCAHMW 1982) and north-west Wales (Gresham 1954), creating significant biases in the distribution pattern. If a single result emerges from the current study it is that the platform as a site type is common across much of central and eastern Wales, and it can be safely assumed that only a small proportion of the existing sites have yet been recorded.

The invariable adjunct to the platform was the natural ground slope which necessitated its creation; the platform was almost always set into the slope with its long axis at right angles to the contour. Such a position facilitated drainage, in that less surface and subsurface water would run off the slope on to the platform (Gresham 1954, 22). During the initial construction work, spoil from the cut into the slope was thrown forward to extend the level terrace. This left a scoop in the rear, its slope termed the 'fan', and a projecting earthwork at the front, the face of which has been termed the 'apron'. A bank, known as a 'hood', was occasionally thrown up around the top of the fan to deflect surface water, but such earthworks were more commonly deployed in north-west Wales than in the border regions. Platform size varies considerably; the length of the level terrace can range from only 4m or so to more than 20m. However, intermediate lengths are prevalent, and nearly half of the Radnorshire platforms fall between 11m and 14m. The vertical height of both the fan and the apron tends to reflect the steepness of the slope; for the fan values of 5m and over are not unknown.

The platform was of course only the earthwork base for a building constructed on it, hence the original label of 'platform house', coined by the Foxes (1949). While many platforms reveal no traces of what was erected on them, a reasonable proportion do show the remains of a rectangular building, but usually only as low foundations. Around 15% of the 300 or more platforms in Radnorshire have building traces on them, a figure rising to near 25% in Brecknock.

Some 580 platforms have now been recognised in the region as a whole. Of these over 250 are isolated sites, there are around 140 pairs where two platforms are either contiguous or sufficiently close to imply that they were elements of the same steading, and there are a small number of groups comprising several platforms in close proximity. Groups are thus quite rare, single platforms much more common. A significant proportion of the upland platforms may reflect seasonal activity, a point we shall return to below (p34), but many others relate to permanent habitation in a range of contexts that must now be examined.

The distribution of all the known platforms (Fig 2.2) reveals significant numbers in the uplands of Brecknock, particularly on Mynydd Epynt and in the Brecon Beacons, a dense distribution in Radnorshire, with a thinner density in Montgomeryshire to the north, and a spread into Denbighshire further to the north-west. But in north-east Wales, from northern Montgomeryshire to the north Wales coast, and also the coastal strip between the valleys of the Conwy and Clwyd, platforms are very sparse. The impact of earlier fieldwork programmes on this picture should not be underestimated. The concentrations in upland Brecknock and also over most of Radnorshire result from fieldwork by the RCAHMW and in recent years by CPAT, whilst the heavy concentration on the western side of the Berwyn in Denbighshire is also a result of recent surveys (Silvester 2000). The distortive impact of this fieldwork can readily be gauged in Radnorshire. Nearly 62% of the known sites were derived either from recent uplands projects, from the search of aerial photography or during fieldwork linked with the current Cadw-funded programme. Thus the almost complete absence of sites in the Wye and Usk valleys in central Wales can perhaps be explained by the absence of field examination of the valley slopes (in contrast to the Dyfi, see below). The same argument might be advanced for Flintshire and adjacent areas, and there is almost a paradox here in the appearance of the only significant nucleated group of platforms, that of Hen Caerwys, where the gentle terrain is hardly conducive to the creation of clear platforms. Nevertheless, the general impression remains that as a morphological type the platform fades out in north-east Wales. This may be not only a result of topographical constraints, but could be underpinned by cultural considerations. Perhaps, too, geographically varying patterns of rural depopulation have some significance, but this remains an under-researched topic.

The majority of known platforms in the region lie in the uplands. That this reflects the impact of recent fieldwork is signalled by other discoveries, cumulatively indicating that platforms are just as likely to be encountered in the lower, farmed lands of the region as in the less exploited hill lands, albeit in a more degraded and usually less distinctive guise. On the eastern slopes of the Dyfi Valley, where it forms the boundary between Meriony and Montgomeryshire, several large and well-defined house platforms occupy ground sloping up from the valley floor, and significantly fall within the same altitude range – no greater than 120m OD – as the present-day farms that lie just above and back from the river. It is a siting that coincides precisely with Smith's favoured location in Montgomeryshire for late medieval hall-houses (1988, 45). In the rolling hills of eastern Montgomeryshire, west of the Severn Valley, where pasture predominates, a recent systematic survey of Trefnant township in Castle Caereinion revealed three pairs of platforms and a further three solitary examples (Silvester 2001), where previously there were no known platform sites, other than that supporting the 15th-century hall-house of Tŷ Mawr (Britnell and Dixon 2001, 60). On this evidence there were more steadings in Trefnant in the medieval era than there are today. All the newly identified platforms existed only as earthwork sites, indicating not only their total abandonment but also a significantly different pattern of rural settlement from that of later centuries.

Platforms occur in both rural and village contexts, and to some commentators they clearly marked the positions of 'peasant habitations' (Griffiths 1989, 237), although their presence beneath more sophisticated, standing buildings such as Tŷ Mawr belies such a straightforward characterisation. Some historic villages in central Radnorshire and Brecknock display a varying number of platforms around the peripheries of their built-up areas, implying not only that these settlements were originally more extensive in past centuries, but also – and not surprisingly – that the communities' response to the topography within their nucleated settlements was the same as in the countryside (Silvester 1997a, 119). What is less readily explicable, but may be a result of a combination of more intensive modern land use, more muted topography, and rather different settlement histories, is that the distribution of these village platform groups does not appear to extend into Montgomeryshire. However, the appearance of the nucleated settlement at Hen Caerwys in Flintshire (Rogers 1979) indicates that the

distribution pattern cannot be rigorously defined, at least for the present, and there are other groups in Radnorshire, most notably the classic site at Beili Bedw, tentatively interpreted as an abandoned 'free' Welsh settlement (Courtney 1991, 250), and also at Cefnllys to the east of Llandrindod Wells, where the concept of the deserted rural settlement as an isolated holding begins to give way to a more nucleated village-like complex. Where platforms do occur within existing village settlements – see for instance the villages of Llanddew and Gwenddwr in Brecknock (Silvester 1997a, 120) – they have been omitted from the present Cadw-funded study, but they form an interesting and potentially informative parallel to any assessment of rural settlement remains.

2.4.2 Platforms with buildings on them

While it can reasonably be assumed that the majority of platforms were designed for houses, contiguous platforms in a permanently occupied settlement might reflect the presence of ancillary structures such as barns or byres, though only rarely has this been collaborated by excavation (eg Gelligaer Common: Butler 1971). Surface evidence, however, can be suggestive. Thus on Rhyd Gethin above Llandrillo (Denbs) the two pairs of platforms lying on the periphery of a block of strip fields both exhibit earthworks of unequal size (Fig 2.3). Solitary platforms, too, could conceivably have served as stances for barns, even in the medieval period, although in the absence of excavation this can remain only a supposition.

Where above-ground structural traces are absent, an original construction in wholly degradable building materials may provide an explanation, but the Gelligaer Common excavations (A Fox 1939) demonstrate the need for caution in any reliance on the surface evidence: although all three houses there were of similar construction with turf walls on low stone foundation walls, only one of the three was visible on the surface of the platform prior to excavation. Post-abandonment destruction through agricultural agencies must also be taken into account, particularly in enclosed farmland. At Beili Bedw (Rads) two platforms have now lost all surface traces of the foundations that were apparent when the site was surveyed by the then Ministry of Works in 1960 (Courtney 1991, Fig 2).

A significant proportion of platforms do have visible traces of buildings on them; in Radnorshire it is in the region of 15%, in Denbighshire more than 23%. Their presence inevitably provides an additional facet to platform morphology, and indeed the visible presence of a

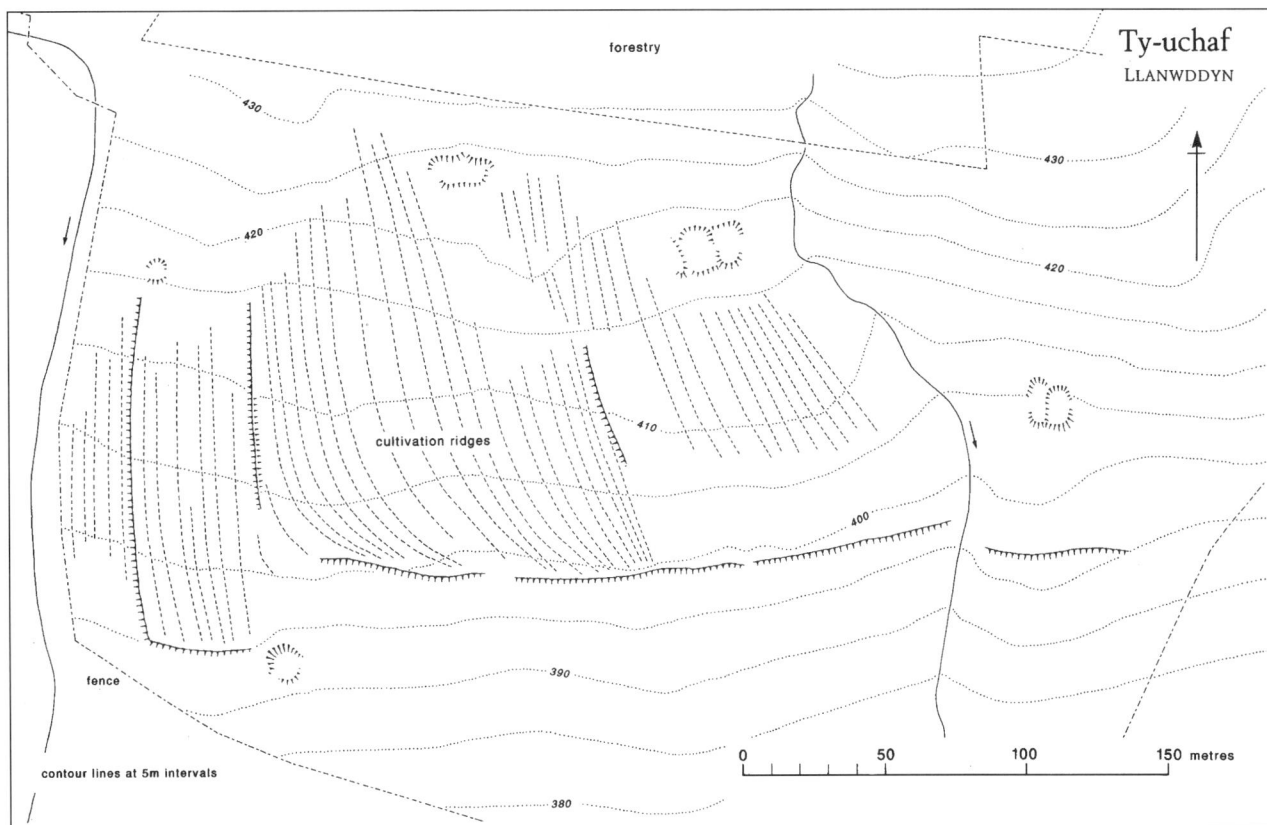

2.4 Ty-uchaf, Llanwddyn

building tends to diminish the significance attached to the earthwork platform itself. However, very occasionally the platform may be considerably longer or wider than the structure it supports, suggesting the secondary construction of a smaller building. This is evidently the case at Cefn Rhysgog, Aberedw (Rads), where a platform of putative medieval date, 23.6m long, is now occupied by a ruined 18th- or 19th-century barn less

2.5 Strip fields on common land at Cefn Wylfre (Aberedw Hill), Glascwm (Crown copyright: RCAHMW)

than 13m long, the level earthwork extending incongruously for more than 7m beyond the end wall of the building. But usually where foundations are visible, they appear to occupy most of the level platform, confirmation coming from excavated sites such as Hen Caerwys (Flints) and Gelligaer Common (Glams).

Without excavation it is impossible to determine whether the platform and the building on it are contemporary elements, and this should also warn us against too precise an interpretation of the building itself based on the earthwork alone, as Butler astutely implied in relation to the excavated platforms on Gelligaer Common (1971, 263). There is, too, little distinguishable consistency in the appearance or non-appearance of building foundations on platforms. There are several examples of paired platforms, where one has visible building foundations and the other lacks them. Equally there are some bare platforms on open moorland where it seems improbable that the building had durable foundations, for these would surely have survived. In summary, little can be read into the presence or absence of visible structural evidence on platforms.

Finally, there is one significant facet of the study of platforms that fell largely outside the remit of the current survey, namely those with standing, and often occupied, buildings on them. Architectural historians have long recognised that a platform was integral to many sub-medieval houses, and Smith was adamant in his belief that 'a distinctive feature of most [late medieval] hall-houses and one which again was retained in the later sub-medieval phase, was the siting of the house down rather than across the slope' (1989, 114), clearly implying the creation of some form of platform. Indeed, the appearance of a platform might be anticipated wherever the local topography demanded it. At Tŷ Mawr in Castle Caereinion (Monts) excavations demonstrated that the extant aisled hall-house of the mid-15th century was preceded by an earlier, 13th-century building (Britnell and Dixon 2001, 77). Only the later construction was certainly established on a platform, but the location of the house set into the base of a steep slope implies that the earlier building, too, would have been platformed.

Where the front and rear walls of a building effectively replace the apron and fan of the supporting platform the earthwork and the structure tend to coalesce into a single unit. The apron can display what appears to be a stone revetment, and excavated late medieval sites such as Tŷ Mawr and also Tyddyn Llwydion in Pennant Melangell (Monts) confirm that the

stonework acted as a sill for the sleeper beam of the timber building above (Britnell and Suggett 2002). The emergence of buildings rising directly above the edge of the platform may have wider, chronological implications, for there is some evidence to suggest a transition from post-hole to sleeper-beam construction in the 13th or 14th century, at least in central Wales, reinforcing the requirement for level ground on which to build (W J Britnell: pers comm).

2.4.3 Platform settlements and fields

Generally, the field systems that provided the agricultural component of many abandoned farming settlement sites at lower altitudes have been modified or even obliterated in later centuries, while higher in the hills conditions were inevitably less conducive to cereal cultivation. Nevertheless, the blanket dismissal by some historians of medieval cultivation over 200m OD (eg Jack 1988, 443) is misleading. Direct associations between platforms and strip-field systems have now been recognised in at least two areas and offer some of the most compelling circumstantial evidence for the interpretation of the platforms as house sites of medieval date. Relict strip fields above Cadwst in Cwm Pennant (Llandrillo, Denbs), on the western periphery of the Berwyn Mountains, have been considered in detail elsewhere; spreading over 65ha and rising to nearly 400m above sea level, the fields are accompanied by nearly a dozen platform sites in two distinct groups lying to the north-west and south of the fields (Silvester 2000, Fig 2). Spatially, the latter might almost be classed as a nucleated settlement. Higher up Cwm Pennant the platforms lie in pairs at field-bank terminals, implying that at least some of the ground was farmed in severalty. The writer has argued that these survivals signal the expansion of the medieval community of Llandrillo on to former grazing grounds on the mountain edge as the pressure on land became acute in the valley below. A similar argument has been advanced for the platforms grouped around a block of cultivation ridges divided into strip fields, above Lake Vyrnwy in Montgomeryshire (Fig 2.4). These must herald an offshoot of the medieval settlement of Llanwddyn which lay about 1km to the south-east and 100m lower (Silvester 2000, 56).

Some commons in Radnorshire are also now revealing evidence of medieval cultivation. On both Aberedw Hill and Cnwch Bank, 10km to the north-east, narrow strip fields which are visible from the air but almost indiscernible on the ground because they are so slight run out from the enclosed lands in the

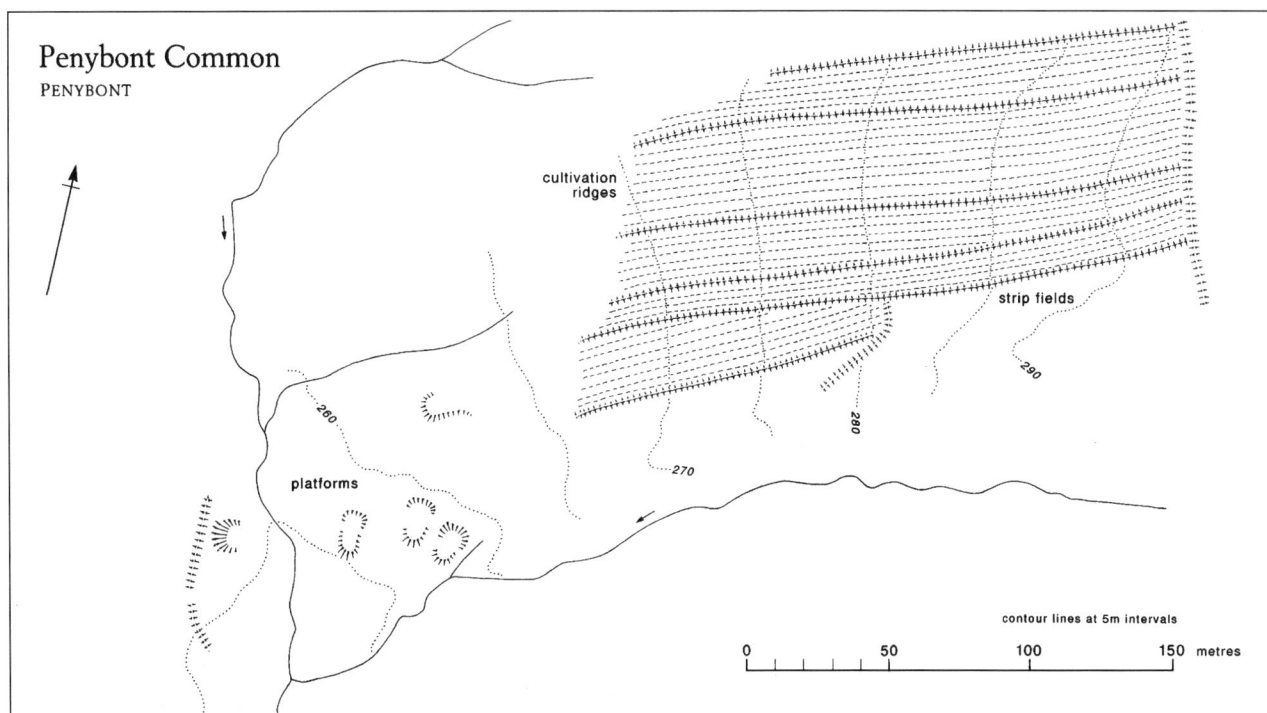

2.6 Penybont Common

valleys on to the unenclosed commons (Fig 2.5). At least one of these groups of fields, above Cwmblaenerw Brook in Aberedw, can be associated with platforms on the basis of geographical proximity. Clearer is the survival on Penybont Common, one of the lower commons in Radnorshire, where little of the ground rises to more than 250m OD. Strip fields, some enclosing ridging, have been identified in three places, the most significant being on the interfluve between small streams where the strip fields terminate immediately above a group of several platforms (Fig 2.6).

Like the platforms, it is impossible to determine on the evidence currently available whether all the known strip fields are specifically medieval in origin and whether any continued in use in the succeeding centuries, as was clearly the case with some of their lowland counterparts.

2.4.4 Platforms with enclosures

The permanent occupation implied by the appearance of field systems at high altitude – 300m to 425m OD – does not extend into Brecknock. The Brecon Beacons, though littered with deserted sites indicative of seasonal usage (see below), have not shown up any indubitable traces of medieval field systems. However, there are at least two places in the northern valleys where the platforms are conspicuously different from the normal range of upland sites, raising the suspicion that they performed a different function. A natural

shelf on the northern slopes of Y Gyrn above the valley of the Tarell supports several platforms, some with rectangular house foundations on them, accompanying two large conjoined enclosures. The overall dimensions of the houses mark them out as being unusual in this area (Fig 2.7). They are comparable, however, with a similar site in the more sheltered valley of the Cynwyn, 5km to the east, where again there is an exceptionally large platform partnered by a smaller, and probably ancillary, platform, as well as a large enclosure. Both these settlements lie at over 400m OD and the situation of the former is not a hospitable one. In the absence of corroborative evidence that might be provided by excavation, neither of these sites can be certainly attributed to the medieval centuries, nor their permanent occupation confirmed, yet the settlement morphology is so distinctive as to suggest that these were permanently occupied medieval farms, and probably typical of others that await discovery in the northern valleys of the Brecon Beacons.

Brecknock is not alone in revealing high-altitude platforms and enclosures, but generally the examples further north are atypical in appearance and appear to have functioned within a monastic economy. A grange of the Knights Hospitallers, the so-called Llanwddyn *Hospitium* (Monts), occupies a natural basin below the summit of a ridge high above Lake Vyrnwy, at a height of about 365m OD. The enclosure contains cultivation ridges and a spring that reputedly had curative proper-

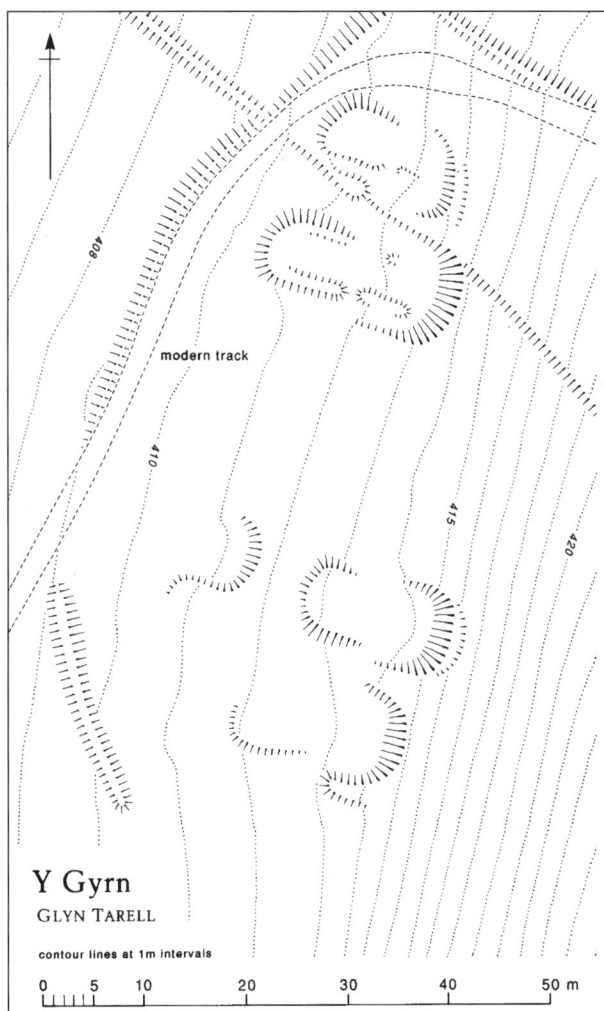

Y Gyrn

GLYN TARELL

contour lines at 1m intervals

0   5   10   20   30   40   50 m

2.7 Y Gyrn, Glyn Tarrell

ties, as well as a substantial platform supporting the foundations of a rectangular building nearly 16m long, one of the largest long huts yet identified in Montgomeryshire. Documentary evidence, albeit tenuous, implies a date in the 13th century (Silvester 1997b). Hen Ddinbych on the Denbigh Moors has also been identified as an ecclesiastical grange (Gresham *et al* 1959). An earthwork surrounds three platforms of extremely large size, one of which has clear traces of a long and relatively narrow structure. The large size – the largest platform is more than 25m in internal length – together with the medieval ecclesiastical links has led Dyer to suggest that one or more of these platforms may have supported roofed sheepcotes of a sort prevalent in western England (Dyer 1995; C C Dyer: pers comm). The paired platforms at Dyrysgol near St Harmon (Rads), though lacking an enclosure, are even larger in size, one earthwork being 36m long, and the structure on it has internal measurements of 33m. Interesting in the historiography of deserted settlement studies because they represented Cyril Fox's first publication on

platforms beyond Glamorgan (C Fox 1939a), they too might have a monastic origin, for the Cistercian grange of Dolhelfa was located in this area (Percival 1993).

2.4.5 Buildings without platforms

It hardly needs to be stressed that even in a predominantly upland region like eastern Wales there are many localities where it was possible to construct a permanent dwelling on level ground, and thus obviate the need for a levelled platform. It follows that platform sites must be only one element – though the most obvious – of the medieval rural settlement pattern. Many other medieval sites may have existed for which all the surface traces have now been completely obliterated, whilst amongst the many stone-foundationed huts discussed in a later section there must be some which originated in the medieval era, though this cannot normally be ascertained from surface evidence alone. On Ffridd Camen in Llandrillo (Denbs), below the Berwyn (Fig 2.8), a long hut with foundations composed of sizeable upright slabs – probably one of the few that can be legitimately interpreted as a longhouse on the basis of its size and visible internal partitions – is less than 1km from platform sites with no traces of buildings on them. Both appear to be associated with strip field cultivation of the medieval period and should be of broadly comparable date (Silvester 1991), but the difference is that the Ffridd Camen hut lies on a natural shelf, littered with surface stone, while the platforms occupy sloping ground which has also been enclosed, and ploughed for pasture improvement.

2.4.6 Chronology

Consideration of the chronology of platform settlement has been left to the end of this section for a good reason. A platform revealing itself only as an earthwork is intrinsically undatable. Where there is a solid association with strip field cultivation of presumed medieval origin, a contemporary date can be assumed, and, while we may suspect that many of the platforms are the bases for former medieval houses, incontrovertible evidence is sparse. Very few platforms have been excavated, yet there is a general assumption that they are broadly medieval or early post-medieval in origin. Fox demonstrated that the platforms excavated on Gelligaer Common were of 13th-century date, and in the study area pottery of broadly comparable date was recovered from a much-degraded platform at Carneddau (Monts). Later dates have, however, been registered for Beili Bedw (Rads), and for Hen Caerwys (Flints).

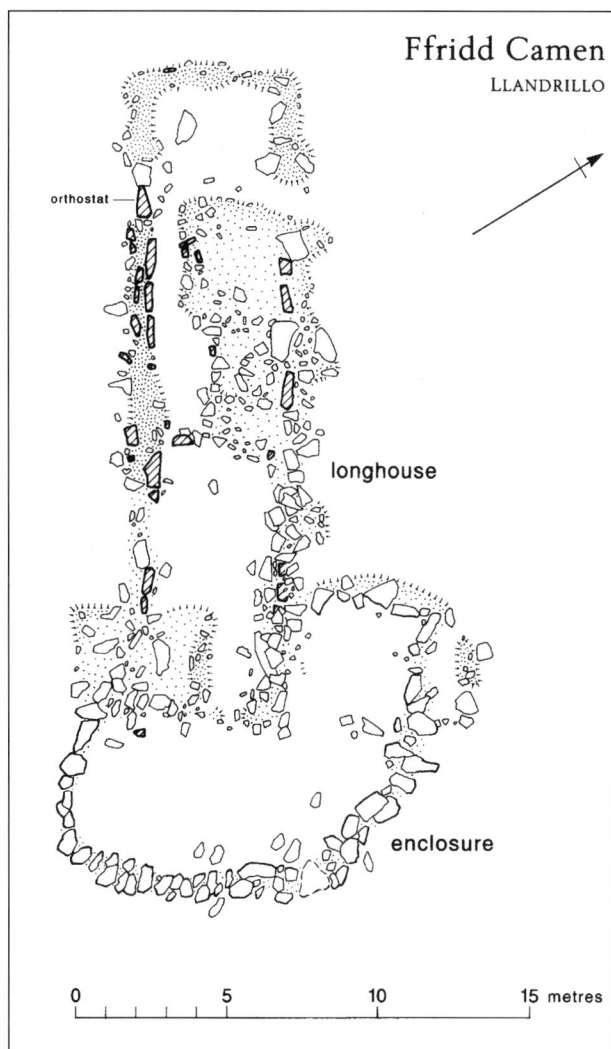

Ffridd Camen
LLANDRILLO

orthostat

longhouse

enclosure

0   5   10   15 metres

2.8 Ffridd Camen, Llandrillo

There is, though, no precise correlation that ties the platform solely to the medieval centuries. From the 15th century a range of standing buildings, noted particularly in Radnorshire, indicate the continuation of the tradition into the sub-medieval era. Ultimately construction of the longitudinal platform set down the slope went out of favour, giving way to its counterpart lying along the contour, and it is generally the latter that has continued to be created up to the present. The first signs of this shift in Radnorshire were in the second half of the 16th century where they are coupled with alterations in house layout (R Suggett: pers comm), but there was no synchronicity in the adoption of these new developments amongst the different social classes and downslope houses continued to be constructed throughout the 17th and into the 18th century. From an archaeological viewpoint a detailed assessment of standing buildings elsewhere might usefully refine this chronology, but overall we should envisage only a gradual shift from one type to the other, and not be surprised if occasionally a contour-following platform appears in a predominantly medieval environment.

2.5 Late medieval deserted settlement

There is general agreement amongst historians that the 14th century witnessed fundamental changes in the socio-economic base of England and Wales, even if the degree of change is sometimes disputed (Astill and Grant 1988, 216; Austin 1989, 234; Dyer 1989, 48). A deteriorating climate, poor harvests and plague led to a marked decline in population and a reduction in the areas actively farmed. The impact of these events in Wales was exacerbated by the widespread destruction associated with the rebellion of Owain Glyndŵr at the beginning of the 15th century (for which see Owen 1991, 99; Davies 1995, 299). Excavations on settlement sites in upland areas of Wales, south-west England and elsewhere have consistently revealed evidence of 13th-century occupation which seemingly terminated thereafter. On the admittedly limited evidence available, there has been a tendency to attribute the abandonment of medieval sites in the uplands to this period of change (Silvester 2000, 57).

The putative retrenchment of settlement, however, appears to have lasted for not more than a few generations at most. Colin Thomas flagged up renewed settlement expansion in 16th-century Merioneth (1964) and this has been echoed in other Welsh studies; and despite a paucity of documentary support, even 15th-century encroachment onto the waste has been postulated by Welsh historians (Owen 1991, 106). Further afield, Winchester (2000, 16) has demonstrated the revitalisation of settlement in northern England and the borders in the 15th century.

Renewed expansion in settlement and farming in the more settled conditions following the Glyndwr revolt can be assumed, then, even if the chronology and level of this expansion is far from clear. Whether new settlements mirrored the form of their predecessors is a matter for consideration. The available

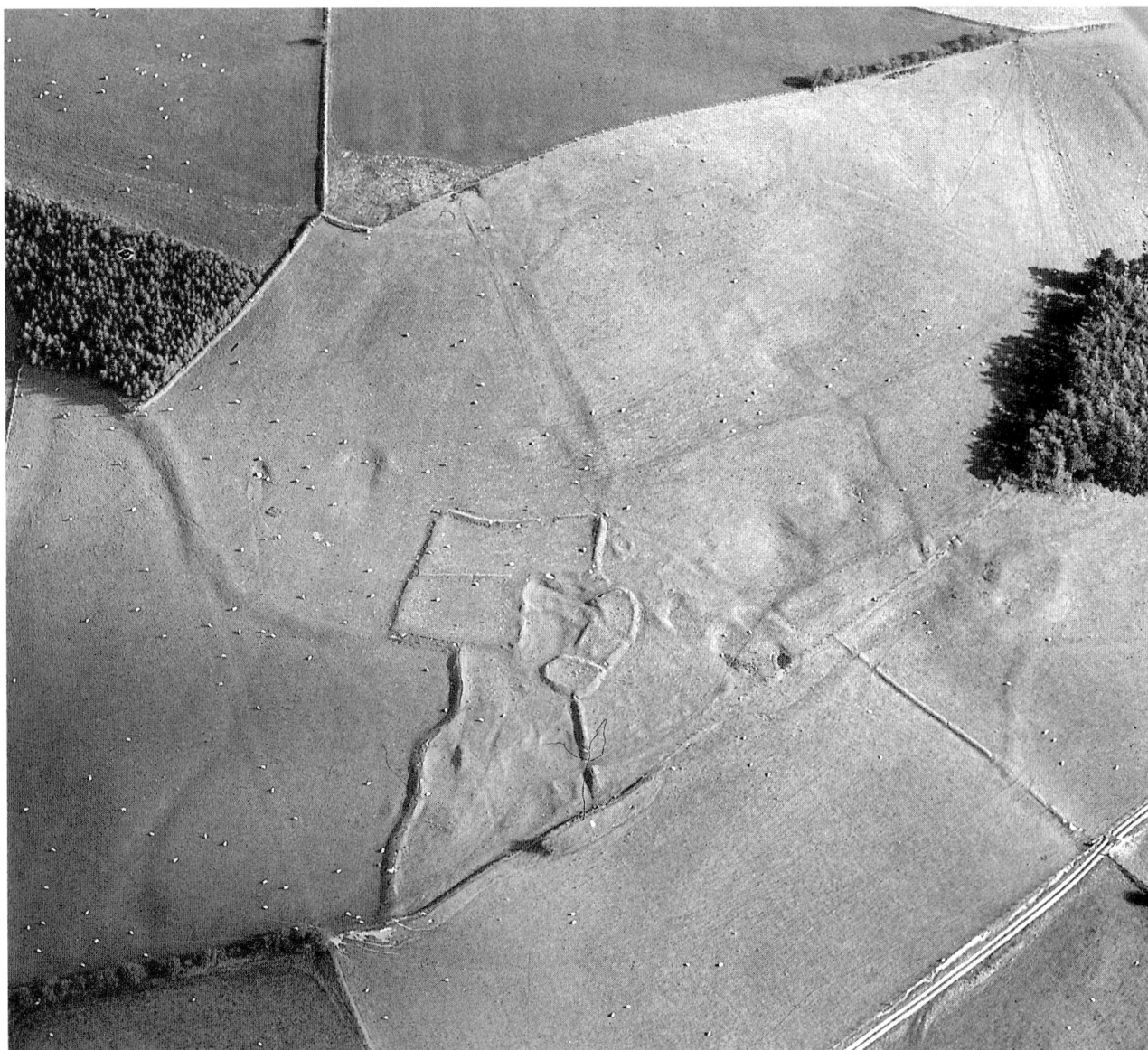

2.9 Beili Bedw, Radnorshire (Crown copyright: RCAHMW)

evidence is slight, yet there may have been a greater emphasis on individual initiative rather than community consensus in the expansion on to lands abandoned in the 14th century and in some places, too, onto the commons. It might reasonably be anticipated that the emergence of different forms of settlement would reflect these socio-economic changes. Griffiths claimed a few years ago that 'open field was taken into severalty and girdle settlements and bond hamlets shrank to be replaced by dispersed *tyddynnod* standing in their own fields, processes that accelerated after 1500' (1989, 233), whilst Suggett's belief (1996, 34) that there was a 'late-medieval transformation in housing which involved the virtually complete rejection of earlier dwellings' is also of potential significance in this context. Settlement change in the 15th century ought thus to be recognisable in the landscape.

Beili Bedw (Rads) offers a useful starting point. Unique in central Wales for the number of its platforms – over a dozen – this nucleated settlement was surveyed by the then Ministry of Works in 1960 and in subsequent years Leslie Alcock excavated three of the platforms, although a final excavation report had to wait for a further 30 years (Courtney 1991). Beili Bedw as depicted by the Ministry of Works consisted of the platforms, some with rectangular buildings on them, and several small, rectilinear enclosures at the centre of the complex with boundaries radiating from them. The various platforms have been considered as integral elements of a complete and coherent settlement (Courtney 1991, Fig 2). However, there is a chronological depth to the earthworks at Beili Bedw which appears to have escaped attention, even in the excavation report. The substantial earthworks of the rectilinear enclosures have been little damaged by later ploughing, and the enclosures immediately to the west show similarities in design and scale, and must be broadly contemporary (Fig 2.9) Between these two groups of enclosures, as the 1960 plan reveals, is a rectangular building, not platformed, which nevertheless remains sufficiently distinctive to signal that it was the focal point of this phase of settlement at Beili Bedw. It emerges clearly on aerial photographs in contrast to the much more muted earthworks of the platforms, a later farmstead set amidst the abandoned earthworks of the Beili Bedw platform settlement. Unfortunately, it was not excavated and datable material from the excavations generally is fairly sparse; late Malvernian pottery suggests that two of the platforms were in use in the 15th or possibly even the 16th century, but Courtney also isolated a fragment of late 16th-century/early 17th-century glass (1991, 241). Surprisingly, there was no earlier material. Taking these finds at face value the simplest explanation is that a platform settlement lasted through the critical years of the 15th century, but was then succeeded by a single farmstead with its accoutrements in the 16th century. This dating throws the concept of Beili Bedw as a bond settlement into doubt, as Courtney, who favoured a freemen's settlement, was at pains to point out (1991, 250), but it also signals the changing nature of settlement, to a farmholding held in severalty.

Assessments of some Radnorshire commons in recent years have revealed the earthworks of small farmsteads consisting of a dwelling each surrounded by several enclosures similar to Beili Bedw. Platforms are still in evidence within these complexes, and in some ways the steadings are rather similar to the encroachments on the waste of later centuries (see below). Nevertheless, they are distinctively different from those numerous cottage enclosures that are depicted across the tithe maps of the mid-19th century. Examples include a settlement on Moelfre Hill, Llanbister (Fig 2.10), where the intermittent foundations of a long hut occupying a platform are surrounded by at least five enclosures of varying size. Access from the common was by a trackway that angled between the enclosures towards the platform. Lying close to the edge of the common and adjacent to a stream, the complex is only a short distance from an agglomeration of cottages and smallholdings which are still recognised by the ironic name of Moelfre City, much as they were in the mid-19th century. There are indicators of other enclosed settlements within the environs of Moelfre City which were later integrated

into the pattern of enclosed fields spreading out from the valleys, but the Moelfre Hill settlement had clearly been long abandoned by the time of the tithe survey around 1843.

Similarly located is a two-celled long hut on Fron Top (Rads) which has small enclosures abutting its south-western side and a larger enclosure filled with cultivation ridges to the east. Other comparable complexes in Radnorshire are Upper House Enclosure I at Glascwm where a platform sports the faint traces of a rectangular building and has both a small appended kidney-shaped enclosure and a larger one containing cultivation ridges (Fig 2.11); and the Garn Fawr settlement on the south-eastern flank of Gilwern Hill in Glascwm, titled even on modern Ordnance Survey maps as a *farmstead*. The latter comprises a deeply terraced platform approached by a track running between enclosures; the settlement lies towards the higher end of land that was being farmed in the mid-19th century, but its position indicates that it had almost certainly been abandoned by the time the land was enclosed.

None of these sites was recorded, let alone functioned, in the mid-19th century, and Garn Fawr appears to have been occupied prior to the enclosure of the slopes that spread upwards from the valley below. An 18th-century date for their occupation cannot be discounted, but an earlier century is more likely. However, all of them come from a limited area of central Radnorshire where the fragmented pattern of commons offered exceptional opportunities for encroachment in the post-medieval centuries (Silvester 2004, 58). There is also little doubt that Radnorshire is exceptional in terms of the effort that has gone into site identification: it has seen sustained fieldwork, and aerial photographic analysis, too, has been extremely fruitful. By comparison other parts of the region have been considerably less researched. Is it possible to detect similar features elsewhere?

Comparable sites can be identified on Mynydd Epynt in western Brecknock. Carnau Bach farmstead, overlooking Afon Dulas on the western side of the plateau, and at a distance from the main enclosed areas on the moor, consists of paired platforms accompanied by a third much smaller platform, four or five enclosures, and a stone-built store for roots or dairy products. Less complex earthworks also appear lower down the Dulas Valley at Topglas, although this appears still to have been occupied at the time of the tithe survey, and at Gardiners Hill East. Further south, towards the head of Nant Gwydderig, lies what

Moelfre Hill
LLANBISTER

long hut

modern tracks

later leat

track

contour lines at 1m intervals

0   5   10   20   30   40   50 metres

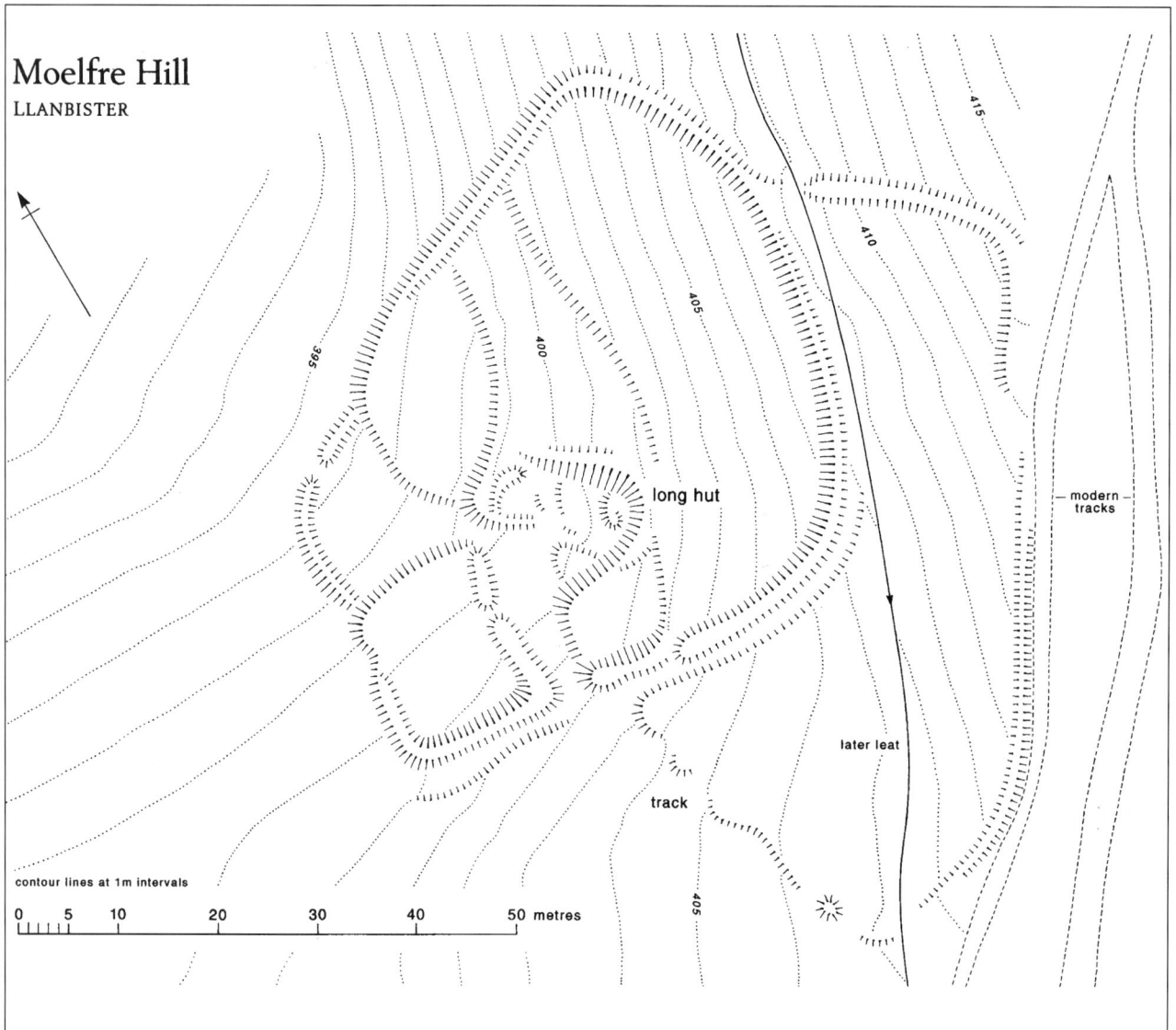

2.10 Moelfre Hill, Llanbister

appears to be another deserted farmstead with one rectangular building on a platform, an adjacent building, a sunken store adapted later to form a shelter, and three discrete embanked enclosures.

Further north in Montgomeryshire and Denbighshire, platforms and long huts accompanied by enclosures are recognisable in the uplands, but these are more likely to be a result of seasonal settlement (see below). Perhaps, however, it is on the enclosed lands that comparable sites should be sought. One aspect of the Trefnant landscape in Castle Caereinion (Monts) emerged through map regression analysis: three of the major farms, still functioning in the township, formed the foci of large, and sub-divided, lobed areas of some 20 hectares (Silvester 2000, 159). Less important than the absolute size, however, was the absence of any direct relationship with the earlier platform sites encountered elsewhere in the township, but these farms did form

primary nuclei in the field patterns that developed across the landscape. One, Pant-yr-alarch, appeared to be an intake from the adjacent common, and implicit in its ownership history was the fact that it had been in existence for two or three generations prior to the first documented reference in 1575 (Silvester 2001, 160). These 'enclosures' could, then, be typical of new steadings held in severalty that developed in the Montgomeryshire hills bordering the Severn after the crises of the 14th century and the gradual breakdown of the open-field agricultural system.

There is more than a little speculation in grouping these settlements. Morphologically they are similar and while there is little direct dating evidence, the relative chronology of the Radnorshire sites and the indirect dating for those in Montgomeryshire is suggestive. Certainly there is scope for much further research on this topic.

2.6 Post-medieval rural settlement

With the progression through Tudor and later centuries, settlement studies increasingly accommodate twin lines of enquiry, with the archaeology and vernacular architecture following converging courses. The latter is reflected in a growing literature on the houses and cottages of the Welsh landscape, from small beginnings in Snowdonia (Hughes and North 1908), to Peate's work, *The Welsh House* (1946), and more recently Peter Smith's monumental work, *Houses of the Welsh Countryside* (1988), Eurwyn Wiliam's studies (1982b; 1986), and the work of the Welsh Royal Commission in Glamorgan (1988) and more recently Radnorshire (Suggett 2005). General trends in the development and distribution pattern of vernacular architecture are thus reasonably well recognised, even if local studies remain uneven.

An obvious conclusion of this research is that at more congenial altitudes a substantial number of houses or at least their sites have seen continuity of occupation since the 15th century. The original house may still be occupied – witness the number of late medieval hall-houses in northern Montgomeryshire (Smith 1988, 38) – or the original house may have been demolished to make way for a more fashionable or commodious successor. In some places the earlier house may have been relegated to the status of a barn or cowhouse when a new house was erected on an adjacent plot. The analysis of these buildings, both as structures in their own right and as contributory elements of the built landscape, is a major study, as Peter Smith has shown (1988). It is also the domain more of the architectural historian than the archaeologist (see J Alfrey, Chapter 8).

While some houses and settlement sites in the lowlands have undoubtedly disappeared, the depopulation of the hills has been considerably more dramatic. Construction and desertion of farms and cottages in the post-medieval centuries were common to every region in the Principality. The hills in parts of central and north Wales are liberally scattered with the sites of such abandoned habitations. Encroachment on the wastes and commons of the uplands, perhaps from the 15th and certainly the 16th century, has already been alluded to, and it is an aspect covered in every volume on the social and economic history of post-medieval Wales. The move away from the hills is equally well charted, whether in the reports of the late 19th-century Royal Commission on Land (1896) or in oral testimony. Colin Thomas (1964) established the

growth in intakes in 16th-century Merioneth and comparable work has produced similar results elsewhere, as in western Denbighshire (Emery 1989, 65), and the Afan Valley in Glamorgan (Griffiths 1989, 237). The consensus is that this particular form of upland exploitation continued and indeed increased over the next three centuries, but whether the 18th century marked the high watermark in such activity as has been suggested remains to be adequately demonstrated.

Virtually every common and the more accessible wastes in the Principality seem to have had their share of intakes, landless labourers, miners, cottagers and other members of the poorest classes each claiming a small patch of common and traditionally erecting a *ty unnos* or 'one-night house' (Peate 1946, 40; Sayce 1942) on it. To maintain any independence the intake had to be detached from the enclosed land, hence the appearance of so many small 'islands' on tithe and more modern maps, but in some places, as cottages and their enclosures agglomerated, the intakes merged with the enclosed lands bordering the common. By the time of the tithe survey in the 1840s, it was only the most remote and inaccessible wastes in central Wales that had not witnessed some encroachment over the previous 300 years. The sheer scale of this expansion is staggering. A Merioneth rental recorded 400 encroachments extending over 10,000 acres of Crown land in the late 16th century (Thomas 1967, 154), while an early 18th-century list of encroachments on the Crown waste in Cantref Maelienydd (northern Radnorshire) revealed 784 encroachments, 421 of which had involved the erection of a cottage (Howse 1955). And when in 1779 Richard Myddelton of Chirk Castle determined to assess the scale of recent enclosures on the waste in the lordship of Ruthin, his surveyor Samuel Minshull mapped 41 cottages with 189 separate enclosures totalling 536 acres, spread over twelve Denbighshire parishes. Clearly the scale of activity was huge, and the subsequent decline and disintegration of the dispersed communities that evolved on and around the commons was probably equally dramatic.

Abandonment, indeed, may have occurred at any time between the 16th century and the 20th century, although there seems little doubt that it was in the 19th century that it reached its peak (see Peate 1946, 88). But it is also worth recalling that different factors may have influenced abandonment up until the recent past, including such exceptional events as the military takeover of Mynydd Epynt in 1940 when 54 dwellings were given up (Hughes 1998, 113).

Some former dwellings in the hills are now distinguished only by their foundations, while others retain their walls to a considerable height, sometimes even retaining a roof. These stone shells, however, will not necessarily represent the original, less substantial structure on the site, and such buildings as are standing are likely to be no earlier than the end of the 18th century (Smith 1989, 95). Their predecessors, whether the traditional *ty unnos* or something more substantial, are less well-known and certainly less immediately recognisable. As Wiliam has shown, few of these 'home-made homes' survive today (1988).

The Cadw-funded programme examined only an extremely small selection of the numerous abandoned homes in the uplands. A decision was taken at an early stage, based on a growing realisation of the scale of the task, to exclude cottages and the like that were considered to be encroachments of 18th-century or later date. It fell outside the remit of the programme to assess standing buildings that were still occupied, whether these lay in the hills or at lower altitudes. But inevitably some sites were visited, largely because the vague descriptions lodged in the regional Sites and Monuments Record frequently failed to clarify the nature of the settlement.

Crowsfoot in Glascwm (Rads) is one example among many. In the mid-19th century it appeared as an island encroachment on an arm of Little Hill Common, since enclosed. Its walls still stand almost to full height, but the enclosure and any other traces of ancillary activities have disappeared. In a re-entrant valley on the opposite side of the Little Hill ridge is Upper Blaen-bedw, shown but not named on the tithe map (and thus presumably already abandoned at that time). It comprises a two-cell structure whose rubble-enveloped walls now stand to rather less than 1m in height, and is surrounded by enclosures and served by a track running up the valley past the ruin. Ty Berth

(Brecs) in the Nant Onneu valley, south of the River Usk, is a ruined farm with the shells of both a house and barn; only the latter appears to have been functioning in the mid-19th century. In addition a third building, slightly upslope from the other two, appears as a rectangular structure defined by low rubble walls and set on a platform raised at the front. Had this been noted in isolation it would have been recorded as a long hut, but its appearance within the farm curtilage raises questions of both its date and function. Rather more can be deduced from the ruins of an unnamed holding above Cwm Pennant in Llandrillo (Denbs), on the western side of the Berwyn. This comprises two buildings, the foundations of which remain, and a series of about nine small enclosures ringed by a drystone wall. The complex post-dates the medieval strip fields (see above, p23) and also arguably the *hafodydd* in the area (Silvester 2000, 55). Yet by the time of the tithe the hill had returned to common.

These four examples, taken from an almost inexhaustible stock, display some of the issues likely to emerge from a study of post-medieval rural settlements. In the absence of comprehensive studies of limited areas such as a parish or even a single large common, it is not even possible to formulate, let alone answer, the wider questions that arise. Expansion and encroachment were a basic way of life in the post-medieval era (Howell 2000, 7). Archaeologically, however, we need to identify how and when encroachment occurred, whether different areas witnessed synchronous activity, whether there was a parallel development with new holdings emerging in already enclosed lands, the form of the ancillary features that went with them, and the nature and evolution of the dwellings themselves. There is also a need to assess the interaction of encroachments on the same common, the survival and loss of structures in the face of more recent enclosure and clearance, and the survival of 'encroachment' settlements down to the present day. Currently, we are a long way from resolving any of these issues.

2.7 Seasonal settlements in the uplands

The concept of individuals or families moving stock to the uplands during the summer months – often termed transhumance, although this term has not received universal acceptance for such seasonal movements in Wales (Kelly 1981–82, 883) – is one that was fundamental to the Welsh way of life in the Middle Ages, continuing as late as the 18th century or beyond

in more remote regions such as Snowdonia (Peate 1946, 127). As late as the earlier part of the 20th century, Iorwerth Peate (1946, 126) was noting, on the basis of personal knowledge, that whole households would move into the hills at Llanbrynmair in western Montgomeryshire, and spend several weeks washing and shearing sheep. The concept of the *hafod* and the

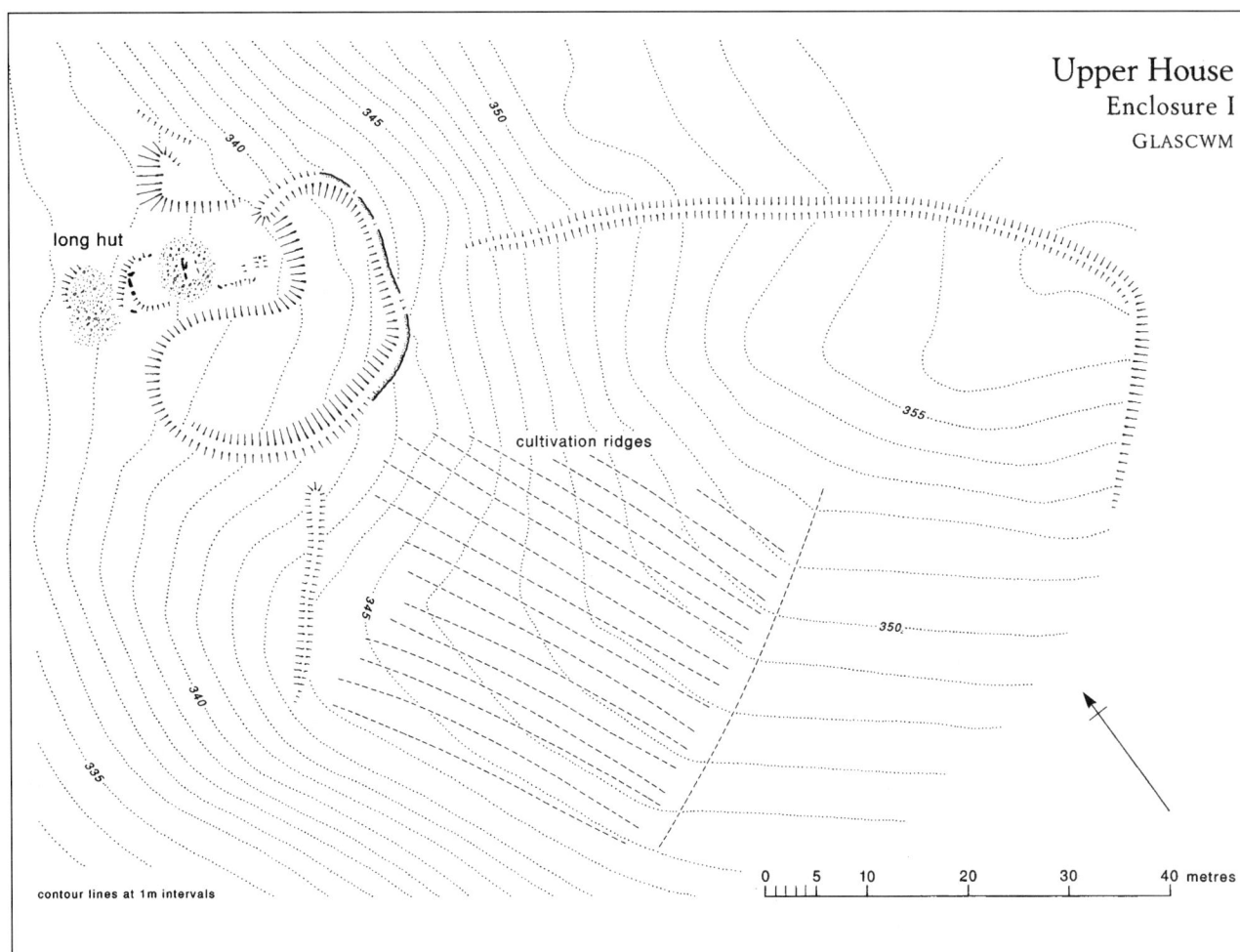

2.11 Upper House Enclosure I, Glascwm

hendre, the summer and winter residences respectively, is thus deeply embedded in any study of Welsh settlement patterns. Furthermore, the *lluest*, particularly prevalent in central Wales, which is variously identified in contemporary documents as a summer house, cottage or dairy (Davies 1980, 8), can also be identified as a shepherd's hut which ultimately might have been occupied throughout the year (Sambrook, this volume). This, too, has significant connotations for pastoral practice in Wales. The nature of seasonal activity varied through the centuries, and the settlement associated with this activity may also have taken different forms. In the absence of the sort of cartographical confirmation so well evinced for Cardiganshire, distinguishing between the field remains of the *hafod* and those of the *lluest* is difficult.

The identification and assessment of large numbers of long huts in some valleys of the central Welsh uplands has been one of the more obvious products of this study. Attention has already been drawn to Sayce's historical approach and Davies' place-name studies. Archaeologically, Crampton's preliminary work in the

Brecon Beacons (1966a) has given way to more rigorous research by the Welsh Royal Commission, and at the northern end of the region the excavations at Nant Criafolen near the Brenig reservoir have brought that area into focus (Allen 1979). Equally relevant is Anthony Ward's work on the Black Mountain (1997) and now Paul Sambrook's work on the *lluestai* of Cardiganshire. But with increasing research (whether historical or archaeological) comes the appreciation that the reality is complex and that no one model will serve to explain all the evidence, even for neighbouring areas. We need to examine various aspects before pulling some of the strands together.

How can we differentiate seasonally occupied dwellings from those inhabited throughout the year? Perhaps not surprisingly, there is no objective and succinct method for distinguishing between the field remains, but what should be of more concern is that even where a settlement has been excavated a consensus can be difficult to achieve. Aileen Fox saw the platforms on Gelligaer Common (Glams) as permanently occupied settlements (1939, 172) while

Iorwerth Peate (1946, 128), perhaps spurred by a point of view not wholly archaeological, preferred seasonal usage, a view shared by Martin Locock (this volume, p00). Conversely, the nature of the most extensively excavated complex in Wales at Hafod y Nant Criafolen (Allen 1979, 46) has been questioned, Stephen Briggs arguing, on the basis of the range of artefacts present, that the site was in permanent use (Briggs 1985, 304). As a result of the paucity of finds, even the status of Beili Bedw (Rads) as a permanent settlement is not beyond question (Ward 1997, 106).

Excavated evidence is not available for more than a handful of sites, leaving site function dependent on a range of characteristics: the topographical and geographical setting of individual sites, their morphology, and negatively the absence of those associated features that imply permanent farming. To these might be added the prevalence of analogous sites in the vicinity, and the occasional place-name or cartographic depiction. Butler (1991, 911) went further, invoking also associated structures such as a stack stand or field kiln for drying grain, though, with the exception of stores for dairy products, such ancillary features are rarely encountered, at least in east Wales. Utilising all the above criteria, a large number of seasonal sites can be isolated with reasonable confidence, although there will always be some which cannot be so readily categorised. However, what should be remembered is that even upland landscapes were not static. What was permanently farmed or occupied land in one century might have been preceded by seasonal usage, and the opposite could also occur: the late medieval platform settlements and their associated field systems above Cwm Pennant in Llandrillo (Denbs) were, for instance, superseded by *hafodydd*, one lying within abandoned strip fields, the others nearby (Silvester 2000, 55).

The evidence for summer settlements appears in three forms. Firstly, there are documentary references to *hafodydd*, summer houses and the like, which are sporadic or rare, depending on the area involved. Elwyn Davies collected much information from readily accessible sources, both medieval and post-medieval, more than twenty years ago (Davies 1980, 6; appendices A–C) and as far as this writer is aware no comparable research has been conducted since that time. Allied with these records are depictions on early maps, although rarely are these earlier than the 18th century (see Sambrook, this volume). Secondly, there is evidence of place-names, but it is unlikely that Elwyn Davies' compilations based on 19th-century Ordnance

Survey, tithe and other maps (Davies 1984–5) will be superseded, for any future research on less accessible sources is likely only to refine his conclusions on the distribution of both *hafodydd* and *lluestai*. Thirdly, there is the archaeological evidence: there is now a satisfactory picture of the appearance of seasonal settlements in virtually every constituent area in this region, even if a full picture of the distribution is still a long way in the future.

Site morphology and association

Both long huts, and platforms lacking any traces of buildings on them, are often to be found in remote locations in some of the highest uplands of central and north Wales, well above the zone of permanent farming. Both types, then, would seem to have been in seasonal use, even though in most of the uplands long huts are considerably more common.

Generally, long huts display a simple rectangular outline defined by low stone walls or grassy banks, although on occasions the walls may be higher and more pronounced. Many are well constructed with facing slabs to the walls, yet the rough boulder-built outlines of others suggest that much less care was taken in the building process (Fig 2.12). Dimensions vary, but the small size of the average long hut can be established from the fact that of some 330 recorded in the survey where the internal length – the best criterion for comparative purposes – can be gauged, over 43% are between 4m and 7m in length. There is normally some evidence of an entrance and, less commonly, partitions or other internal features. Detailed studies of such huts have been completed by Ward for parts of the Black Mountain contiguous to south-western Brecknock (1991, 5) and Leighton for some areas in the Brecon Beacons (1997, 100), and in due course comparable analyses for other regions might conceivably reveal regional variations in construction and morphology.

Variation, however, frequently comes less in the structure itself or its siting than in its associations with other features such as enclosures, ancillary structures and further long huts. Any inclination to view these seasonally occupied dwellings as isolated features in our upland landscapes should be tempered by the appearance of dispersed or sometimes even nucleated groups of long huts, though even excavation cannot, it seems, distinguish between sites in contemporary occupation and those that were successive. There were three or even four *hafodydd* on Ffridd Camen above Llandrillo (Denbs) distributed across the 40ha of the enclosed spur, and one of these was clearly of two phases (Silvester 1991, 13). Long huts in the Brecon Beacons tend to congregate along the floors of some valleys but not others; by Nant Crew there are at least eight long huts along a 2km-length of the valley, yet in the adjacent valley of Nant Ddu, little more than 1km away not a single example has been identified.

Nucleated groups are not common but they do exist. Hafod y Nant Criafolen near the Brenig Reservoir (Denbs) consisted of seven rectangular huts, six of them spread across an area 120m long around a stream confluence, and the final one about 100m further downstream. All except one had appended enclosures surviving, and this last may have been destroyed by ploughing. Curiously, Hafod y Nant Criafolen stands alone on the Denbigh Moors, for no other groups of similar complexity have been identified. But in north-western Brecknock around the Elan Valley three such groups have been identified in recent years in an area restricted to a few square kilometres. Small groups of four or five were located beside Nant Chwefri and in the valley of Nant Rhyd-goch and rather more, seven or eight, spread up a north-facing hillside below Cerrig Llwydion.

Some long huts interpreted as *hafodydd* (or *lluestai*) have associated enclosures around or adjacent to them: over 100 examples have been recorded to date, and the geographical distribution is fairly uniform across the region. Less convincing are long huts that appear superficially to be associated with the boundaries of fields or large enclosure complexes – the juxtaposition is as likely to be coincidental as synchronous. There are, though, other associations that do appear to have a regional flavour: stores, some partially sunken, occur close to long huts, particularly in the south of the region. These are particularly prevalent in the northern valleys of the Brecon Beacons and they appear, too, on Mynydd Epynt; occasional examples have been identified in southern Radnorshire but on the evidence currently available they do not generally feature further north. Usually drystone-built, the chambers probably had an important role in preserving dairy products. Exemplifying all three aspects is the settlement site at Pant-y-Blodiau East towards the south-western end of Mynydd Epynt (Fig 2.12). The long hut of orthostatic build occupies about a quarter of a stone-banked enclosure and also within this is a small embanked store, while a further two possible stores or clamps lie outside it, a short distance to the east. Intermittent scarp banks of unknown origin lie downslope.

The focus up to this point has been on long huts as the physical manifestations of seasonal settlement.

Yet on the unenclosed commons of Radnorshire platforms are a frequent phenomenon and, while these are associated with the trappings of permanency on the commons of Penybont and Aberedw as shown above, there are many other places where the platforms stand in isolation, in small groups, or are accompanied only by an enclosure. On Cilfaesty Hill in the north of the county more than a dozen platforms were identified close to its boundary during a survey in 1999, but at most there were two rectangular stone-built huts further into the interior. Likewise, there are considerable numbers of platforms around the edge of Aberedw Common, and the situation at the head of the Cefnhinog Brook is particularly illuminating. Congregating immediately outside the limits of the enclosed land is not only a cigar-shaped enclosure containing an encroachment cottage known as King's Palace and apparently already abandoned (and ignored) by the time of the 1843 tithe survey, but also a long hut in an enclosure, another long hut, and a line of four platforms, none with a trace of a building on it. To adduce a sequence here is at best hypothetical, but it is most likely that the platforms were succeeded by the long huts, and later by the encroachment.

Further south in Brecknock similar distribution patterns emerge. The three groups of platforms on Partrishow Common in the east of the county lie at a greater distance from the head dyke surrounding the enclosed land, but all are set to provide good views of the ground running into the valleys below; of the eleven platforms only two show fugitive traces of buildings on them. Superficially, the Brecon Beacons present a different picture (Fig 2.13), though here the site distribution pattern is based on sporadic and non-systematic fieldwork. South of the mountain ridge that forms the watershed, stone-foundationed huts lie along the main valleys close to the streams as in Nant Crew; very few lie higher up the steep slopes or, with one or two exceptions, the smaller tributary valleys. Platforms are less frequent (except for their unexplained prevalence in the valley of Afon Llia in the western part of Fforest Fawr) and there is a tendency for them to lie up the slopes away from the valley floors. The northern flank of the Beacons reveals a small concentration of long huts and more appear well above the valley floors, a reflection perhaps of the occurrence of natural shelves on the valley sides. Platforms are as common, showing not only above the valleys but also just beyond the boundaries of the enclosed ground as in Radnorshire. Possibly these distributional differences could reflect differences between the practices of the communities of the Usk Valley on the one hand and the Glamorgan valleys on the other, but this is an aspect requiring rather more research.

Northwards, in Montgomeryshire and Denbighshire, comparable platform sites are fewer; there are some around the tributaries leading into the upper valley of the Vyrnwy, but where sites do appear in the unenclosed uplands they tend to be long huts rather than platforms. However, in view of the smaller overall number of sites, it is questionable how much can be read into this dichotomy.

The appearance in the same uplands of both long huts and earthwork platforms (as well as platforms with the remnants of huts on them) requires an explanation, and the chronology of seasonal land use offers one possible solution. An interpretation of the Gelligaer platforms as seasonal sites, contrary to the view of the excavator, was first voiced by Peate (1946, 128) and has received more credence recently (Locock, this volume). This, together with the medieval attribution of the majority of excavated platforms at lower altitudes, strengthens the argument for a similar timespan for those on the commons. The absence of structures on many of these platforms points to the widespread use of timber for the buildings at a time when this material was readily available, in continuance of the traditions established in the construction of permanent dwellings in the valleys below; these are similar yet often smaller versions of the platforms at lower altitudes. While caution is required in invoking purely chronological factors to explain the variation in the use of raw materials, one possibility is that when timber became scarce builders did resort to stone, perhaps in the late medieval or sub-medieval period. Stone is not a rare commodity on the Radnorshire Commons or in the Brecon Beacons: surface quarries are visible around many of them, whether used in the past for the construction of the boundary walls or in recent times by local farmers. Further, the hypothesis receives broad support from the general trends evinced by architectural historians and others (Emery 1967, 138), and using the sparse historical data such as Leland's oft-quoted comments on the pressures on woodland in the 1530s (Emery 1989, 67). Platform sites might, then, precede those long huts where stone was the sole building material.

Time and again platforms are found immediately inside the common boundary, often close to streams, and this in turn implies that that boundary must have been in existence when the platform was in use.

However, the precise date at which the boundary of any particular common was formalised usually remains unknown, except in those instances where parliamentary enclosure occurred in the 19th century. Can these numerous platforms set just above the upper limits of farmed land be accommodated within the conceptual framework that has been developed for the seasonal use of the uplands? The idea that summer settlements had to be established in the pastures of distant upland valleys far from the winter homesteads is one that pervades the literature on transhumance. It can be sustained for areas such as the remote valleys in the Brecon Beacons or even the remote and inaccessible valleys running through the Elan Valley catchment, but there was probably no inherent need for medieval communities to go deep into the hills to find summer grazing. Seasonally occupied settlement sites could function equally well on the edge of the unenclosed waste as in a distant valley, and on the Radnorshire Commons, on Epynt, and on the northern flanks of the Beacons such gently graded locations would provide much if not more accessible pasture than a rocky steep-sided valley deeper into the mountains. This can be seen above Cwm Pennant, Llandrillo (Denbs), where the *hafodydd* are generally no more than a few hundred metres from the edge of the slopes leading down into the valley. Perhaps the only point of contention is why summer settlements would have been required at all, given their proximity to the home farms, but the necessity of keeping stock on the unenclosed hills throughout the summer and not having to take them back to the homestead every evening would have provided motive enough.

Distribution and Date

On the basis of what has been said above and with the proviso that neither past fieldwork nor documentary research has been consistent across all the upland areas of central and north-east Wales, we can assess the patterns of seasonally occupied settlement (Fig 2.14). In the extreme south in the Brecon Beacons, on Mynydd Epynt and, to a lesser extent, in the Black Mountains, the archaeological evidence is plentiful. For these areas there is virtually no place-name evidence (Davies 1984–85, 90) and historical documentation relating to seasonal activity appears sparse in the extreme. Theophilus Jones, the county historian of Brecknock in the early 19th century, makes no mention in his voluminous writings, and the lack of references from other documents of the period, either to the concept of summer pasturing or to the

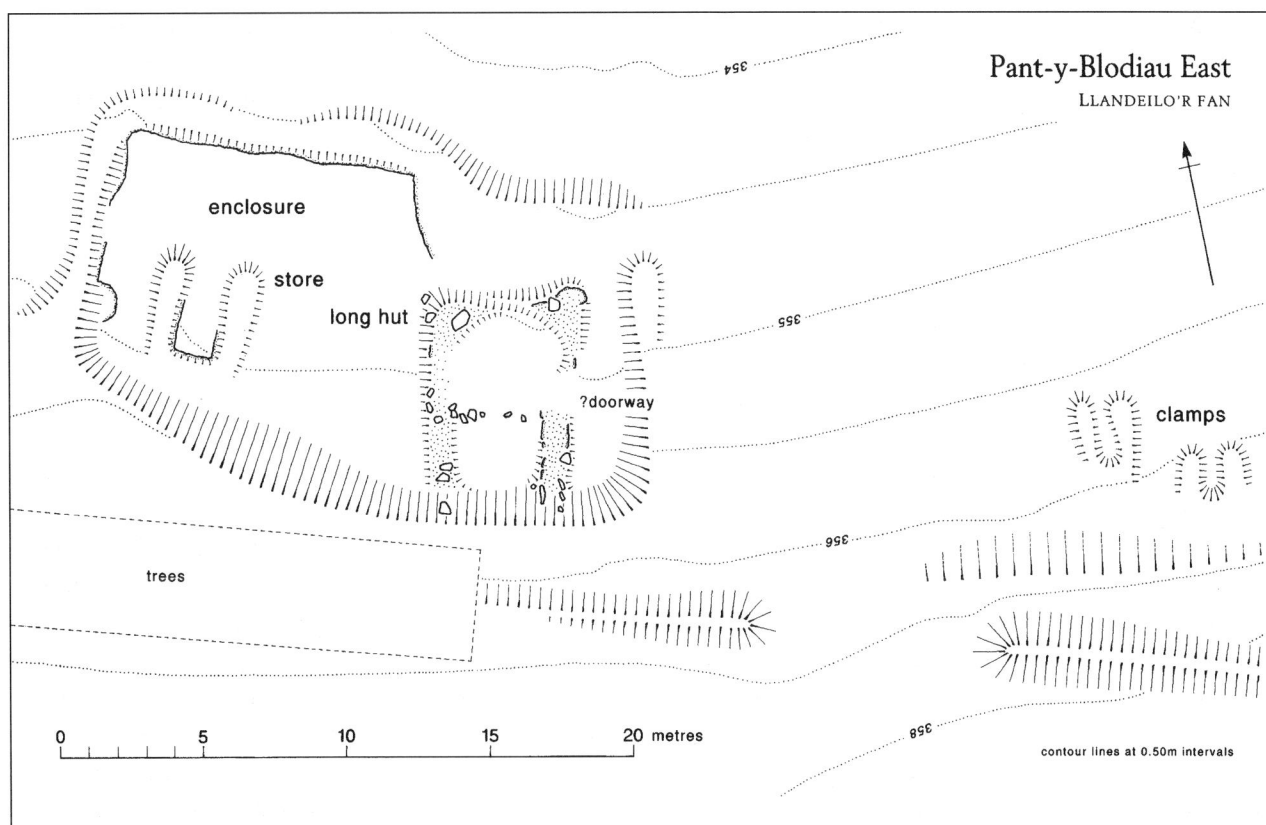

2.12 Pant-y-Blodiau East, Mynydd Epynt

structures that were generated, seems to confirm that the demise of transhumance had already occurred. The earliest detailed maps of Brecknock – those in the Badminton Manorial Survey of 1587 (*NLW Maps: Badminton 3*) – instance only or two places or areas called 'havod', and if the increasing number of later 18th-century maps are a reliable guide, the tradition of summer pasturing had faded by that date.

A similar situation obtains in Radnorshire. Jonathan Williams at the beginning of the 19th century was unaware of the summer use of the hills, and while on the Radnorshire Commons there is plentiful evidence of platforms and some long huts, the early documentary evidence of 16th- to 18th-century origin (see Suggett 2005) is confined largely to areas further west, in the Elan Valley. The latter accords with the evidence for both *hafodydd* and *lluestai* in neighbouring Cardiganshire from the likes of John Evans at the beginning of the 19th century and Samuel Morris in the 18th (see Sambrook, this volume), as well as more generally with the evidence from the Cambrian Mountains in central Wales. Thus in the western Montgomeryshire uplands and the Berwyns the documentary, place-name and archaeological evidence come together to indicate the continuation of the practice into the 18th century.

The Denbighshire Moors likewise offer this combi-nation of source material, and in view of the fact that historically, north-west Wales remained true to the practice of transhumance for longer than other areas, on the evidence provided by the likes of Thomas Pennant and E Owen (Peate 1946, 127), it is no surprise that cumulatively some of the most substantive evidence comes from the adjacent parts of Denbighshire. Yet further east, there is a remarkable dearth of data for the Clwydian Hills, and only a few physical remains on Ruabon and Llantysilio Mountains.

Cumulatively, the evidence reveals the pattern of transhumant pasturing throughout the Welsh uplands, but its demise occurred in eastern areas more quickly than further west. By the 16th century it may have declined to insignifice on the commons of eastern Radnorshire, and the same must have happened by the early 18th century in the Brecon Beacons and the Black Mountains. This argues for a retreat from a traditional way of life, but whether this should simply be attributed to farming methods from the east influencing contemporary practice, as seems to be the message from Winchester's analysis of northern England and the Borders (2000), or whether there are more complex interwoven processes at work is a question that still needs to be addressed.

Brecon Beacons Survey

Tai'r Bull

Llanfrynach

Tarell

Nant Cwm Llwch

Cynrig

Nant Menasgin

300

009

Senni

F f o r e s t   F a w r

600

600

Lila

Dringarth

400

500

500

Ystradfellte
Reservoir

Beacons
Reservoir

Taf Fawr

Nant
Crew

Cantref
Reservoir

800

500

700

600

700

600

500

Upper Neuadd
Reservoir

Taf Fechan

400

unenclosed
enclosed land

platform   o

long hut   ●

long hut on platform ◉

contour lines at 100m intervals

0   1   2   3   4   5 km

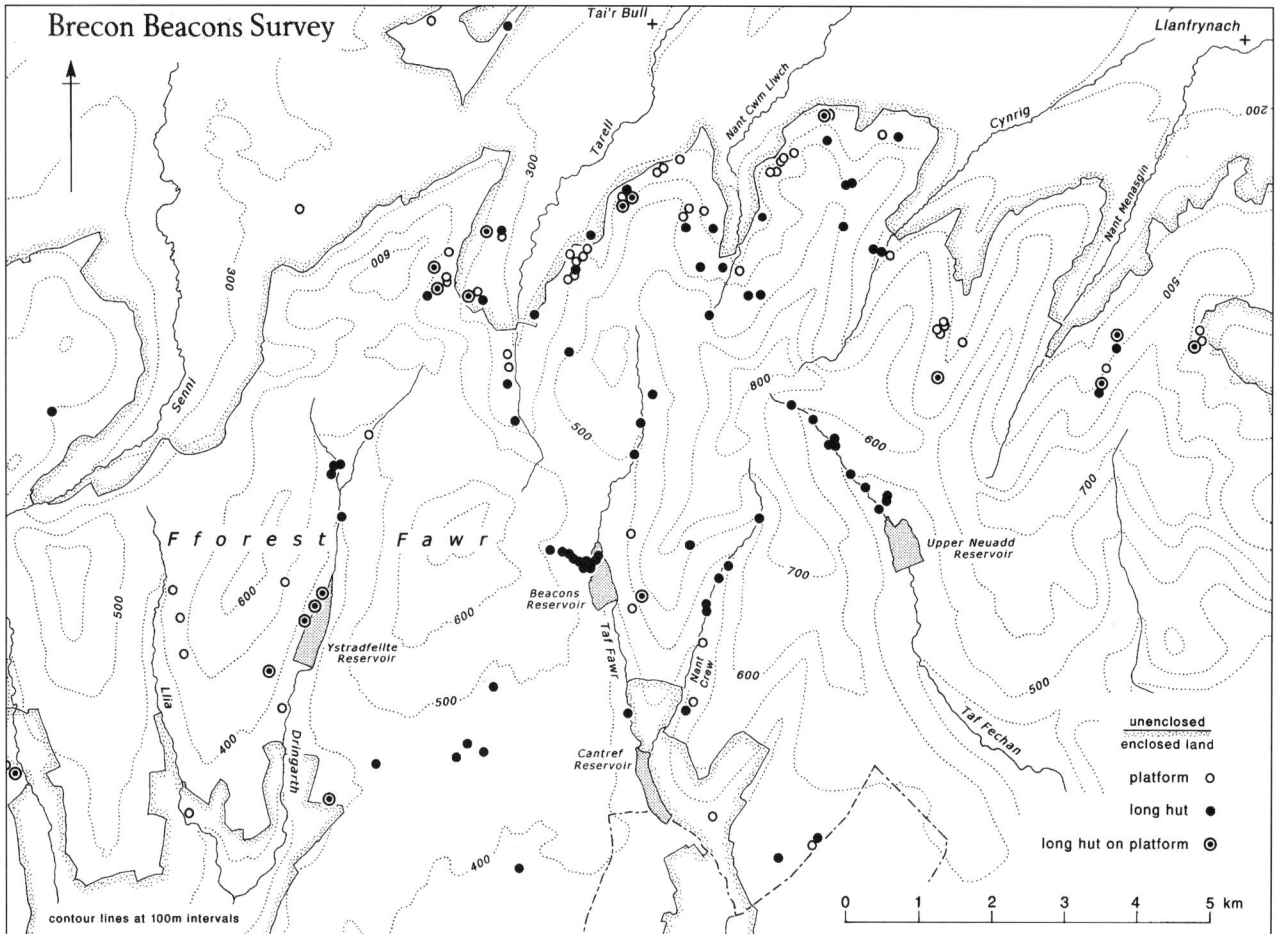

2.13 Brecon Beacons Survey

2.8 Conclusions

Emerging strongly from the issues developed in the foregoing sections is our recognition that wider patterns of medieval and early post-medieval rural settlement are fundamentally dependent on modern systematic fieldwork. We can only guess the overall number of deserted rural settlement sites in the Principality – virtually every survey undertaken in Powys in recent years, whether on the commons of Radnorshire or the enclosed grazing lands bordering the Severn in Trefnant township, has revealed their presence in meaningful numbers. Settlement has never been static; over the centuries it was dynamic in the lowlands, even more so in the uplands, and to gain any appreciation of the location and distribution patterns, thorough fieldwork is required. The emphasis has been very much on the unenclosed commons, and even more so on the uplands in general. Over 85% of the proven sites in central and north-eastern Wales are located above the 244m OD contour, the level generally taken as marking the uplands, and this introduces an unavoidable bias in the evidence.

The key to our appreciation of the location of medieval settlement in rural areas is the slope-set platform. It was not of course the only morphological form, for there was no necessity for the platform on level ground, but it appears to have been ubiquitous throughout the region, except perhaps in the extreme north and north-east. That the platform is now such a recognisable earthwork form is due largely to the fieldwork of recent years: numbers have almost doubled in the last decade. Taken in the context of the better known evidence from Glamorgan and Merioneth the distribution pattern of these earthworks can now be seen as a truly countrywide phenomenon, running in a wide sweep from the south of Wales through to the north-west, and perhaps spreading beyond into the border counties of Herefordshire and Shropshire, though this remains to be established.

However, the earthwork platform cannot be divorced from the building that occupied it. To the architectural historian the platform is but a minor

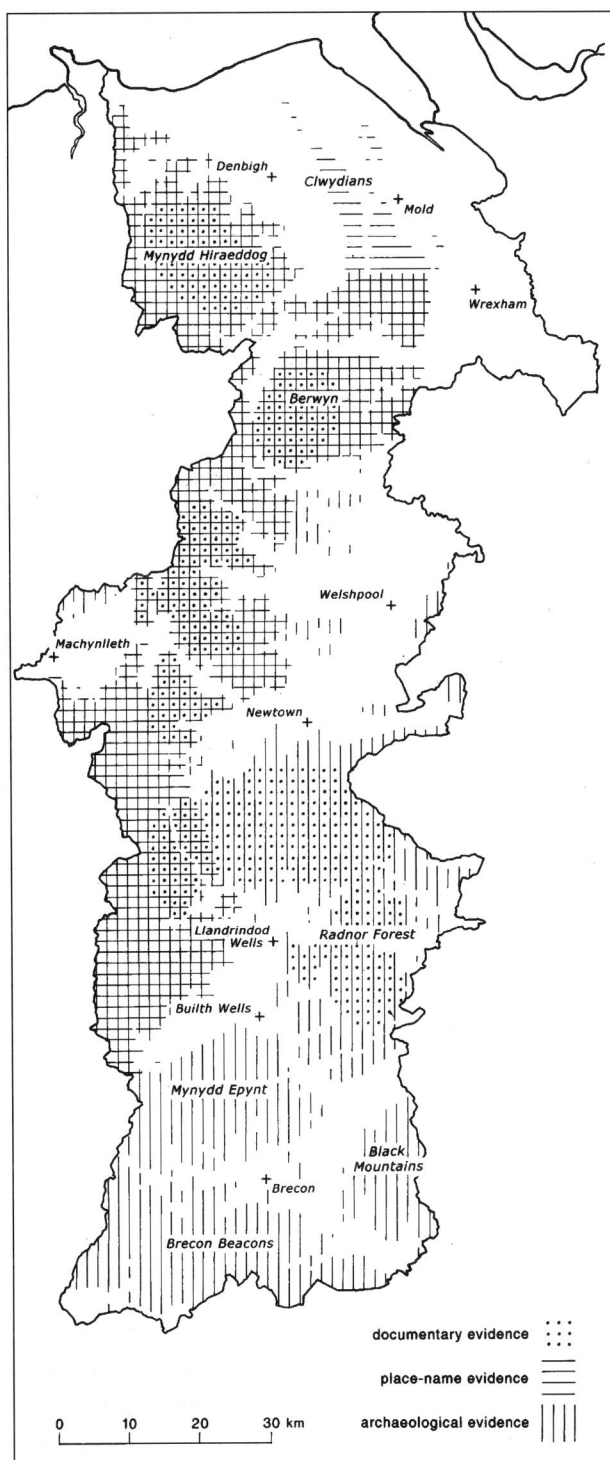

2.14 Geographic distribution of source material for seasonal settlement

with the introduction of what might be termed 'self-contained farmholdings' held in severalty, and by the late Tudor period encroachment on the open commons was well under way. Not that the platform was rendered wholly obsolete; morphologically it remained as the base for dwellings set down the slope for a prolonged period, probably into the 18th century. What can be termed the centuries of encroachment may be clearly understood as a socio-economic and historical phenomenon, but their archaeology is as yet ill known.

Finally, the problem of distinguishing between permanently and seasonally occupied settlements has been considered above. This is much more than simply a question of nomenclature. It has an impact on site typology and even more importantly on the agricultural processes in the Welsh landscape. That the interpretation of some of the best known excavated sites – Gelligaer Common, Beili Bedw, Hafod y Nant Criafolen – is still confused by alternative theories reveals a fundamental weakness in what should be a developing field of study.

Acknowledgements

My thanks are due to: the many owners throughout Powys and the old county of Clwyd who permitted access to their lands; Cadw who funded this programme and particularly Mike Yates and Kathryn Roberts for their assistance throughout; my colleagues at CPAT, Richard Hankinson and Glyn Owen who shared much of the fieldwork with me; Richard Suggett of RCAHMW for helpful discussion and provision of a copy of his Radnorshire text on summer houses prior to publication; and Bill Britnell, the director of CPAT, Martin Locock, Kathryn Roberts and Judith Alfrey for their advice on an early draft of this text.

element in the appreciation of the medieval or sub-medieval house. For the medieval period it remains in most cases the only visible element of that house, particularly since so very few Welsh houses pre-date the middle of the 15th century (Suggett 1996, 32), but in later centuries its importance as a key element is generally superseded.

The late medieval period appears to mark a change,

3 Deserted rural settlements in south-east Wales

By Martin Locock

Abstract

The historic counties of Glamorgan and Monmouthshire contain approximately 200 sites falling into the definition of sites adopted by the project; these include excavated groups at Gelligaer and Cefn Drum. They are distributed throughout the area, but are clustered on high ground, often in groups. In contrast to the rest of Wales, associated features are few. There appears to be an association between Cistercian monastic land and the distribution of sites, perhaps reflecting organised exploitation of upland pasture for sheep rearing. In other cases, a later, early post-medieval, date is suggested, and in some cases continuity from (seasonally occupied) platform to longhouse can be demonstrated. A later phase of commercial sheep-pasturing is represented by the related class of 'tarren' sites. The examples from south-east Wales demonstrate a range of functions, dates, and contexts, and a single explanation applicable to all is rejected.

3.1 Introduction

South-east Wales, for the purpose of this study, comprises the old counties of Glamorgan and Monmouthshire (from 1974 to 1996 divided into West, Mid- and South Glamorgan, and Gwent, and now administered by twelve Unitary Authorities), corresponding to the area covered by the Glamorgan-Gwent Archaeological Trust (GGAT) Sites and Monuments Record, a total of 3622km². Topographically, it comprises two main zones: the Glamorgan uplands, characterised by deeply incised steep-sided valleys running north into a heavily dissected *massif* rising to 400m OD, and the lowland belt, from Gower in the west, through the Vale of Glamorgan, to Monmouthshire in the east. Along the fringe of the coast between Cardiff and Chepstow the reclaimed alluvial plain of the Gwent Levels lies close to 0m OD.

Most of the area was in Norman control by the 1070s, but in the medieval period there remained a clear distinction between the Anglicised areas of the Vale, Gower and south Monmouthshire, with their landscape of nucleated villages and arable open fields, and the 'Welshry', to the north, which remained predominantly pastoral and dispersed. This pattern was carried forward into the post-medieval period, but was reversed in the 19th century by the intensive industrialisation of the valleys, masking the previous agricultural landscape. More recently, there has been the development of the urban centres of Chepstow, Newport, Cardiff, Neath, and Swansea, and associated industry in the lowlands. The area has seen extensive redevelopment over the last 30 years, although in the upland areas there remains much unenclosed moorland on the summits and enclosed pasture on the slopes. There has also been widespread afforestation by the Forestry Commission.

The Cadw-funded survey of deserted rural settlements in the old counties of Glamorgan and Monmouthshire was carried out between 1999 and 2001, following the methodology and terminology established by the work elsewhere (GAT 1996; Yates 2000; this vol.). The study excluded consideration of deserted medieval villages, larger houses, or conventional farms, and was focused on the class of monuments now comprising earthwork platforms, known variously as 'long huts' or 'platform houses'. One aim of the study was to establish a more precise definition and terminology. Although it was essentially a descriptive exercise, some analysis and interpretation was undertaken. Key research questions identified for south-east Wales were:

- Is the distribution of sites as reflected on the SMR accurate?
- Are the sites related to specific land use and pastoral patterns?
- What dates and functions can be ascribed to them?
- How does the field archaeology evidence compare to that of documentary sources?
- Do the sites in the area represent the same phenomena as those elsewhere?

The general distribution of sites had been reviewed relatively recently (see below); the predictable strong representation throughout the upland areas included some surprising gaps and clusters, and therefore four study areas were selected for intensive prospection through desk-based searches in order to check the validity of the observed pattern. It was concluded that the irregular distribution was indeed a true reflection of the location of sites, and the second stage of the study focused on visiting the known sites and describing them to a standard format. In the nature of such a study, some sites have yielded considerably more detailed and reliable evidence than others, and in this account the former have been discussed at greater length than the latter. In particular, surface examination of the physical remains has revealed very little about their date and purpose, and it has proved possible to address the broader questions of interpretation only where contextual information can be obtained. Wherever possible, previous work was reviewed in order to provide additional comparative data.

3.2 Previous work

South-east Wales holds a special place in the study of 'platform houses', since it was during fieldwork in the uplands of Glamorgan that Sir Cyril Fox and Aileen Fox first identified and named them, and their subsequent excavations have provided the most complete evidence of date, function and structure. Initially, the sites were interpreted as being of pre-Norman date, but after excavations on Gelligaer Common, a medieval date was preferred. Fox and Fox continued to identify further examples, and detailed studies of the Neath area and East Gower added more (Green 1954; Morris 1954). In 1960 the RCAHMW commenced fieldwork for the preparation of the Glamorgan inventory of medieval sites (published in 1982), involving visits to all known examples of what they called 'platform houses' (aligned down the slope) and 'long huts' (rectangular buildings aligned across the slope) of suspected medieval date; it should thus be noted that the Royal Commission's use of this term is different from that adopted by the current project. The RCAHMW also considered a class of upland structures identified by Fox and Fox as 'tarren sites', upland complexes of stone walls associated with stock management. The RCAHMW's examination of post-medieval sites in Glamorgan has been restricted to standing buildings and industrial sites. Rescue and developer-funded projects since the mid 1970s have identified a small number of certain and a larger number of possible sites, and surveys in the Rhondda and Rhigos areas have added further examples (Davis 1988; 1989), while some of the known sites lying in Forest Enterprise land were visited recently as part of the Welsh Heritage Assets survey (CAP 1999a–c).

In parallel with the Cadw survey, GGAT undertook an extensive survey of the uplands of Blaenau Gwent (north-east Monmouthshire), the areas above 244m OD, as part of the RCAHMW-sponsored 'Uplands Initiative' (Yates 1999). At the start of the survey there were no recorded deserted rural settlements recorded on the Sites and Monuments Record (that is, of site types 'long hut' or 'house platform' as used by RCAHMW). The survey identified a total of 678 new sites of which there were 11 earthwork sites likely to be deserted rural settlements and a further 53 buildings pre-dating 1881. These discoveries demonstrate the partial nature of the record and potential for prospection survey in areas devoid of previously identified sites.

In addition to these surveys, there have been excavations (Table 3.1; Fig 3.1), commencing with the work of Cyril and Aileen Fox on Gelligaer Common, Glamorgan. Their work covered two groups of platforms, on the west, on the upper slopes of the Bargoed Taf Valley, and on the north-east slope of Twyn y Fidffawydd overlooking the Bargoed Rhymni valley (discussed below). It is perhaps unfortunate that these sites have formed the basis of subsequent discussions of the date and function of the type, since they can now be seen to be unrepresentative in their size, arrangement, date, function, material culture, and landscape context. Aileen Fox rejects any association between her platform houses and 'Iowerth Peate's *hafods*' (Fox 2000, 86).

Table 3.1. Excavated deserted rural settlements in south-east Wales

Site	Date excavated	Ref. nos. (RCAHMW 1982, SMR)	Reference
Gelligaer West (Coly Uchaf, Dinas Noddfa)	1936–8	PH 30–31; 505–506m	Fox 1937
Gelligaer East A	1938	PH 36–38; 977m	A Fox 1939
Cefn Drum	1996–8	PH 6, 8; 369w, LH 1; 373w	Kissock 2000; Kissock and Johnston 2000

The University of Wales College, Newport, has undertaken a survey and excavation programme on Cefn Drum, to the north-east of Pontarddulais, Glamorgan (Kissock 2000). The work has identified a regular occurrence of platforms in groups of three or four, usually a pair close together with the others standing a little further away. Slight clearance cairns were also examined and found to lie in a systematic arrangement suggestive of variations in the intensity of cultivation (presumably for arable). Excavation of two of a group of four platforms revealed the remains of buildings with stone and clay walls and postholes; phosphate analysis from one seemed to indicate that one of the two compartments of one structure had been used almost exclusively by animals. No dating evidence for the cairns or platforms was found, but a medieval date was assumed by the excavators. Elsewhere on the hill, a long hut was excavated, and was shown to have been a sheep house. Nearby structures included a hay barn and a small dwelling; all are thought to be of 16th-century date (Kissock and Johnston 2000).

Other medieval buildings have been excavated in Glamorgan (discussed and compared by Robinson 1982), including round-cornered stone buildings at Rhossili, (Davidson et al 1987), and Barry Old Village (Thomas and Davies 1972; Thomas and Dowdell 1987), and conventional rectangular buildings at Highlight (Thomas 1966; 1967; 1970); these fell outside the scope of the field study, but were examined for comparative purposes.

3.3 Methodology

The present study comprised two elements: a 'condition survey' of field visits to the sites recorded on the SMR, and a 'prospection survey' examining a range of sources with follow-up fieldwork in order to identify additional sites not previously recorded in selected areas. The sites were visited and described using the standard terminology adopted for the project. They were also photographed, and any threats or other management issues were recorded. The data were transferred into a master project database, based on the SMR structure with additional fields, which formed the basis of gazetteers in the reports. The dataset for the project comprised 215 records described by the Regional Sites and Monuments Record at the time as 'platform house', 'longhouse' and 'long hut'. A trawl was also made for other sites with descriptions mentioning 'platforms' (the precise number of individual sites was larger than this, since many of the records covered groups of two or more platforms and other related features); some of these records related to more than one site, and the dataset represented 238 sites. The SMR dataset was fairly consistent, since the sites had been correlated to the terminology adopted in the RCAHMW Inventory.

For the prospection survey, four study areas were selected in order to test the reported distribution of deserted rural settlement sites, which was typified by a patchy pattern with dense clusters on some ridges and absences nearby. It was also hoped that close examination of early maps would provide a better resolution of the question of date of use and desertion. The areas selected were Neath, Glyncorrwg, Pontypridd, and Barry. Of particular importance to the study was the availability of the Neath Abbey, Briton Ferry and Wenvoe Castle estate surveys of the 18th century; these supplemented the full cover for the mid-19th century provided by the tithe maps.

Table 3.2 Site densities in prospection study areas

Location	Area (km²)	No. of known sites at start of survey	No. new sites identified during survey	Total sites studied	Sites classified as relevant following survey	Density (site/km²)
Neath	108	16	4	20	16	0.148
Glyncorrwg	120	14	1	15	14	0.117
Pontypridd	120	8	0	8	8	0.067
Barry	64	15	0	15	4	0.063
South-east Wales	3622	238	20	258	219	0.060

The prospection survey also examined vertical aerial photographs held by the Central Register for Air Photography in Wales, Cardiff, but it was found that the limited cover was generally at too small a scale to allow the positive identification of known or new features. As will be seen from Table 3.2, this relatively intensive desk-based work identified a number of new sites, but confirmed the variation in distribution as a genuine phenomenon, reflected in the range of site densities.

In practice, it proved impossible to visit all known examples. Permission was sought from the landowner to visit sites on private enclosed land, and this was not in all cases forthcoming. Sites located in dense forestry were visited whenever possible, but in a few cases they proved inaccessible. A total of 51 sites were not visited (24.5%).

The initial Sites and Monuments Record trawl yielded of 215 records; the desk-top study identified a further five sites, and fifteen were noted during the field visits. There were 47 records which when visited were either rejected as archaeological sites or reassigned to a different site-type, leaving 188 sites or locations as types coming under the scope of deserted rural settlements, representing 219 individual archaeological features (since some sites incorporated more than one structure).

3.4 Distribution, types, and dating

Known deserted rural settlements are found throughout south-east Wales (Fig. 3.2), with concentrations on Cefn Drum and Graig Fawr in the west, Mynydd Glyncorrwg and Mynydd Margam south of Neath, Mynydd-y-Glog and Gelligaer Common in the north, and Mynydd Machen north of Cardiff. The distribution is characterised by clustering on some ridges and absence from others nearby. Some areas seem to be entirely blank, including modern Cardiff and the eastern part of the Glamorgan uplands, and there are very few in Monmouthshire. Although Fox and Fox (1934) described the type as characteristic of uplands, in fact they occur at a wide range of altitudes: 42% lie below the 244m (400 feet) 'uplands' contour, and 8% lie below 100m OD (including a longhouse on the Gwent Levels at 8m OD). At the other end of the range, 9.6% occur between 400 and 499m OD,

and the highest example lies at 490m. Although present land use cannot be directly correlated to earlier exploitation of the landscape, it is notable that 46% of sites lie in what is now unenclosed heath and moorland, 21% in enclosed pasture, and 13% under woodland and forestry, emphasising the concentration of identified sites in areas of marginal land use, even at low altitude.

In addition to clustering at a macroscopic scale, there is considerable evidence for grouping as multiple platforms, and some complexes of platforms associated with other features (there are also a small number of features noted which were not linked to a platform). Sites closer than 200m apart were considered to form part of the same group for Table 3.3; the figures have been adjusted to account for single records on the Sites and Monuments Record which relate to multiple sites.

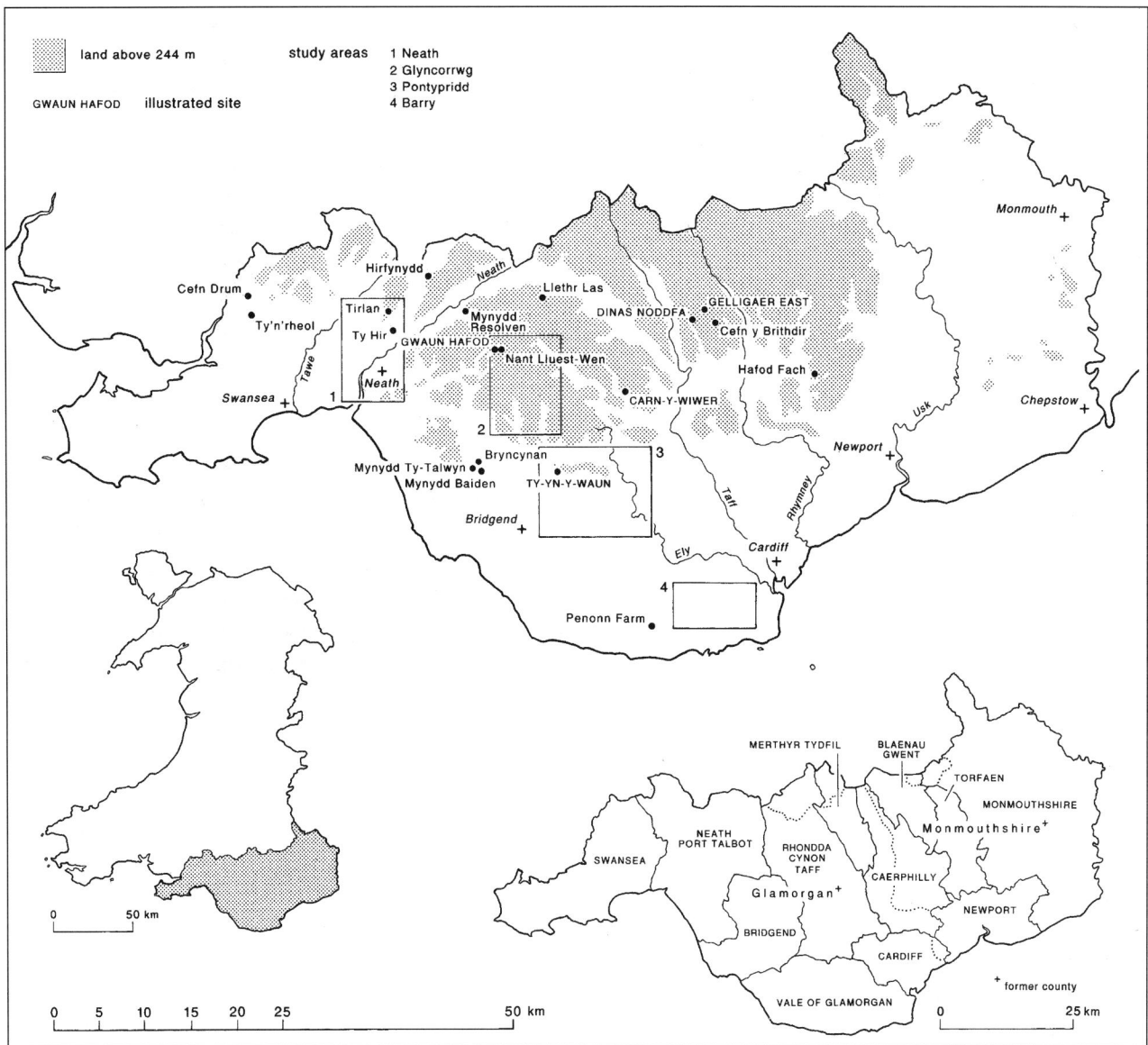

3.1 Map of south-east Wales showing principal sites and survey areas

The precise nature of the relationships between sites is unclear; it is impossible to establish whether occupation was contemporaneous. Although it has been proposed that paired platforms longitudinally aligned represent a precursor to the longhouse (Morris 1954, 40) and that a group of three platforms represents a settlement unit (Kissock 2000, 225), the regularities of number and disposition across south-east Wales are not striking. Rather it would appear that the 'long hut complex' (a rectangular building, usually aligned down the slope, on a platform with opposed entrances in the long sides) was established as one of the *schemas* for buildings available in the medieval and post-medieval period, constructed for use for a range of functions whenever convenient.

The spatial relationship between platforms has some regularities; typically a group will be located along a

track running diagonally up a slope, in a sheltered position below the summit area. Platforms side-by-side, with doorways directly opposite, are relatively rare; a diagonal arrangement is more common, presumably because it gave easier access to either platform without being restricted by the proximity of the other, particularly important in livestock handling. There does not seem to be a preference for a particular aspect of slope; ease of access from the valley seems to have decided the sites chosen.

The 219 sites can be categorised in terms of the standard glossary adopted for the project: 115 are platforms with no visible structural evidence; 92 are long huts, retaining evidence of a rectangular building on the platform, 5 are longhouses (all standing buildings: no ruins with two floor levels were found). It does not

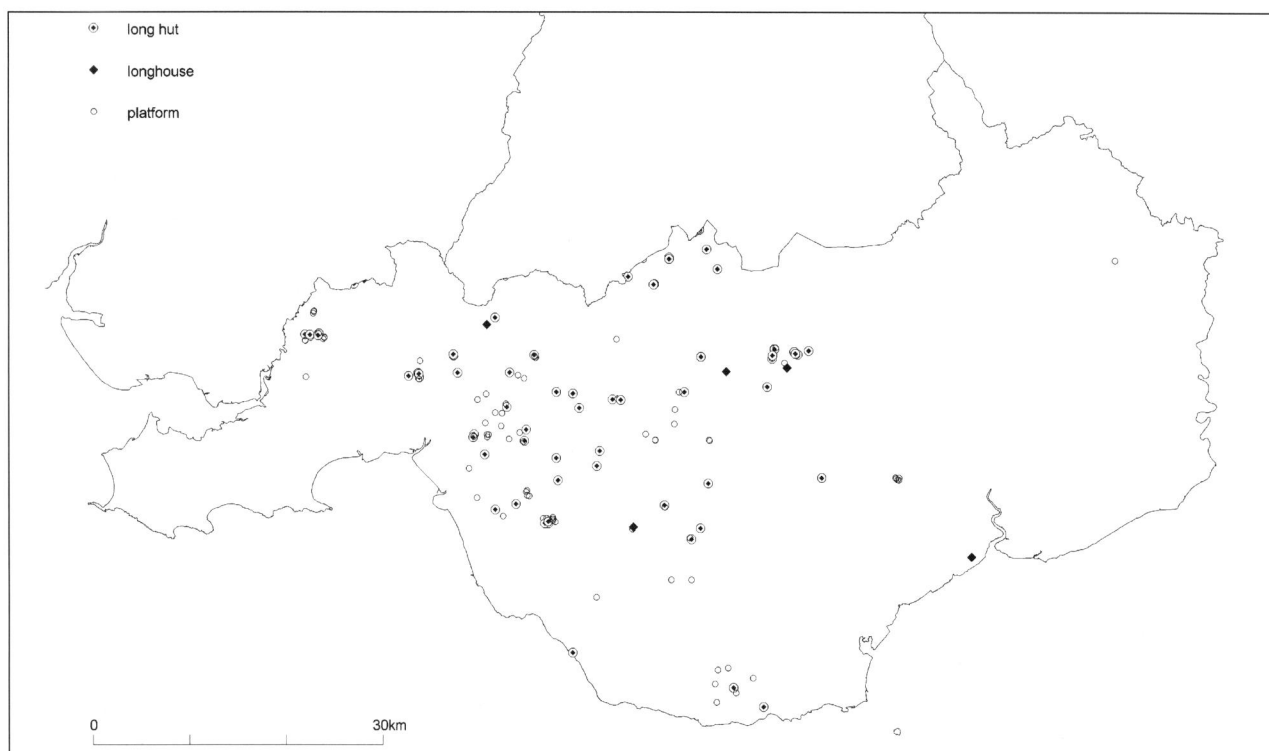

3.2 Distribution map of known sites

appear that there is any significant difference between the distributions of long huts and platforms, and the variation in form is probably a function of after-use of the site. Two examples are lateral to the slope (one platform, one long hut).

Table 3.3 provides an indication of the extent to which platforms and long huts were found in association with other features. They have been divided according to the number of proposed platforms or long huts present.

Most of the sites with associated features were long huts, and the most common features were enclosures (9), pillow mounds (5), yards (2) and folds (2). There were 15 shelters (10 not associated with a platform or long hut), 7 folds (3 without a 'parent' site), and 1 goose pen, at Tarren Ferch Du. Only one possible storage clamp was found, on Cefn-y-Brithdir, comprising a rectangular depression 14m x 5m x 1m deep, with a bank at the south-west (downhill) end, between two conventional platforms.

Table 3.3 Grouping of long huts/platforms and presence of other features

Number of platforms and/or long huts at site	Number with associated features	Number without associated features	Total
One	12	25	37
Two	3	39	42
Three	1	12	13
Four	2	8	10

Most of the sites lie above the limit of land enclosed in the 19th century, although more recent enclosure and forestry has altered this pattern. As a result it has been assumed that their function is associated with

exploitation of summer pasture, although seasonal occupation has not been demonstrated. In fifteen cases, there is evidence for field banks apparently contemporary with the sites, now abandoned. Such intakes have been discussed by Leighton in the context of Mynydd Du and Mynydd Mallaen (Carms) (1997, 31). He suggests that such encroachments are more likely to be retained where they are added to nearby enclosed landholdings rather than isolated within the moor. It is perhaps misleading to think of these intakes as 'failed' encroachments; they may simply have been short-term in conception, execution and use, and may therefore be the product of a much wider range of factors than simply climate change.

Field banks need not imply arable or horticultural use, and may simply have assisted stock control. There is some indication of arable cultivation, in the form of ridges, although they are notoriously difficult to identify under dense vegetation cover. Two areas are well marked, at Tirlan, Mynydd Marchywel, north-east of Neath, Glamorgan, and on the east side of Gelligaer Common, Glamorgan. In the latter case, the ridging seems to respect but post-date the platforms, running down the steep eastern slope to the walls of the enclosed land, covering an area of several hectares. The ridges appear as 0.3–0.5m wide, up to 0.1m high, forming a gently rounded profile. In view of the steepness and restrictions of the ground, spade cultivation, perhaps for potatoes, is more likely than ploughing. At the Tirlan site the ridges are less well defined and less extensive, and may be contemporary with the platforms. They lie within enclosed pasture, and may represent drainage improvement.

Perhaps the most problematic features are the clearance cairns often found interspersed with platforms, taking the form of piles of stones 2–5m in diameter, 1m high, spaced 5–20m apart. Those on Cefn Drum, Pontarddulais, Glamorgan, have been surveyed in detail, and Kissock (2000) argues that they must be associated with the platforms and thus of medieval date (the RCAHMW had earlier argued against a prehistoric date: 1976, 119, no. Ri). In contrast, the RCAHMW examined the platforms on Carn-y-Wiwer, east of the Rhondda, Glamorgan, and concluded that the cairns probably resulted from prehistoric clearance, while the platforms were medieval, and the cultivation ridges post-medieval in date (Fig 3.3) (RCAHMW 1982, 39–41); previously, these cairns had been categorised as 'doubtfully sepulchral' (RCAHMW 1976, 119, no. 513). The precise nature and date of the activity leading to the creation of the cairns is unclear; the areas are usually unenclosed by earthworks, and would be incompatible with ploughing. Hoe cultivation may be one explanation.

The direct dating of these earthwork sites remains a major difficulty. The limited excavation evidence suggests a medieval date, but only Dinas Noddfa (Gelligaer West), Glamorgan, has produced pottery in any quantity. The absence of later material (including clay pipe and pottery) implies either an early date or an extreme paucity of material culture, but in this context either alternative is plausible. A more fruitful line of enquiry is the relationship of the sites to other landscape features, in order to derive at least a relative chronology. In contrast to some of the related features (shelters, folds and enclosures) which continued to be used and maintained into the recent past, and in some cases into the present, long huts and platforms do not form part of the modern landscape, except where paths which once led to their entrances have survived as moorland tracks. The sites cluster around the upper limit of old enclosure, usually just outside, but sometimes within.

Unfortunately, the chronology of enclosure in south Wales is as yet poorly established. As a model, initial enclosure is assumed to be concentrated on the better

3.3 Carn-y-Wiwer, Rhondda, Glamorgan (after RCAHMW 1982)

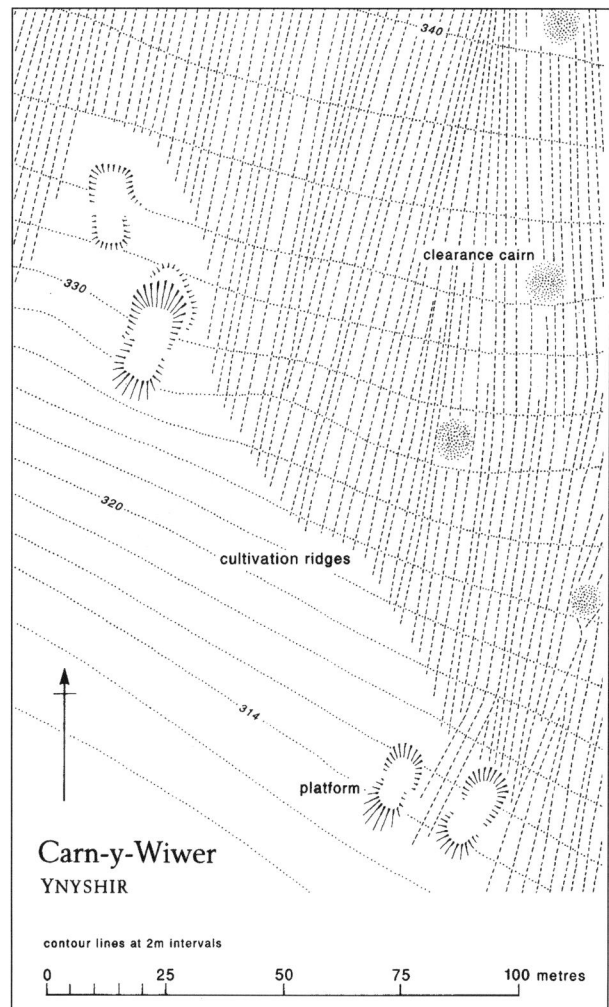

Carn-y-Wiwer
YNYSHIR

contour lines at 2m intervals

0   25   50   75   100 metres

agricultural land in the valley bottoms, either around individual farmsteads or as part of a manorial system. Later, further intakes were made, protecting pasture and woodland from grazing stock on the commons, and perhaps 'privatising' the land. There is, as noted above, some evidence for a subsequent retraction from the maximum limit of enclosure. The spread of long huts has been correlated to the climatic optimum of the medieval period, in the 12th–13th centuries (Leighton 1997, 25, 31) and land-hunger and population expansion prior to the Black Death (A Fox 1939), but the main periods of enclosure in the area are substantially later, notably in the 16th–17th centuries.

There are definite examples of much later date, including Ty Hir (longhouse), Cilfrew, Glamorgan, which is shown on the 1840 tithe map for Cadoxton-juxta-Neath as an unroofed walled structure, named as 'Ty hir' (ruins). This site is in enclosed pasture and is now an earthwork. Were it not for the name and the map, which indicate a stone structure abandoned in the mid-19th century, the site would now be indistinguishable from the many other long hut earthworks investigated.

There is, therefore, no single unified phenomenon of deserted rural settlements, with a common function and date; rather, platform, long hut and longhouse

sites are a feature of medieval and post-medieval landscapes with individual histories of establishment, maintenance, and abandonment. In many cases (as set out in the case studies below) a late medieval origin is proposed, but in general, the 17th and 18th centuries are preferred as the date for their creation and use.

Place-name evidence for individual sites is scarce; in contrast to other types of site, they have left little trace either as settlements proper, as topographic names (eg Nant Hafod), or field names reflecting past use (eg *Cae Hen Dy-hir*, meaning 'old longhouse field'). This contrasts with *lluest* names, whose relatively recent date can be adduced from their survival as topographic names for features on the moors, and their use for still-extant structures. '*Hafod*' names, referring to the area of summer pasture rather than necessarily to the *hafodty* (house), are fairly common, and were certainly current by the 17th century, but there is minimal correlation between the names and long hut sites. It would appear that the rights of common pasture or customary practice that permitted use of the pasture by a community or family were of greater and more long-lasting significance than the precise location and nature of associated shelters, perhaps another indication of the impermanence of their intended use, and in contrast to the *hendre* (main or winter settlement).

3.5 Discussion with case studies

3.5.1 Monastic estates

The extensive holdings of the Cistercian houses at Neath, Margam, Llantarnam, and Tintern were exploited for stock management, combining cattle pasturing with the rearing of thousands of sheep. There is some evidence for cattle transhumance and the construction of *vaccaries* or monastic cattle ranches, on the summer pasture (Williams 1984, 302). Similarly, sheep-rearing involved the construction of folds, and shelters for the shepherds (in the 13th century these were *conversi* (the lay brethren), but by the 15th century, paid shepherds) (Williams 1984, 386). The monastic grange (in the strict sense) would be a substantial structure providing permanent accommodation for monks, including elements such as an oratory, a barn, and accommodation for the *conversi* (Williams 1984, 227). Granges are also fairly well documented. It is therefore important to examine structures of appropriate date on monastic estates with care before identifying them categorically as granges.

The Dulais Valley runs north-east from the Neath

Valley at Tonna, forming part of the extensive holdings of Neath Abbey. There are documentary references to a grange at Crynant, ravaged in the 13th century and later exchanged for lowland manors with Gilbert de Clare (Williams 1984, 223). The grange has not been located, although RCAHMW suggest that it may lie at Gelli-benuchel, on the north-west-facing slope of the valley, surrounded by walled fields (RCAHMW 1982, 252, MG 3). A group of platforms and related features occupy the brow of the ridge to the north of the enclosed fields, 800m north of Gelli-benuchel, in what is now fenced moorland; the area has seen extensive coal extraction in the 20th century. The southernmost site, although noted as a platform by the Ordnance Survey, could not be located; it may be a later industrial feature. The summit area is occupied by a large rectilinear ditched enclosure with an internal bank. The enclosed area is little different to the remainder of the hilltop, comprising poorly drained tussocky grassland; there are some indications of widely spaced ploughing running down the slope in

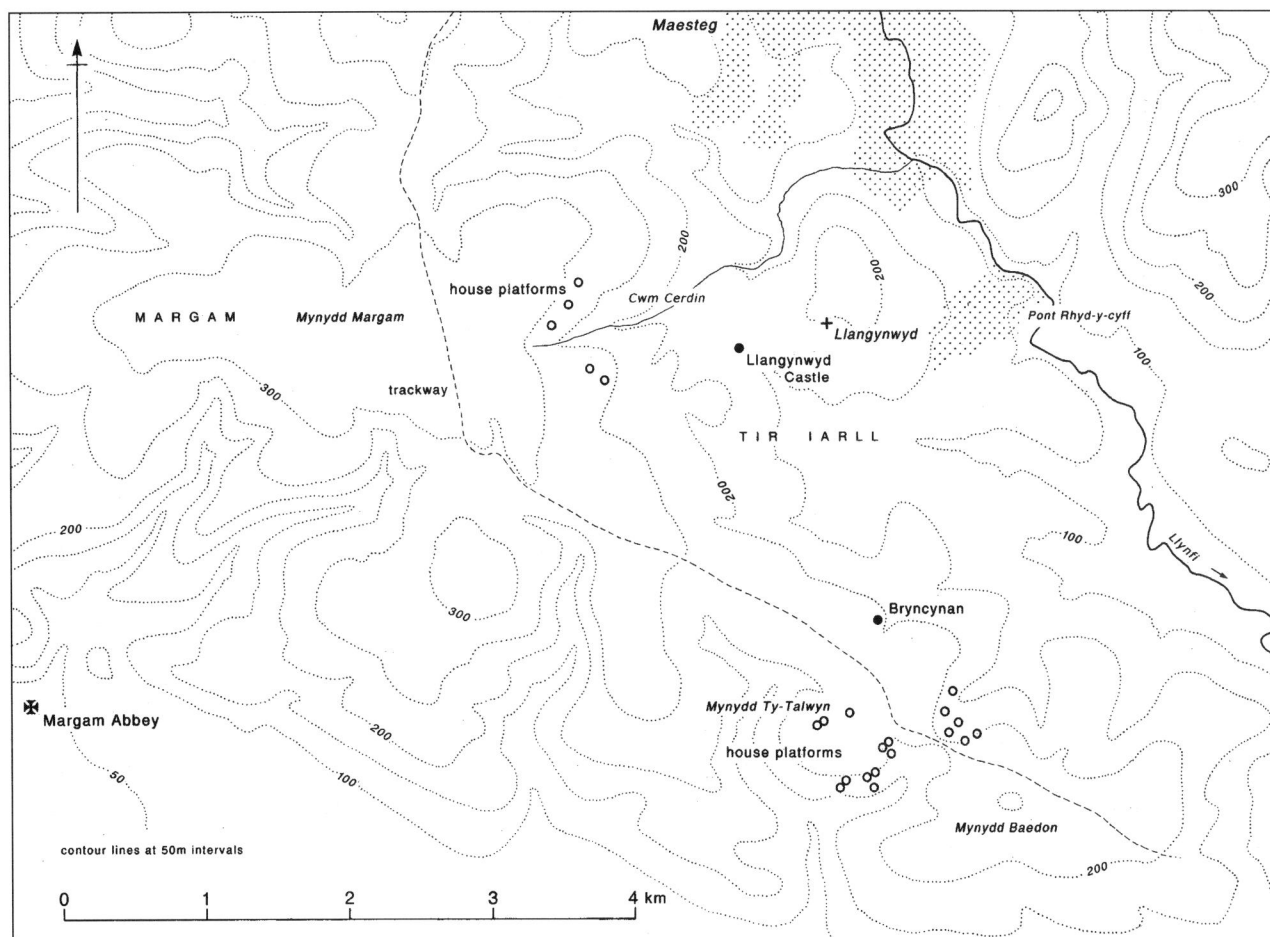

3.4 Mynydd Margam

the south-east part of the enclosure. In the south-west corner there is a well-defined platform, 16.8 x 9.8m, with well-marked wall banks 1m wide. The doorway in the external wall is the only break in the enclosing bank. The second well-defined platform lies 30m to the south-west, at the same elevation, with a similarly well-defined wall bank on the north side. Dating evidence is largely absent. The 1840 tithe map (NLW, Cadoxton-juxta-Neath) shows the enclosed fields of Gelli-benuchel and Coed-du to the south much as they survive today; two sides of the enclosure define the boundaries of a large undivided field, but there is no indication of the platforms. The earthworks, with their substantial wall banks, would imply well-built masonry buildings. The map therefore reflects their status in 1840 as long vanished, and a medieval origin seems likely. The sites and enclosure may have formed part of an outlying land use from the farm centres to the south, perhaps as part of the *friddoedd* zone of unenclosed land (Alfrey 2000, 127), or may have been an attempt at a pioneer settlement that was later abandoned. Although the abandonment may reflect contraction in times of lower population pressure (as

Alfrey 2000, 127, suggests for Carmarthenshire), the complex history, and in particular the series of traumatic events in the 13th–15th centuries, may have rendered the sites unwanted or unoccupied.

Pen-Onn, in the south-west of the parish of Llancarfan, Glamorgan, is described by RCAHMW (1982, 303, MG 49) as a possible grange of St Peter's Abbey, Gloucester. The site occupies the southern shoulder of higher ground overlooking the incised valley of the River Waycock to the south, just east of its junction with the Nant Carfan. The settlement of Pen-Onn is now a cluster of buildings halfway between the village of Llancarfan (site of a major early medieval monastery) and Penmark. The earthworks form two terraces, enclosed to the north by a field boundary and marked on the west by a track. The upper terrace is occupied by one main long hut (at the west end), two smaller platforms, and a circular depression (perhaps a pond). The second terrace contains a square platform at the west end, alongside the track. Penonn Farm, to the north, is a post-medieval house, presumably a successor to the earthwork. The identification as a possible grange seems likely; again, the trigger to

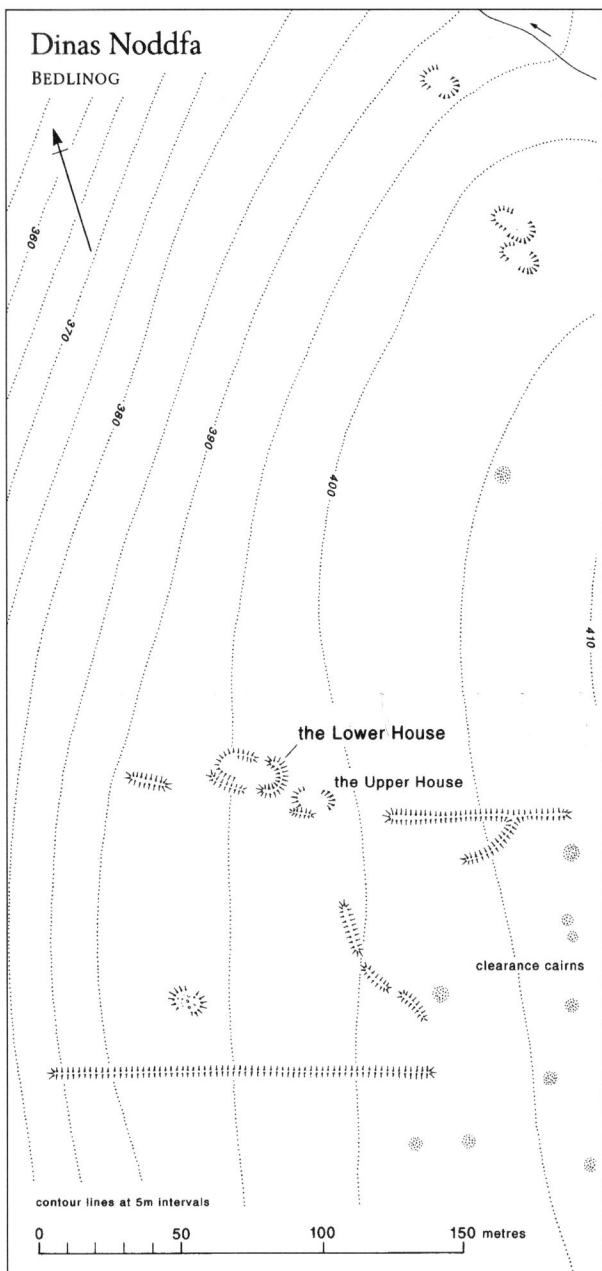

3.5 Dinas Noddfa: plan (after RCAHMW 1982)

overlooking the Clydach Brook (RCAHMW 1982, 26–7, PH25 a–e). They are now in poor condition, situated in dense forestry, and affected by industrial working, but they present a range of forms, including typical platforms, a building in a walled enclosure, and isolated stone buildings. There is considerable evidence for pre-forestry enclosure, in the form of surviving field walls and banks. The land lay within the Ty'n-y-cwm Grange of Margam (RCAHMW 1982, 266–7, MG 18); it has been suggested that the sites may represent peasant encroachments during the period 1291–1329 when the grange was held by Gilbert de Clare. This explanation is perhaps too simple: some of the sites can be shown to have survived into, or been created in, the post-medieval period, and relate to the enclosure of land at that time. It is possible that some of the simple platforms are survivors of an earlier phase of upland exploitation, but in their current condition the evidence is equivocal.

The identification of long huts and platform houses with the medieval monastic economy may thus mask a more complex pattern in which some sites survive – some are created late, and others are deserted; the explanations for such variation might be better sought in the history of ownership and land use than in long-term environmental change or population growth.

At the west end of the Vale of Glamorgan, the coastline runs north-west to leave only a small coastal plain between the Glamorgan uplands and the sea. This area formed the boundary of the Marcher lordship of Glamorgan, and control was disputed between the Norman and Welsh lords for much of the medieval period. The Earl of Gloucester granted extensive lands within this area to the abbeys of Margam and Neath. North of Bridgend lies the Llynfi Valley, defining a triangular area comprising Mynydd Margam and the long ridge of Mynydd Baedon and Mynydd Ty-Talwyn; this ridge formed the boundary between the lands held by Margam and that forming the secular lordship of Tir Iarll ('Earl's land') (Fig 3.4). A well-marked trackway follows the ridge, becoming extensively braided in the saddle between Mynydd Baedon and Mynydd Ty-Talwyn. Margam's lowland lands were farmed from an extensive system of granges, but there is a cluster of platforms on the slopes of Mynydd Ty-Talwyn, comprising fifteen sites. The land is now enclosed pasture, but was probably unenclosed in the medieval period. It is possible that the cluster represents displaced or earlier Welsh settlement, but it seems more likely that it formed part of the abbey's system of stock management; Margam held more than

abandonment may have been the direct or delayed effect of a change in landholding, in this case the readjustment of land units following the Dissolution of the Monasteries. The site is a reminder that even in the Norman landscape of the Vale, with its arable open fields, nucleated villages, and lowland topography, the long hut form could be adopted within a complex site. There is no reason to suppose that the complex represents anything other than a detached permanently occupied farmstead of the medieval period.

A further group of sites with a monastic connection are those on Mynydd Resolven, at the north-east end of the Neath Valley, Glamorgan. The sites form a scatter of platforms on the south-west-facing slope

Dinas Noddfa
The Lower House

drainage gully

upper bank

pit

collapse+

orthostat

entrance

entrance

stone+ heap

paving slabs

stone+ heap

entrance

limit of excavation

stone+ stylised

posthole ●

| 0 | 1 | 2 | 3 | 4 | 5 | | 10 | | 15 | | 20 metres |

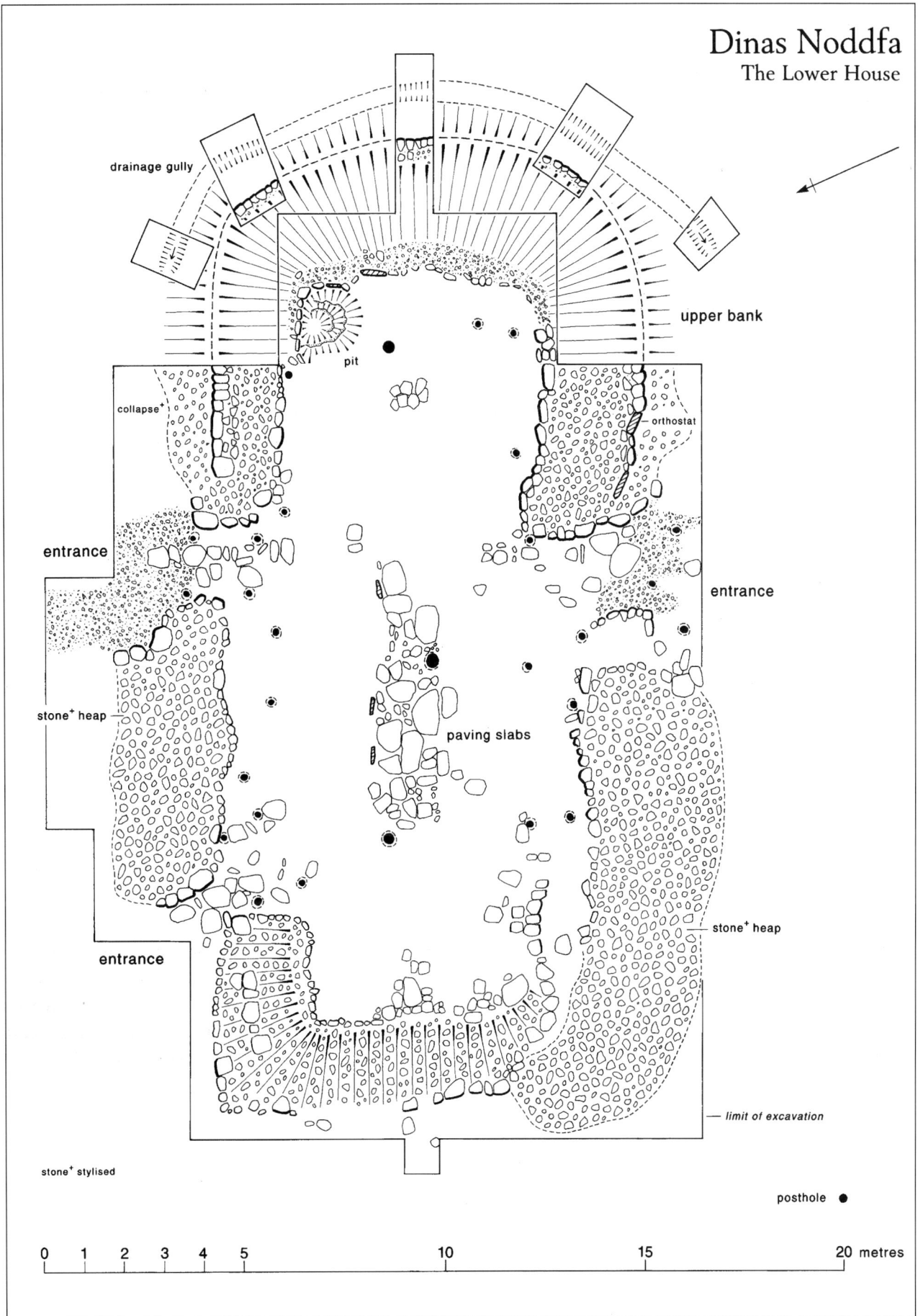

3.6 Dinas Noddfa: lower house

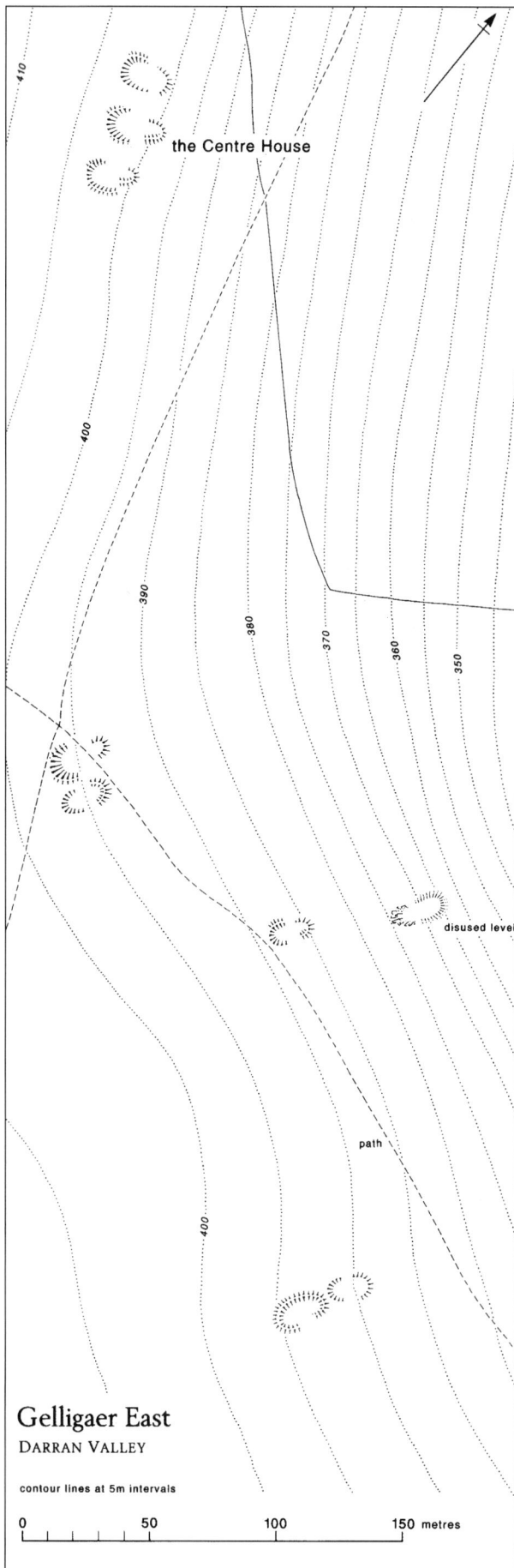

the Centre House

disused level

path

Gelligaer East
DARRAN VALLEY

contour lines at 5m intervals

0   50   100   150 metres

3.7 Gelligaer Common: plan (after RCAHMW 1982)

5000 sheep in 1291 (Williams 1984, 305). It is tempting to correlate the large number of platforms on Mynydd Ty-Talwyn with the eleven recorded granges in Margam (Williams 1990, 48–50); perhaps each grange sent its stock under the care of a shepherd who occupied a house built on the platform for the summer. It is possible that the cluster marks the 'entry point' onto the upland pastures from the south, where in the autumn the sheep were herded and sorted prior to their return to the lowlands *via* the track.

The neighbouring parish of Llangynwyd was the site of the seat of the Tir Iarll lordship, Llangynwyd Castle (RCAHMW 1991, 258–63), to the west of Llangynwyd village. The distribution of platforms forms two clusters, at the head of Cwm Cerdin and on the east side of the saddle between Mynydd Baedon and Mynydd Ty-Talwyn, the latter only a few hundred metres from the Margam cluster on the other side of the ridge. This pattern is similar to Margam (the southern cluster might be Llangynwyd's shepherds claiming their stock).

There is also, however, the anomalous site of Bryn-cynan Farm, to the north, which is a clearly visible earthwork platform, with a large central building of longhouse form indicated by wall banks, surrounded by yards and shelters, enclosed by a substantial bank. The site is clearly more sophisticated than the humble platforms to north and south, and can perhaps best be interpreted as an upland manorial centre, either as a summer residence for the lord, or else as the house of his reeve. The role of the *maerdy* in the administration of common rights has been noted elsewhere in south-east Wales (Locock 1998). This use of the long hut form as a unit within a complex of different function parallels that at Pen Onn.

The sites in this area are assumed to be medieval in date, since post-Dissolution the granges of Margam ceased to be a single land-holding unit, and each became a separate farm.

3.5.2 Gelligaer Common: permanent and temporary settlement

Gelligaer Common lies in the Glamorgan uplands, to the south-west of Merthyr Tydfil and north of Caerphilly. It takes the form of a north–south plateau at 400m OD, between the valleys of the Bargoed Taff and Bargoed Rhymney. The settlement of Gelligaer lies at the south end of the ridge, in enclosed fields. The lower valley slopes to the east and west had been enclosed by the 18th century (Hill 1999), but the summit area is still unenclosed common. The area lay

Gelligaer East
The Centre House

revetment
wall

posthole

orthostat

hearth stone

entrance

stone⁺ heap

entrance

drainage gully

drainage gully

paving slabs

pit

stone⁺ and turf

— limit of excavation

stone⁺ stylised

burnt layer

rock outcrop

0 1 2 3 4 5   10   15   20 metres

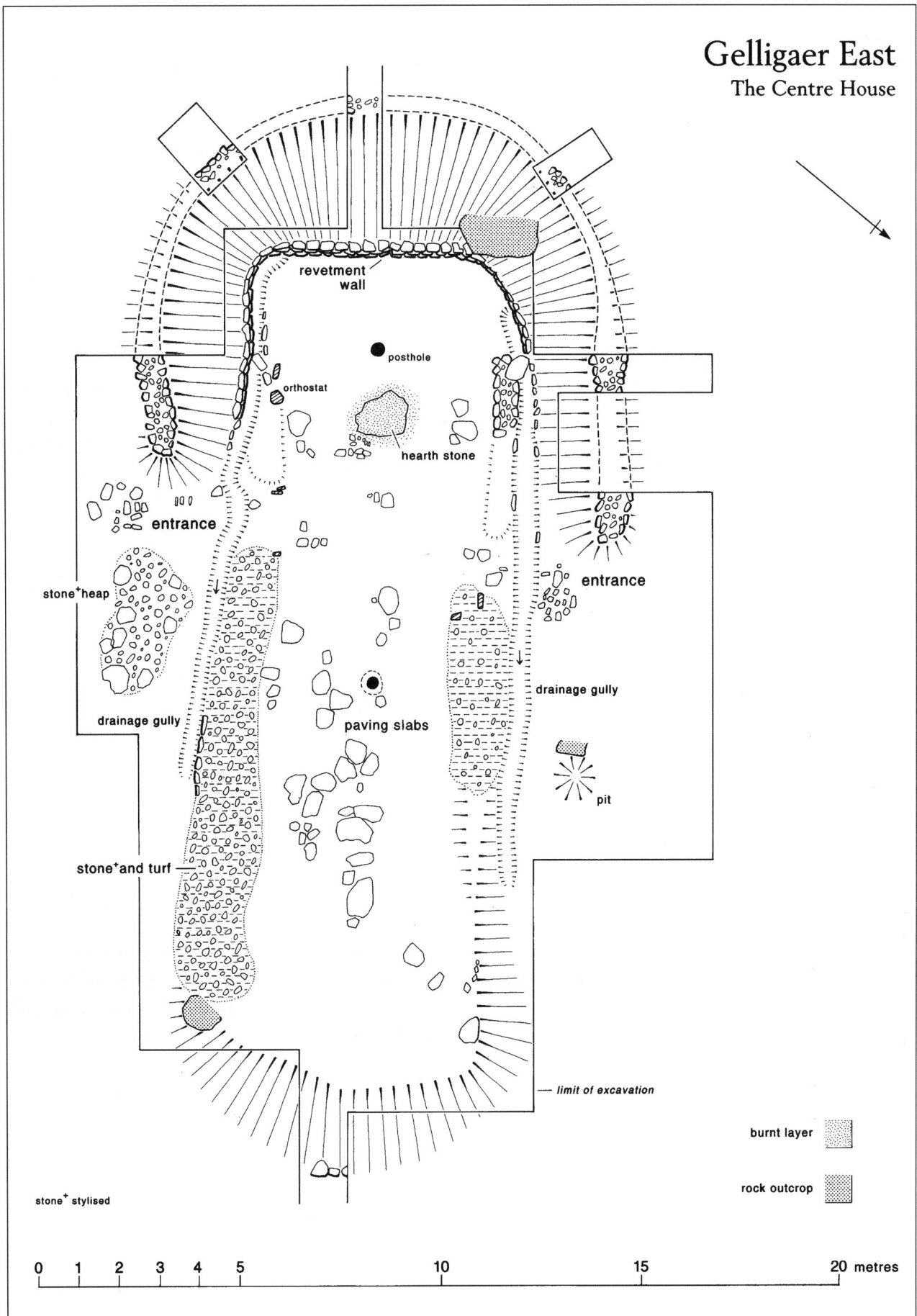

3.8 Gelligaer Common: centre house

within the medieval lordship of Senghenydd, the north part of which remained under Welsh control until Gilbert de Clare ejected Gruffydd ap Rhys in the 1260s, and built Caerphilly Castle in the 1270s (Rees 1974). Control continued to be disputed, and in 1316 Llywelyn Bren, of Gelligaer, attacked the Castle and town, while the 1320s saw further warfare between the Marcher Lords and Edward II. In the peace that followed, Caerphilly developed into a small but prosperous market town, but the remainder of Senghenydd remained undeveloped until the 19th century. This historical background becomes significant in the context of the platform sites and their date, since the troubled history provides a number of windows for encroachment and corresponding periods of

manorial control, and possibly reduction in population.

The group on the western side of the common, overlooking the Bargoed Taff Valley, was partly excavated by Aileen Fox in 1936–8 (as 'Dinas Noddfa' or Col-y-uchaf) (Figs 3.5 and 3.6). The Lower House proved to be a posthole timber structure with opposing doorways, effectively filling the platform. The Upper House was a smaller building, with only one doorway. No indication of a hearth or fire was found in either building. Clearly associated with these sites is a pair of linear field banks to the south, running up the slope, terminating in a scatter of cairns which may be medieval or prehistoric (A Fox 1939; C Fox 1939b). The finds from the excavation were sparse: no pottery was found, and the only artefacts were a whetstone and

3.9 Ty-yn-y-waun, Heol-y-Cyw, Glamorgan

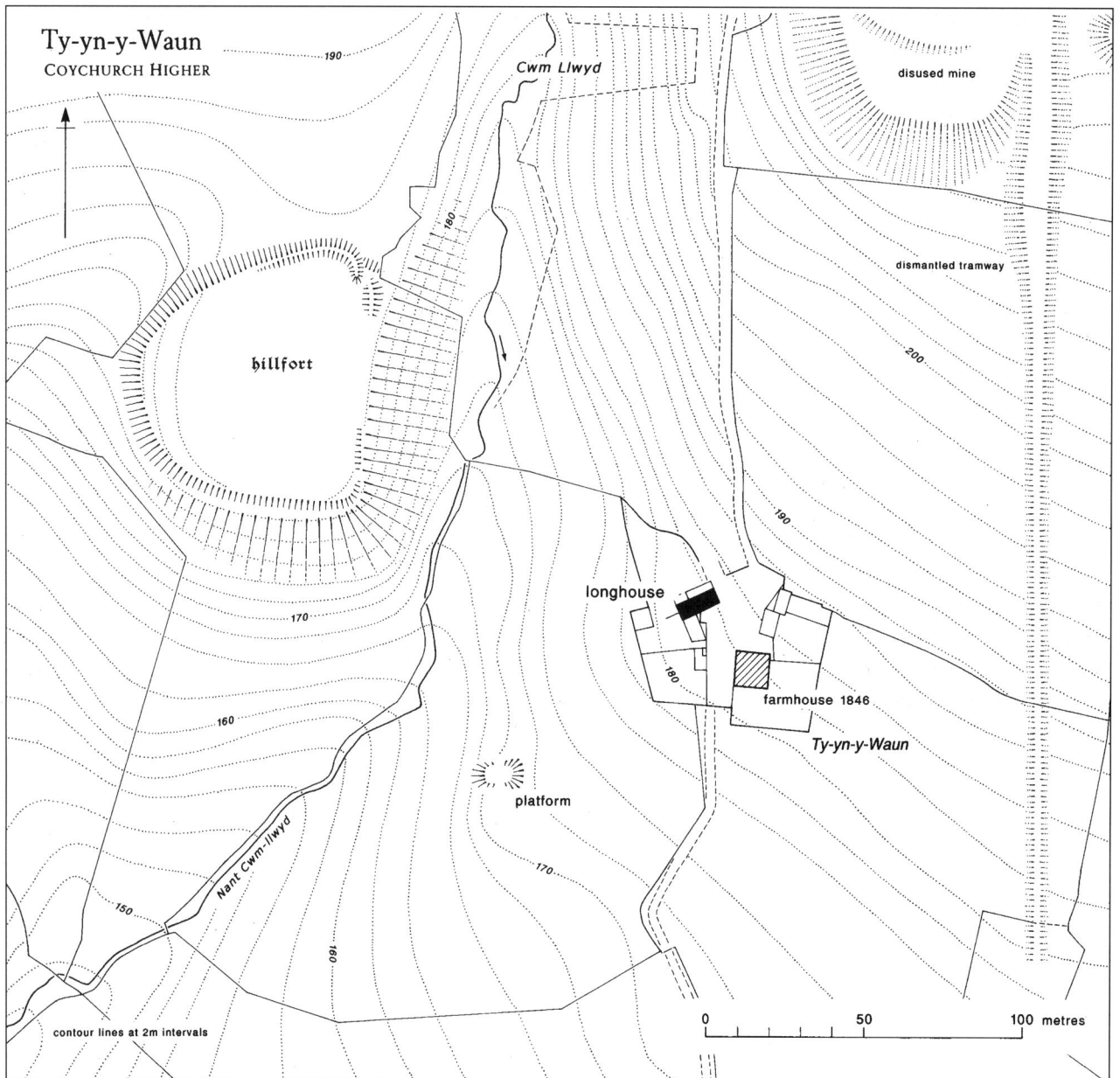

'12 pieces of iron slag … embedded in the surface of the floor … there were no signs of burning or smelting near them' (Fox 1937, 257). Thus, despite the presence of the field banks and cairns, there is no evidence of permanent occupation here. The same is true of the group of three platforms to the north. Indeed, the apparent relationship between the platforms and adjacent enclosures may be misleading, since there are further platform sites to the south-west, well within the enclosed land.

On the eastern side of the Common there is a group of platforms running along the contour to the west of the modern enclosed fields on the steep valleyside (Figs 3.7 and 3.8). The northernmost group of three was excavated in 1938 (A Fox 1939); the north and south houses proved to be simple rectangular structures; the southern had a yard area at the hood end. The central house (Fig 3.8) was more complex and substantial, including a hearth slab at the hood end and opposing doorways. It is worth noting that even this building would not qualify as a longhouse (strictly defined) since there is no evidence for stock use of the lower part of the building. This site is critical to the history of the interpretation of the type, since it was the recovery of pottery sherds (of coarseware and a glazed jug) from the house that provided a date, of the 13th–14th centuries, and led Fox to suggest that it was occupied all year round. The floor also produced a whetstone, iron slag, fragmentary iron objects, and a stone mould for casting a dress ornament. Thus the assemblage was a typical domestic group, with indications of occupation and craftworking somewhere in the vicinity (although no evidence for ironworking within the building was found). If this does indeed represent permanent occupation, it would appear to be unusual. The lack of contemporary enclosures and the number of platforms are much more similar to the groups elsewhere in south-east Wales, assumed to represent seasonal exploitation of pasture, than to posited medieval encroachment.

While there are indications for permanence from the excavations at Gelligaer East, they are not comprehensive or compelling. It seems more likely that any seasonally occupied medieval platforms which did develop into permanent occupation sites were those in the now-enclosed land to the south, rather than those on the common, which may be the summer end of a transhumance pattern, either from the valleys to east and west or from Gelligaer to the south. It can be hypothesised that the entire lordship of Sengehenydd was involved, and that the trigger for abandonment of

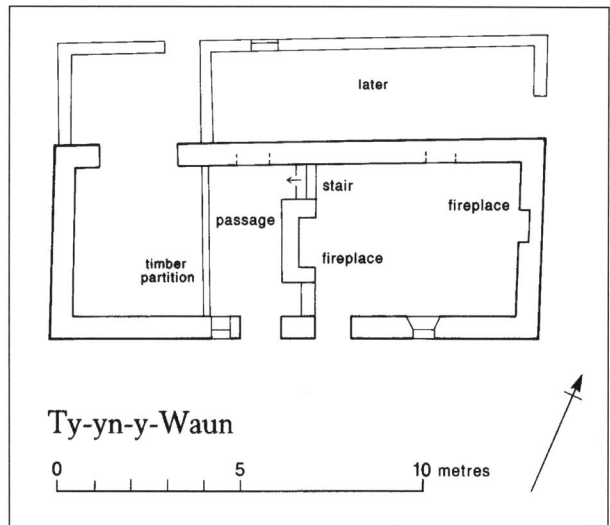

3.10 Ty-yn-y-waun longhouse

the sites was the replacement or disruption of the *hendre* end in the course of the Norman offensive in the Caerphilly area. If this were the case, then the enclosure of the valleys may represent a change in exploitation pattern in which long-distance transhumance ceased to play a part, and thus a shift in economy directly resulting from the political context of the late medieval period.

3.5.3 From platform house to longhouse: Hafod Fach and Ty-yn-y-Waun

The project has adopted Peate's (1946) architectural definition of a 'longhouse' as a three-unit building with a drop in floor level at the lower end (used for stock) and an entrance into the middle unit (a cross-passage or feeding walk); he considered this to be a 'common 17th-century type' (Peate 1946, 59). He noted that in the late 19th century there were many examples in Glamorgan, but that the great majority have since been abandoned or reconditioned (Peate 1946, 66). This observation is apparently borne out by the small number of longhouse sites represented in the SMR (fewer than 20). He also discussed *hafod* and *lluest* sites, describing them as simple structures, and the spread of squatting and the creation of *tai unnos* (houses built in one night, a customary method of encroachment on a common); it is notable that he rejects any connection between these activities and the longhouse form. (See also Sambrook, this volume).

There is some confusion in the literature between a longhouse in Peate's sense (endorsed by Alcock and Smith 1972; Meirion-Jones 1973; Gardiner 2000) and the broader sense of 'any three-unit building in which the third is used for farm purposes' (Hurst 1971, 113).

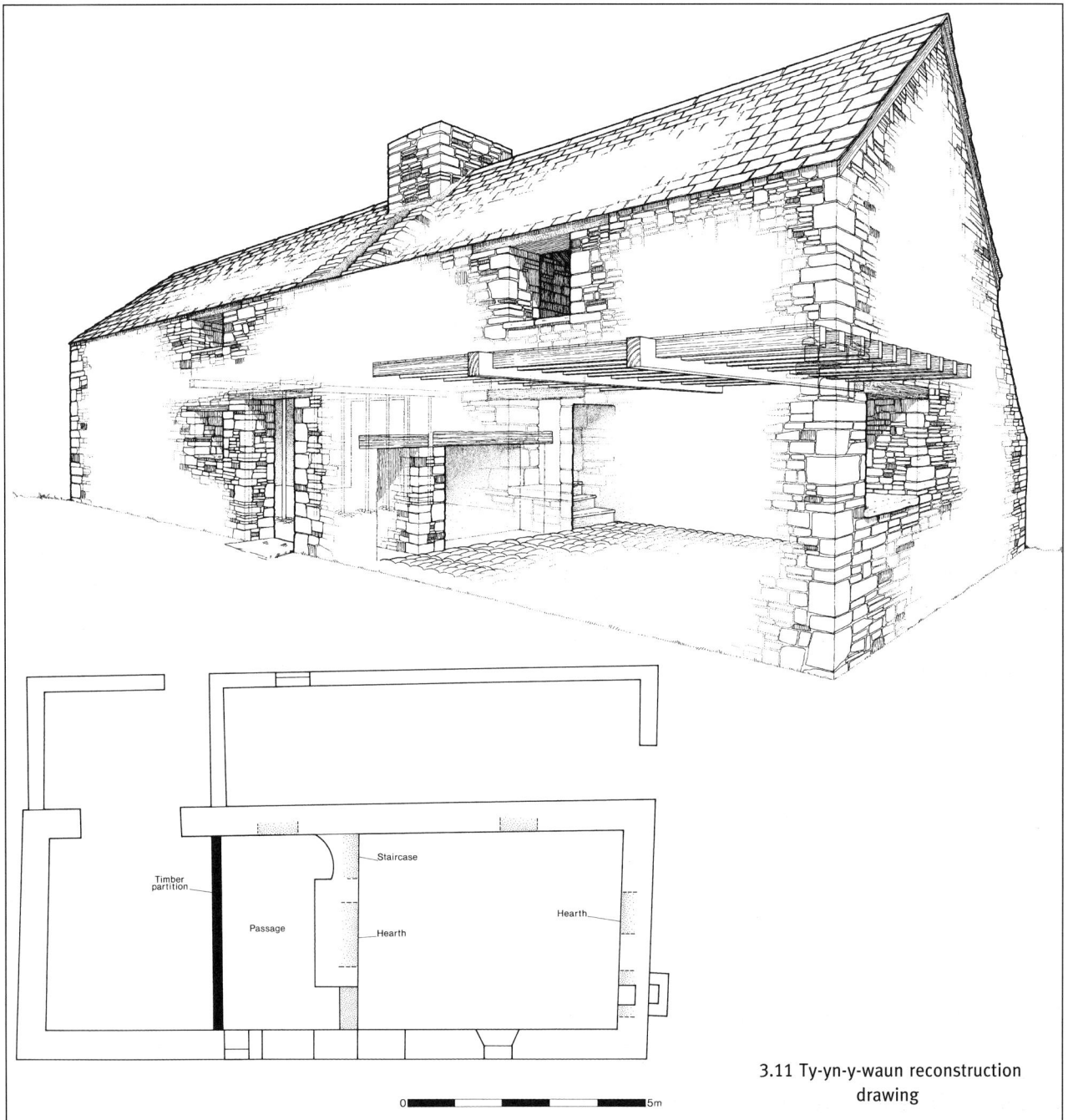

Timber
partition

Staircase

Passage

Hearth

Hearth

0   5m

3.11 Ty-yn-y-waun reconstruction
drawing

Jones and Smith (1963) proposed three terms: the *true* longhouse, with access from house to byre; the *false* longhouse, with separate external access but no internal access; and the *vestigial* longhouse, in which the byre element is no longer present. In order to evade these difficulties, Smith (1988) and RCAHMW (1988) use the term regional house B or BL to describe buildings which retain a three-unit plan, with a hearth- or cross-passage, but do not have a byre element (and therefore fall outside Peate's usage). It is perhaps unfortunate that the precise function of the lower third of the building has become so critical. Alcock's examination of three-unit buildings in Devon revealed a complexity of layout and use masked by this

distinction: 'Physical structures give little direct evidence for the social spaces they contained … a common plan form does not necessarily reflect common room use' (Alcock 1994, 210). The issue is important, though, since Morris (1954, 40) has proposed that the longhouse developed from a transitional form in which a pair of longitudinally aligned platforms were used as a single two-unit building, in turn a development from a single house on a platform. Platforms may well represent a different type of building (temporary, less substantial), rather than an earlier (or necessarily seasonally occupied) one. The proposed sequence probably fails on chronological grounds, since paired platforms are contemporary with longhouses, and raises structural difficulties with the position of doorways and links between the units. The identity of platform sites and longhouse form can be demonstrated in some cases, implying that the byre element was required, in turn suggesting that cattle were over-wintered in the building and not in the valleys.

Although no certain earthwork longhouses were identified in south-east Wales, two standing buildings are worthy of discussion. Hafod Fach, Caerphilly, Monmouthshire, was surveyed by GGAT prior to its demolition in 2000; it overlooks the south-east-running valley of Cwm Hafod Fach, on the western edge of the Mynydd Maen *massif* east of Newbridge. The house lay within enclosed pasture, immediately south of the medieval grange of Cil-lonydd (Weeks 1998). The area was probably enclosed from the common pasture on the summit in the 17th century, when there is recorded encroachment at Hafod Owen, in the adjoining side valley to the east (Bradney 1993, 138). The building (ruinous and unstable when surveyed) was located laterally on a large level terrace, and had seen extensive alterations in the 19th century, but retained sufficient early features to permit its identification as a hearth passage house with a secondary unit to the south and a stair to an upper floor south of the hearth, a plan typical of the 16th–17th centuries. The house as such is probably contemporary with enclosure of the fields. The place-name and any associated platform must relate to the previous phase of medieval transhumance; the change in agricultural regime may have resulted from the switch from monastic to secular control. It appears to be a rare example of the logical sequence from temporary to permanent settlement accompanied by a shift from long hut to longhouse type and from open common to enclosed fields, dating to the early post-medieval period. As such it would confirm a medieval date for its presumed predecessor, although no predecessor site has been identified.

The second site studied in detail is Ty-yn-y-waun, Heol-y-Cyw, Glamorgan. It lies on a plateau at the foot of Mynydd-y-Gaer, on the east bank of the Nant Cwm-llwyd, which runs south to Hirwaun Common (Bridgend) and the east–west ridge of Cefn Hirgoed (Fig 3.9). The farm comprises enclosed pasture, with the remains of woodland along the valley bottom; it is overlooked by Cwm Llwyd Iron Age hillfort. The presumed earliest feature is a poorly defined platform facing west, 11 x 5.5m. A further, bowl-shaped, platform, to the west of the river, measures some 5m

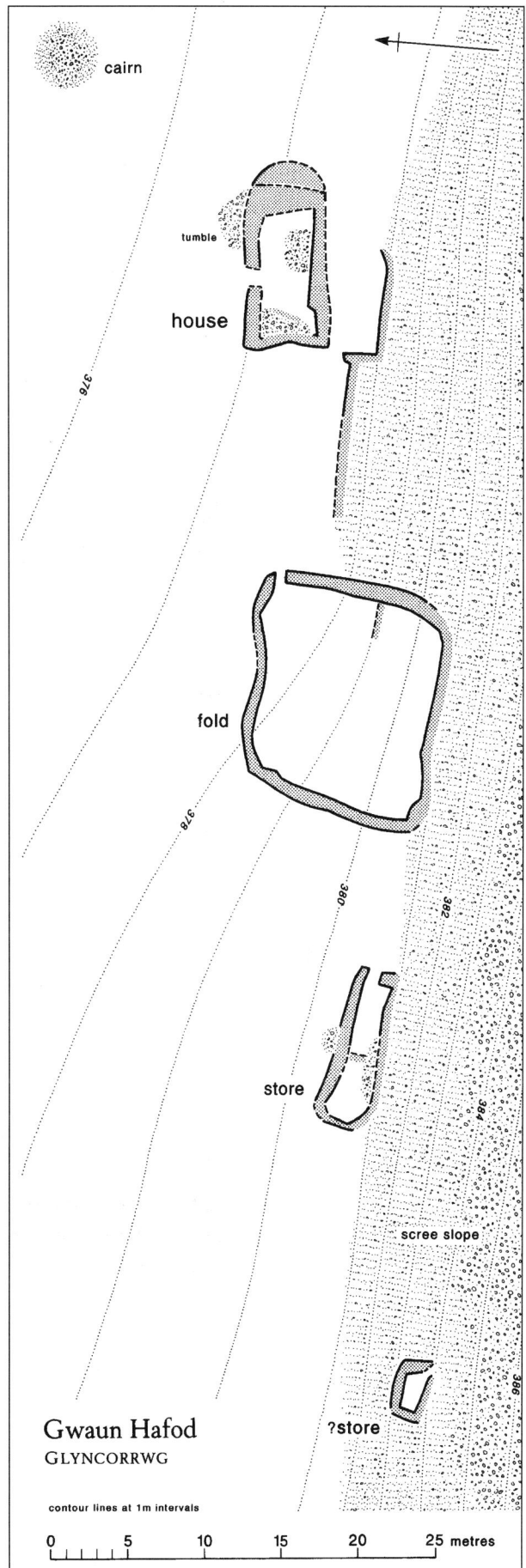

Gwaun Hafod
GLYNCORRWG

contour lines at 1m intervals

3.12 Gwaun Hafod, Glyncorrwg

across; it is interpreted as a charcoal-burning platform, from the post-medieval period. The farmstead complex has developed over a long period, and now includes both a longhouse and a farmhouse (Ty-yn-y-waun built in 1846). The longhouse, now an outbuilding, is a much-altered hearth passage house, running down the slope, with a stair to the upper floor on the north of the fireplace at the lower end of the east unit. Later changes involved the construction of a new hearth in the east gable and the insertion of a doorway in the gable to give access to the loft from the track outside (Fig 3.10). Despite several episodes of fire damage and extensive repairs, many of the elements can still be identified (Fig 3.11). There is no direct dating, but a 17th-century date seems likely; the building was demoted when the new farmhouse was built in the 19th century.

The structural evidence is fairly complete, and a link to the landscape context can be proposed. It seems reasonable to suppose that the early platform represents use of the area prior to enclosure; it is notable that the Cwm Llwyd Valley leads to a saddle in Mynydd-y-Gaer, and therefore would be a preferred access route from lowland to upland. The name for the later farm, meaning 'house in the meadow', might reflect this enclosure. The construction of this presumed predecessor of the hearth passage house would logically accompany the enclosure of the surrounding fields, and there followed alterations and improvements on the same site until the move to the new house in the 19th century (perhaps reflecting growing prosperity as industrial activity in the locality began). From Cefn Hirgoed there is pollen evidence for woodland which was cleared in the early medieval period, replaced by pasture; the change in vegetation may have initiated the substantial peat growth observed (Walker *et al.* 1997). It is possible that this sequence reflects pressure on the common land of Coety Wallia arising from this enclosure of Mynydd-y-Gaer to the north.

It would seem from these two examples that the construction of longhouse forms is associated with enclosure of the surrounding pasture; this would fit with the need for shelter for over-wintering cattle indoors, in contrast to the simpler type of platform buildings needed as a summer shelter or dairy. It is unfortunate that such examples are rare; more generally, it appears that in south-east Wales enclosure led to new building in a different tradition, the gable-entry house (Wiliam 1986, 18–19), perhaps because separate buildings were provided for such purposes.

3.5.4 'Tarren sites', sheepfolds and later features

Although the focus of the study was on sites of possible medieval date, many upland sites are poorly dated, and some later sites were included since there was insufficient evidence positively to exclude them. Fox identified complexes of stone-built features, typically including sheepfolds, guidewalls, and related shelters or huts, often located on open moorland at the foot of exposed scarps and named them 'tarrens', from the Welsh word for the crag with which they appeared to be associated. As a group they have been discussed by the RCAHMW which has proposed a late post-medieval (perhaps 19th-century) date for them and noted a common association with *lluestau* (RCAHMW 1982, 65–8).

There is evidence for a long chronology for these sheepfold complexes. Mynydd Ynyscorrwg lies south-east of the mining village of Glyncorrwg, in the upper Afan Valley. At the foot of the main slope is a large gently sloping bench, with very poor drainage. Until recently the mountain was unenclosed. Two separate complexes comprising structures and enclosures are present; their relative age was suggested by their condition and construction details. The older, Gwaun Hafod, lies to the south-west (Fig 3.12). The main building (the RCAHMW's 'house') has a north doorway and an 'apsidal' east gable; a narrow yard is defined to the south by a low revetment wall. A large squarish fold and two smaller structures (stores or shelters, perhaps) lie to the west, and a cairn to the north-east. The site lies at the southern (uphill) extent of an area of enclosed ground recorded on the 1840 tithe map as 'Gwaun Hafod'. It is interesting to note the use of 'gwaun' here for unimproved pasture rather than meadow. The nature of the enclosure is not clear, but since it is no longer visible it may have been fenced or with a low bank. There is no evidence for guidewalls in the complex, which is not shown on the map. It would appear that the name of the enclosure carries forward a tradition of unenclosed land use as a *hafod*, placing the complex in that earlier, perhaps transhumant, context.

To the east, across an incised stream valley, is the second group of features, Nant Lluest-Wen, occupying a similar topographic location, at the base of the slope. There are traces of guidewalls from the mountain to the south. The principal feature is the large walled enclosure, enclosing some 4ha, with a well-built drystone wall up to 1.8m high. There are two entrances, at the south end, adjoining a large building (running down the slope; it has no chimney), associated with a series of internal and external folds. The walls, which are significantly higher than most field walls, may be intended to provide some protection for the stock from the weather as well as simply preventing escape. It is possible that the enclosure was used (in the relatively recent past) as a shelter for sheep after lambing, prior to their release onto the moor or transport for sale. Thus it would appear that the two complexes are of different date and function but reflect a continuity of upland stock management which may extend back into the early post-medieval period or before. Osborne (1978), working from documentary sources, notes the exploitation of the coalfield uplands for sheep-rearing in the early post-medieval period, and the development of specialist sheep farms and shepherds caring for stock from farms in the Vale of Glamorgan without access to pasture. Activity on this scale may well have resulted in the development of tarren-type structures.

On Hirwaun Common, the unenclosed moorland at the foot of the main slope is scattered with more than 30 structures (Davis 1989), ranging from small buildings (with hearths and chimneys) to pens, folds and possible long huts. Davis relates the structures to continued exploitation of the right of free common of tenants of Miskin Manor. Apart from a probable 17th-century cottage at the foot of Craig-y-Llyn, now under forestry, there is little evidence for permanent occupation or attempted encroachment, perhaps reflecting the ability of the commoners to protect their rights against individual transgressors.

3.6 Conclusions

Function
There is evidence for a range of functions for long hut sites; the vast majority would appear to be related to temporary occupation as part of pastoral farming in or close to unenclosed land. There is relatively little evidence for their use as part of a process of encroachment and enclosure *de novo*. What evidence there is implies that some sites which may have started in an unenclosed landscape remained in use and were overtaken by the expansion of enclosure. The emphasis on temporary settlement perhaps explains the absence of the full 'longhouse' form, since the provision of shelter for stock at the lower end would have been unnecessary in buildings intended solely for summer use. The minimal evidence for heating can be similarly explained.

There are several cases where long hut buildings were used as a component in a complex with other structures, particularly monastic farmsteads; it would appear that these examples reflect the use of a template of a building type rather than a development of function. There remain a few cases where long huts appear to represent encroachment and enclosure, but this use of a form need not imply a functional alteration.

Land tenure
There is little evidence for these sites forming a separate tier of settlement within the medieval and post-medieval landscape, for example, providing housing for 'squatters' or as overflows from established settlements. Rather, they appear to perform a role within an established system of land exploitation in which maximum use is made of the upland pastures. The resistance to the fragmentation, encroachment or enclosure of these areas was powerful, perhaps reflecting a unity of interest between the manorial lord and those with rights of common which effectively discouraged alternative land use. Evidence for cultivation and other activities is very limited.

The grouping of platforms in clusters on the edges of the commons presumably reflects the need for kinship groups to maintain some kind of presence to oversee their stock; the pattern appears to be essentially egalitarian, without much variation between the different clusters.

Desertion
It is perhaps inevitable that in studying the phenomenon of deserted rural settlements much attention is paid to the process and causes of desertion. Philosophically, this may be unnecessary. Many sites may be intended to have only a short duration, and to assume that continuity of use is typical may be misleading. Perhaps more can be learnt from the various histories of each site: some continued in their original form, others developed into more substantial buildings, and others were abandoned. The range of dates to which these sites belong makes it dangerous to seek a single cause or process that led to desertion: as has been demonstrated, the explanations for individual sites seem to lie in tenurial, political or economic changes of *local* relevance. The temptation to conflate all these factors into a process of desertion, in order to identify a single cause (such as environmental change or the Black Death) needs to be resisted.

Deserted Rural Settlements in context

When first identified, long huts were interpreted as a thing apart, a type of site lying outside the normal pattern of settlement and land use. The existence of the current study is perhaps an echo of this view. On the basis of the case studies examined here, it would be more useful to consider them alongside other elements of the medieval and post-medieval landscape to which they are related, either closely (as in transhumance) or more generally as part of the sequence of enclosure and encroachment.

Acknowledgements

The project was managed by Andrew Marvell (Principal Archaeological Officer Contractual) and undertaken by Martin Locock (Projects Manager), with assistance from Paul Graves-Brown (Sites and Monuments Record Officer), Susan Hughes (Heritage Management Officer), Terry Davies (Photographer), Kate Howell (Project Officer), and Jo Mackintosh, Claire Davies, Penny Jefferson, Andrew Sherman, and Natalie Swords (Project Assistants). Illustrations were prepared by GGAT Illustration Department.

The Trust is grateful to Mike Yates and Kate Roberts (Cadw: Welsh Historic Monuments), Paul Sambrook (ACA/DAT), Richard Knight (Cooke and Arkwright), John Blundell, Adrian Wilcox (Monmouthshire County Council), Mark Redknap (National Museums and Galleries of Wales), Trevor Warren (Lafarge Redland Aggregates Ltd), and Jonathan Kissock (University of Wales College, Newport) for their help, and to the staff of West Glamorgan Record Office, the National Library of Wales, and Glamorgan Record Office.

The Trust is also grateful to the landowners and tenants, including David H G Thomas (Tyn-y-waun Farm, Heol-y-Cyw), Mr and Mrs Parry (Ross Kear, Penonn, Llancarfan), Jeffrey Howell (Bryncynan Farm, Llangynwyd), Chris Griffiths (Ffermdy Lluest Wen, Llangynwyd), and Mrs Parry (Penarth Farm, Llanishen) for their assistance with the project.

4 Deserted rural settlements in north-west Wales

By David Longley

Abstract

There is a class of field monument in the landscape of north-west Wales categorised by Gresham (1954) and the RCAHMW (1956; 1964) as 'rectangular buildings, now reduced to their foundations [representing] abandoned dwellings ... varying in date from the middle ages to the 18th-century' (RCAHMW 1964, clxxviii). Individual examples have in the past been described as 'platform houses' where a terrace into a hill-slope has been created to provide a level foundation (Fox 1939) or 'long-huts' (RCAHMW 1956, xxxiii–iv; 1964, clxxviii), describing their elongated proportions, with no implication in respect of function.

Between 1995 and 1999 the Gwynedd Archaeological Trust undertook an assessment, in the field, of all previously recorded monuments of this class as represented on the Regional Sites and Monuments Record. The process of fieldwork increased this total by 30% with the result that over 1200 sites were actually visited. A number of potential sites lacked sufficient surviving field evidence for any meaningful identifica-tion to be made and certain others were clearly more appropriately classified in a different category, such as, for example, cottage or barn, with no certain evidence for earlier use. Six hundred and seventy-one sites could be confidently classified as deserted rural settlements against the defined criteria. These formed the basis of the following assessment. Part One discusses the character and structural form of the monuments, topo-graphic setting, aspect, distribution and land use. Part Two considers the social and economic context within which such structures might have been erected. A distinction is sought between those structures of possible medieval date which might be considered to have formed part of the core settlement of townships, albeit on the periphery, and those, beyond the limit of historic enclosure, which might represent the seasonal exploitation of the *ffridd*. Other structures, again, are considered to have been associated with the process of estate building, expansion and intake on the *ffridd* during the 15th, 16th, and 17th centuries.

4.1 The character of the monuments

The character of the monuments was considered with reference to the surviving evidence of structures including wall foundations and platform size and shape; the evidence of land use in the immediate vicinity; topographic setting; the altitude at which sites were recorded and their aspect. The distribution of the monuments was considered with reference to the alti-tude bands within which they occurred. Figure 4.1 identifies sites mentioned in the text; figure 4.2 illus-trates some examples and contexts.

4.1.1 Topography and altitude
The landscape of north-west Wales is one of consider-able contrasts. The large island of Anglesey, off the north-west coastline, is generally low-lying and rela-tively flat. The immediately adjacent mainland of Arfon and Arllechwedd rises steeply from the shore of the Menai Straits and the coastal strip of the Arfon plateau to the heights of central Snowdonia and the Carneddau at over 1000m within 10km. The Llyn Peninsula, by contrast, is a more gently undulating landscape which is, nevertheless, punctuated by a string of peaks from Bwlch Mawr to Carn Fadrun, which reach, at their highest, over 500m.

To the south, Ardudwy and Meirionnydd exhibit similar extremes, with narrow west-facing coastal lowlands backed by the frequently inhospitable uplands of the Rhinogau, Cadair Idris and, inland, the high wet moorland of Trawsfynydd and the Migneint. This region, the 'Land of Cynan', was described by Giraldus Cambrensis as 'the roughest and most dreadful territory in the whole of Wales ... wilder and less accessible than other regions' (Itin. Kamb. 2.5; Descrip. Kamb. 1.6). The south-eastern limit of the survey area is defined by mountain ranges of Yr Aran and the Berwyns at over 800m.

The high ground, however, is transected by steep-sided river valleys which facilitate communication and sustain pockets of nucleated settlement. Principal among these are the Conwy in the north and its tributaries, the Lledr at Dolwyddelan and the Llugwy; the Dwyryd and the Glaslyn entering the sea at Tremadog Bay in the armpit of the Llyn, and the Dysynni and the Dyfi opening into Cardigan Bay. In the east of our area lies Llyn Tegid at Bala and the tributary of the Dee, the Meloch. The high mountains of central Snowdonia are cut and separated by glacial valleys at Nant Ffrancon, Nant Peris, the valley of the Gwyrfai and Nant Gwynant. Important as these valleys are, however, it is the high watersheds that are more likely to define the boundaries of communities and, often, also the regional boundaries of medieval administration and politics. For descriptive purposes within the discussion, twelve topographic regions are identified, based largely on the principal watersheds. These are mapped in Figure 4.3.

The monuments under review extend over a considerable altitude range, rising from 5m at Ystumllyn, near Criccieth, to over 500m at Pant y Griafolen, near Llyn Dulyn, and 750m at Ffynnon Caseg below Carnedd Llywelyn. On the subjective assumption that altitude might be related to function, or that form might be influenced by altitude, the siting of surveyed monuments was considered in respect of four altitude bands. These bands (1–4), from sea level to 185m OD, from 186m to 299m, from 300m to 412m, and from 413m to the highest peaks, were selected with reference to the curve of distribution of the monuments ranked by altitude. The ground surface areas occurring within these bands are: Band 1: 1914sq. km; Band 2: 683sq. km; Band 3: 619sq. km and Band 4: 640sq. km.

4.1.2 Wall foundations and platforms

The foundations of walls, perhaps always low and supporting a timber superstructure (cf. Kelly 1981), survive at most sites (78% of the total). Otherwise the former presence of structures is indicated by the plat-forms, terraced into sloping ground, on which they once stood. Platforms are predominantly aligned perpendicular to the contour. Not all monuments of the class under discussion required, nor were provided with, platforms, but a significant minority (47%) display evidence of both wall foundations and plat-forms together.

Smith has noted, in considering the more substantial houses of the Welsh countryside, that the dominant agricultural units of the later Middle Ages are represented by 'isolated farms, mainly sited on the lower [and intermediate] slopes of hills' and 'that the old farmhouses tend to be sited down rather than across the slope' (Smith 1988, 45). The creation of a level base (that is, a terraced platform) for construction is a more critical requirement in a timber-framed building and alignment perpendicular to the slope rather than along it would aid stability. An equally, if not more, important consideration, however, lies in the advantages for facilitating drainage that a perpendicular alignment contributes. Normally a space would be left at the uphill end, between the building and the slope into which the building platform was cut, achieving a hood-like effect around the upslope gable for the purpose of drainage. At St Tudwal's Isle, Llanengan, a building of 14th-century date, a rock-cut drain achieved the same result (RCAHMW 1964, No. 1591). An additional enhancement in the context of platform structures would be to raise the height of the 'hood' above the ground surface of the prevailing slope. This feature was recorded in 147 instances (23%) of the sites surveyed. As might be expected, moderate or steeply sloping locations gave rise to a proportionally greater incidence of sites with drain hoods than those without this provision. Thirty-seven per cent of all platforms with hoods were sited on steep or moderate slopes compared to 27% of sites without hoods. No differentiation was observed between the incidence of platforms with hoods and those without hoods on gently sloping ground.

The height of platforms is determined by the degree of slope and the extent to which a platform might be terraced out or recessed into the slope. Most have a platform height of around 0.5m and a corresponding depth, as represented by the depth of a drain hood, of 0.5 to 0.6m. It has been argued that as the platform is incidental to the principal element of the construction, the house which stood on the platform, too much emphasis should not be placed on the platform itself as a means of analysis. Nevertheless, there are consistent elements across the range of dimensions

Castell, Trefadog

Great Orme

Gorddinog
Aber / 5 Penmaenmawr
Ffridd Ddu Allt Wen
Wig Maes y Gaer
Plas Berw 1 2 Tal y Fan 4
Bwlch y Ddeufaen
Aber ffriddoedd Afon Goch Castell
Afon Ffrydlas Pen y Gadair
Cororion Afon Ddu 6
Rhosyr Afon Caseg
Cwm Eigiau
Llanrug Trefriw
Caernarfon Dolbadarn
Waunfawr Dolbadarn Bryn Tyrch
ffriddoedd Cwm Clorad
Cwm Dyli Moel Siabod
Bala Deulyn
Nanhwynan Dolwyddelan
ffriddoedd Dolwyddelan
Cefn Graeanog Nant Gwynant ffriddoedd
Bwlch Mawr Moel Penamnen
Elernion 3 Moel Bronmiod Pennant
Llanaelhearn Cwmystradllyn
Llithfaen Dolbenmaen
Gwynnus Gesail Gyfarch

Carn Fadrun
Prysor Amnodd Y Bala
Trawsfynydd Nanfach
Ardudwy Ffridd Trawsgoed
ffriddoedd Y Feidiog
Penarfynydd St Tudwal's Isle Penllyn
Bryn Coch ffriddoedd
Dyffryn Ardudwy Wenallt Cwm Ffynnon
Cwmdadi

Gwanas
Pennantigi

Talybont
ffriddoedd
Ffridd Pennant

0 50 km

land above 200m

Illustrated sites

1 Ffridd Ddu
2 Hafod y Gelyn
3 Farm Yard Llanaelhaearn
4 Maen y Bardd, Caerhun
5 Penmaenmawr
6 Ardda, Dolgarrog

0 5 10 15 20 25 50 km

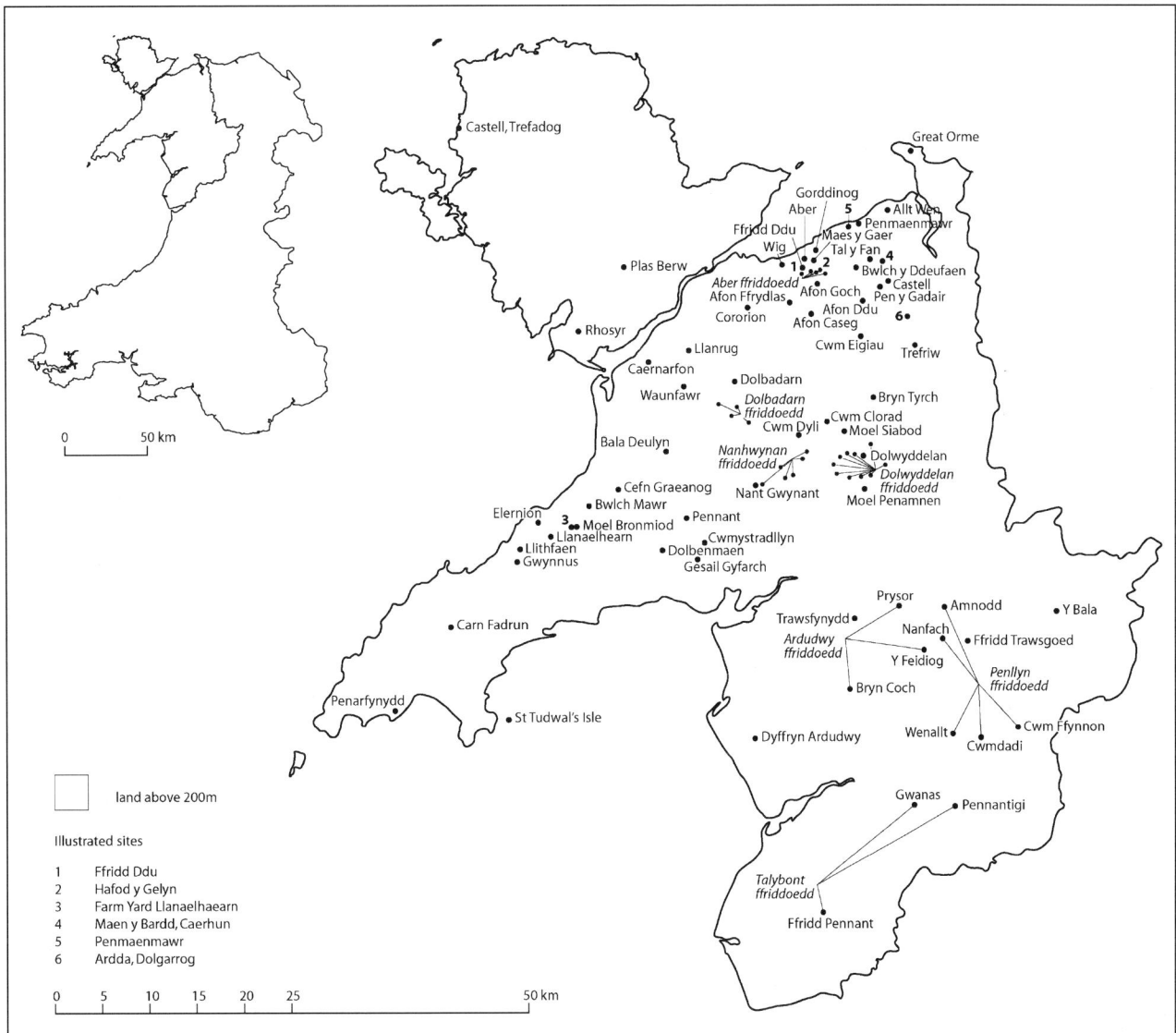

4.1 Map of north-west Wales showing principal sites mentioned in the text

represented and there are also indications of a proportional relationship between platforms and their houses, where the evidence for buildings survives. Although there are extremes of length and width (the largest recorded platform extends to over 20m, with a width of 13m, albeit with no visibly surviving evidence for a house), the most commonly recurring lengths are in the range 8–10m with corresponding widths of 4–5m.

In respect of individual monuments there is a overwhelming preponderance of both platforms and the foundations of structures in the width:length ratio of between 1:1.6 and 1:1.8 with, perhaps, a small group of narrower platforms, around twice as long as they are broad. The mean dimensions of houses in the ratio of 1:1.6 are 7.6m long by 4.8m wide and this may be taken to represent the characteristic shape of structures within the class. However, there is an identifiable tendency for length to increase in proportion to width

in the higher altitude bands. This does not necessarily give rise to an increase in surface area however, as the sites themselves are predominantly small. Additionally, there is a clutch of rather more square sites, which may be industrial, in the highest altitude band. The proportions are anomalous and one explanation may be that they are to be associated with upland industrial activities such as quarrying although this was not demonstrated during the course of the survey. There is a predominance of proportionately larger structures in altitude bands 1 and 2 with, on balance, those in band 2, in the range 186–299m OD, best representing the average as identified above.

There is an imputation that platforms and structures with the characteristics described above are of medieval or late medieval date (Smith 1988, 45; Fox 1939, 163–99; RCAHMW 1982, 20–1). The lack of extensive excavated evidence inhibits any certain

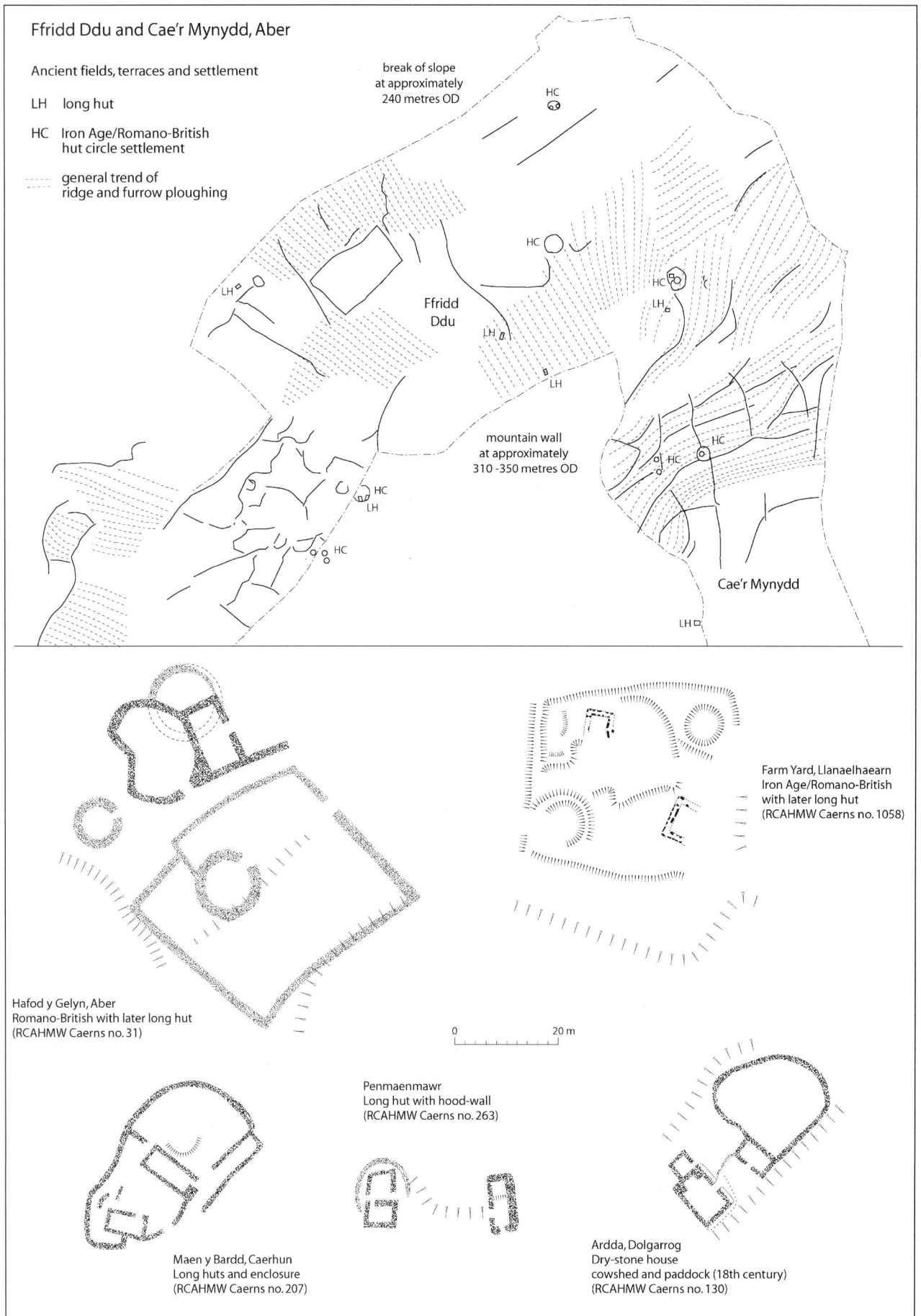

Ffridd Ddu and Cae'r Mynydd, Aber

Ancient fields, terraces and settlement

LH   long hut

HC   Iron Age/Romano-British
        hut circle settlement

----   general trend of
        ridge and furrow ploughing

break of slope
at approximately
240 metres OD

Ffridd
Ddu

mountain wall
at approximately
310 -350 metres OD

Cae'r Mynydd

Hafod y Gelyn, Aber
Romano-British with later long hut
(RCAHMW Caerns no. 31)

Farm Yard, Llanaelhaearn
Iron Age/Romano-British
with later long hut
(RCAHMW Caerns no. 1058)

0   20 m

Penmaenmawr
Long hut with hood-wall
(RCAHMW Caerns no. 263)

Maen y Bardd, Caerhun
Long huts and enclosure
(RCAHMW Caerns no. 207)

Ardda, Dolgarrog
Dry-stone house
cowshed and paddock (18th century)
(RCAHMW Caerns no. 130)

4.2 Examples of sites surveyed and one wider context, Ffridd Ddu

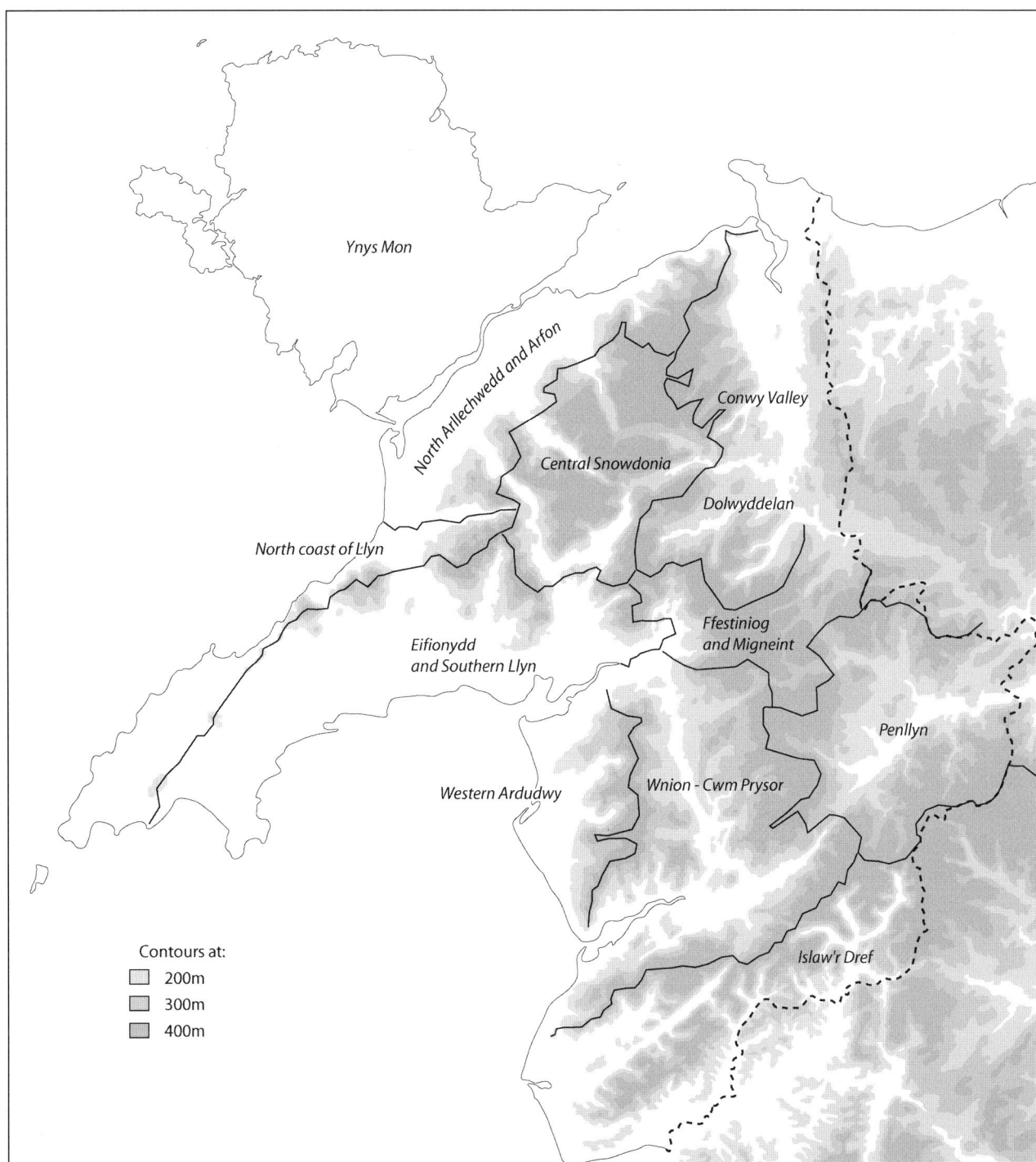

4.3 Physical topography of north-west Wales

conclusion but the suggestion gains some support in the association of 13th to 14th-century pottery at Dinas Noddfa, Glamorgan; the presumed 14th-century date of the structure on St Tudwal's Isle, Llanengan, Caernarvonshire; and the excavated evidence of 13th-century occupation at the group of rectangular structures at Cefn Graeanog, Llanllyfni, Caernarvonshire (Kelly 1981). A change in alignment of house relative to the prevailing contour may be perceived at certain lowland gentry houses as much as

at small upland settlements. At Plas Berw, Llanidan, Anglesey, for example, a 15th-century hall with its main axis following the declination sloping gently down towards Malltraeth marsh, was replaced in the early 17th century by a substantial new mansion, adjacent, but aligned with the prevailing contour rather than across it. Inevitably, persistent drainage problems ensued (Longley 1991a).

On the other hand, there are classes of building which stand perpendicular to the prevailing contour and which continued to be built, replaced or added to, into the 18th and 19th centuries. These fall into two principal groups. The first comprises certain 'longhouses' as defined by Peate and discussed by Fox (Peate 1946). These, in general, are the focus of small farms, comprising house and byre, and possibly additional farm buildings (Smith 1988, 144–5). They do not invariably occupy platforms but follow the lie of the land. These classic longhouses are well represented in south Wales but are rare in the north. Nevertheless, it is possible that the type was once more common than the surviving evidence allows. In this respect, Wiliam quotes a document of 1607, referring to the Machynlleth area, which suggests that it was common practice at night to inspect cattle tied up 'in the lower part of the house' (Wiliam 1992, 13). Examples also survived to be recorded at, for example, Hendy, Waunfawr and Cefn-buarddau, Llanaelhaearn, of probable 18th-century date (RCAHMW 1960, Nos. 1428a; 1036).

The second group is represented by the field byre. This stood as a single structure housing animals and carrying hay in a loft. The location of field byres is generally in areas of formerly open pasture, latterly enclosed and often, by nature of the prevailing topography, on sloping ground. There was also a practical reason for choosing a site on a slope. By terracing the byre into a slope direct access to the hay loft could be provided in the uphill gable at a level with the surface of the field, minimising the labour required in stacking it. Many field byres are of 18th- or 19th-century date. However, some show evidence of cruck-framing and the type may be of considerably earlier origin (Smith 1988, 145).

House-and-byre structures should be distinguishable by their elongated plan, although in a ruinous condition chronological differentiation may not be possible, and, perhaps, by the association of adjacent ancillary structures. A key feature which distinguishes field byres from platform houses as described above is that platform structures are, in general, designed so that a space is left between the uphill gable of any building on the platform and the hood. Field byres, on the other hand, require that the ground surface at the uphill gable abuts the wall of the byre to facilitate access to the loft. Nevertheless, the dilapidated condition of the majority of monuments surveyed again renders certain identification difficult. The general distribution of field byres also corresponds to the predominantly upland distribution of the monuments under review, including, as noted above, areas of seasonal pasture or *hafodydd*, subsequently enclosed.

A further distinctive characteristic of certain structures is the presence of rounded external corners (314 sites, 49%). This feature may be suggestive of a medieval date but not necessarily exclusively so. Excavated examples of rectangular structures with well-formed rounded external corners and squared internal angles are known from north Wales at Castell, Porth Trefadog, Anglesey, of 12th-century date; at Llys Rhosyr, Newborough, Anglesey, of 13th-century date and at St Tudwal's Isle, Llanengan, Llyn, of presumed 14th-century date (Longley 1991b; Johnstone 1999; RCAHMW 1964, No. 1591). Two of the structures at Hafod Y Nant Griafolen, Clwyd, had rounded corners. The general currency of this site, on the basis of excavated evidence, was placed in the 15th and 16th centuries (Allen 1979).

4.2 Land use in the vicinity of the monuments under review

It is accepted that the precise chronology of the structures surveyed is a matter of speculation which will not be determined without excavation or detailed documentary analysis on an individual site basis. It is, however, possible to establish a relative context describing earlier and later components within the landscape they inhabit. Establishing contemporaneity is more difficult.

4.2.1 The earlier landscape: Iron Age and Romano-British settlement

It has frequently been observed that long huts and platforms occur near or adjacent to Iron Age and Romano-British hut circle settlements. This perceived association may, to some extent, reflect the particularly good survival of both classes of monument in marginal areas, less intensively developed agriculturally. However, the pattern of distribution of hut circle settlements displays a real differentiation between, on the one hand, nucleated and enclosed settlements, possibly representing the equivalent of a 'home farm', and, on the other, unenclosed, dispersed and single isolated sites (Fig 4.4). Figure 4.5 presents the distribution of hut circle settlements against the distribution of long huts and platforms, within the altitude bands identified above.

Long huts or platforms have been observed in the vicinity of about 28% of all hut circle settlement

(Smith 1999, 19). In a limited number of instances (c. 4%) long huts can be seen to have been built directly over the sites of earlier hut circle settlements. At face value there is little to distinguish numerically between the association of long huts with nucleated/ enclosed hut circles and those near the sites of dispersed/isolated hut circles. However, when the proportionate incidence of each group, nucleated/ enclosed, dispersed/isolated, and long hut/platform is plotted against the four identified altitude bands,

weighted to compensate for the disproportionate surface area of the landscape occurring within each band, a more interesting pattern emerges. Nucleated/enclosed hut circle settlements are strongly represented within the two lower altitude bands (up to 299m OD). Unenclosed and dispersed hut circles occur most commonly within the two central altitude bands (between 185m and 412m). This pattern of density through altitude, as presented in Fig 4.5, is most closely matched by the incidence of long huts

4.4 Distribution of Iron Age and Romano-British hut circle settlements

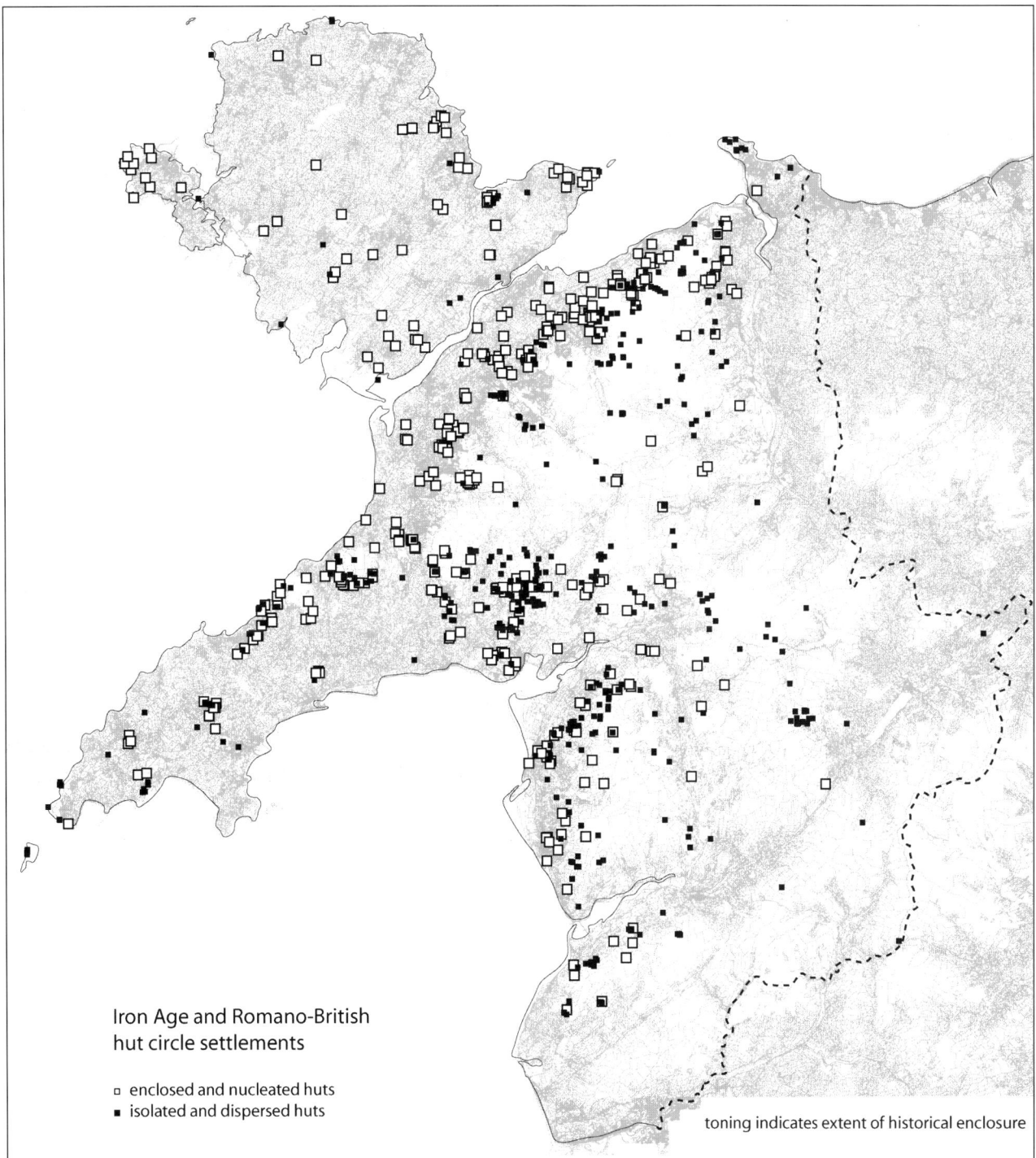

Iron Age and Romano-British
hut circle settlements

□ enclosed and nucleated huts
■ isolated and dispersed huts

toning indicates extent of historical enclosure

and platforms and stands in contrast to the incidence of enclosed and nucleated hut circle settlements. The significance of this observation may be that the distribution of nucleated and dispersed hut circle settlement represents a complementary and broadly contemporary use of a cross section of the landscape which finds similar expression in the complementary distribution of medieval core settlement and long huts. Both series of distributions may be a response to a persistent economic imperative, that of maximising the potential of a very varied and frequently inhospitable topography.

4.2.2 Medieval agriculture

Ridge and furrow ploughing was recognised in the vicinity of 10% of all sites and within an altitude range that extended from 40m to 385m. A particular concentration of association was recorded between 285 and 340m. The settlements identified in the immediate vicinity of ridge and furrow ploughing displayed a higher than average incidence of structural features potentially indicative of a medieval date such as houses aligned perpendicular to the contour, rounded corners at the external angles, and drain hoods. Two or more such features were present in combination at 76% of the settlements within the altitude range of greatest density of ridge and furrow (between 285 and 340m), and at 52% of the remainder. The average incidence of these features across the settlement type as a whole is 45%. It was also noted that a large proportion (60%) of the sites with ridge and furrow adjacent are settlements comprising more that one structure. The average incidence of multiple structures is 29%. This

combination of features, albeit in circumstantial association, may be a pointer to medieval smallholdings with an arable component, notwithstanding the higher altitudes recorded.

4.2.3 Recent land use

The evidence for later land use and activity around and upon the sites of deserted rural settlement is more diverse. Ditches, fences, walls, stone dumping, quarrying, tracks, a pipeline, and even a disused railway are recorded. Through the entire altitude range, with the exception of the highest band, over 412m, there are numerous instances of later field banks and boundary walls, superimposed on and crossing these settlements. They occur at between 10% and 13% of recorded sites. There are fewer instances of later agricultural buildings on the earlier settlements. These occur, surprisingly, more frequently at higher altitudes but even there at no more than 4% of the total. A number of the settlements have subsequently been quarried, and the walls used in the construction of sheep pens and shepherds' shelters. As might be expected the frequency of occurrence increases with altitude so that, in the lowest band, sheep pens occur on 2% of sites; between 185 and 299m the frequency increases to 5%, and at higher altitudes, above 300m, 12% of all settlements have sheep pens superimposed. At these altitudes many of the sites under review are likely to have been associated with livestock management on the high pastures during all periods. Field clearance was recognised in the immediate vicinity of between 30% and 40% of all sites, the lowest frequencies occurring in the highest altitude range.

4.3 Setting, altitude, and aspect

The topographic setting of these monument's extends from the coastal plain to the upper reaches of hill slopes. The most commonly recurring location is mid-slope on the sides of hills and valleys (53%) with, nevertheless, a notable proportion on upper slopes and ridges (23%). Twenty-four percent were recorded on the floors of valleys. Where these structures have been recognised on the valley floors, most (62%) are at relatively high altitudes, over 300m. While sloping ground is clearly preferred, the gradient is generally gentle or moderate (85% of locations) and rarely steep.

As these monuments are a predominantly upland phenomenon, at least in their survival, local topography and the influence of altitude and climate on land use is likely to have been a significant determinant of

siting. In mapping the monuments, the major watersheds are indicated, as is the interface between the historically enclosed and improved landscape and unenclosed moorland and mountain. As a generalisation, the sites under review can be seen to occupy the margins of enclosed land at this interface. This siting stands in contrast to the focal points of medieval core settlement as represented by the survival of township names (see below). The differentiation is striking and the distribution almost mutually exclusive (Fig 4.6). It is possible, of course, if not probable, that the operation of a more intensive agricultural regime and the continuity and replacement of settlement on the lower ground has had a deleterious effect on the survival of evidence. This point will be addressed below. It has

Iron Age and Romano-British
hut circle settlements
altitude band 0-299m

Iron Age and Romano-British
hut circle settlements
altitude band 185-412m

■ enclosed and nucleated huts
□ isolated and dispersed huts

■ enclosed and nucleated huts
□ isolated and dispersed huts

All 'Long Huts' and 'Platform Houses'
Principal areas of associated
ridge and furrow ploughing circled

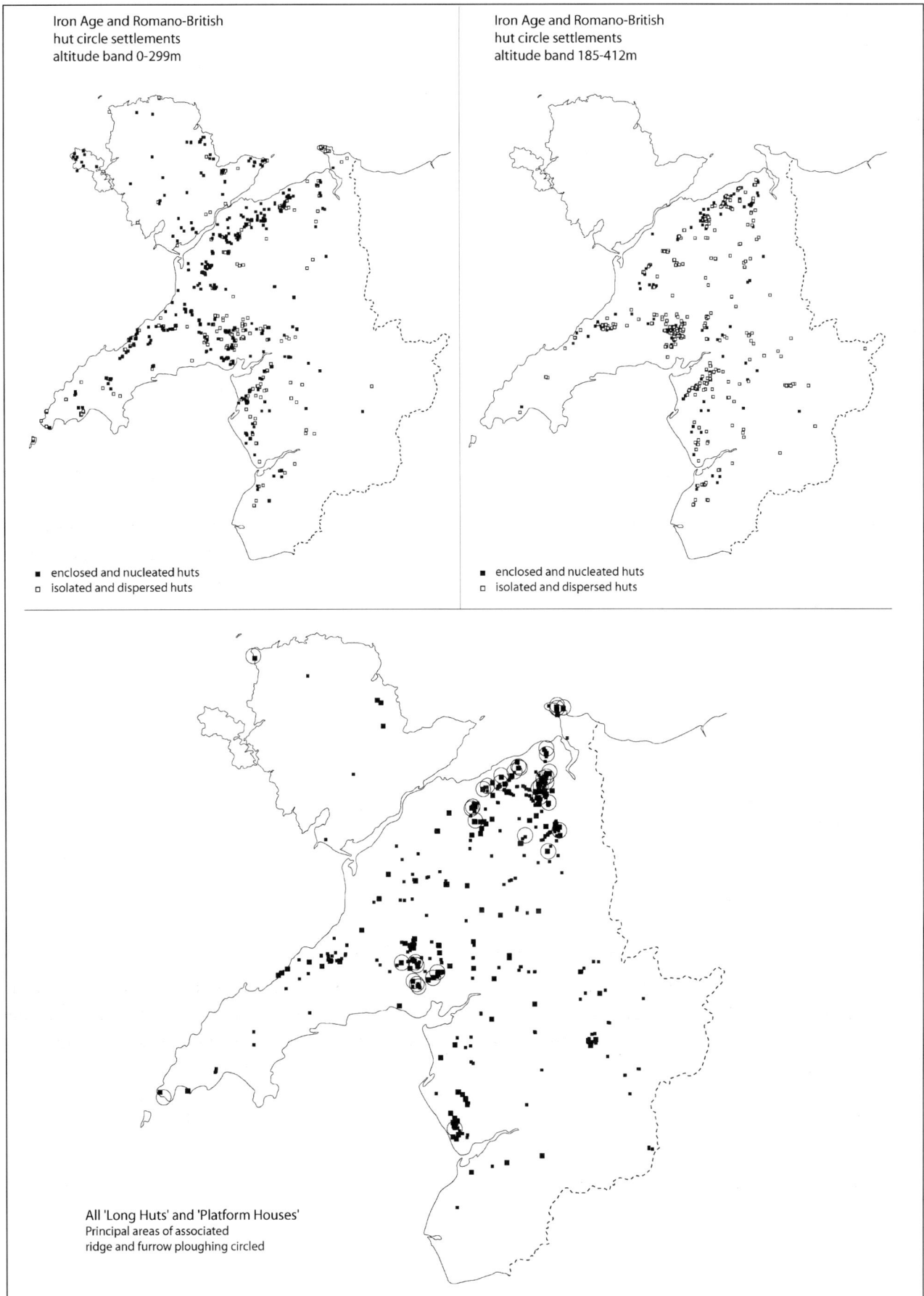

4.5 Distribution of Iron Age and Romano-British hut circle settlements compared to that of long huts and platforms
recorded during the survey

been argued above that the monument class is most strongly represented between the 185m and 412m zone. A similar observation was made by RCAHMW in 1964 on the basis of a smaller sample of Caernarvonshire sites.

Despite the altitude at which these settlements lie, most have the benefit of some degree of shelter. In 80% of recorded instances the availability of shelter was seen to have been fair or good. Few sites have poor shelter or none at all. Siting, with regard to aspect, would need to be chosen carefully too, as a protection against the prevailing weather and to maximise access to sunlight, particularly if agriculture was to be a component of the regime. In north-west Wales the prevailing wind is south-westerly, whence comes the rain. The lower Conwy Valley and parts of the north coast are in rain shadow as much of the rain falls on the Snowdonia *Massif.* Nevertheless, one might antic-ipate a preference for an easterly or south-easterly aspect. In practice the circumstance is more complex.

The choice of location for settlement, quite apart from any tenurial considerations, must take local and regional topography into account. For example, in the topographic area described in this analysis as the Arllechwedd Uchaf and Arfon coastline, 77% of settle-ments have an aspect within the arc west through north-east, reflecting the predominant prospect from the coastal upland towards the north-west. There is only one site with a southerly or south-eastern aspect.

In contrast the uplands of the west bank of the Conwy Valley (Arllechwedd Isaf) look east. The watershed runs in a general north–south direction with rivers draining north-east to the River Conwy. Seventy-three percent of settlements, here, have a north-east/south-east aspect. Only two sites look west.

Taking the monument class as a whole there is a tendency towards an east-north-easterly aspect but not overwhelmingly so. However, the pattern changes with progression through the altitude bands. In the lowest range, up to 185m, if it is possible to detect any pref-erence at all, it would be in the arc swinging from north-west to east. From 186 to 299m the tendency, again, is towards the northern arc of the compass. In the higher altitude ranges, however, from 300 to 412m the preference for an east-south-easterly aspect is more pronounced and becomes even more so above 412m. Aspect would appear to be less of a consideration at lower altitudes, even up to 300m, but becomes critical above this line.

A further consideration, in respect of altitude and the agricultural potential of certain upland locations is that some deep valleys and parts of the north coast barely see the sun at certain times of the year. Tracts of medieval ploughland on shoulders of the upland, even on north-facing slopes as at Aber, on the north coast, or on the south side of the Nantlle Valley, may be more advantageously situated than lower-lying but shadowed valley bottoms.

4.4 Distribution

It must not be assumed that all the data collated during the Deserted Rural Settlement assessment represent evidence for contemporary settlement. However, on the basis of those very few sites for which objective dating evidence is available, together with circumstantial detail from a small number of sites (as suggested at Maes Y Gaer, Aber, for instance, RCAHMW 1965, 15), and drawing on the evidence for comparable structures elsewhere or beyond the remit of this assessment, it is possible to introduce a level of discrimination to the analysis.

Neither can it be assumed that the evidence repre-sented by the distribution of recorded sites is complete. It is probable that evidence has been lost in areas of continuing and intensive arable agriculture. Anglesey is particularly devoid of recorded sites meeting the criteria for inclusion on the database. Similarly, the coastal plain and the lower reaches of major valleys show a very low incidence of these sites.

There is a further bias in the distribution, which reflects different levels of archaeological fieldwork across the area. Caernarvonshire benefits from very good survey work undertaken during the 1950s and early 1960s by RCAHMW. Merioneth, on the other hand, has no recent Royal Commission Inventory to draw on. The dearth of evidence from Talybont and Ystumanner is particularly noticeable. Hot-spots in the pattern of distribution can, in certain instances, be attributed to particular targeted campaigns of field survey. Upland surveys at Trawscoed, above Llanuwchllyn, and on Moel Bronmiod, Llyn, are cases in point. Targeted rapid survey as part of the Deserted Rural Settlement Project at Castell in the Conwy Valley and Pennant in Eifionydd highlighted the level of under-representation by more than doubling the number of previously known settlements. Nevertheless, the distribution is distinctive in its predominantly upland representation, which appears not to be simply a function of disproportionate survival or targeted fieldwork.

Certain characteristics have been identified which, it is suggested, are potentially indicative of a medieval or late medieval date. They include an alignment perpendicular to the prevailing contour, the presence of a drain hood at the upslope end, and rounded external corners on buildings. Two or more of these features are present at 45% of the total number of sites. Using this criterion the settlements were mapped against the general distribution of the monuments. No spatial clustering or distinct patterning was observed. However, at a further level of discrimination, the monument class as a whole was mapped within the altitude bands described above. Settlements within the altitude range up to 185m were noticeably lacking in potentially diagnostic medieval features. Sites within altitude bands 2, 3, and 4 displayed these characteristics to broadly the same degree. Within band 2, however, encompassing the altitude range 186m to 299m, a slightly higher representation was observed at 56% of the total number. The high representation of these features (76%) in the vicinity of ridge and furrow ploughing, within the more restricted range of 285m to 340m, has been discussed above. A more general assessment of the distribution of monuments follows.

Altitude band 1

There are 104 recorded settlements within the lowest altitude band, from sea-level to 185m (Fig 4.7a). These comprise 152 structures in total. Seventy-one are single houses; 24 sites are represented by pairs of structures. The remainder comprise groups of three or more buildings. Two-thirds of the total sites have associated annexes or enclosures. One settlement, the probable site of the historically documented Gesail Gyfarch, destroyed by Owain Glyndwr in 1409, may have as many as five buildings on its several platforms (this vol., 00). Gesail Gyfarch is in the medieval township of Penyfed in Eifionydd and it is in this region that the densest concentration of these low-lying settlements is represented. Significant smaller clusters are to be found on the northern Llyn coastline near Lithfaen and on the Great Orme.

Altitude band 2

This second altitude band, from 186m to 299m, best typifies the monument class (Fig 4.7). One hundred and seventy-one settlements are represented, comprising 249 structures or house platforms. Approximately half are single structures. There are 34 pairs of

buildings and 16 further settlements comprising three or more structures. Fifty-seven percent of the total show evidence of associated enclosures or annexes. Forty percent have field clearance in the immediate vicinity, and ridge and furrow ploughing is recorded at 14% of the sites, in some cases up to the limit of the altitude band.

The densest concentration of recorded sites is again in Eifionydd. There are also important clusters in the lower Conwy Valley from Allt Wen near Conwy to the slopes below Tal y Fan and Llanbedr y Cenin; above the north coastline on the slopes between Llanfairfechan and Aber; on the southern slopes of Moel Bronmiod and Bwlch Mawr on the Llyn Peninsula and in southern Ardudwy between Dyffryn Ardudwy and Llanaber. A particularly significant feature of the distribution of these settlements is the way in which they occupy the marginal zone at the limit of the historically enclosed areas. This is equally true above the west bank of the Conwy Valley, along the lowland-upland interface above the Arfon plateau between Aber on the north coast and the Nantlle Valley, skirting the upland margins of Garnedd Goch and Cwm Pennant and west-facing slopes of Mynydd Egryn.

Altitude band 3

The third altitude band, between 300m and 412m, sees some settlement established beyond the zone of enclosure and onto open moorland. Distribution is generally more dispersed. One hundred and eighty-two sites are recorded, comprising 245 structures (Fig 4.7). Approximately half of the sites stand alone. Nevertheless, there are 35 recorded settlements where pairs of structures are known and 14 other sites composed of clusters of two or three buildings. Sixty-two percent of sites are associated with an enclosure or annexe and even at the altitudes at which these sites lie, 37% show evidence of field clearance, while ridge and furrow is recorded at 8% of locations. Among the most elevated instances of ploughing are two long huts lying at 350m OD on south-east facing slopes of Ffridd y Ddwyffrwd above Rowen in the Conwy Valley, and within an area of ancient terraced fields and hut circle settlements. Lazy beds and a garden are recorded in four instances, for example, at Cwm Eigiau, at over 380m OD, within a constricted cwm at the south end of Llyn Eigiau, below the eastern face of Carnedd Llywelyn and the northern slopes of Pen Llithrig y Wrach. There are few locations in Eifionydd and western Arfon. There are, however, clusters of sites at Moel Bronmiod on the Llyn Peninsula and at

Medieval core settlement
and surveyed 'long huts' and platforms
compared

□   townships (trefi)
■   'long huts' and platforms

toning indicates extent of historical enclosure

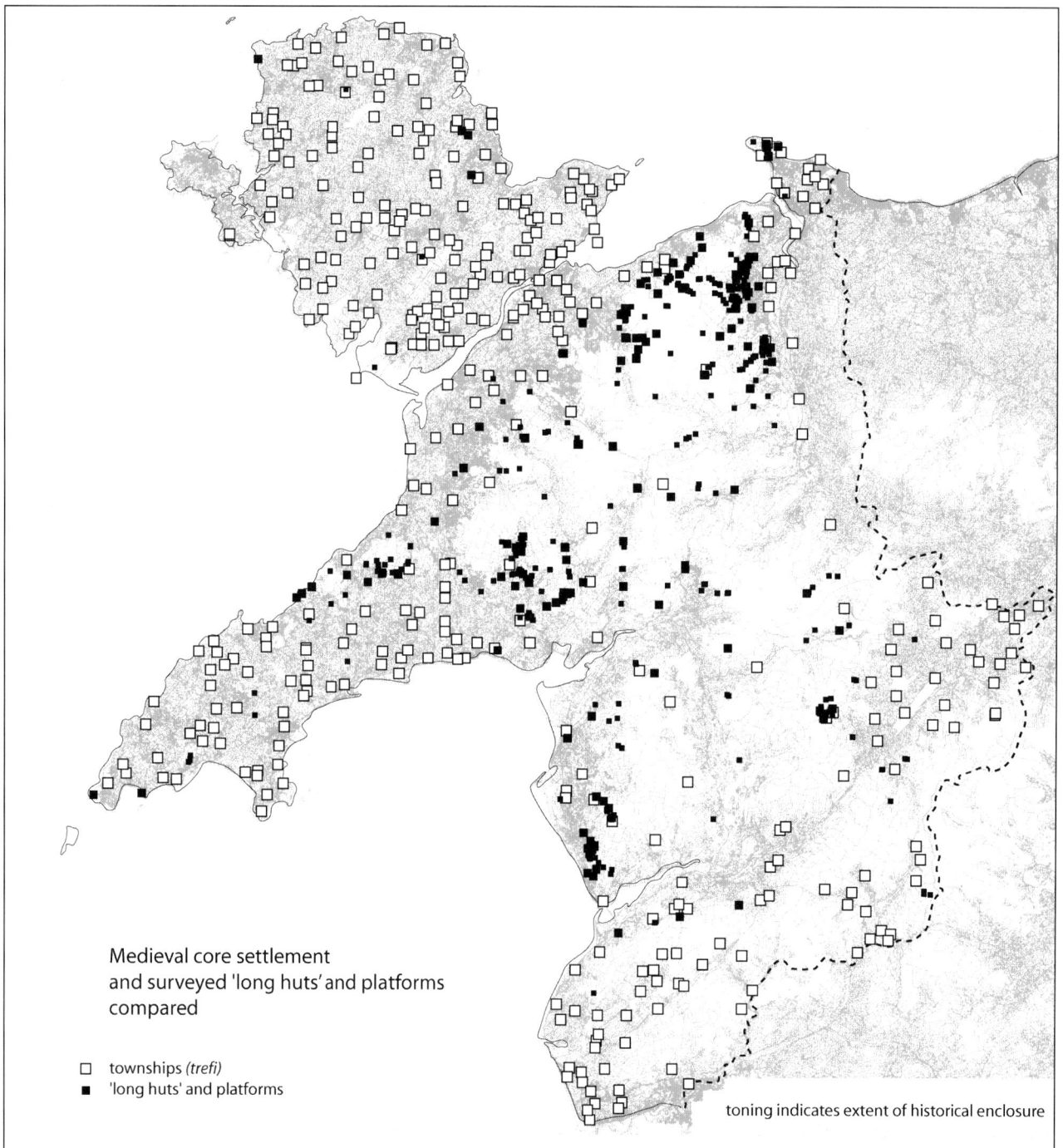

4.6 Medieval core settlement and settlements recorded during the survey

Trawsgoed on the western margins of Penllyn. Penllyn is otherwise largely devoid of evidence for monuments of this class in the lower altitude ranges. Both Trawsgoed and Moel Bronmiod have been the subject of recent Upland Survey which helps to explain these two local high-altitude clusters and points to the potential for further work in other areas which might benefit from similar survey.

In the northern part of the study area the pattern is significantly different. There are concentrations of sites in Arllechwedd Isaf, right up to the Tal y Fan watershed

where the distribution is mirrored on the north-facing slopes of Arllechwedd Uchaf. There are further concentrations near Bethesda, below Moel Wnion and Moel Faban, along the Afon Ffrydlas, and along the Afon Caseg where the distribution spills over into the Snowdonia Massif. Another major concentration occurs in the Afon Ddu/Cefn Cyfarwydd area above Dolgarrog and Trefriw in the Conwy Valley. Here, and in Castell township to the north, Upland Survey and targeted rapid survey for the Deserted Rural Settlement Project have undoubtedly enhanced the distribution pattern.

Altitude band 4

The distribution of sites within altitude band 4, above 412m, is essentially a continuation of the pattern of occupation represented by the higher altitude sites around the Tal y Fan watershed and in the Bethesda area (Fig 4.7). A small cluster south of Arenig Fawr on Ffridd Trawsgoed, north-west of Llanuwchllyn, is explained as a product of the Upland Survey referred to in describing the distribution of band 3. Only 21 sites are represented at these altitudes, comprising 25 individual structures. The majority stand alone. Nevertheless enclosures or annexes are recorded in the vicinity of twelve sites and field clearance at eight.

There is an important cluster near the ancient mountain trackway across Bwlch y Ddeufaen, mostly on the north-eastern slopes of Carnedd y Ddelw in the area known as Ffridd Cwm Ithel and Buarth Cwm Ithel. There is a nucleated sheepfold in Cwm Ithel and others in the general area. Huts occur, following the same general contour from Llannerch Fedw on the north-western slopes of Drosgl, round the north-eastern slopes of Foel Lwyd, to the south-south-eastern slopes of Pen y Gadair, 1km west of the hillfort of Pen y Gaer. There is a group of three huts at Pen y Gadair, another within 100m and a fifth 500m to the west. These eleven structures are all sited between the 420m and 450m contour.

A further small concentration of high-altitude huts occurs between the northern end of Llyn Eigiau at Clogwyn Yr Eryr and Llyn Dulyn at Pant y Griafolen. At Clogwyn Yr Eryr, two huts stand adjacent; a third lies 120m to the east. All three lie between the 420m and 460m contour. A nucleated sheepfold stands 200m to the north-east. At Pant y Griafolen a single hut is recorded on the south-eastern slopes of Foel Fras at 520m.

Along the streams that flow east and north-east from the Drum–Carneddau watershed lie a further cluster of high-altitude huts: within Cwm yr Afon Goch, above Aber Falls; at the headwaters of the Ffrydlas along Ffos y Foelgraig and along the Afon Caseg; north-east, south-east and east of Bethesda respectively.

Within Cwm yr Afon Goch and Cwm Caseg the huts are closely hemmed in by steep, if not precipitous, crags. Along the Afon Goch, two huts lie within 150m of each other near the floor of the cwm. There is a nucleated sheepfold within the same cwm, 350m to the north-west. At Cwm Caseg the hut lies at 750m near the northern shore of the lake, enclosed on all sides by the steep slopes of Yr Elen and Carnedd Llywelyn.

All of these high-altitude sites lie beyond the limit of agricultural enclosure in the historical period, with the exception that the cluster of sites at Pen y Gadair at around 425m above the Conwy Valley is close to upland intakes and small farms at Bwlch y Gaer and Tan y Bwlch on south-east facing slopes above Llanbedr y Cennin.

4.5 Discussion

4.5.1 The relationship to core medieval settlement

The majority of monuments classified in this assessment are presumed to have been built and used within the medieval and immediately post-medieval centuries. Some may be as late as the 18th century but none is considered to be of the modern period, with the exception that a small group of square structures at high altitude may be industrial and related to quarrying.

A comparison with the distribution of documented medieval core settlements in the area under review, rather than providing a correspondence with the spread of the monuments mapped above, on the contrary, displays a complementary and almost mutually exclusive pattern (Fig 4.6). The basis on which core settlement is identified for the purposes of this comparison is principally that of documented townships (*trefi*) and hamlets represented in royal and ecclesiastical extents, surveys and taxation of the 13th and 14th century. It is acknowledged that, by the 13th century, the *tref*, or township, could not be simply defined as a fixed location but could, and frequently did, extend over very large tracts of land and could accommodate a complexity of tenurial arrangements. Nevertheless, it seems also to be the case that of those settlements which might exist, dispersed or nucleated, within the bounds of a township, the ancient core survived, in name, as the title of a single farm or small group of farms, on land on or close to the original settlement nucleus.

The discrimination apparent in the pattern of distribution between documented core medieval settlement and 'platform houses' and 'long huts' visible on the ground suggests that while, clearly, the monuments surveyed must operate within the administrative framework of a township or its successor, in the majority of those sites which have survived to be recorded they represent an activity complementary to, or distinct from, that of the core settlements. A

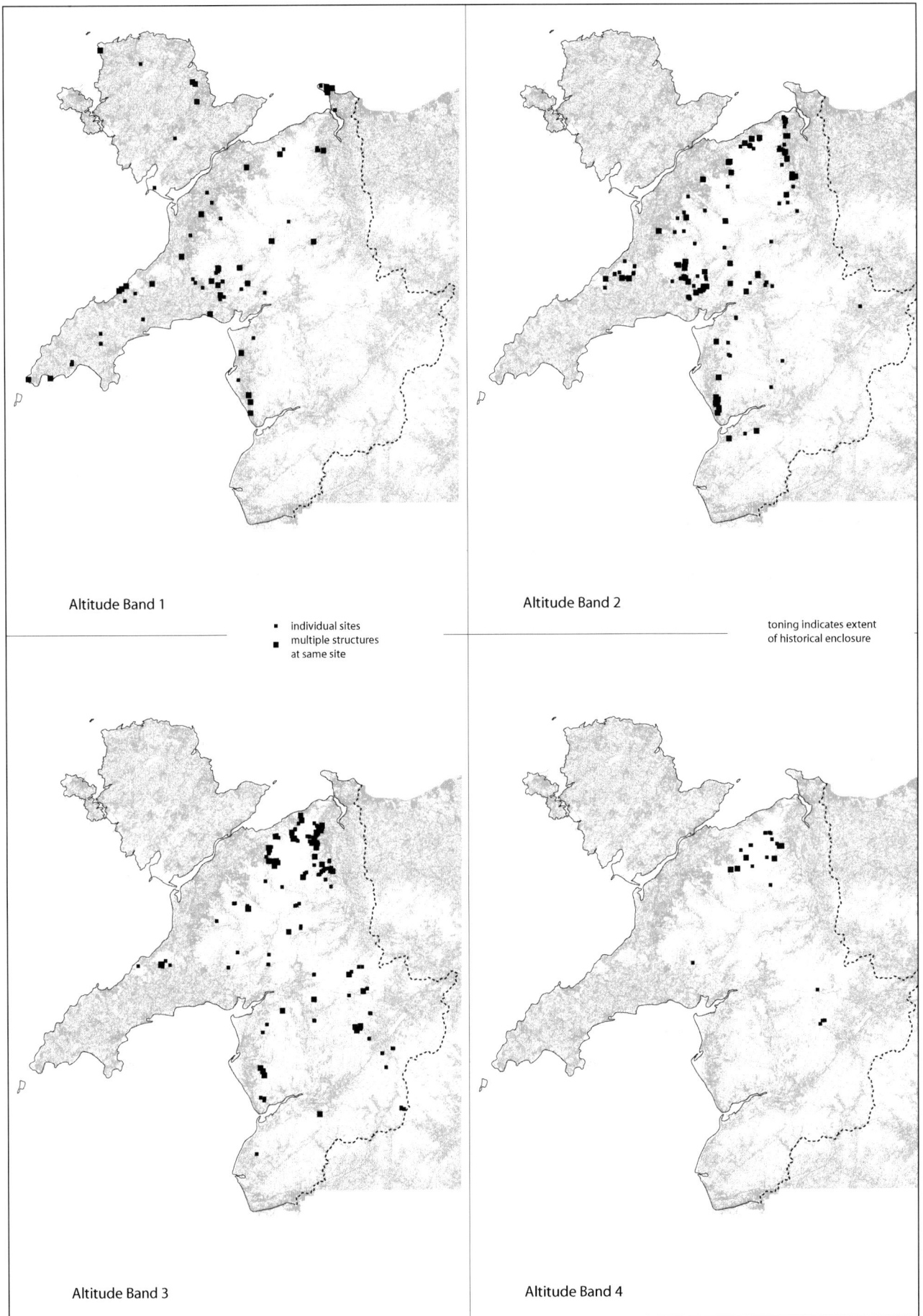

Altitude Band 1

Altitude Band 2

■ individual sites
■ multiple structures
at same site

toning indicates extent
of historical enclosure

Altitude Band 3

Altitude Band 4

4.7 Distribution of recorded settlements by altitude band

significantly distinguishing characteristic of these settlements is their predominantly upland location.

Topographic regions were chosen for convenience in describing the monuments under review. Rivers and watersheds provide convenient boundaries. Similar limits defined the administrative and territorial boundaries of the Middle Ages (Fig 4.8). In considering the distribution of settlement against natural boundaries it may be relevant to take into account the imposed boundaries of political and proprietorial concerns. There is some indication of such constraints in the mapped distributions. For example, the Tal y Fan–Foel Fras watershed is also the boundary between the two medieval commotes of Arllechwedd Uchaf (north coast) and Arllechwedd Isaf (lower Conwy Valley). The clustering of sites either side of this divide presumably reflects the upland manifestation of the respective territorial associations of the townships within each commote. The core settlement areas of Arllechwedd Isaf and Arllechwedd Uchaf respectively were the lower reaches of the river Conwy close to the valley floor and in particular the extensive free township of Castell, focused on Caerhun and the commotal administrative centre near Tal y Cafn, and the north coastal strip around Aber, where the *maerdref* of that commote lay. Other important townships lay north-west of present-day Bethesda in the lower Ogwen Valley. The resources of the uplands were exploited from these centres and it is not surprising to find that the distribution of recorded deserted rural settlement, beyond the nucleus of the parent township but still within its bounds, fans out from the immediate vicinity of these documented centres so that, if medieval in date, the sites along the north coast would appropriately have sprung from the townships of Aber, Wig, Bodsilin, and Gorddiniog, for example. Those in Cwm Caseg and the Ffrydlas would represent a component of the townships of Bodfaeo and Cororion. Similarly, the notable concentration of sites in Eifionnydd may be seen to be contained within both administrative and topographical boundaries, extending into the upland around Cwm Pennant and Moel Hebog from a point of origin near the maerdref of Dolbenmaen and in the dense concentration of core settlement nuclei to the south-west. On the other hand, across the watershed, settlement in the uplands of Moel Tryfan, Cefn Du, and Snowdon itself would seem to represent an extension, from the north-west, of settlement from core townships of Uwch Gwyrfai and Is Gwyrfai respectively (for townships and boundaries, see Richards 1969).

One particularly important aspect of medieval exploitation of the uplands is the seasonal pasturing of animals by the community of a township. This aspect will be treated more fully below. For the present purpose it may be relevant to note that the township and royal estate centre (*maerdref*) of Aber maintained pastureland (*ffriddoedd*) in the uplands above the core settlement in the valley bottom (Rec. Caern., 140–1). Similarly, the royal township of Dolbadarn maintained extensive *ffriddoedd* on the slopes of Snowdon, as did the township of Dolwyddelan on the slopes of Moel Siabod and Moel Penamnen (Rec. Caern., 10, 18). The cow pastures of Dolwyddelan were particularly extensive and two, additional, summer pastures (*hafodydd*) extended over the Moel Siabod watershed into Dyffryn Mymbyr and the Lligwy Valley. Four long huts lie close by one of these, on the south-facing slopes of Glyder Fach. Despite the apparent circumstantial association, the long huts should not be associated with the documented *hafodydd*, if for no other reason than that these *hafodydd* lie within the commote of Nant Conwy and the long huts lie in the commote of Arllechwedd Uchaf. It is a consideration to be borne in mind that while it might be tempting to match the results of fieldwork with historical documentation on the basis of juxtaposition, tenurial constraints also have to be satisfied.

Similarly 13th–14th-century *hafodydd* are documented on the Llyn Peninsula at Gwynnus near Lithfaen to the south-west of Yr Eifl and Elernion on the north-east slopes of Yr Eifl (Rec. Caern., 22, 35). Deserted settlements occur in the vicinity of both sites and a significant cluster is recorded on the adjacent upland of Moel Bronmiod and Bwlch Mawr to the east. While it is possible that extensive pastures extended across this belt of upland they must represent the exploitation of an upland resource by two separate communities as the commotal boundary runs between the two zones, separating Gwynnus in Dinllaen from Elernion in Uwch Gwyrfai.

4.5.2 Upland settlement and the seasonal pasturing of animals: hafod and ffridd

It has been suggested and is sometimes assumed that certain of the monuments that comprise the class under review might be *hafotai*, houses associated with the summer seasonal pasturing of animals. The following discussion considers this concept as one possible context for the settlements recorded in this survey. Any approach to this subject must acknowledge a debt to Davies' two seminal studies of the development of hafodydd, in Caernarvonshire and Merioneth (Davies 1973; 1979).

The *hafod*, literally summer-dwelling-place, is first documented in the 13th century but the concept is likely to be ancient (BBC, 70). In 14th-century royal surveys the *hafod* is closely associated with both '*ffridd*' and '*vaccary*'. A vaccary (Lat. *vaccaria*) is a cattle ranch, used in particular with reference to grazing lands and attested from the late 11th century. *Ffridd* is a rather more difficult concept. Although, in modern usage, *ffridd* is a well-established term synonymous with upland grazing, it is, in fact, a borrowing from Middle English *frith* (Old English *fyrhthe* – 'land overgrown with brushwood, scrubland on the edge of forest'; Gelling 1984). The Anglo-Saxon usage, in a land use context, is indicated in an 11th-century document where *weald, freyth* and *heyninga* are distinguished as forest, heathland and enclosed arable, respectively (Gelling and Cole 2000, 225). The earliest documented Welsh use of *ffridd* is in the 14th century where the meaning would appear to be comparable to English usage. It is also found in a literary context as a descriptive term applied to a particular characteristic of landscape. However, *ffridd* at this date did not carry a specifically or universal upland connotation. On Anglesey, in royal surveys of the mid-14th century *ffridd* is used to describe land lying waste or uncultivated, generally through lack of tenants or heirs to that land (Carr 1971–2; Rec. Caern. *passim*). The context is the aftermath of the Black Death. Uncultivated upland, however, made suitable summer pasture and at the thirteen locations described as *ffridd* in 14th- and 15th-century royal surveys of Caernarfon and Meirionnydd, seven are also described as *havotiroedd* (summer-pasture-lands) while an eighth is described as woodland pasture (Rec. Caern. *passim*). In Meirionnydd the term *havotreffrith* is used to describe a townland characterised by summer pasturelands on *ffridd* – that is, on uncultivated scrub. Thirteenth-century manuscripts of lawbooks, referring to royal rights and prerogatives, recognise a provision for summer pasturing, away from the *maerdref* or commotal administrative centre, and describe these grazing lands as 'hafotir' and 'diffaith' – 'summer-dwelling-land' and 'waste' (Jenkins 1986). This is a designation that closely matches the term 'havotreffrith'. These 'lawbooks' further refer to winter-houses (w: *gaeafdy*; Latin: *mansio hyemalis, id est hendref*) making the association between a winter-house and the core settlement in contrast with a house on the summer pastures (Jenkins 1986, 236 n40.12). The relatively slight

nature of a summer-house may be inferred from its legal worth of between 15 times (*Llyfr Iorwerth*) and 17.5 times (*Llyfr Cyfnerth*) less than that of a winter house (Jenkins 1986, 190; 297 n22.4). It may be such summer-houses that Giraldus Cambrensis described in what is taken to be a disparaging commentary on the 'wattled huts' of the Welsh, 'on the edges of the forest', put up with little labour or expense, but strong enough to last a year or so (Descrip. Kamb., 1.17). Gerald wrote in the late 12th century. Nearly 400 years later the Court of Exchequer Commissioners could describe transient upland settlement in the commote of Talybont, and cottages 'in great ruin and utterly decayed, for want of repair' on void and barren ground, previously occupied by freeholders thereabouts and other inhabitants, some one year and some another (*Rec. Court of Augment*, 29 Nov. 1568)

In medieval Wales there was both a requirement and a necessity for the animals of a community to be removed from the core settlements, the *hendrefi*, where stood the winter-houses, to alternative pastures. This ensured that, in open field, crops could ripen and be harvested without risk of encroachment. It also ensured that the potential of pastures unavailable during the winter months might be fully exploited during the summer and that full use was made of the productive capacity of as much of the landscape as possible. These summer pastures might include areas of marshland and bog although, over much of the mainland of north-west Wales, topography and climate dictated that they would invariably include tracts of unenclosed upland. The period of removal spanned the summer months from Calan Mai (May Day) to Calan Gaeaf (All Saints' Day).

Several references to actions in local courts confirm that seasonal pasturing was a social and economic reality and not simply a theoretical concept. Legal censures ensured compliance. On 10 June 1326 Iorwerth Gethin was fined 2s. at Harlech for keeping his cattle on the common pasture of the *hendref* beyond the due date (Lewis 1927–9, 162). As late as May 1552 certain men of Gwydir were indicted for overstocking the common summer pastures of Moel Siabod and *Dolloiaon* (? Dolwyddelan) to the injury of the communities of Gwydir and Penmachno. The practice was not confined to the north. In 1256 certain tenants of the Norman manor of Abergavenny were indicted for similar transgressions.

The presence of *hafodydd* in north-west Wales, and their location, is best documented on lands in the hands of the Welsh Princes of Gwynedd. It is also clear

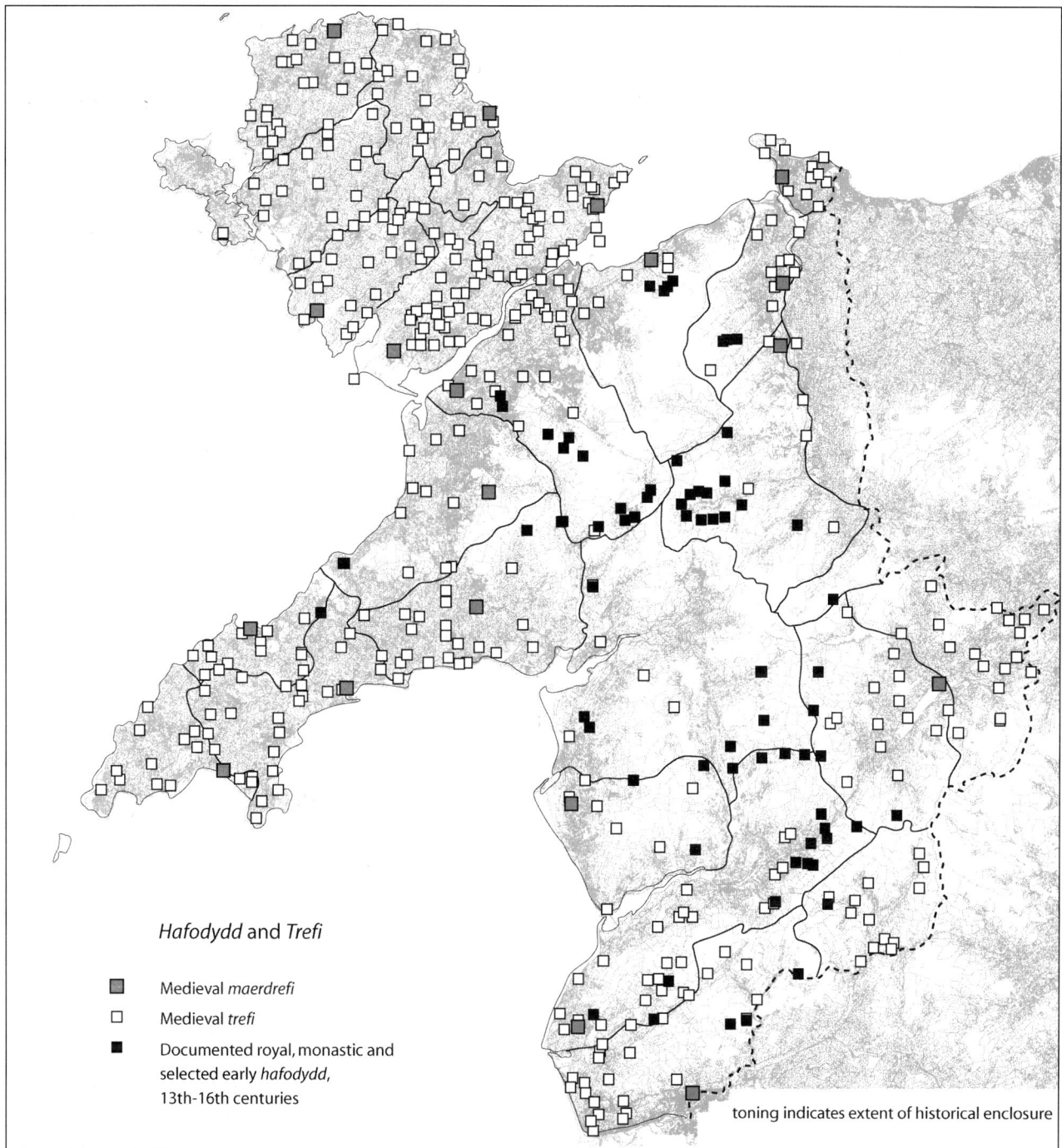

Hafodydd and *Trefi*

- ■ (grey) Medieval *maerdrefi*
- □ Medieval *trefi*
- ■ (black) Documented royal, monastic and selected early *hafodydd*, 13th-16th centuries

toning indicates extent of historical enclosure

4.8 Medieval territorial boundaries, *maerdrefi* and documented *hafodydd*

that major monastic institutions ran cattle farms and, although the evidence largely eludes the documentary record, it is highly probable that the communities of free townships made use of seasonal pastures in a similar way.

The Princes' arable demesne was located at the *maerdref,* a counterpart of the *hafod.* Figure 4.8 maps the documented royal *hafodydd,* the location of the commotal *maerdrefi,* monastic *hafodydd* and other early documented *hafodydd* and may be compared with *ffridd* place-names as they appear on the modern map

(fig 4.9). There are some notable omissions. It is not clear where the royal *ffridd* of Uwch Gwyrfai was located. In the 13th century the lordship centre may have been at Bala Deulyn in the Nantlle Valley. The *ffridd* may have occupied the valley sides; a farm at the south-western end of Llyn Nantlle Uchaf still bears the name Ffridd. Additionally, a parcel of demesne land in Elernion on the northern flank of Yr Eifl was known as Ffridd Fawr in the 14th century (Rec. Caern., 22). This location is right at the south-western extremity of Uwch Gwyrfai but very close to the extensive royal *ffriddoedd* of Dinllaen where nine 'havotri' lay on and around the slopes of Moel Gwynnus in the 13th and 14th centuries. Neither are the *ffriddoedd* of Eifionydd documented. The lordship centre in the 13th century was at Dolbenmaen, before the building of Criccieth Castle. Clusters of *ffridd* names survive on the modern map north of Dolbenmaen and particularly on the slopes to the east of Cwmystradllyn, and may indicate the location. Similarly a cluster of *ffridd* names, including one 'Ffriddlys' on the eastern slopes of Tal y Fan and Cefn Maen Amor between 300 and 400m above the west bank of the Conwy Valley, may indicate the otherwise undocumented royal *ffriddoedd* of Arllechwedd Isaf.

At the southern tip of the Llyn Peninsula, as on Anglesey, evidence for upland summer pastures is slight, predicated to a large extent by topographic considerations. Coastal *morfeydd* (sea strand), low-lying moorland or *rhosydd* and marsh may have provided comparable opportunities for seasonal pasturing. Nevertheless, an arc of *ffridd* place-names in the commote of Caflogion to the south of Carn Fadrun may be significant in the context of the documented 12th-century stone castle on Carn Fadrun. Again, a community holding their land under *tir cyfrif*, a particularly restrictive tenure indicative of direct exploitation of land by a lord, at Penarfynydd on the northern slopes of Mynydd Penarfynydd, rising to 177m above the southern Llyn coastline, may provide a context for a counterpart of the *maerdref* at Neigwl (Rec. Caern., 36).

The primary royal *hafodydd* of Ardudwy (Ffridd Prysor, Y Feidiog, and Bryncoch), Penllyn (Wenallt, Cwmdady, and Cwm Ffynnon in the south-west, Amnoth, Gwernllyn, Bradfos, and Nanfach in the west and around the River Meloch, north of Bala), Talybont (Ffridd Pennant, Gwanas, and Pennantigi) and Ystumanner (ffridd y Foeldrys) are documented even if certain of the locations lack precise identification (Rec. Caern., 292; 269; 276; Carr 2001, 712; 713). However, in order to understand the extent of the resource, its economic significance and the degree to which the Princes of Gwynedd managed and exploited the potential of seasonal upland pastures it is necessary to focus on the *hafodydd* and *ffriddoedd* of central Snowdonia. At Pen y Gwryd, 5km to the east of the summit of Snowdon, the boundaries of the three commotes of Arllechwedd Uchaf, Is Gwyrfai and Nant Conwy coincide. The *maerdref* of Arllechwedd Uchaf at Aber on the north coast was run on traditional lines (Jones Pierce 1972a). The upland pastures at the

hafodydd of Y Cras, Meuryn, Nanheskele (Hafod y Gelyn), Nanmawan (in the Anafon Valley) and Nanteracadrat (near Rhaedr Fawr on the Afon Goch) were all relatively easily accessible from the demesne lands of the lowland settlement (Rec. Caern., 140–1). In the commotes of Is Gwyrfai and Nant Conwy, however, *hafodydd* had been established at some considerable distance from the royal estates at the traditional commotal centres. The *maerdrefi* of Is Gwyrfai and Nant Conwy were at Caernarfon and Trefriw respectively. In the otherwise free township of Llanfair Prysgol, in Is Gwyrfai, the Princes held four *hafodydd* along the west flank of the Snowdon massif between Llanrug and Waun Fawr (Rec. Caern., 18–19). More particularly, in Dolbadarn township there lay four further *hafodydd* on the northern slopes of Snowdon itself between 300 and 400m at Llyn Dwythwch, Helfa-aelgarth, Cwmbrwynog and Maesgwm (Rec. Caern., 18). In Nant Conwy the Princes' *hafodydd* were concentrated around Dolwyddelan in the Lledr Valley, some 12km as the crow flies and much further by mountain track along the ancient Sarn Helen, from the commotal centre at Trefriw (Rec. Caern., 10). Here, above both banks of the Lledr, on the slopes of Moel Siabod and Penamnen, extended no less than ten contiguous *hafodydd*, comprising 11,000 acres of moorland and mountain. In the 14th century royal surveyors assessed their carrying capacity at 552 beasts. In the 16th century, in Wynn hands, these same *hafodydd* supported 1280 cattle (NLW MS, Llanstephan 179b). A further two royal *hafodydd* lay across the Moel Siabod watershed in Dyffryn Mymbyr at Cwm Clorad and on the upper Llugwy at Bryn Tyrch (Rec. Caern., 12).

Between the royal *friddoedd* of Dolwyddelan and Dolbadarn lay Nanhwynan, now known as Nant Gwynant. Here, extensive lands were granted by Llewelyn ap Iorwerth to Aberconwy Abbey, perhaps as early as 1199, perhaps a little later. Six *hafodydd* are recorded among the former properties of the Abbey in the 16th century, extending from Hafod Wydr and Hafod y Porth near the confluence of the Glaslyn and Colwyn at Beddgelert to Hafod Llwyfog and Hafod Rhisgl north-east of Llyn Gwynant. It is possible that Cwm Dyli and Gwastadannas, on either side of the valley at its northern limit, and which were in the Abbey's hands, were also maintained as *hafodydd* at this period. Central Snowdonia was a huge cattle ranch with royal *hafodydd* and *hafodydd* on former royal lands extending over a continuous run of some 17km from Dolbadarn to Dolwyddelan, unbroken except for the highest slopes and the peaks of Snowdon and Moel Siabod. Gerald's comment that 'If all the herds in Wales were driven together, the mountains of Snowdonia could supply them with pasture' is very apposite (Descrip. Kamb., 6). It cannot be without significance that stone castles of the late 12th and early 13th centuries are strategically disposed close to the valley floors that gave access to these cow lands at their north-western, southern and south-eastern extremities.

It is important to realise that seasonal pastures were a managed and not an incidental resource. As Professor Smith has observed, 'the Princes' bond and free tenants [exploited these pastures] in the manner in which social custom decreed' and appropriate dues went to the Prince (Smith, J Beverley and Smith, L L Beverley 2001, 35). However, it would appear that, in addition to providing pasture for the Prince's own stock the *ffriddoedd*, in the hands of the Prince, could also be leased out to individuals as a source of revenue (*ibid*, 189). It may even be the case that inroads into the 'Forest of Snowdon' were made in deliberate exploitation of this resource. *Quo Warranto* proceedings of the 15th century, enquiring into the rights of agistment, pasturage, dairies, hay in the forests of the lord, and hunting rights, frequently consider these aspects together, suggesting that the management of the 'Forest of Snowdon' and the management of the *ffriddoedd* were associated. The 'forest' need not be dense and a 'sparse, savannah-like structure' is implied by the uses to which the forest was put (Rackham 1995, 487). Certain documented 14th-century *hafodydd* retain names that suggest such an origin. These include elements such as *helfa* (hunting chase as in Helfa-aelgarth, Dolbadarn), *coed* (wood, as in Coed Mawr, Great Wood, Dolwyddelan), and *gelli* (woodland grove as in Ffriddgelli, Dolwyddelan). What remains uncertain is the extent to which relatively permanent structures, albeit seasonally occupied, were built on the summer pastures, in contrast to those slight constructions and temporary habitations on the edges of the forest of Gerald's commentary and the lawbooks.

The conquest of Gwynedd in 1283 initiated certain fundamental changes in the organisation of communities. Several *hafodydd* and *ffriddoedd* are recorded in extents, surveys, accounts, and legal proceedings of the late 13th, 14th, 15th and 16th centuries. They chronicle a world in transition as rights which had formerly been part of a community's exploitation of a township's resources were leased to individuals for their revenue value. True, it seems that the Princes also leased out surplus resources and the issue is a complex one. Never-

theless, the interests of the leaseholders of the *ffridd* revenues were now divorced from those of the communities who utilised these resources. By the middle of the 14th century John of Chirbury held the ten *hafodydd* of Dolwyddelan and that of Cwm Clorad in Dyffryn Mymbyr. Robert Pollard, *camerarius*, held the remaining royal *ffridd* of Nant Conwy at Bryn Tyrch. Thomas Missenden held the four *hafodydd* of Dolbadarn and the four *hafodydd* in Llanfair Prysgol, thereby controlling the royal *hafodydd* of Is Gwyrfai. He also held rights in some of the *hafodydd* of Dinllaen on the Llŷn Peninsula at Gwynnus. Walter de Manny, custodian of Harlech Castle, held all the royal *hafodydd* of the new county of Merioneth, comprising those in the commotes of Ardudwy, Ystumanner, Talybont, and Penllyn, possibly as many as fourteen in all. During the 15th century, prominent local Welshmen came to acquire certain of these leases. For example, during the first quarter of the 15th century, the Derwas family, father and son, drew income from the farm of the *ffriddoedd* of Penantigi, Gwanas and Pennant (Thomas 2001, 109) in Talybont. During the 1460s the Coetmor family had begun to purchase rights in property in the upper Conwy Valley in Trewydir township, similarly consolidating their position with the acquisition of Crown leases (Jones 1995, 28). In 1547 Rhydderch ap Dafydd ap Rhys and Cadwaladr ap Robert were demised the pasture rights of the 'forests' of Amnodd, Nanfach, Bradfos, and Gwernllyn, the *ffriddoedd* of Western Penllyn. These lands 'lying open' are described as barren pasture and mountain but by the 1540s the *ffriddoedd* of Amnodd and Gwernllyn already contained 20 acres of newly enclosed meadow.

Towards the end of the 15th century, Maredudd ab Ieuan began to 'find elbow room' for himself 'in that waste country among the bondmen' in the Lledr Valley (HGF 52 n30.2). In similar fashion he had acquired rights in the Crown leases of the *ffriddoedd* of Dolwyddelan. Maredudd also leased monastic land from the Abbey of Aberconwy in Nanhwynan, at Bwlch Murchan, Llyndy, Glastrain and, particularly, Gwastadannas, Hafod y Porth, Hafod Tan y Graig, and later, Hafod y Rhisgl. At the dissolution most of these were retained by his son John and Hafod Llwyfog was added. These were important cattle pastures. At about the same time, during the early 16th century, Maredudd acquired Gwydir by purchase and began to settle able men on his holdings as a protection for his own interests and for the better economic exploitation of his lands, 'filling every empty tenement with a tenant or two where of most was the king's land whereof

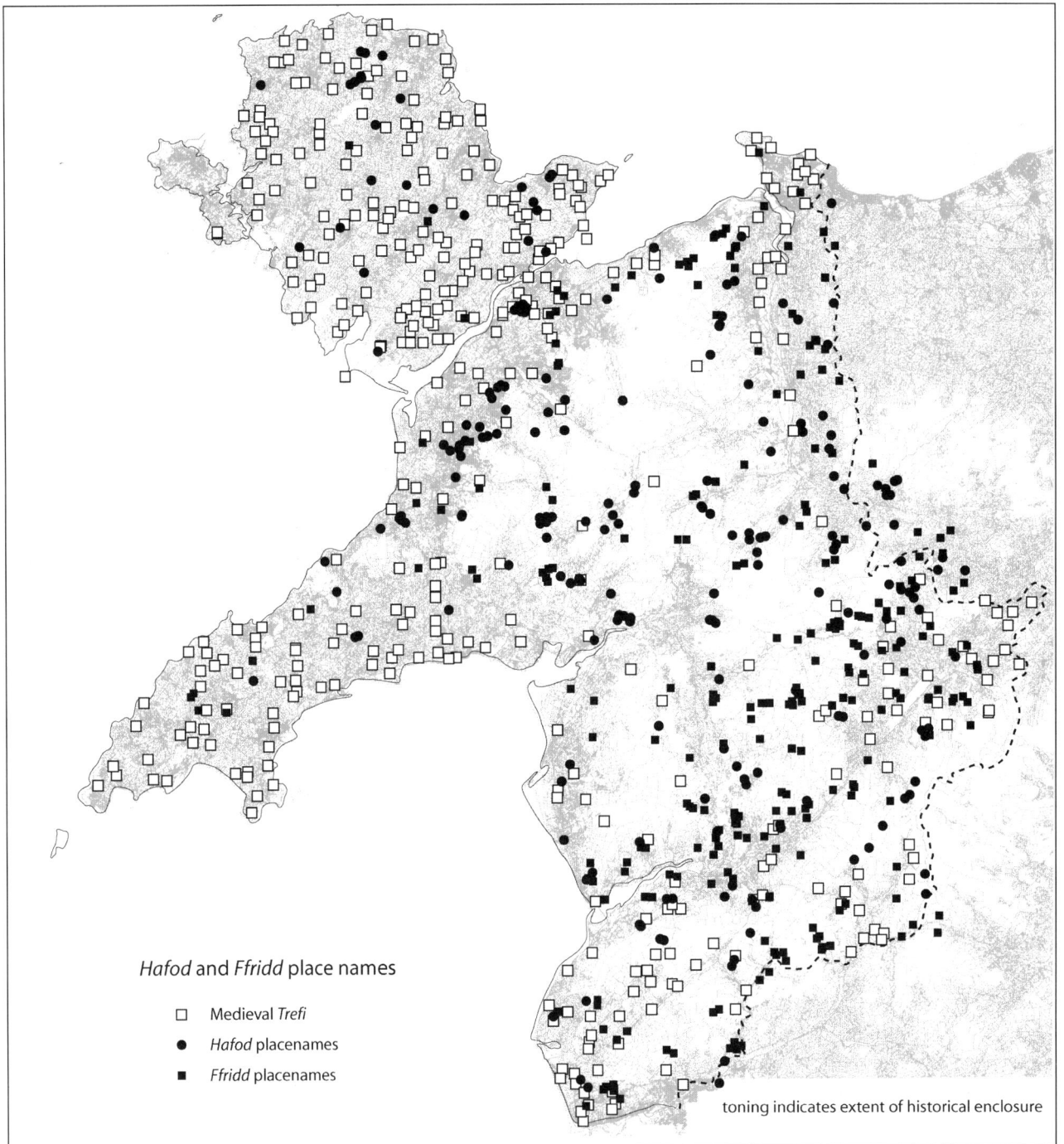

Hafod and Ffridd place names

☐ Medieval *Trefi*

● *Hafod* placenames

■ *Ffridd* placenames

toning indicates extent of historical enclosure

4.9 Distribution of *hafod* and *ffridd* place-names

many of their posterity remain to this day' (that is, 1616) (HGF, 56–7).

Some indication of the nature of the process of settlement may be gauged from the detailed account of leases kept by Morris Wyn, grandson of Maredudd ab Ieuan, where, for example, in 1568, a tenement called Llwyn y Bettws was demised for four of five years on condition that the tenant should make a beudy (cowshed) of 23ft length and where provision was also made for slating the roof of the dwelling house. Elsewhere Gweirglodd y Crynnawd was

demised on condition that the tenant make a house 24 foot long, 15 foot broad, and 2 yards in height. At Cenglog the tenant was to make a great house and to 'install the whole round-abouts' with wall and ditch. At Erw'r Crowach in 1569 the land was to be enclosed with quick set hedges, and provision was made for repair and maintenance by yearly replanting of saplings (NLW, Llanstephan MS 179b, 12–19). Specific references to *hafodydd*, now tenanted, include Hafod y Mynydd in Ffestiniog and Llandecwyn, where repairs were to be made and the spring wood nourished,

Bwlch Gwarnog and 'the higher havoty' in Llanfrothen and Hafod Ffraith in Nantconwy (*ibid*).

Traditional *hafodydd* were still maintained during the 16th century and *ffriddoedd* utilised in the customary way. The free tenants and other inhabitants of Gwydir and Penmachno continued to use the common grazing of Moel Siabod during the summer months and contested their rights in this respect. In a particular instance in 1552, William ap Ieuan ap Gruffydd and other yeomen of Gwydir and Penmachno were indicted for taking 100 of the beasts and cattle of strangers on to these *ffriddoedd* for profit, keeping them there over summer to the detriment of the rest of the community who had only ever been accustomed to pasturing their own animals (*Rec. Caern. Quart. Sess.* 97 (164), May 1552). Similarly a survey of the Commission of the Court of Exchequer in 1568 found, in Tal y Bont, properties in void barren ground, neither hedged nor ditched, and cottages there in great ruin and utterly decayed. These had been timber habitations (there was 'no timber within 4 miles to repair the same') and temporarily occupied (they were never let by lease before ... always occupied by freeholders thereabouts, some one year, some another). The account appears to describe temporary structures on *ffriddoedd* which had still to be encroached upon.

In 1548 royal surveys found at Brynllyn y Cwmcedryn, in Trawsfynydd, a former property of Cymer Abbey, 'one cottage or dairy house for summer (that is, a *hafod-ty*), and no other buildings standing, for the more part in two barren mountains and, between the same, a valley of well moorish ground, very difficult to measure' (*Rec. Court of Augment*, Survey, 2 Ed. VI). In 1563 an assessment of the 'Havottreffrythes' with their herbage in the forest of Snowdon included the commentary that it was not known how many acres the possessions contained, never having been measured, open without wood and never enclosed. Here, 'all the Queen's tenants adjoining have had common pasture for the summer season, for in winter by reason of the coldness of it and long

continuance of snow there, the same can maintain no cattle' (*Rec. Court of Augment*, 21 June 1563). Nevertheless, the 16th century saw a significant increase in encroachment and the establishment of permanent settlement on these lands. The 16th-century tenants of Hafod y Rhysgl in Nanhwynan, for example, occupied land which may have been royal *ffridd* in the 12th century, subsequently granted to Aberconwy Abbey and leased to Maredudd ab Ieuan, formerly of Dolwyddelan, then of Gwydir, in 1520. Those tenants petitioned in 1585, after two generations in Wynn family tenancies, that they had turned the mountain and barren ground to fruitfulness and profitability at great cost to themselves and had built houses and hedges about the premises (Jones 1995, 83).

At Gwynnus on the royal *ffridd* of Dinllaen, a dwelling house had been built at 'Gunneth havot' also known as Rhos Gwyniasa, following a lease of Henry VIII (*Rec. Court of Augment*, 32/25). In 1548 Rice Thomas was demised tenements, including dwelling houses and their appurtenances which already existed, on the former royal *ffridd* of Bryn Tyrch in Trewydir township, Nantconwy. This is the location of one of Maredudd ab Ieuan's settlement of tenants a generation earlier. Rice Thomas and his associates went further and encroached on the adjacent lands of Bryn-llys where several houses had been lately built. Three years later, the Caernarvonshire Quarter Sessions heard the indictment of certain yeomen who, in the same township, unlawfully enclosed a parcel of mountain common within the King's Forest of Snowdon, driving the cattle of others out of the common (Rec. Caern. Quart. Sess., 82.110, 15 June 1541).

Crown surveys of the later 16th century and early 17th century found several instances of concealment of and encroachment on 'certain lands and tenements, both parcels of Principality of North Wales and of wastes of the Forest of Snowdon, concealed, subtracted and unjustly detained' (Rec. Court of Augment, April 1568). It is not without significance that a number of these encroachments bear the names of 'Cae Newydd' (new enclosed field) (*ibid*).

4.6 Conclusions

The distinction between the operation of the royal *hafod* in the 13th century and the leasing of *hafodydd* and *ffriddoedd en masse* to eminent individuals after the conquest has been noted. The significant aspect of this distinction would seem to be in the potential of the *hafod* as an individual financial resource rather than a

communal resource. Initially, it would seem, the benefit to the lessee lay in the revenue from pasture rights. Progressively, however, these lands were re-let and sub-let whereupon they became assimilated within the process of 16th-century estate building, settled with tenants and run as individual farms rather than as components of a wider agricultural landscape. Some, as in the case of the *ffriddoedd* of Dolwyddelan and Nanhwynan, clearly retained their territorial integrity. Nevertheless, each was run as an individually tenanted farm, albeit primarily pastoral, but carrying a range of stock. This does not negate the significance of access to high-altitude seasonal pasture within the context of each such farm. The proprietorial nature of the operation should tend towards a greater degree of permanence in the buildings represented.

In the context of the monuments surveyed, the majority of sites identified, with features potentially characteristic of medieval date and occurring within altitude bands 1 and 2, up to 300m, should, most probably, be considered to form part of the pattern of core settlement within the township in which they occur, though not necessarily at the nucleus of settlement, rather than representing any aspect of seasonal use. Those sites with indicative medieval structural components and circumstantially associated with ridge and furrow agriculture at altitudes above 300m should, perhaps, also be considered to have formed part of the core township, albeit at the margin of permanent settlement.

It must be admitted that there is no certain evidence for permanent structures on the *ffriddoedd* during the 12th and 13th centuries. Nevertheless, structures with medieval characteristics, no association with contemporary agriculture, and a topographic location beyond the limit or at the margin of historical enclosure (generally above 300m), might be considered to have been associated with the exploitation of the *ffridd*. The same might equally be proposed for the slighter, less clearly defined structures in this altitude range, corresponding perhaps to those 'utterly decayed' and transiently occupied cottages in open barren ground

recorded by the Court of Exchequer Commissioners in Tal y Bont in 1568 or to the summer dairy house, standing alone on mountain and moorland in Cwmcedryn. Otherwise the remaining structures in altitude bands 2 and 3 might appropriately be regarded as elements of the expansion of settlement and tenancies following the disturbances of the early 15th century when 'the whole country was but a forest, rough and spacious ... waste of inhabitants and all overgrown with woods' (HGF, 51). These structures might then be seen to be associated with the process of estate building on the margins of previously enclosed land and at higher altitudes, encroachment on to the commons and Crown *ffriddoedd* characteristic of the later 15th, 16th and 17th centuries.

By the 18th century the traditional *hafod*, as an institution, was in terminal decline. Thomas Pennant recorded an evocative impression of summer occupation of a 'hafodty' or 'summer dairy house' in Cwm Dyli, Nant Gwynant, in the 1770s (Rhys 1883, 325–6, 339; Davies 1979, 18–7–18). Within a generation very few observers could confirm such continual residence during the summer months. As late as the 17th century, 'hafod' could still refer to 'a summer's dwelling' and also carry the meaning of 'dairy house'. By the late 18th and early 19th centuries, however, alternative meanings were in use as of 'a farmhouse at a distance from neighbours' or, applied to 'peat houses', as 'a small building or shed in a remote place for storing peat late in the season'. Hafotai were still maintained as an adjunct to upland farms, but appear in general to have been used on a daily basis with return to the *hendre* in the evening (Davies 1979, 18–19). Few of the sites recorded in the DRS survey are likely to have been constructed as late as the 18th century.

Acknowledgements

The Deserted Rural Settlement project in NW Wales was initiated by David Thompson who also undertook the preliminary fieldwork. The bulk of the fieldwork discussed in this chapter was undertaken by Susan Jones and David Hopewell.

5 DESERTED RURAL SETTLEMENTS IN SOUTH-WEST WALES

by Paul Sambrook

Abstract

The diverse geography of south-west Wales, combined with periodic climatic and economic changes, has resulted in a complex regional settlement history which provides a fascinating field of study. There are few places where deserted settlements have not been identified and at the start of the project the regional sites and monuments record held in excess of 7000 records of potential relevance to the study. A selective fieldwork strategy was adopted, concentrating initially on 21 study areas, results subsequently being extrapolated throughout the region. This paper presents and discusses the results of those studies. Particular consideration is given to the relationship between upland and lowland settlement and the evidence for upland settlement in south-west Wales as represented by the medieval *hafod* and, in later centuries, by the more permanent *lluestau*. The fortunate survival of a detailed 18th-century survey of the Crown Manor of Perfedd, Northern Ceredigion, presents a unique opportunity to investigate a group of datable *lluestau*, many of which can still be identified as field monuments. The study provides a useful insight into the occupation and eploitation of an upland landscape.

5.1 General Introduction

South-west Wales is a distinct geographic region, separated from the rest of Wales to the east by the Cambrian Mountains and the Black Mountain (Figs 1.1, 1.2, 1.3). The region comprises the counties of Carmarthenshire, Ceredigion, and Pembrokeshire (united as the county of Dyfed between 1974 and 1996). The major towns – Llanelli, Carmarthen, Pembroke, Milford Haven, Haverfordwest, Fishguard, Cardigan, and Aberystwyth – have a coastal or estuarine distribution, and secondary towns either lie on the coast or on rivers. The human exploitation and management of natural environments, influenced by altitude, degree of exposure, geology, and other factors, has led to the creation of rich and varied landscapes.

The richest farmland of the region occupies a fairly low-lying zone of undulating ground stretching from the Pembrokeshire coast, through mid- and south Pembrokeshire, mid- and south Carmarthenshire and eastwards up the Tywi Valley past the towns of Llandeilo and Llandovery. Improved pasture is the dominant land use, but with a high arable content to the far west on the Pembrokeshire coast. Topographically, south-east Carmarthenshire is similar to mid- and south Carmarthenshire, but with rougher pasture on the poor soils over coal measures. Coal-mining, iron and steel production and other heavy industries developed here, exploiting the coal and iron ore reserves, and settlements such as Llanelli and Ammanford grew to serve them. Eastern Carmarthenshire is dominated by the open moorland of the Carmarthenshire Vans, the westernmost arm of the Brecon Beacons, which rise to a maximum of 781m.

High ground running eastwards from the Preseli Mountains, at a maximum of 468m, towards the Cambrian Mountains dominates the landscape of north Pembrokeshire and north Carmarthenshire, and separates the Tywi Valley to the south from the Teifi Valley to the north. Improved pasture is present over much of this region, with some extensive areas still characterised by moorland, most notably perhaps on the Preseli Mountains, at its western extremity, and the more plateau-like and bleaker Mynydd Mallaen to the east. Some areas that survived as open moorland until the 20th century are now hidden by thick coniferous plantations, dating to the latter half of the 20th century, most notably in the area of the Brechfa Forest in Carmarthenshire.

Rich farmland lies in the western coastal zone, running northwards from Newport in north Pembrokeshire, past Cardigan and on to Aberporth in Ceredigion. However, most of southern Ceredigion between the Teifi valley and the coast comprises hilly pasture and boggy hollows between 30m and 200m, with rounded summits of moorland at over 320m. The coastal zone of north Ceredigion stretches inland for c. 15km and is bisected by deeply incised, west-flowing rivers, such as the Ystwyth and Rheidol. It becomes increasingly higher to the north, with many rounded peaks at over 300m. Here, apart from the highest points, improved pasture is the dominant land use. Further to the east lies the Ceredigion ore-field, and

traces of numerous old metal mines (mostly lead) are scattered across the landscape.

The eastern side of Ceredigion is characterised by the high, open moorlands of the main Cambrian Mountain range that rise steeply from the valleys of the Teifi, Ystwyth, and Rheidol. Generally this is a bleak, exposed landscape, lying between 350m and 550m, and broken only by modern coniferous plantations. North-eastern Ceredigion is dominated by Pumlumon, the highest peak in mid-Wales at 752m.

Clearly, with such diverse environments, exaggerated periodically by climatic changes or economic changes, the settlement history of the region is a complex and challenging field of study. The processes of rural settlement desertion are similarly varied and dependent on the many factors that have caused rural depopulation or internal population shifts. This paper attempts to present some of the reasons why settlements were abandoned and examines the physical evidence left by abandonment.

5.2 Previous work

A small number of valuable deserted settlements studies have been undertaken in the past, but there has been no overall analysis. A considerable body of information relating to deserted settlements in upland contexts has been accumulated during recent decades through the Uplands Initiative, and a number of new sites have been identified and recorded, for example on the Black Mountain (Leighton 1997).

There have also been area studies such as the work of Dr Anthony Ward, which focused on the evidence for upland settlement within the medieval commote of Perfedd in eastern Carmarthenshire (Ward 1991; 1995; 1997). This work marked the first concerted attempt in the region to survey deserted settlement sites within a defined historic administrative unit and thereby put the sites themselves into an historical context. The Blaencaron Survey (Williams and Muckle 1992) focused on an upland area east of Tregaron, Ceredigion, and similarly took an historic unit as a study area, although this survey was not confined to settlement-related sites. Importantly, this survey proposed a typology of site types, the first attempt in the region at standardising the descriptive terminology applied to deserted settlement sites.

The Preseli Survey (Drewitt 1983; 1984; 1985) identified a large number of deserted settlement sites of possible medieval or post-medieval date. However, the time-depth of the Preseli landscape and the

complex grouping of some archaeological features can make clarity of recording and interpretation difficult for a survey using rapid-recording techniques. Thus the settlement history of this remarkable historic landscape remains far from clearly charted.

A rather different project was the Cardiganshire Marginal Land Survey (Metcalfe 1979) that created records for hundreds of settlement sites located on marginal land in Ceredigion. Many of these sites were relatively recent post-medieval cottages, which had become abandoned during the 20th century as the population of agricultural and industrial workers in the Ceredigion landscape declined. However, the area also included examples of earlier post-medieval or medieval settlements.

Relatively few deserted settlements have been excavated in south-west Wales to date (Table 5.1) and few of these excavations have produced firm evidence for the dating and function of the settlements in question. Consequently, the information provided by these excavations is limited. However, it is worth passing some comment about the nature and conclusions of those listed in Table 5.1.

Bwlch yr Hendre, Blaenrheidol, Ceredigion (Butler 1963), was described as a longhouse when fully excavated by L A S Butler in 1963. It was interpreted by Butler as a *lluest* or shepherding cottage, with a possible secondary use as a peat-cutting shelter, and it

5.1 Map of south-west Wales showing principal sites and study areas

was dated within the period 1550–1750. The site has since been flooded by the Nantymoch Reservoir.

A site of an apparent medieval settlement, described as being to the west of Llanddewi Brefi, was excavated in 1926. The excavator described the buildings as being '. . . rectangular in plan with "lean-to" outbuildings, the walls being of local stone and roughly built without mortar. The only datable material is some fragmentary late 14th-century pottery' (Lewis 1927). The pottery mentioned as being of 14th-century date is further described as being, 'a soft reddish paste ... (with) yellowish brown glaze on both sides'. There is an element of uncertainty as to the exact location of this excavation although it might correspond with the site at Cors y Clochydd, Llanddewi Brefi. This is a long hut surviving only as wall bases and associated with ancillary structures. Although the description of the excavation does not exactly correspond with this site, there is evidence of ground disturbance suggesting a previous excavation.

Another possible excavated long hut site stands on a spur alongside a mountain stream at Cefn y Bryn, Cynwyl Gaeo (Hook 1970). Although no datable evidence was produced, the site was interpreted as a Roman outpost associated with the nearby Roman fort and gold-mine at Dolaucothi, Pumsaint. However, the essential characteristics of the site are very much those of a classic upland medieval or post-medieval long hut. The physical appearance of the single dwelling and its streamside location is comparable with many of the post-medieval shepherding cottage sites of the Cambrian Mountains area.

Several buildings, associated with over 30 pillow mounds, were excavated in 1979 in advance of land improvements at Bryn Cysegrfan, Llanddewi Brefi, Ceredigion (Austin 1988). Three rectilinear buildings were examined and they were all found to have been robbed out and damaged in the past. It was only possible to record the wall lines of the structures and examine what little remained of the internal floor surfaces. These were of earth and stone composition, although there was some evidence that they may have originally had some flagstones. Phosphate analysis suggested that one building might have been divided into a domestic section and an animal byre. There was no dating evidence, although small fragments of pottery recovered were thought to be of possible medieval date. However, a sherd of 19th-century brown-glazed basin was found in a similar context. A radiocarbon date of between 1315 and 1415 was obtained for a sample taken from beneath one of the pillow mounds. This led the excavator to suggest that the site might have had origins as a seasonally occupied medieval *hafod* settlement.

The partial excavation of a medieval settlement was undertaken at Llanerchaeron, Ceredigion, in 2000 (Latham *et al* 2001). The 12th-century 'Brut y Tywysogion' refers to a vill at Llanerchaeron, and a geophysical survey undertaken for the National Trust showed the sites of at least two buildings and other features beneath the grass of a flat pasture field between the mansion and the parish church. Excavation of one building showed it to be a house site. Pottery of 13th or 14th-century date and an Edward III silver penny (1363–67) were found on a beaten clay floor inside the house.

A small excavation in 1976 at Cwrt, Myddfai, by the Rev. H Roberts revealed three sides of a stone built enclosure, with internal paving. These features were interpreted as being representative of a building. However, no dating evidence was found, nor any indication of the site's function. The unpublished report of the work is held in the Regional SMR.

Several standing post-medieval structures were excavated during the latter half of the 1980s in the Newport and Nevern area in North Pembrokeshire (Mytum 1985; 1986; 1988). These included single-roomed 18th- and 19th-century cottages at Fron Haul, Newport, and at Berry Hill, Nevern and the partial excavation of four 19th-century cottages at Cwm Clydach, Newport, Pembrokeshire. One of the cottages was at Llystyn Mill, where excavation showed evidence for a possible earlier mill building and wheel-pit, which apparently pre-dated the 19th-century mill complex (Mytum 1988).

The partial excavation of an upland deserted rural settlement at Tro'r Derlwyn, Quarter Bach, Carmarthenshire, in 1998 is described elsewhere in this volume.

Table 5.1 Excavated deserted rural settlements in south-west Wales

NAME	Year	Excavator
Ceredigion		
Bwlch yr Hendre, Blaenrheidol	1962	LAS Butler (Butler 1963)
Cors y Clochydd, Llanddewi Brefi	1926	T Lewis (Lewis 1927)
Bryn Cysegrfan, Llanddewi Brefi	1979	David Austin (Austin 1988)
Llanerchaeron, Ciliau Aeron	2000	Nicky Evans (Latham *et al* 2001)
Carmarthenshire		
Cwrt, Myddfai	1976	Rev. H Roberts (Roberts 1976)
Cefn y Bryn, Cynwyl Gaeo	1969	David Hook (Hook 1970)
Tro'r Derlwyn, Quarter Bach	1998	Pete Crane (Crane, 1999)
Pembrokeshire		
Berry Hill Cottage, Nevern	1985	Dr Harold Mytum (Mytum 1985)
Fron Haul, Newport	1985–6	Dr Harold Mytum (Mytum 1985; 1986)
Cwm Clydach, Newport	1987–8	Dr Harold Mytum (Mytum 1988)

5.3 The condition survey in south-west Wales

At the start of the project the regional SMR contained records of over 7000 sites of potential relevance to any study of deserted rural settlements in south-west Wales. All of these records were reassessed during the project and, where necessary, appropriate amendments were made. Table 5.2 lists the amended totals for each site type following the desk-based assessment of the whole region and the fieldwork within specific study areas.

Table 5.2 Potential deserted rural settlement site types recorded on the regional SMR as at July 2002

Site type	Definite sites	Possible sites	Total
Building	164	13	177
Cottage	2450	152	2602
Dwelling	1221	33	1254
Farmstead	925	45	970
Hafod	2	86	88
Longhouse	79	13	92
Long hut	371	78	449
Platform	244	12	256
Unknown	1102	-	1102
Deserted rural settlement (group record)	208	66	274
TOTAL	6766	498	7264

These 7264 sites represent a wide variety of settlement types, potentially ranging from the huts of medieval herdsmen to the cottages of post-medieval peat cutters, agricultural labourers or industrial workers. There are also complex reasons behind the foundation and abandonment of different settlement sites and in the majority of cases it is simply not possible to ascribe a specific date or function to any given site, without detailed excavated evidence. In a number of cases the definite identification of specific site types was not possible and, in the absence of excavated evidence, alternative interpretations could be given. For example, several of the platforms identified appeared to be building platforms although they could also be interpreted as natural terraces. In a significant number of cases the descriptive record that exists was insufficient to assign a particular deserted rural settlement to a specific site type. These sites are simply listed in Table 5.2 as unknown.

It was recognised that the definition of the site types listed in Table 5.2 does not necessarily correspond with structures of specific periods. It is possible that platform sites, long huts, and the more complex longhouse sites are a reflection of the medieval rural settlement pattern. However, the actual situation is likely to be considerably more complex. For example, a cottage site with standing walls might have medieval origins whereas a platform site might be the location of a recently cleared 19th-century building. Consequently, it was considered necessary to include all potential structures within the study, both poorly preserved ruins and relatively well-preserved buildings, in order to assist in an understanding of the changing settlement history of rural south-west Wales. It was recognised that deserted settlements relate to historic settlements. They also relate to definable and determining systems of agrarian and social organisation. Changes to these systems have caused growth, contraction or abandonment of settlement in the past and present.

Elsewhere in Wales it was felt that to include all abandoned homes in rural areas and to include structures, such as 18th-century and later cottages, was beyond the scope of the study. However, in south-west Wales it was suggested that specific study areas could be examined in detail using a combination of desktop research, documentary and cartographic sources, and field survey. This allowed an attempt to be made to use available historical sources to assist in the dating and the interpretation of deserted settlement sites within the region. However, this was a relatively rapid and largely field-based survey exercise. The detailed study needed properly to understand and explain the settlement history of a single community would undoubtedly require considerable time and resources.

The study areas examined are listed in Table 5.3 and shown on Figure 5.1. They were mostly based on historic units of administration, such as parish boundaries, in order to attempt to make sense of wider settlement patterns and to help contextualise identified deserted settlements. However, some were chosen for other reasons, such as their status as areas of former common land within of medieval commotes or areas where sites recorded by previous archaeological field-work were felt to be in need of re-evaluation. Another factor considered in the selection of study areas was to provide a wide geographical spread, with the intention of including a representative sample of site types across the three counties of south-west Wales. It should be noted that the study areas shown in Figure 5.1 are approximate areas. With the exception of whole parish surveys in Llansadwrn, Troedyraur and Eglwyswrw, and the condition survey of sites within the Pembrokeshire Coast National Park, the study areas represent zones within which various small blocks of land were visited during the field survey periods.

Between 1996 and 1999, eighteen study areas were examined. However, it was realised that by 1999 there had been a marked bias towards studying the resource in upland areas. This was due to the fact that the past study of deserted settlements in the region has been closely linked to the study of the medieval *hafod* phenomenon and the 'long hut', both essentially related to settlement evidence on upland or marginal land. Therefore, in 1999–2000 attention was paid to three essentially lowland study areas and a condition survey of known sites within the Pembrokeshire Coast National Park. This provided an opportunity to address issues specifically related to the nature and survival of deserted settlement sites away from the uplands.

The table demonstrates that a combination of historical research and field visits has led to a significant increase in the total number of known sites within each of the study areas. Overall the numbers of recorded sites has increased by nearly 100%.

5.2 Distribution map of known sites

Table 5.3: Number of sites visited by Study Area

No. on map	County	Study Area	Definition of Study Area	Sites previously recorded	New sites identified
1	Carms	Mynydd Du	The township of Quarter Bach, part of the commons of the Lordship of Cemaes	30	3
2	Carms	Mynydd Mallaen	A large part of the commons of the medieval commote of Mallaen	23	6
3	Carms	Myddfai	The commons of the lordship and parish of Myddfai	17	6
4	Carms	Llanddeusant	An area focusing on the parish commons	63	39
5	Carms	Llanllwni and Llanfihangel Rhos y Corn	Adjacent commons of the parishes of Llanllwni and Llanfihangel Rhos y Corn	6	2
6	Carms	Cynwyl Gaeo	An area including a combination of common and enclosed farmland	15	33
7	Carms	Llansadwrn	The parish of Llansadwrn	-	54
8	Cered	Caron Is Clawdd	The upland townships of the parish of Caron Is Clawdd, formerly part of the commons of the Lordship of Tregaron	28	4
9	Cered	Cwmystwyth	The Monastic grange of Cwmystwyth, a grange of Strata Florida Abbey	13	-
10	Cered	Perfedd	The former commons of the Crown Manor of Perfedd	4	31
11	Cered	Caron Uwch Clawdd	Parish of Caron Uwch Clawdd	11	35
12	Cered	Gwnnws	The commons of the historical parish of Gwnnws	19	20
13	Cered	Llanbadarn y Creuddyn	A detached portion of the main parish, including lands along the Castell and Rheidol valleys north of Devil's Bridge	42	-
14	Cered	Llanddewi Brefi	The historic parish of Llanddewi Brefi, once an estate of the Bishop of St David's	4	49
15	Cered	Mynydd Bach	A area of upland in central Ceredigion, detached from the Cambrian Mountains and mostly enclosed during the 18th and 19th centuries	22	16
16	Cered	Ysgubor y Coed	The northernmost parish in the county of Ceredigion	-	11
17	Cered	Troedyraur and Llangynllo	The parishes of Troedyraur and Llangynllo	-	76
18	Pembs	Preseli	The historic commons of the Lordship of Cemaes	19	5
19	Pembs	Preseli II	Carningli Common and the commons of the Maenclochog area	4	13
20	Pembs	Eglwyswrw	Desk-based survey of historical sources for the parish of Eglwyswrw	-	33
21	Pembs	Pembrokeshire Coast National Park	Condition survey of known sites in the Pembrokeshire Coast National Park	123	-
		TOTALS		443	436

5.4 The character of deserted rural settlements in south-west Wales

5.4.1 Settlement form

Assessing the form of settlement types within the region is not always an easy undertaking. Where the spatial form of a deserted settlement complex can be identified on an historic map, the associations between buildings and other features can be inferred. For example, the development of a farmstead shown on an early estate map can be followed until its abandonment. Supporting documentary evidence or oral testimony may also exist, helping explain the purpose and relationship of now derelict or ruined structures. However, this is not possible for those sites that have no cartographic record. A group of several long huts or platforms may be related although in the absence of excavated evidence it cannot be said with any certainty that they are even contemporary. Similarly, a single structure may look isolated, although it is quite possibly a component of a larger settlement complex. For example, in one case a small, ruined shelter was recorded on a hillside 500m from a house site. This structure had no meaning or context until an informant explained that it had been used, within living memory, by the occupants of the house as a goose pen and was therefore an integral part of the settlement complex.

However, some basic observations can be made of some commonly encountered settlement forms in the region. The sites listed as farmsteads in Table 5.2 can be defined as a farmhouse with ancillary buildings arranged around a farmyard and presumed to have been set within a land holding. The cottage sites are usually a single, detached dwelling, with one or more ancillary buildings, standing in or attached to a small plot of land, such as a garden or paddock. Although these are definitions that are familiar today, other site types are not so easily defined.

Figures 5.2 and 5.3a–c illustrate the distribution of the three main site types (platforms, long huts and longhouses). The use of the term longhouse conforms with the definition used by Iorwerth Peate (Peate 1946, 51–84), ie a structure divided internally between a *pen-llawr* (upper floor level) and *is-llawr* (lower floor level), often with a cross passage or storage compartment between the two. It is also implicit that longhouses are former dwellings or farmhouses and are often, but not always, associated with ancillary structures, and are the focus to a farm complex. Ninety-two longhouses have now been recorded (Table 5.2; Figures 5.2 and 5.3c). Long huts are

generally single-cell, rectilinear structures with only the wall bases of the dwelling surviving above ground and no clear surface evidence as to their function. There are currently 449 long huts recorded across the region (Table 5.2; Figures 5.2 and 5.3b). If two or three long huts stand in close proximity, it cannot be said which, if any, was the dwelling and which were ancillary to the dwelling, unless there is supporting cartographic or documentary evidence. However, in many upland contexts, long huts occur singly and can be identified as the dwelling component of the deserted settlement complex. This is particularly true of the '*lluest*' type settlements discussed below. Smaller structures, defined as shelters, will usually occur singly. They must be seen to be ancillary structures to a dwelling elsewhere, even though the relationship is rarely apparent in the field. A shepherd's shelter would not necessarily be intervisible with the cottage or farm from which the shepherd was working.

In many cases there are no surface traces of a building, the only evidence for a deserted site being a level platform, with 256 such sites now recorded across the region (Table 5.2; Figures 5.2 and 5.3a). Often pairs of platforms will be encountered, typically one larger than the other, suggestive of a dwelling and an ancillary structure. Single platforms are also common and, more rarely, groups of more than two platforms are found. However, little interpretation can be drawn from surface evidence, as we have no indication as to whether such structures are even contemporary or simply represent rebuilding close to an original site.

The dwelling components of deserted settlement sites are always rectilinear in plan. They survive as drystone structures (which may have rubble-build or well-coursed stone walls surviving to a metre or more in height), as stone and earth remains or as simple earthworks. The majority of buildings are single or two-roomed structures although multi-celled structures are also found. However, in many cases timber, or even peat, would have been used to create internal divisions. Such divisions are unlikely to leave any surface trace and so any attempt to quantify structures on the basis of such divisions is likely to be problematic.

The availability of particular building materials is likely to have influenced both the form and location of rural settlement sites and often explains the variations found between the different study areas. For example, where the only evidence for a former site is

a

b

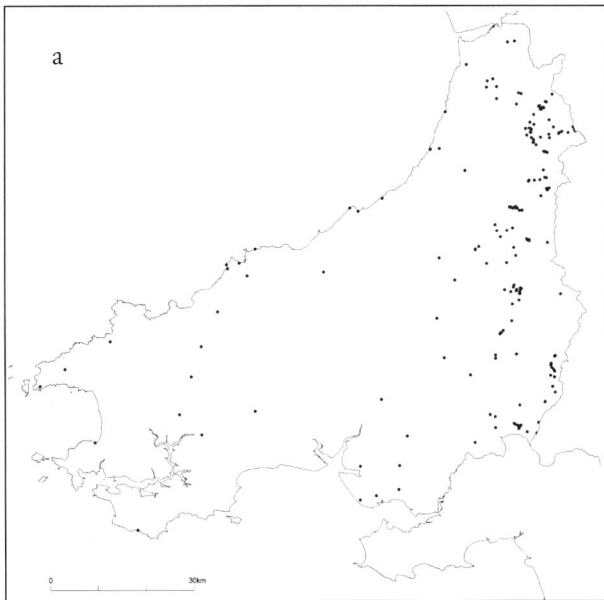

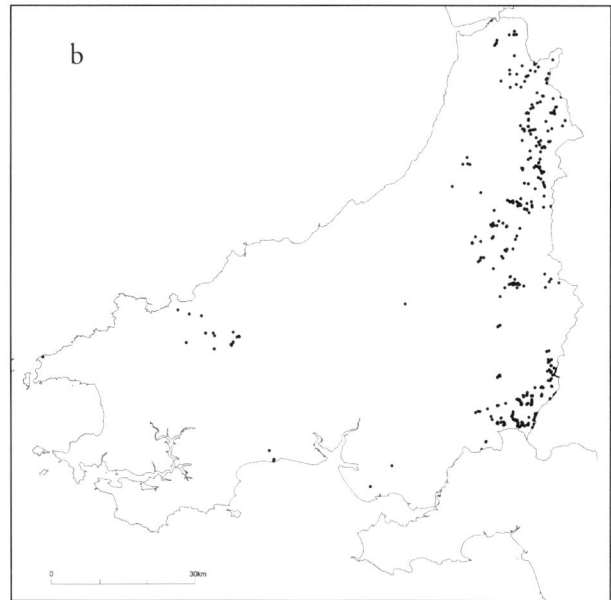

Clockwise from top left:
5.3a Distribution map: platforms
5.3b Distribution map: long huts
5.3c Distribution map: longhouses

c

now an empty platform, it seems probable that the structure was largely constructed of timber or clay and turf. Therefore, the absence of surface stone associated with long hut sites on the commons of Mynydd Mallaen in north-east Carmarthenshire is almost certainly explained by the scarcity of outcropping rock over large parts of the mountain. In some areas, the absence of stone may help in dating some sites as it is possible that timber was more abundant in the past and there was no need to quarry building stone even if it was readily available. At sites where the only surviving evidence is a denuded earth bank with little or no visible stone component, it may be that walls were originally constructed using clay or *clom* on a stone foundation. This may reflect a limited choice of materials available to the builders, rather than a particular preference for those materials.

Table 5.4 Percentages of structures of various build recorded during the field survey. This excludes sites visited during 1999–2000 that were predominantly 19th-century cottages (further detail for which can be found below in Tables 5.8 and 5.9)

Type	Total	%
No structure (bare platform)	85	14
Mostly earth	27	5
Earth and stone	188	32
Coursed drystone	209	35
Rubble build	40	7
Uncertain	43	7
TOTAL	592	100%

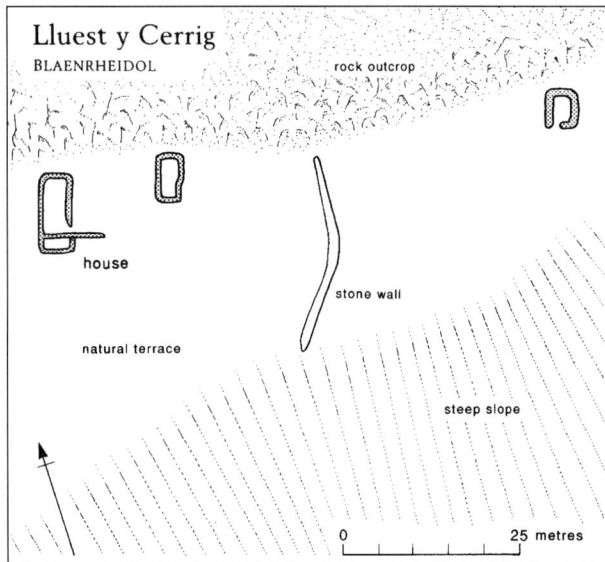

5.4 Lluest y Cerrig, Perfedd

Where stone walling survives, the stonework is usually earth-bonded or reasonably well-coursed drystone walling. Even in the case of known 19th-century abandoned dwellings, lime mortar was extremely uncommon in any of the areas studied and presumed to be of relatively recent date. Examples where structures had unbound, rubble, drystone walling, were often, but not always, encountered at sites where the stonework of a ruinous dwelling had been roughly rebuilt to form a later fold.

Most stream valley sites utilised exposed bedrock or rock and boulder debris washed down by the streams. For example, the roughly built structures of the Nant Garw Valley in Quarter Bach, Carmarthenshire, utilised the abundant supplies of loose boulders and stone washed down by the Garw stream. Even sites described as having 'earth and stone' wall bases are suspected to have a more substantial stone component beneath the surface. The excavated long hut at Cefn y Bryn, Cynwyl Gaeo, Carmarthenshire (Hook 1970), provides an interesting example. The unexcavated parts of the site appeared to be defined by grassy earth wall bases. But those parts of the site where the turf had been stripped during excavation over 20 years previously remain exposed and show that beneath the turf are well-coursed drystone wall bases.

Ephemeral features and roughly constructed buildings are in a small minority, reflecting the fact that most structures, however small or simple, were built with care and purpose by those who intended either to dwell within them or make use of them. The description given by the Rev. John Evans (Evans 1804) of a hut near Strata Florida, Ceredigion, inhabited by a poor peat-cutter and his family, indicates how simple the construction of some homes could be even in recent times and how resourceful people were at using available materials to create a home. Perhaps, more importantly, it also serves to remind us of the importance of the home to its occupants, however humble:

It was one of those poor huts that are thinly sprinkled by the sides of the hills, inhabited by peaters and shepherds … It was partly formed by an excavation in the slate rock, and partly by walls of mud mixed with chopped rushes, covered with segs, and having a wattled or basket work chimney. The entrance was in the gable end, facing the southeast, which was defended during the night, or in very cold weather, by a wattled hurdle, clothed with rushes. A wall of turfs for fuel served as a partition for the bed-room, furnished with a bed of heath and dried rushes in one corner. The furniture was such as necessity dictated: some loose stones formed the grate; two large ones, with a plank across, supplied the place of chairs; a kettle, with a back stone for baking oaten cakes, answered every culinary purpose; and two coarse earthen pitchers stood by for the preserving or carrying of water and dodgriafel, the usual beverage of the family … Now, my friend, collect what they had to maintain a family of seven, a man, his wife, and five children!! The mother looked in health, and the children, though thinly clad, ruddy and smiling … Indeed, there did not appear any thing like the misery and filth observable in the dwellings of the English poor, whose weekly income is four or six times as great. Though the floor was formed of the native rock, it was regularly swept with a besom made of segs, bound with a band of the same, and the fuel was as regularly piled as bread on a baker's shelves.

5.4.2 Dating

Very few deserted rural sites in south-west Wales have been securely dated. There is often a temptation to date a site on the basis of the extent of the surviving remains. For example, a very ruinous or earthwork structure might be considered older than an almost complete, standing building. In reality, of course, this can be a very simplistic generalisation. Some abandoned buildings of relatively recent date may have been demolished and cleared, leaving simple platforms that might give the impression of early sites in the absence of any other dating evidence. Conversely, at some of the most interesting settlement complexes, relatively well-preserved structures were recorded that may in fact be earlier or contemporary with sites that survive in much poorer condition. This point is particularly well illustrated in relation to two neighbouring sites visited in the Mynydd Bach study area, the Bryn-yr-ychain farmstead and Hafod Gou 'long hut'. Cartographic evidence shows Bryn-yr-ychain, which includes relatively well-preserved ruined structures, pre-dates the 19th century. However, despite being in a much poorer condition and possessing a *hafod* place-name, Hafod Gou is in fact more recent (late 19th-century in origin).

Ultimately, archaeological excavation is likely to be the only way that secure dating evidence can be obtained. However, there is a relative absence of excavated evidence (Table 5.1) and this has produced relatively few credible dates. Radiocarbon dating has suggested medieval occupation at Bryn Cysegrfan (Austin 1988) and pottery reputed to be 14th century in date was retrieved at Cors y Clochydd in 1926 (Lewis 1927), although this needs to be re-examined. At Llanerchaeron, (Latham *et al* 2001) excavation uncovered the remains of a clay-walled dwelling with a beaten clay floor. Into this floor was set an Edward III silver penny, possibly evidence of 14th-century occupation. Early post-medieval occupation was suggested by radiocarbon dates from Tro'r Derlwyn (Crane 1999), whilst Mytum (1988) recovered abundant evidence of post-medieval occupation, particularly 19th-century activity, at Cwm Clydach.

It is possible that bare earthwork platforms may once have been the sites of timber houses. Given the scarcity of building timber in many areas in post-medieval times, it could be assumed that timber houses (and thereby earthwork platforms) should be viewed as earlier (i.e. medieval) settlement sites. However, this is a questionable assumption. Table 5.4 indicates that at least 75% of structures examined in the field were of partly drystone construction and at present it is simply not possible to know whether this reflects the widespread availability of stone for building, or that most deserted settlements examined are in fact post-medieval in origin, built when timber was scarce.

5.4.3 Distribution

Probably the most striking aspect of the deserted settlements study in south-west Wales was the wide distribution of the recorded sites (Fig 5.2). There are very few places where deserted settlements have not been identified. From the higher slopes of Pumlumon to the Pembrokeshire coast evidence survives that charts the ebb and flow of rural settlement over the past millennium. However, some significant variations can be detected in the location, situation and density of sites from area to area or, more accurately, within different landscape types. There are, for example, certainly variations in the distribution of sites between lowland and upland environments, and within the farmed lowland

5.5 Squatter settlement at Rhosygell, Devils Bridge, Ceredigion (Crown copyright: RCAHMW)

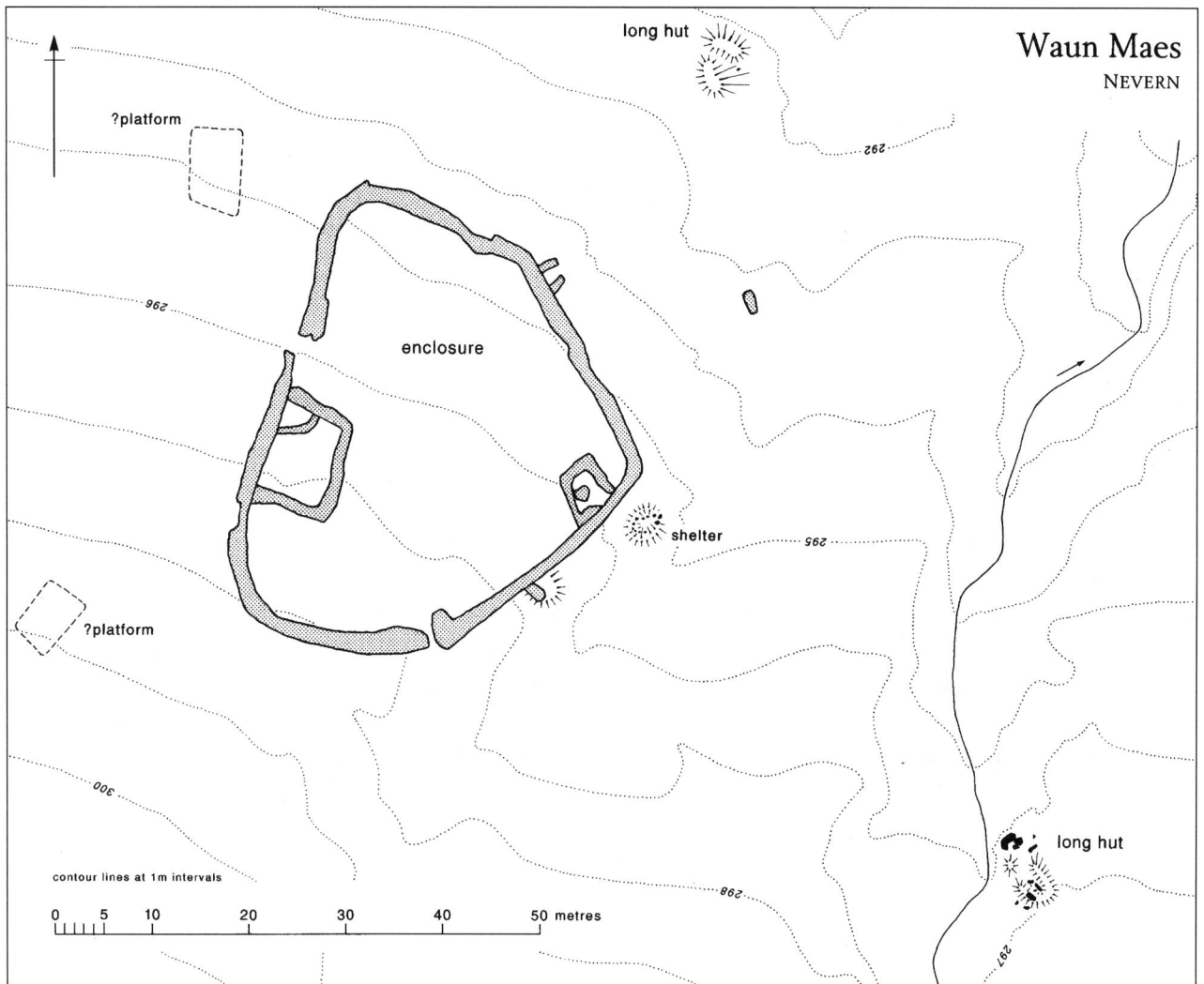

5.6 A possible *hafod* at Waun Maes, near Brynberian, Pembrokeshire

landscape as opposed to marginal lowland landscapes. It is perhaps inevitable that topography and climate have had a major influence on historic settlement patterns. In upland contexts, there is a predominance of deserted settlements over occupied settlements. However, as deserted upland settlements are also often left undisturbed by later development or agricultural activity, the survival rate of deserted upland sites is also markedly higher than that of the lowlands. It is evident from the fieldwork undertaken that even where afforestation has taken place in the uplands, many sites have survived; unlike ploughed fields, forest plantations can often shelter and preserve settlement sites.

The distribution map (Fig 5.2) demonstrates that the upland areas of the region are packed with valuable evidence of past settlement. Distribution patterns also indicate that the locations of sites are heavily influenced by local topography. There is a clear tendency for upland deserted settlements to be found in sheltered locations, particularly alongside stream and river

courses. Other favoured spots in upland areas have been observed to include the leeward side of hillocks, rocky outcrops, escarpments and cliffs, almost any location that offered shelter from the prevailing winds. This careful selection of location means that, even today, a deserted settlement site can offer good shelter on a windswept mountainside for example at Lluest y Cerrig (Fig 5.4). Occasionally, upland sites are located on exposed hill slopes, and it may be that such sites were temporary or seasonal dwellings. In varying contexts, they may even have served as drying platforms for peat stacks or hayricks. It should not be assumed on the basis of surface evidence that all platforms are former dwelling sites. However, human endeavour is of course more than capable of overcoming physical or environmental barriers to development, if even only for a short period of time and ultimately unsuccessfully. Consequently, barren moorlands can be enclosed, farmed and settled but then abandoned if the experiment fails, the climate deteriorates or economic or social problems militate against continued settlement. Therefore, open moorland and marginal land around mountain fringes are often the location of short-lived 18th- or 19th-century farmsteads or sometimes more extensive squatter settlements. These may include tens of cottages spread out over a portion of moorland that had been carved out of the wastes, drained, and farmed (Fig 5.5).

The distributions shown in Figures 5.2 and 5.3a–c may hint at the distribution of pre- 18th- and 19th-century deserted settlement sites within the study areas although the difficulty of dating sites has been highlighted above. It is likely that many of the sites recorded on the SMR as buildings, cottages, dwellings, farmsteads or as unknown (see Table 5.2) had medieval origins. However, the majority of these sites have been identified from documentary and cartographic sources dating to the last 200 years and probably represent the homes of 18th- and 19th-century industrial workers or agricultural labourers.

In the lowland areas of the region, mid-19th-century parish tithe maps provide a 'snapshot' of the countryside at a time when population levels in many rural areas were at their peak. In south-west Wales the principal farmsteads in each parish employed significant numbers of agricultural labourers and were supported by craftsmen and other workers. The metal orefields of mid-Wales, and the Carmarthenshire and Pembrokeshire coalfields also supported a much larger population than at present in many parishes. They attracted, and for a time sustained, a population larger than that which could normally be expected to be supported by the natural resources of the land. These short-lived industrial settlements might appear as small nucleations of settlement or as scattered cottages, and then disappear with subsequent decline of the industry, unless alternative work was available. This explains the higher density of deserted cottages scattered across

marginal land in the Ceredigion metal-ore mining district (which ceased production in the early 20th century), than at the margins of the Carmarthenshire coalfield (which continued to offer employment until the 1980s). The effect of industrial expansion within the rural landscape was both to create new settlement and to ensure the utilisation and modification of many earlier settlements. This resulted in a more complex arrangement in these areas, with another layer of settlement needing to be identified and understood, although the careful examination of cartographic evidence can be of great assistance.

With population growth peaking during the late 18th and early 19th centuries, it is not surprising that the distribution pattern of lowland settlements in non-industrial areas also changed. Settlement was no longer focused on the best farmlands; tithe maps show that the landscape had quite literally filled up and that cottages and dwellings were to be found in field corners, along roadsides and in occasional small nucleations. The sharp decline of the rural population during the later 19th century has left a legacy that is equally striking. It is this decline that has resulted in a significant number of deserted settlement sites being present in every lowland community in the region and their distribution in the lowlands is therefore greatly skewed by these recent events.

As a consequence of settlement expansion and decline during the 18th and 19th centuries, the process of locating and mapping medieval or early-post medieval sites in lowland or even marginal upland landscapes can only be undertaken through detailed historical investigation. The impact of later post-medieval and modern settlement change has to be understood before the earlier patterns can be identified. In south-west Wales an attempt has been made to achieve this through detailed, localised studies.

5.5 Discussion: deserted rural settlements in upland south-west Wales

5.5.1 The Hafod in south-west Wales
Hafod is a term and a phenomenon of great significance to settlement studies in Wales, and one of the most important themes of relevance to settlement studies in the region's uplands is that of the medieval *hafod/hendre* model. The basic mechanics of the *hafod/hendre* system were that animals were moved from their winter pasture around the homesteads or *hendrefi* to the summer pastures or *hafodydd*. Members of the community would move with the stock and reside in summer-houses or *hafotai* until the end of the

summer grazing season, when people and animals would return to their homesteads. Although usually taken to refer to upland summer pastures on the commons and wastes, *hafod* is more properly a term that was applicable to any summer pastureland, regardless of altitude. Indeed, an example of a farm called Hafod is found at 1m OD, at the edge of the coastal bog of Cors Fochno in the community of Ysgubor y Coed, Ceredigion.

Hafod is a common place-name element in south-west Wales. It is often used in the names of existing farmsteads, but also applied to some deserted settlement sites as well as relatively extensive blocks of upland pasture. It is perhaps significant that farms with *hafod* place-names in the region tend to be found at the edge of marginal land or on the upland fringes, not on the higher mountain ground. It may be that the *hafod* was in some ways a 'base camp' and that smaller satellite settlements or camps were also used, where herdsmen could stay close to the animals on the hill pastures. The main *hafod* could perhaps become subsumed into the enclosed landscape in later centuries as the enclosure of mountain wastes occurred and thereby become a viable farmstead. The cottages or huts on the mountain ground might thereafter be retained as seasonal shepherding stations, or even become permanent homes in later centuries. However, our present level of knowledge makes this a matter of conjecture.

The *hafod* has long been considered a characteristically medieval site type (Davies 1980, 4). However, despite the presence of several hundred sites recorded as '*Hafod*' in the regional Sites and Monuments Record, there are very few, if any, sites currently known in the region that are proven medieval *hafotai*. Most of the sites recorded as possible *hafotai* are based on *hafod* place-names, taken from map sources, or of deserted settlement sites which have only been examined briefly in the field and of which little is known beyond visible surface features. The identification of a genuine medieval *hafod* is not easy. Much has been written about documentary sources and theoretical models relevant to the *hafod*'s place in medieval agricultural systems (eg Davies 1980), but it would appear that more consideration needs to be given to what the archaeological remains of a *hafod* would look like in the field.

The archaeological evidence for a *hafod* is likely to include a cluster or dispersed group of long huts and ancillary structures; evidence for the dwellings and shelters of the cowherds and shepherds who tended the animals, along with animal folds or pens, which might include anything from large corrals for bovine stock to small shelters for fowl. Examples of such complexes have been recorded throughout the region, from the Preseli hills to the Carmarthenshire Fans and up onto the Ceredigion hills. The survey recorded a very well-preserved example of such a site at Waun Maes, on the commons of the parish of Nevern, Pembrokeshire (Fig 5.6). The sub-circular fold at Waun Maes is a drystone construction, now in a ruinous state. A number of certain or suspected long huts and/or ancillary struc-

tures close to the fold may be contemporary and these may represent the sites of temporary shelters used by shepherds or cowherds during their time at the fold.

One of the main activities at the *hafod* was dairying. Therefore, cool-stores for dairy products would have been essential. The medieval *hafod* was part of a well-organised agrarian system, where the production of meat, dairy produce, wool, and leather was not simply carried on at a subsistence level, but with a mind to producing a surplus. Many *hafod* sites might leave evidence that reflect this complex organisation.

In the neighbourhood of Strata Florida Abbey, the project identified a series of substantial upland settlement complexes, which may be indicative of such organisation. Within a few kilometres east of Strata Florida Abbey itself, complexes at Hafod Eidos, Hafod Frith, and Troedyrhiw (Fig 5.7) include dwellings, ancillary structures, and substantial enclosures which may have been stock corrals associated with large-scale pastoral activity on the abbey's home grange. However, sites of this kind, on monastic granges, may have been unusual in their size and scale of operation.

On a smaller scale, Craig-lan-las on Cae'r Meirch Farm, near Devils Bridge, Ceredigion (Fig 5.8), illustrates the relationship between dwellings and their ancillary features, which in this case included a fine example of a 'sunken shelter'. Sunken shelters have been noted during the field survey at a number of deserted settlement sites in eastern Ceredigion and, although they are not fully understood (there are no known excavated examples), they are thought to represent the remains of some form of underground cool-stores. The examples recorded tend to measure between 10m and 16m long, 2–3m wide and can be well over 1m deep, with upstanding earthwork banks forming a U-shaped structure in plan. The downslope end is usually left open, suggesting that access was possible into the low chamber that was formed. It can only be assumed that these structures had a simple thatched roof.

The Craig-lan-las complex included the wall bases of a rectilinear building or long hut set on a levelled platform. The large sunken shelter was 16m long and was located 80m to the north-west. A smaller, circular ancillary structure was located to the south-west of the sunken shelter. No fold or stock corral was identified, suggesting that there were not large numbers of stock animals kept here. Neither was there any evidence of crop-raising or field enclosure contemporary to the settlement. Today, a large and unbroken stone and earth boundary bank now separates the ancillary

5.7 Troedyrhiw, near Pontrhydygroes, Ceredigion (Crown copyright: RCAHMW)

structures from the presumed dwelling of the settlement complex. A stone field boundary wall also divides the settlement area from a small pocket of raised bog immediately to the west. A number of small quarry pits in the vicinity may have been used to obtain the stone to build the stone wall. It is not known if these boundaries post-date the settlement, but it seems unlikely that a large and inconvenient bank would be raised between a dwelling and its ancillaries during the time of occupation.

It may be argued that platform house sites associated with these sunken shelters are medieval or early post-medieval in date and possibly associated with the *hafod* tradition. However, our lack of knowledge of the sub-surface archaeology of such sites makes such opinions speculative. Dating this type of site from surface features alone is difficult. The site at Craig-lan-las is not shown on any known cartographic source, the earliest known of which are the early 19th-century Ordnance Survey Surveyors Drawings (Sheet 311, c. 1820–1). If the interpretation of a sunken shelter as a form of cool-store is correct, we can perhaps suggest that this settlement was associated with dairying (of cattle or sheep), and that the sunken shelter provided storage for perishable produce such as milk, cheese or butter. However, the comparative scarcity of such structures is at odds with the notion that they were important structures at upland settlements involved in dairying. It is known that sheep were milked at the post-medieval shepherding stations or *lluestau* of mid-Wales (see 3.5.2 below), but there are no known sunken shelters recorded at settlements of the *lluest* type in the region, nor at later post-medieval farmsteads in the uplands. Another characteristic of Craig-lan-las is that it was not sheltered, but rather it was located on an exposed natural terrace which is open to the south-west. This may indicate that the site was only seasonally occupied. Life would have been difficult during the winter months at such an exposed site.

All the sites of possible *hafotai* discussed above have left substantial surface remains of buildings and ancillary structures, and animal pens or corrals. However, the surface evidence for a *hafod* might be very limited and might simply consist of one or more building platforms with little or no visible surface evidence. An empty platform with no visible structural remains suggests that timber or wattle and daub may have been used as building materials. It is possible that such materials may have been used at a time when timber was commonly available. Consequently, an assumption could be made that empty platforms are relatively early (possibly medieval) when found in upland contexts.

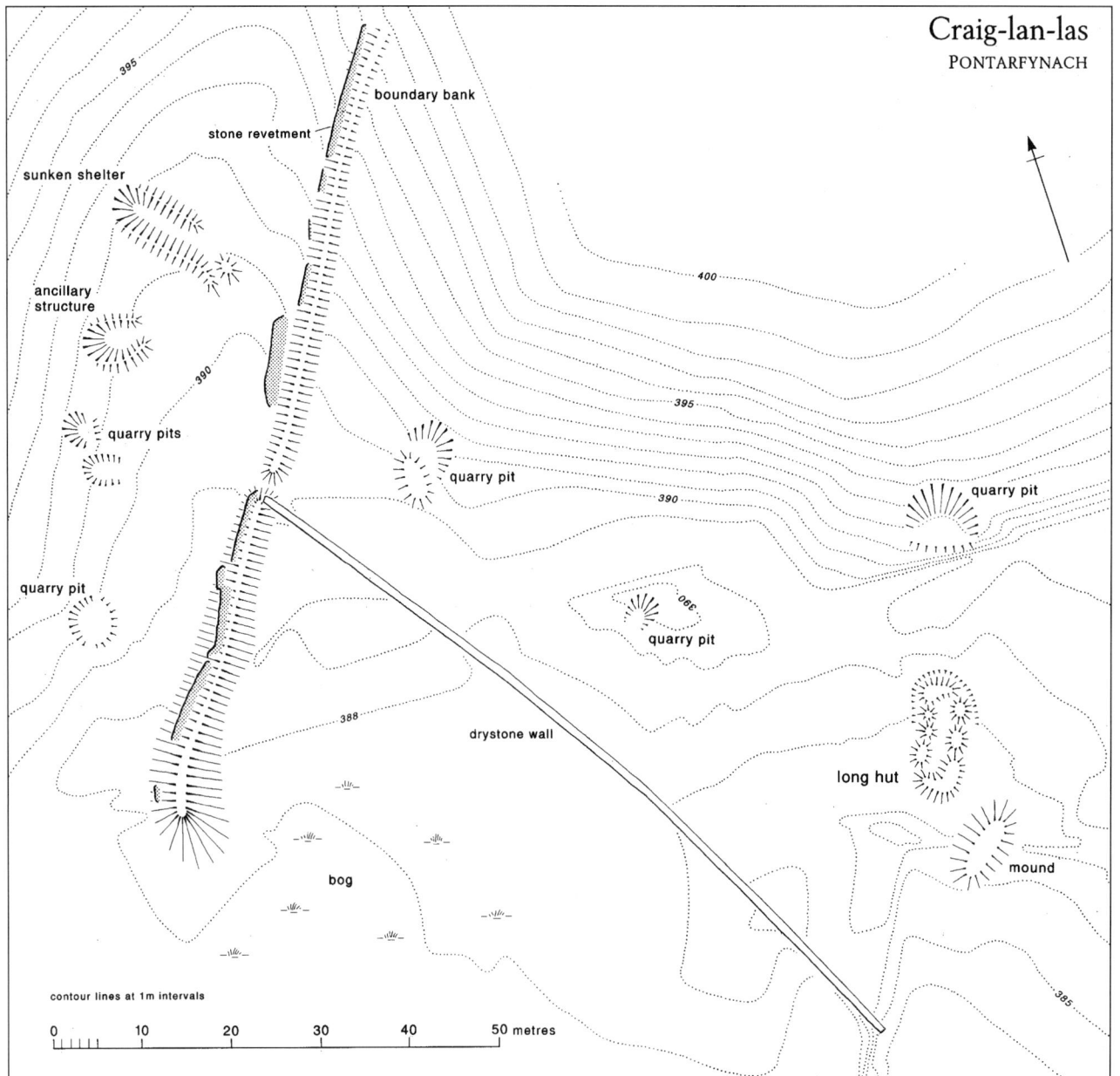

5.8 Craig-lan-las, Devil's Bridge, Ceredigion

Examples of single platforms, platform pairs or, more rarely, clusters of platforms are known throughout the uplands of Carmarthenshire and Ceredigion although they appear to be less common in Pembrokeshire (Fig 5.3a). A group of three platforms was recorded on an exposed hillside at Disgwylfa Fach, Ceredigion. The three platforms varied in size from 9 x 4m to 12 x 7m and may have served different functions. These platforms had no obvious ancillary features and are markedly different in character to the post-medieval shepherding settlements that are common in the same area, which typically include stone structures and associated enclosures. Of course, the interpretation of platforms in upland locations as *hafotai* is tenuous and in reality many of these features may not be medieval in

date and might not even be associated with settlement. Such structures clearly need further investigation if their potential for informing settlement studies is to be fully realised. However, the evidence for seasonal activity from excavated evidence can be ambiguous (Silvester this volume).

Despite the decay and ultimate abandonment of the *hafod/hendre* system by the early post-medieval period (Davies 1980, 24), the term *hafod* became synonymous with almost any form of upland settlement in Wales. John Leland passed through central Ceredigion during the late 1530s (Toulmin-Smith 1906). Whilst crossing the Afon Claerddu he looked northwards and observed '*ii very poore Cotagis for Somer Dayres for Catel*' (Williams 1889). Leland may well have witnessed genuine communal *hafotai* or '*Somer Dayres*' towards the end of the medieval tradition. However, when the Rev. John Evans passed through the same area in the early 19th century, he still referred to the cottages dotted about the hills as *hafotai*: 'The surrounding hills afford, up their sides, fine pasturage for cattle; and during the summer months numerous havotys are ranged amidst the mountains ... They have scarcely any idea of demarcation, ranging with their cattle for grazing where situation may induce, or inclination lead'.

The use of the term *hafod* by Evans almost certainly does not refer to the existence of the communal *hafodydd* of the medieval model, but rather to the post-medieval tradition of 'keeping a *hafod*' (*cadw hafod*). The *havotys* that Evans refers to may be synonymous with the *lluestau* of other sources. As will be shown below, the *lluest*, a type of shepherding station, may account for a large number of deserted settlement sites in the region, particularly in Ceredigion, and appears to be an essentially post-medieval phenomenon.

5.5.2 The Lluest in south-west Wales

The origin of the term *lluest* (pl. *lluestau* or *lluestydd*) is as ancient as that of the *hafod* and the term has similarly undergone a subtle, but significant, change of

5.9 Pen Cefndyrys, Ceredigion

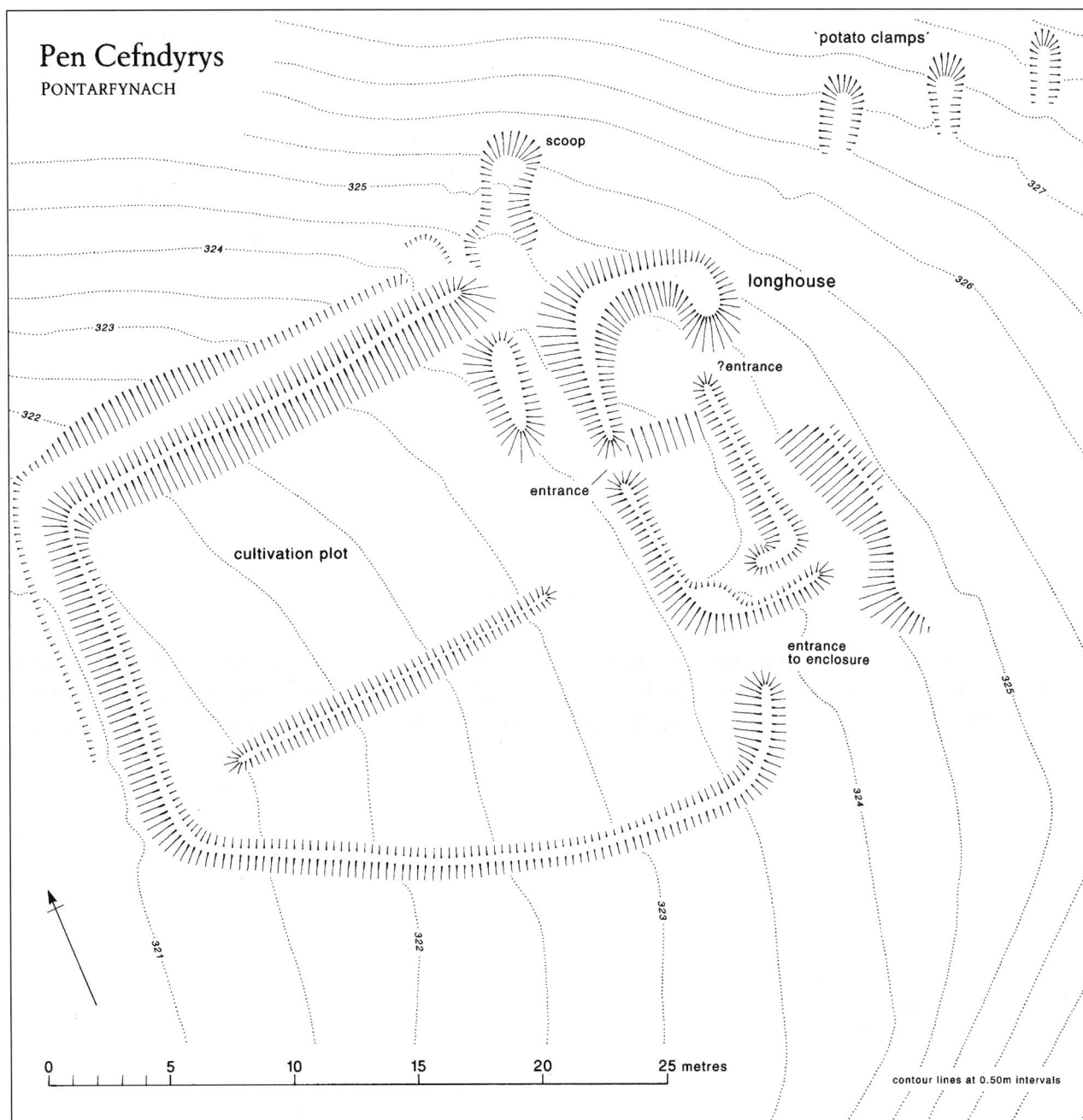

Pen Cefndyrys
PONTARFYNACH

'potato clamps'

scoop

longhouse

?entrance

entrance

cultivation plot

entrance
to enclosure

0   5   10   15   20   25 metres

contour lines at 0.50m intervals

meaning since medieval times. *Lluest* appears as a term in medieval Welsh law codes traditionally held to have been first codified during the reign of Hywel Dda, King of Deheubarth in the 10th century. The Gwynedd Code of these laws makes reference to *lluestau* which clearly indicates that they were a form of temporary encampment: '*E brenhyn a dele o pob byleyntref den a march a bueall e wneythur lluest e'r brenhyn*' (The King has a right to a man, horse and axe from each township of villeins to make his *lluest*) (Wiliam 1960, 23).

An example of the early use of the term occurs in a medieval account of the Battle of Mynydd Carn, fought in Pembrokeshire in 1081. The forces of Gruffudd ap Cynan of Gwynedd had marched to face the armies of Caradog ap Gruffudd, Meilyr ap Rhiwallon, and Trahaearn of Arwystli:

'*A guedy kerdet dirvaur emdeith diwyrnaut, yg kylch gosper wynt a doethant y venydd, en y lle yd oedd lluestau y dywededigyon vrenhined uchof*' (And after a long day's march, towards evening they came to a mountain, where the aforementioned kings had their *lluestau*) (Evans 1977, 15).

Whatever the medieval usage of the term, there are numerous documentary sources available to show that, by the 17th century, *lluest* was being used to describe shepherding settlements in the Cambrian Mountain district of mid-Wales. Today, the term *Lluest* is a common place-name element in the Cambrian Mountain area of the counties of Ceredigion and Powys (Davies 1980), although it becomes increasingly rare as one moves away from that region. At what point the term *lluest* came to be associated with shepherding, and to have a wider application than the original medieval definition, is difficult to assess. Indeed, it may well be the case that the term had always been applied to any type of impermanent shelter or settlement regardless of purpose. This is perhaps implicit in the evidence of the law books.

The noble associations of the *lluest* certainly seem to have disappeared by early post-medieval times. The Welsh princes and their armies no longer defended the hills and the Tudor monarchs had established a new legal order. By the time Thomas Jones published his 'Dictionary of Welsh and English' in 1688, the term *lluest* can be seen to have more than one meaning, being defined as 'A shepherd's Cottage, also a Tent'.

Amongst early references to *lluestau* observed at the National Library of Wales is a deed that dates to the early 17th century and relates to two settlements within Llanddewi Brefi parish, Ceredigion. These are a *tythyn* or farmstead named as *Tythyn John David Vain* and its associated upland shepherding cottage. This upland cottage is referred to in a deed dated 26 October 1616, in which it is described as 'one cottage or turf house called *Lluest John David Vain ynhalken y bryn Rhydd*' (NLW Schedule of Glan Paith Documents, 2–3, No. 59). The location of the *lluest* is specified in its very name – *ynhalken y bryn Rhydd* – 'at the end of Bryn Rhudd' (Bryn Rhudd is a hill that overlooks Llanddewi Brefi village from the north-east). Although it is not possible to be certain of the exact position of the *lluest*, it is worth noting that only one long hut was recorded by the field survey at either end of Bryn Rhudd, and this is a strong candidate for the site.

The Glan Paith deed also gives an insight into the character of the dwelling at an early post-medieval *lluest* and concurs with the physical evidence of the long hut recorded on Bryn Rhudd, which is a single-celled structure with grassed over, drystone wall bases. The rest of the structure was presumably of timber, clay, and turf. A small ancillary cell is attached to the southern end of the long hut, but there are no other associated features. If this is indeed the site of the *lluest* built by David Vain, the absence of ancillary features requires explanation. Perhaps a short-lived *lluest* would not have required ancillary features and perhaps not all *lluest* sites developed into anything more that a single, temporarily occupied hut.

The relationship between *lluestau* and *tyddynod* is commonly referred to in documentary sources between the 16th and 18th centuries in the region. The location of *Tythyn John David Vain* is not known, but it is likely to have been a farmstead away from the parish commons, with the *lluest* serving as a shepherding station on the common. This relationship compares in some respects with the *hafod/hendre* model of transhumant practice, although limited to private holdings rather than communal grazing land. This model is supported by deeds dating to 1615, that indicate that lowland and valley floor farmsteads or *tyddynod* were in possession of *lluestau* on the parish uplands of Ysgubor y Coed, Ceredigion. In that year there is a reference to *tythyn ucha ymlaen Eignion* (probably the present farmstead of Blaeneinion) which held the dairy or summer-house called *lliest ymlaen Eignion* (NLW Harold Hughes Deeds, No. 27). The physical evidence for the latter is as yet unidentified and it is possibly hidden in the extensive forest block of the south-eastern corner of the parish.

Another early reference, dating to 1589, relates to a *lluest* on the ridge of Craig Twrch, Cynwyl Gaeo,

Carmarthenshire, named as *llyest morgan griffith ar kraig twrche*, the lluest of Morgan Griffith on Craig Twrch. This is defined in the document as a *domus lactearius or cottage, part of a tenement of Tir Erw Willim or Tir Owayn, Cynwil Gaeo*. The description of this *lluest* as a *domus lactearius* or dairy house is consistent with oral tradition in the Cambrian Mountain area that the *lluestau* of the uplands were places associated with milking sheep. However, this example is also described as a cottage and therefore a dwelling, and as belonging to a larger tenement or *tyddyn* the location of which is not given (NLW Index to Edwinsford Deeds and Documents I, 141, No. 879). There are several deserted rural settlements recorded on Craig Twrch, the identification of *llyest morgan griffith* is not possible at present.

The dwellings at *lluest* sites tend to be simple single-cell long huts, although this can vary. At Pen Cefndyrys (Fig 5.9) a division into two cells is apparent, with a step down from one room to the other, a feature more often associated with longhouses and possibly indicating that the dwelling included an animal byre. The material used in constructing these dwellings can also vary. At Pen Cefndyrys, low, grassy earthwork banks represent the dwelling, although the grass may cover a stone wall base. As the local bedrock is very slatey in nature, it seems likely that clay walling around a timber frame, set on a stone footing, would have been preferred. In areas where better building stone is available, it is likely that drystone walling would have been used. The aptly named Lluest y Cerrig, literally 'The Lluest of the Stones' (Fig 5.4), is a good example of such a site. The dwelling at Pen Cefndyrys is in a sheltered location in an upland stream valley and associated with evidence for cultivation within an adjacent enclosure, an ancillary building and several 'potato clamps' for storing root vegetables. Where such 'potato clamps' are found at upland settlements, a post-medieval date can be suggested. They are notable features at many 19th-century cottage sites and they were still used in upland areas well into the 20th century. They are also useful indicators of permanent occupation, as the need to store root vegetables over winter seems unlikely at seasonally occupied sites.

Immediately to the east of the area shown in the plan is an unenclosed, level terrace with further evidence for cultivation and a small sub-rectilinear building. Both the cultivation ridges and the building are thought likely to be associated with the isolated Pen Cefndyrys deserted settlement and suggest that the relatively favourable position of the south-west-facing terrace made some arable farming possible. Many *lluestau* had small areas of improved, cultivated ground associated with them. These were often enclosed and might have been used for crops such as potatoes or oats.

An opportunity to study a group of datable *lluestau* was provided by the Perfedd study area in Ceredigion. This focused on the area of the former commons of the Crown Manor of Perfedd in northern Cardiganshire. The area includes Pumlumon, one of the highest peaks in the region, and is characterised by high, open moor and mountain pasture with many craggy outcrops. More favourable pasture is located along the lower slopes and valley floor of the Rheidol Valley to the west. The historical legacy of the administration of these commons includes a cartographic survey (Fig 5.10) carried out in 1744 by Lewis Morris, then Deputy Steward of the Manor (Morris 1744). Morris's map and the accompanying manuscript, *An Account of the Lead and Silver Mines in the Kings Mannor called Cwmwd y Perveth* (Bick and Davies 1994, 16–19), show and name 48 *lluestau* (shepherding cottages) and other dwellings dotted across the manorial commons (see also Vaughan 1966). A number of these have now either been lost under the waters of Nantymoch Reservoir or obscured by forestry plantations. Some have been replaced by 19th-century farmsteads and remain in occupation. Of the sites identified, 22 were visited by the project (Table 5.5).

Morris recorded that, according to local tradition, the *lluestau* of the area were originally only occupied during the summer months. 'In this Mannor interspersed all over the Common there are small cottages which were originally summer houses for shepherds and have an inclosure of a few acres of ground annexed to them ... These cottages are called by the natives Lluestai to distinguish them from the freeholds' (Vaughan 1966, 257).

This evidence provides a snapshot of life on the hills in what is now an empty and remote corner of the region. However, in 1744 it was well populated and it may be postulated that the same may have been true of the uplands of the whole of the region. What is unclear is how old the *lluestau* of Perfedd were when Lewis Morris described them. They are plainly at least early post-medieval in origin and their seasonal occupation may point to roots in the medieval *hafod* tradition. The statement by Morris that the *lluestau* were originally seasonal shepherding stations suggests a continuity of use that might extend back to medieval

5.10 1744 Map of Perfedd by Lewis Morris (by permission of Llyfrgell Genedlaethol Cymru/The National Library of Wales)

times. It seems possible that the *lluestau* were originally associated with a form of transhumant farming and only later did some become the permanent homes for shepherding families.

It is not just the origins of the Perfedd *lluestau* that are of interest here, but also the timing of their demise. By coincidence, a second map was produced in 1794 by David Davies, one of Lewis Morris's successors as Crown Steward of Perfedd. Of the original 48 *lluestau* and cottage sites named by Morris, only thirteen remain. It is noticeable that these are the sites in the most accessible and sheltered locations. Clearly, life on the mountain pastures was becoming less tenable. The documentary and map sources do not account for this abandonment. Possible factors may have included climatic, economic or agrarian change. All three may have played a part. The generally poor climate of the

mid-18th century may have made life difficult on the slopes of Pumlumon (Caseldine 1990, 94) and it is possible that increased mining activity in the Ceredigion ore-field during the mid- to late 18th century may have drawn young men away to more rewarding work in local industries.

The presumed dwellings recorded at the sites visited during the survey were typically drystone, rectilinear structures. Most of the wall bases were less than 1m high. However, there were some variations of structural form. For example, at Lluest Nant y Clychau there was no trace of a substantial dwelling, only a small building platform associated with the faint traces of a small rectilinear structure set within a series of enclosures. The range of ancillary structures associated with the *lluest* settlements also showed some significant variations (Table 5.5).

Table 5.5 *Lluestau* and cottages visited in Perfedd

NGR	Name	Form/Condition	Ancillaries
SN75158560	Lluest Helfa Las	Drystone wall bases	Platform on opposite side of stream
SN75508580	Lluest y Cerrig	Drystone wall bases	Two small shelters; stone boundary wall
SN79318504	Nant yr Hydd	Drystone wall bases	Possible small pen or extension to dwelling
SN77688760	Lluest y Meinciau	Drystone wall bases	Enclosure; two shelters, one with two cells
SN77038671	Lluest Carreg Wreiddyn	Earth and drystone wall bases	Sheepfold complex; sheepwash in stream
SN74828466	Lluest Nant y Clychau	Earth and drystone wall bases on platform	Stone wall; enclosure bank
SN77438234	Lluest Nant Graeanog	Hollow; slight drystone wall bases	Lazy bed cultivation; boundary banks
SN79108380	Nant Nod	Built over	
SN78408270	Lluest Troedrhiw-wyddon	Built over	
SN79588917	Lluest Fawr Hengwm	Ruinous farmhouse	Ancillary buildings
SN80688905	Lluest y Graig	Drystone wall bases	Drystone enclosure
SN79758931	Lluest Fach Hengwm	Not located	Sheepfold (may overlie dwelling site)
SN78308906	Nant y Llyn	Ruinous drystone farmhouse	Ancillary buildings
SN77468808	Lluest Maesnant	Standing farmhouse	Modern ancillary buildings
SN80809033	Lluest Gelli Gogau	Ruinous drystone cottage	Ancillary building; sheepfold
SN69808472	Lluest Newydd	Drystone wall bases	Ancillary building; pen; garden
SN71838384	Lluest Thomas John Griffith	Ruinous drystone cottage	Ancillary building
SN71258283	Lluest Pencraig Ddu	Earth and drystone wall bases	Lazy bed cultivation; field enclosures
SN72998350	Lluest Glanydwr	Destroyed	Enclosure; possible lazy bed cultivation; shelter
SN72658610	Lluest Gwarygraig	Not located	
SN73108310	Bwlchystyllen	Ruinous farmhouse	Ancillary buildings
SN72678445	Syfrdrin	Ruinous farmhouse	Ancillary buildings

There are close parallels between the Perfedd *lluestau* and groups of deserted settlements in other parts of south-west Wales, particularly in the Black Mountain and Cwmystwyth study areas. Although these areas are not supported by such good documentary and carto-graphic evidence, the physical form of the dwellings and ancillary features that were recorded and the shel-tered locations are similar. It seems likely that such groups of sites had a similar function and period of use. As recently as the early 19th century, shepherds in the Preseli Mountains in Pembrokeshire were described as living in simple huts in the shelter of stream valleys around the mountain fringes: 'Numerous flocks are here constantly attended by shepherds … They reside in adjacent vales in self-erected huts, built of loose stones and covered with rushes; which also serve them as beds for their nightly repose: doors they have none, but when the keen blast and howling storm approach, a rush-clad hurdle set on end affords the wished for shelter' (Evans, 1804).

This scenario bears a marked similarity to the typical location and form of the Ceredigion *lluestau*. Likewise, in the hills of central Carmarthenshire long huts and ancillary structures are seen in the shelter of mountain stream valleys. Local oral history indicates that such settlements were the summer-houses of lowland farms, where family members would spend the summer tending stock on the commons. There-fore, although the term *lluest* is not commonly encountered in either Carmarthenshire or Pembrokeshire, historical and archaeological evidence suggest that a similar form of upland settlement was present during recent centuries in the hill areas of both counties.

By the mid-19th century the number of *lluestau* and other upland settlements throughout the region had declined. Across Ceredigion, late 19th-century Ordnance Survey maps show numerous rectilinear sheepfolds on the hills. The field survey indicated that many of these were originally settlement sites similar to the Perfedd *lluestau*. It seems that by the late 19th century their former use as dwellings had been forgotten and their ruinous walls reused by a new generation of shepherds to pen and shelter sheep.

It is suggested that the historic information about the Perfedd *lluestau* is, in some respects, a potential 'Rosetta Stone' for the study of deserted settlement in south-west Wales and beyond. Certainly, the dating of a group of deserted settlements, such as those described by Lewis Morris, to the 18th-century, with possible pre-18th century origins, is of great signifi-cance. It questions any assumption that the majority of deserted sites of the regional uplands are medieval *hafotai* and it demonstrates the complexity of the history and origin of upland settlements.

5.5.3 Deserted rural settlements in lowland south-west Wales during the post-medieval period

Much of the previous discussion has focused on deserted settlements in the regional uplands. The project also focused on the evidence for deserted settlement sites in a selection of lowland communities: Llansadwrn in Carmarthenshire, Troedyraur and Llangynllo in Ceredigion, and Eglwyswrw in Pembrokeshire (Fig 5.1). The information on settlement patterns within these study areas was supported by significant historic and cartographic information.

In the Eglwyswrw study area it was possible to identify an expansion in rural population during the post-medieval period with the Elizabethan antiquary, George Owen of Henllys, Pembrokeshire, proving a particularly valuable source. As Marcher Lord of Cemaes, Owen fought continuously to kept his feudal rights and maintained detailed records of his properties. The survival of a rent roll of properties in northern Pembrokeshire in 1592, known as 'The Extent of Cemaes' (Howells and Howells 1977), is particularly informative about the nature of settlement in the parish of Eglwyswrw. Furthermore, information on settlement and population is available from census returns made for the Privy Council by the Bishop of St David's in 1563, the Hearth Tax returns of 1670 (Howells 1987, 2–3), and later national census data.

The resulting data suggest a significant increase in population between the mid-16th century and the mid-19th century (Table 5.6). Although the figures can only be a rough guide to true population and household numbers, the steady rise in population must have implications for the post-medieval settlement pattern of the parish. If the population genuinely quadrupled between 1563 and 1670 there must have been a significant amount of new building taking place. A further doubling of the population between 1670 and 1801 would have had a similar impact on settlement. Presumably, a significant percentage of the settlement sites (and by implication, deserted settlement sites) in Eglwyswrw and other parishes in the region are likely to be of post-Elizabethan origin.

Table 5.6 Post-medieval population figures for Eglwyswrw

Year	Source	Households	Population
1563	Bishop's Census	11	48*
1592	Extent of Cemaes	31	134*
1670	Hearth Tax	48	209*
1801	Census	97	420*
1831	Census		563
1841	Census		560
1871	Census		490

*A model is provided by Howells which suggests that the number of households recorded in early post-medieval sources can be multiplied by 4.33 to give an approximate idea of the contemporary population (Howells 1987, 11).

Clearly, the landscape of south-west Wales was beginning to fill up during the early post-medieval period. The new homes are likely to have appeared on newly enclosed and farmed lands, perhaps utilising unenclosed lowland common or waste, significant areas of which would have remained in many lowland parishes at the time.

The 31 Eglwyswrw tenements that are listed in the *Extent* are generally described as being of 4, 8 or 12, or other multiples of 4, Welsh acres; the acre of the Welsh lawbooks is c. 1440 square yards, much smaller than the English acre (Jenkins 1982, 4–5). The names of many of these tenements are remarkably similar to those of the farmsteads of the parish in modern times (Table 5.7). Significantly, some names on the list represent holdings that survived until the 19th century, which are named in sources such as the 18th-century parish Land Tax returns or the later tithe survey, but which have since disappeared from the landscape (eg Esgair Wilym). However, fourteen of the 31 do not appear in any of the later records or maps consulted. Consequently, the actual geographical location of these 'missing' settlements is not known. These sites clearly have archaeological potential and might give an insight into the nature of settlement desertion in the parish.

The *Extent of Cemaes* demonstrates that a high proportion of the deserted settlement sites dotted throughout the lowland landscape represent a class of dwelling, the *tyddynod*, above that of the landless

labourer's cottage and earlier in origin than many such cottages shown on 18th- and 19th-century maps. Clearly, any understanding of changing rural settlement patterns must be dependent upon a consideration of a combination of such early historical records, later map evidence and archaeological information.

The field identification of more recently abandoned settlements is made easier by the existence of 19th-century tithe maps. In the parishes of Llansadwrn in Carmarthenshire and Troedyraur and Llangynllo in Ceredigion the field survey attempted to identify those dwelling sites that were depicted on the parish tithe maps dating to between 1839 and 1842 but not shown on the modern OS maps. The disappearance of these sites from the map evidence was presumably associated with a decline of the rural population from the 1840s onwards.

This decline in population during the late 19th century can also be identified historically and indeed it is well documented in the census returns for rural parishes in the region. It has already been shown that in Eglwyswrw the rural population continued to increase well into the early part of the 19th century. However, by the middle of the century the situation began to change. This trend is also reflected in Llansadwrn, where the census returns indicate that the population of the parish grew from 807 in 1801 to 1221 in 1831, an increase of over 50%. However, by 1891 it had dropped back down again to 849.

Presumably, many of the new houses built to accommodate the rising population had a very short lifespan and were subsequently abandoned.

The location of the new dwellings associated with the initial population increase is reflected in the evidence from the tithe maps of the mid-19th century. The new houses were built along roadsides, on marginal land and in the corners of fields. In some areas the landless poor attempted to squat on common land, an activity that was generally not tolerated. However, this was often the only option for the rural poor and it was often associated with the *tai unnos* tradition of squatters' cottages built in a single night. It is not always easy to identify genuine squatter settlements because records of their establishment are often difficult to locate. One example is found on the northern slopes of the Preseli Mountains, in Eglwyswrw parish. Here the parish tithe schedule of 1839 refers to a group of cottages, shown on the fringe of the parish commons on the accompanying tithe map, as 'Encroachments on the common',

indicating that they were illegal settlements.

The legitimate enclosure movement of the late 18th and early 19th centuries also provided new opportunities for settlement and agriculture as large areas of traditional common land were fenced in and improved. For example, the Llansadwrn parish tithe map of 1839 shows new farmsteads and cottages on what had been open mountain pasture some 40 years previously.

The cottages of the rising rural population (including those of small farmers, agricultural labourers, general labourers and practitioners of a variety of crafts and trades), were often poorly built. This factor is likely to influence the survival of settlement sites. Poorly built structures were much more likely to be swept away following desertion and often no surface evidence will survive of such cottages. In two of the study areas over 50% of the cottages shown on 19th-century parish tithe maps, but which had become deserted by the late 20th century, now have no obvious surface evidence (Table 5.8).

Table 5.7: Eglwyswrw tenements listed in the 1592 Extent of Cemaes and modern farmsteads

No.	Name in the Extent of Cemaes	Modern name	Description
1	Berllan	Berllan	In the tenure of David Gytto
2	Carnhean	Carnhuan	
3	Carnhean Ycha	Not known	Where John David formerly lived
4	Castell	Tyddyn Castell?	One of two tenements of Lewis Mathias
5	Castell	Not known	One of two tenements of Lewis Mathias
6	Coorte, The	Cwrt	Tenement
7	Esker Wilim	Not known	Where Rhys ap John ap Rhydderch lives (known as Cefen yr Esker in 1583)
8	Glangafran	Blaengafren?	Newly built tenement near Glangafran built by Eynon Llewellin Powell where he lives
9	Gweun y Givir	Not known	One tenement where William John lives
10	Yr Hendy, or Place y Llestrach	Not known	Messuage in decay (is this the old Manor House?)
11	Henllan Issa	Henllan Owen Isaf?	One tenement held by Miles Thomas
12	Henllan Owen	Henllan Owen Uchaf?	Where Richard James lives

13	Keven Diannell	Not known	John Mathias holds a tenement where he lives
14	Llannerch Fychan	Not known	One tenement where Lewis Morgan lives alias Place Llanerch Vychan
15	Melin Jordan	Felin Wrdan (ruin)	Held by Griffith ap Ievan
16	Tenement near Melin Jordan	Not known	One tenement near the mill where Rees and Phillip Lewis Phillip live
17	Nant Hean	Huan?	Tenement where Lewis ap Jevan lived
18	Tenement at Nanthean issa	Not known	One tenement where Owen Lewis lives
19	Tenement at Nanthean issa	Not known	Where Miles Thomas, clerk, lives
20	Tenement at Nantyrhelygen	Nantyrhelygen Isaf	One tenement where John Charles lives
21	Tenement at Nantyrhelygen	Nantyrhelygen Uchaf	One tenement where Robert Rhydderch lives
22	Tenement at Nantyrhelygen	Not known	One tenement where Rees James lives
23	Penkelly Vawr	Pengelli	Tenement where Thomas ap Rees lives
24	Tenment at Penkelly village	Not known	One of two tenements late in tenure of Mathew Jenkin
25	Tenement at Penkelly village	Not known	One of two tenements late in tenure of Mathew Jenkin
26	Penycoed	Penycoed	Where Griffith William Powell lives
27	Sighpant	Not known	Tenement where Phillip Mathias lives (near Esker Wilim)
28	Tenement at Treclyn	Treclyn	Land of James Lewis where he lives
29	Tenement at Treclyn	Treclyn	Land of Thomas Gytto where he lives
30	Trewilim Issa	Trewilim Isaf	
31	Trewilim Ycha	Trewilym Uchaf	

5.11 Abandoned cottage, Mynydd Llansadwrn, Carmarthenshire (photo: Paul Sambrook)

Table 5.8 Condition of deserted sites visited in Llansadwrn and Troedyraur and Llangynllo

Study area	No surface evidence	Slight earth-works	Reduced to wall bases	Badly ruined stone building	Well-pre-served stone building	Total sites visited
Llansadwrn	32 (53.5%)	10 (16.5%)	8 (13.5%)	6 (10%)	4 (6.5%)	60
Troedyraur/ Llangynllo	38 (58.5%)	9 (14%)	9 (14%)	3 (4.5%)	6 (9%)	65

Of the deserted cottages and farmsteads that survive within the modern farmed landscape, it is rare for buildings and features to survive in anything other than a fragmentary state unless they are located on small parcels of unimproved land. However, even at these sites the remains will often be simply wall bases or slight earthworks. In many cases the evidence will be similar to the remains of long huts in upland and marginal landscapes, suggesting similarity of building techniques and house styles. For example, some of the settlements that are known to have appeared on Mynydd Llansadwrn, Carmarthenshire, during the 1820s and were abandoned by the mid-20th century, now only survive as fragmentary ruins (Fig 5.11).

The survey that was undertaken in these lowland communities has demonstrated that in many cases historical evidence can provide a clear context for deserted settlement sites. Census returns and carto-graphic sources can often provide the names of the dwellings and even the names of those who once occu-pied them. It also demonstrated that many deserted sites were post-medieval or even 19th century in origin, occupation and abandonment, even though the surface evidence may be slight or non-existent. Unless this historical context is fully understood there is clearly a possibility that such sites will be mistaken for earlier medieval settlement.

5.6 Conclusions

The survey in south-west Wales has demonstrated the extent and varied nature of deserted rural settlements in terms of physical characteristics, chronology, func-tion, and condition. The term 'deserted rural settle-ment' encompasses a varied range of archaeological sites. However, they all serve to demonstrate human perseverance and ingenuity in attempting to master the environment, whether to farm the land or exploit its natural resources. These 'lost homes' indicate that settlement has been located in almost every part of our rural landscape over the past 1000 years. The resulting archaeological resource in south-west Wales is varied and rich. However, the process of interpreting the evidence and understanding has only begun with this regional survey.

When a site is identified in the field there is a temp-tation to apply an instant interpretation to it depending on its form and condition. For example, an empty building platform or the low wall bases of a long hut might be thought of as the remains of seasonal shelters of shepherds, perhaps a medieval *hafod* or an early post-medieval *lluest*. However, in some circumstances such a structure might just as easily be the former home of an early 19th-century squatter attempting to exist on the margins of settle-ment. It has been seen that many of these 19th-century structures often leave very little trace. Conversely, a deserted site with substantial, surviving standing walls might be thought of as the former home of a more recent inhabitant. However, such a site might have much earlier origins and might itself have originally been occupied only on a seasonal basis. For example, we have seen how many modern farmsteads in the Perfedd area were originally seasonal *lluestau*. There are often surface clues that might help interpret a site and the survey has also shown that there is a need for careful examination of some of the associated histor-ical and cartographical evidence. All of this might provide a context from which an interpretation can be made. However, there will be occasions where excava-tion may be the only way to provide supporting evidence.

More research, fieldwork and excavation may be required to allow future discussion to be based on fact rather than supposition. There is a need for the exca-vation of selected sites, representing the main site types identified in the field. This would provide much-needed dating evidence and would assist in a greater understanding of the dynamics of deserted settlements in terms of their origin, function, and abandonment. The deserted settlements of the region are a major archaeological resource, a significant monument type, and an integral element of the region's social, cultural, economic, and landscape history.

Section Two: General themes

6 RESULTS OF THE PROJECT EXCAVATIONS

By George Smith and David Thompson

6.1 Introduction

The initial pilot study report compiled by Gwynedd Archaeological Trust at the outset of the project in 1995 identified only seven deserted rural settlement sites (out of a possible total of a thousand sites recorded on the sites and monuments record) which had been excavated in north-west Wales. These sites were at Penmaenmawr (Griffiths 1954), Bodafon (Griffiths 1955), Cefn-y-fan (Hogg 1954), the Aber Valley (Butler, 1962), Hendai, Newborough Warren (Adams, 1973), Erw Wen (Kelly 1988) and Cefn Graeanog (Kelly 1982b), of which only the latter two were carried out under what might be termed 'modern conditions'. Excavation has, of course, also been carried out elsewhere in Wales, but has nevertheless been limited, with little interest being shown in sites of this type and period compared, for example, with prehistoric and Roman sites. Fox (1939) examined a number of platform houses on Gelligaer, Glamorgan, while a series of upland *hafodydd* were examined in Brenig in advance of the construction of a reservoir (Allen 1979); more recently Kissock (pers comm) has excavated sites on Cefn Drum and Evans has excavated a site at Llanerchaeron which comprised *inter alia* a rectangular structure with a beaten clay floor which yielded a 14th-century silver penny (Latham *et al* 2001). The building was surrounded by other remains including trackways and evidence for iron-working.

However, despite these recent initiatives, our understanding of such sites is still slight. Discussions concerning date, function and social status of the sites have tended to hinge on evidence from the (very limited) material culture discovered during the excavations, from documentary references, from analysis of site location (local land use and altitude), and relationship to known historical medieval townships. However, often few conclusions were reached regarding the type of settlement (temporary or permanent) represented, or its precise economic and social function.

The excavation programme described in this chapter was designed to support the Deserted Rural Settlement Survey Project by undertaking limited evaluation exercises at a small selection of sites; none were full-scale excavations. There were four aims: to provide a better understanding of the variety of structural types observed during the survey; to record the levels of survival of buried archaeological remains associated with the sites; to assess their vulnerability to damage from a range of land use threats; and to assess their potential for providing environmental evidence. Four sites were excavated in north-west Wales (by Gwynedd Archaeological Trust) and one in south-west Wales (by Cambria Archaeology) (Fig 6.1).

The sites investigated in north-west Wales were Ynys Ettws, previously identified as a typical *hafod* site in marginal, upland pasture; Gesail Gefarch, one of a scattered group of platforms in lowland pasture previously identified using historical documents as the home of the lord of the local township; Llystyn Ganol, largely buried below field clearance, thought to be one of the only surviving elements of a once extensive medieval settlement; Hafod Rhug Uchaf, a small long hut lying amidst a system of field walls, but much obscured by scrub encroachment. In south-west Wales the site investigated was Tro'r Derlwyn, an upland, farmstead complex in the Nant Garw Valley, Black Mountain, Carmarthenshire which was being actively eroded by a stream. Before excavation, detailed contour surveys were made of each site and its immediate vicinity. In addition, trials were made of different geoprospection techniques: magnetometry at Gesail Gyfarch and Tro'r Derlwyn; phosphate sampling at Llystyn Ganol; metal detection at Ynys Ettws, Gesail Gyfarch and Hafod Rhug Uchaf. At Tro'r Derlwyn purpose-flown aerial photography was carried out by RCAHMW, enabling the production of detailed rectified plots.

6.2 Ynys Ettws, Nant Peris, Gwynedd

6.2.1 Description and background

The site lies on a small shelf behind a knoll on the north-facing side of the Llanberis pass, historically an important route from Roman times on, just below the scree of the steeper valley sides and some 200m above the valley floor (Fig. 6.2). The settlement consists of two rectangular, stone-built buildings, both lying on a similar orientation, approximately north to south, and situated c. 50m apart (Fig 6.3). The two buildings had previously been thought to be contemporary (Crew 1979), although the visible remains are of somewhat different construction and have been subject to modification. The site was chosen for excavation since it has often been regarded as a classic example of medieval platform houses, the *hafodydd* dwellings used in conjunction with upland summer grazing (Lynch 1995, 159–60). The surrounding land shows signs of stone clearance, in the form of small cairns, but there are no boundary walls or enclosures of any description related to the buildings, although there are small springs nearby.

6.2.2 Excavation

One building was investigated (Fig 6.3, house 1). It was a rectangular structure, c. 10m by 6m overall, built on a terrace cut into, and perpendicular to, the hillslope, with a large 'hood' bank around the uphill end. Approximately 50% of the area of the building was excavated to subsoil levels in two opposing quadrants. The walls were left *in situ*, except in two trial sections where they were dismantled to study the structure and stratigraphy.

The work confirmed the original impression that there were two phases of construction, the earlier phase being obscured and largely destroyed by the later rebuilding (Fig 6.4). The later walls had been built on little more than the footings of the earlier walls, which must therefore have been entirely collapsed at that time. The footings of the walls of the earlier building showed as relatively neatly laid and aligned remnants beneath the irregular rebuilding work.

The earlier walls had delineated a single room measuring c. 8m by 3.8m internally, with an entrance in the centre of the (long) east side. In the middle of what was assumed to be the floor of the earlier phase there was a large heat-cracked flat slab, presumably for an open hearth. A small pit (pit 33), partly sealed under an inserted partition wall of the later building, probably belonged to this phase. It contained some charcoal of birch and oak, as well as hazelnut fragments, seeds of sheep's sorrel, dock, bramble, and fragments of burnt bone. This charcoal produced a radiocarbon determination of 780 +/- 70 BP (Beta–127671) with an intercept with the radiocarbon calibration curve of cal AD 1260. The range of this date fits with other dates received from the site and is taken to identify the period of the first phase of occupation of the house.

Above the scarp of the platform on which the building sat there was a hood bank of soil, presumably thrown up during the construction of the platform, supplemented (probably in the later phase) around part of its length by a stone-faced earth wall which was probably built as protection from the prevailing wind. These banks are regarded as characteristic of this type of building (Gresham 1954, 22) and are usually assumed to be designed to provide drainage, since such buildings are commonly built on hill slopes.

An excavated section through this revealed buried soil and a small pit, both containing charcoal of oak, birch, alder, and ash, suggesting a quite well-developed woodland in the area at the time when the hood was constructed. This charcoal produced a radiocarbon determination of 880 +/- 70 BP (Beta–127669), with an intercept with the calibration curve of cal AD 1175. The pollen analysis of the buried soil supports the above evidence, suggesting that hazel woodland dominated the immediate surroundings, with other tree species not far away.

In the second phase, the building consisted of a small, approximately square room, or cell, measuring 3.6m by 3m internally, built over the low remains of the north end of the earlier building. The remainder of the original building then appeared to have been used as a small annex or yard. The walls of this later building were quite haphazardly built, with no real attempt at regularity of layout or style of construction, and probably originally stood no more than c. 1m high; there was no evidence of a proper doorway.

The main internal feature of the room was a low wall of slabs that divided off the south-west corner and which showed discolouration and cracking from heat; these were interpreted as probable fire-bars for a raised corner fireplace. The floor of the room was partly thin,

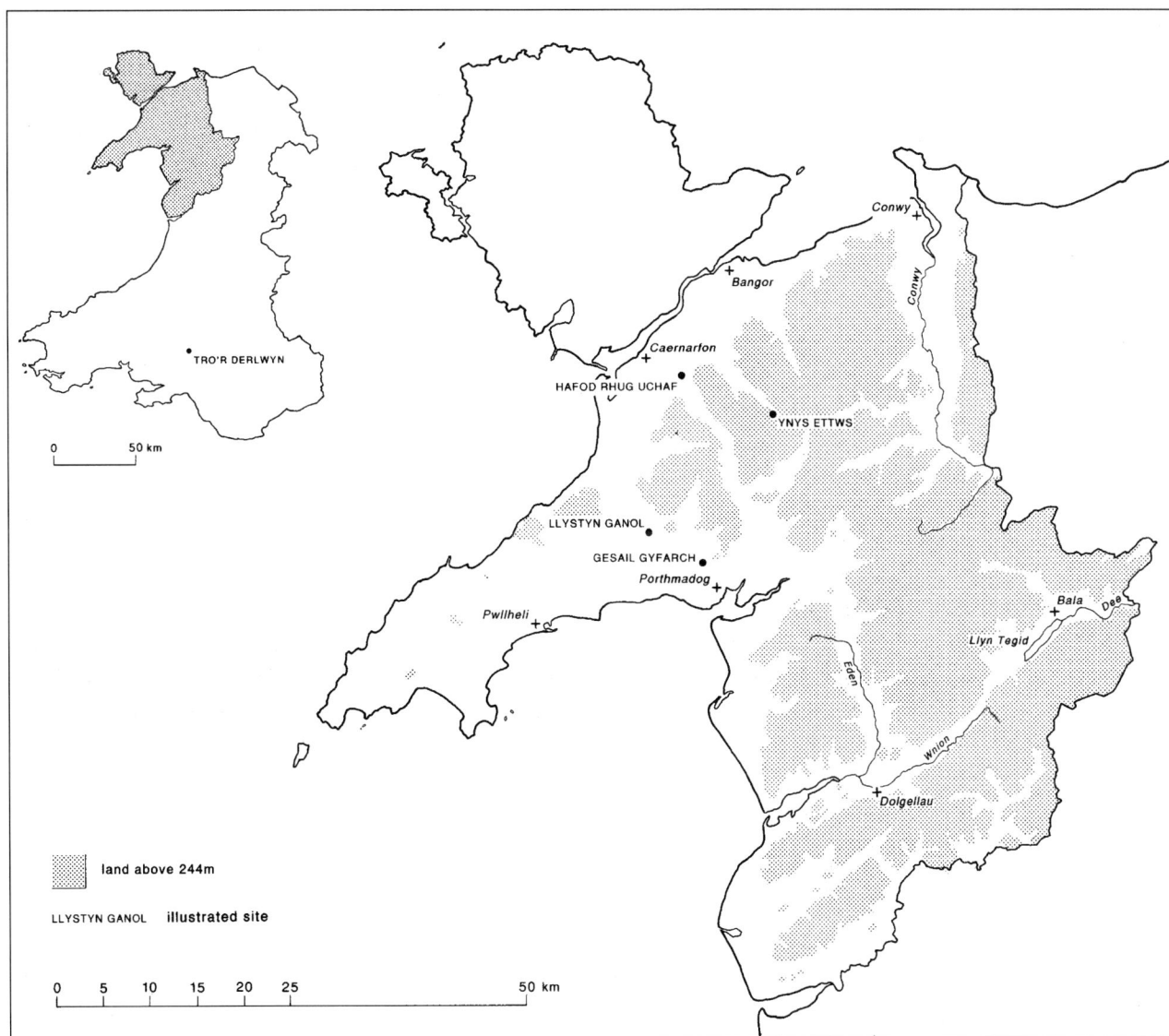

6.1 Project excavation site location map

randomly laid slabs and partly exposed ground rock. The innermost corner comprised a deliberately made recess in the north wall which was interpreted as possibly being for a bed. Removal of the floor slabs revealed a thin soil level with a scatter of birch and oak charcoal which produced a radiocarbon determination of 240 +/- 70 BP (Beta–127670) with an intercept with the calibration curve of cal AD 1655. This was taken to relate to the actual period of use of the second phase of the building.

The clay floor of the adjoining annex (or yard) of this period produced the only artefact from within the building that probably related to this phase of occupation – a single body sherd of brown-glazed earthenware of the mid-17th to 18th century (matching the range of the radiocarbon determination). Other finds included three ponyshoes, two pieces of waste lead and a copper alloy button (all found by metal detector in the topsoil),

as well as a flint blade (either mesolithic or neolithic), several worked stones, and a piece of worked wood.

Outside the building, a small test pit was excavated for the removal of a peat pollen column in a spring-fed, flat marshy area to the south of the house (Fig 6.3). This provided a complete environmental sequence which spanned from the time of the first occupation of the house to the present day (see Caseldine, 7.11 for details).

6.2.3 Discussion

There was no direct artefactual evidence for the date or function of the building in its earliest phase. Its location, the nearby small-scale clearance, and the absence of any enclosures for stock or cultivation suggest that, together with the adjacent building, it could have functioned as a *hafod*. Two nearby circular features may be bases for circular ricks to store fodder

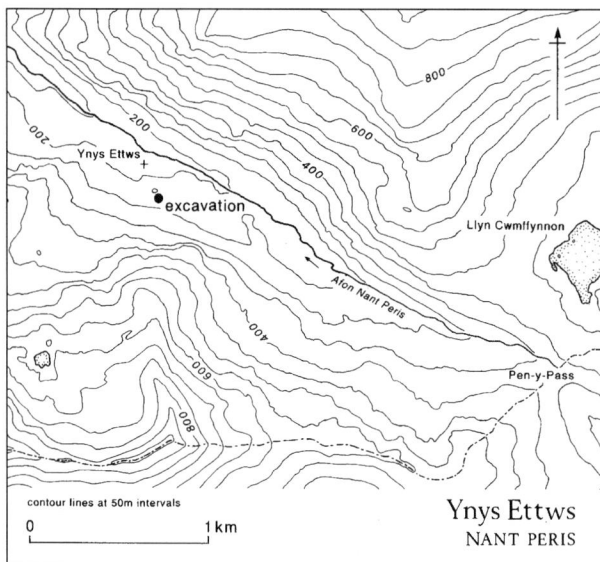

6.2 Ynys Ettws location map

or bedding, such as bracken. Alternatively (or even additionally), its siting, at the head of the pass which was an important route, historically, allows for the possibility that it was connected with a thriving pack-horse and drove trade.

The three radiocarbon determinations suggest construction possibly as early as the middle of the 11th century, and the environmental sequence from the spring basin implies use continuing until around the middle of the 17th century, when the area finally became the treeless upland that it is today. However, the paucity of archaeological evidence of activity tends to suggest that periods of occupation were short.

Usage may have lasted until around 1660 when it is possible, as happened elsewhere, that cooler and wetter weather made conditions less favourable for cultivation in the area and led to the abandonment of the site in its initial form. Some woodland had survived up until this time, providing shelter and a fuel resource, but now was apparently cleared, resulting in the very open landscape of today, and an intensification of pastoral activity followed.

The environmental evidence is very full and demonstrates the quality of information that can be retrieved from such a small and relatively shallow peat deposit. Its value lies in being a pool close to an inhabited building, which was therefore probably the recipient of the direct detritus of activity, such as crop-processing waste, cereals, and weeds of cultivation as well as fodder and wood. The evidence suggests that at the time the settlement was first occupied some birch and hazel woodland still persisted near to the site. Alder possibly grew in the valley below with perhaps the

occasional oak and ash. Cereal, notably oats, may have been grown not far away and was probably being processed at the site, although it is not clear whether it was for human or animal consumption. Gorse and holly may also have been used as fodder, in addition to crop-processing waste, and bracken as bedding. The question of whether occupation was seasonal, however, is unresolved.

The oak and birch charcoal shows that fuel wood was being used in the first phase and was easily available close by, to judge by the pollen evidence, in contrast to the treeless valley today. The hearth of the later building, however, produced no charcoal, suggesting that only peat was being burned (implying that that the landscape then was more like the present day). The interpretation of the stone-built corner feature is far from certain; if it was not a hearth, an alternative interpretation might be that of a fodder-rack, implying that the later building could have been an animal shelter, possibly a milking shed. The lead pieces, probably waste from smelting, are an unusual find, especially if associated with the earlier house, as the nearest lead mines are at Llanllyfni, 16 miles away.

The second phase of building was evidently much later than the first, as its walls were constructed on low ruins. If the 17th- to 18th-century date is correct for the later phase then a medieval date for the first phase house is quite likely. The small and ramshackle nature of the later building suggests impermanent occupation, possibly more appropriate to a single shepherd's or cowherd's shelter than a family *hafod*.

In his *Tour in Wales*, published in 1770, Thomas Pennant describes (Kirk 1998, 169) 'havodtai, or summer dairy houses', above Cwm Brwynog on the slopes of Snowdon. It is worth quoting his description at some length. 'These houses consist of a long, low room, with a hole at one end, to let out the smoke from the fire, which is made beneath. Their furniture is very simple: stones are the substitutes of stools; and the beds are of hay, ranged along the sides ... During summer, the men pass their time either in harvest work, or in tending the herds: the women in milking or in making butter and cheese. For their own use, they milk both ewes and goats. Towards winter, they descend to their *hen dref*, or old dwelling, where they lead, during winter, a vacant life.'

This description of a building could be applied to the remains of the first phase of occupation at Ynys Ettws. The earlier remains are of a single, rectangular room and there was no direct artefactual evidence, although the fire was placed at one end. However, during the second phase (which was dated to c. 1655, about a hundred years before Pennant's observations) the building became smaller and square in shape, with an attached annexe, perhaps occupied by a single shepherd rather than the classic *hafod* described by Pennant. As he only described a single building, however, it is entirely possible that there was a wide variety of building types in use in the uplands at this time (see Tro'r Derlwyn below).

6.3 Gesail Gyfarch, Penmorfa, Gwynedd

6.3.1 Description and background

The settlement at Gesail Gyfarch is located in a field of improved pasture at 170m OD on the side of a projecting spur of land between Penmorfa (the original head of a sea inlet) and Cwm Ystradllyn. It consists of a scattered group of three rectangular house platforms on a slightly sloping hillside with associated paddocks or enclosures, and covers several acres (Fig 6.5). Two recent 'shelter walls' had been built over it.

The site had previously been surveyed and described by Colin Gresham (1954), and identified as a high-status settlement, the seat of the lords of the township of Penyfed in the 14th century. The excavation concentrated on the largest platform in the complex, identified by Gresham as probably the site of the principal house of the settlement. This was therefore likely to be the house of the Lords of

Penyfed Township and specifically of Maredudd Ap Hywel, named in the Record of Caernarfon of 1352 (Gresham 1973, 80–2). His family supported the Lancastrian cause and Owain Glyndwr burned Gesail Gyfarch in 1403. The history of Gesail Gyfarch ('cosy nook' or 'sunny corner') is well documented and recorded extensively by Gresham (1954; 1973) and Gwynfor Jones (1990), and the association of a fairly complete settlement with documentary references gives the site great historical value. The settlement site survives because at a later date the house of Gesail Gyfarch was relocated to the south.

The site was chosen for excavation because of its high archaeological potential (especially with its documentary history) and because it was perceived to be at risk, from both large-scale land improvement and the actions of vehicles eroding the main platform. A

6.3 Ynys Ettws site plan

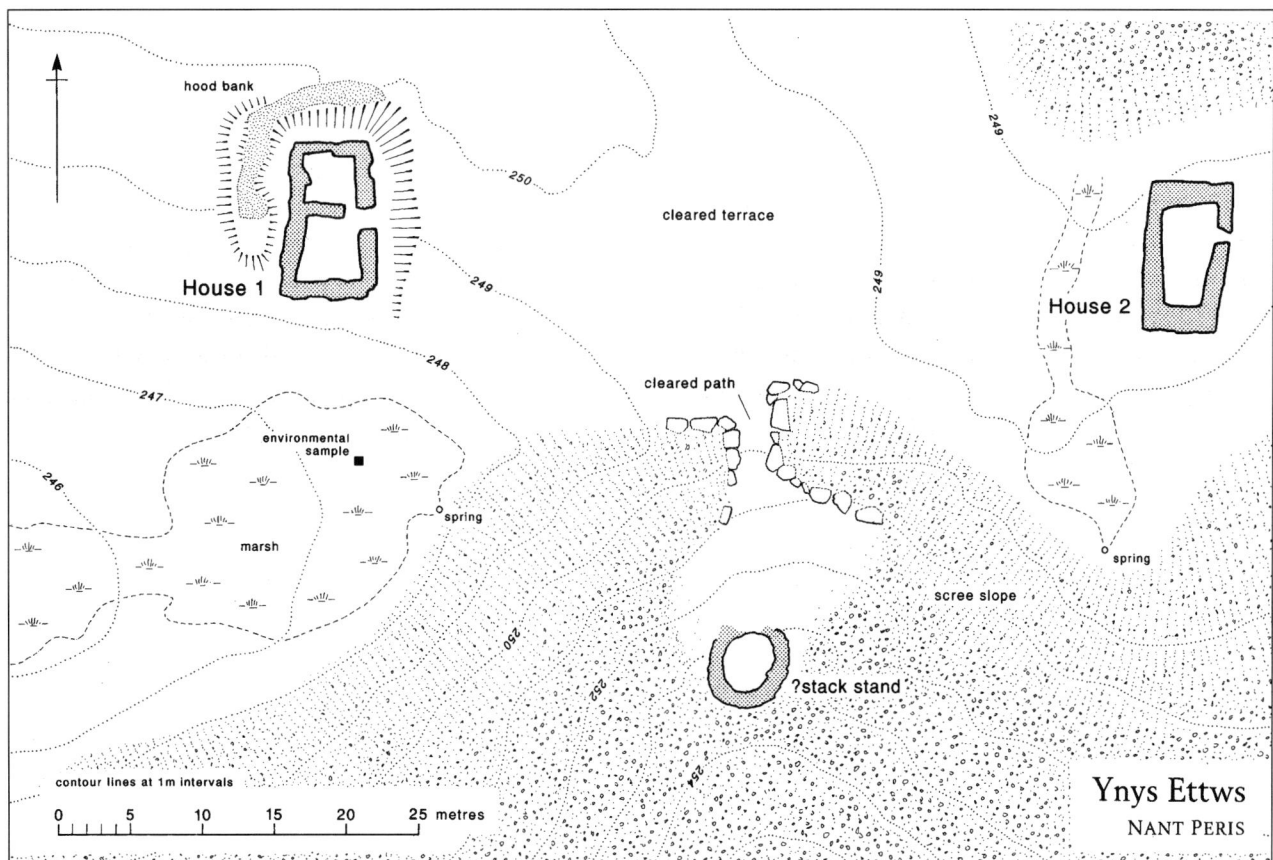

Ynys Ettws
NANT PERIS

Ynys Ettws
House 1

pit 32

later phase bank

hood bank

drainage gully

recess

bedrock

bedrock

bedrock

hearth
stone

fireplace

pit 33

doorway

excavated
to subsoil

later phase walling

limit of excavation

later walling removed

0   1   2   3   4   5   10   15 metres

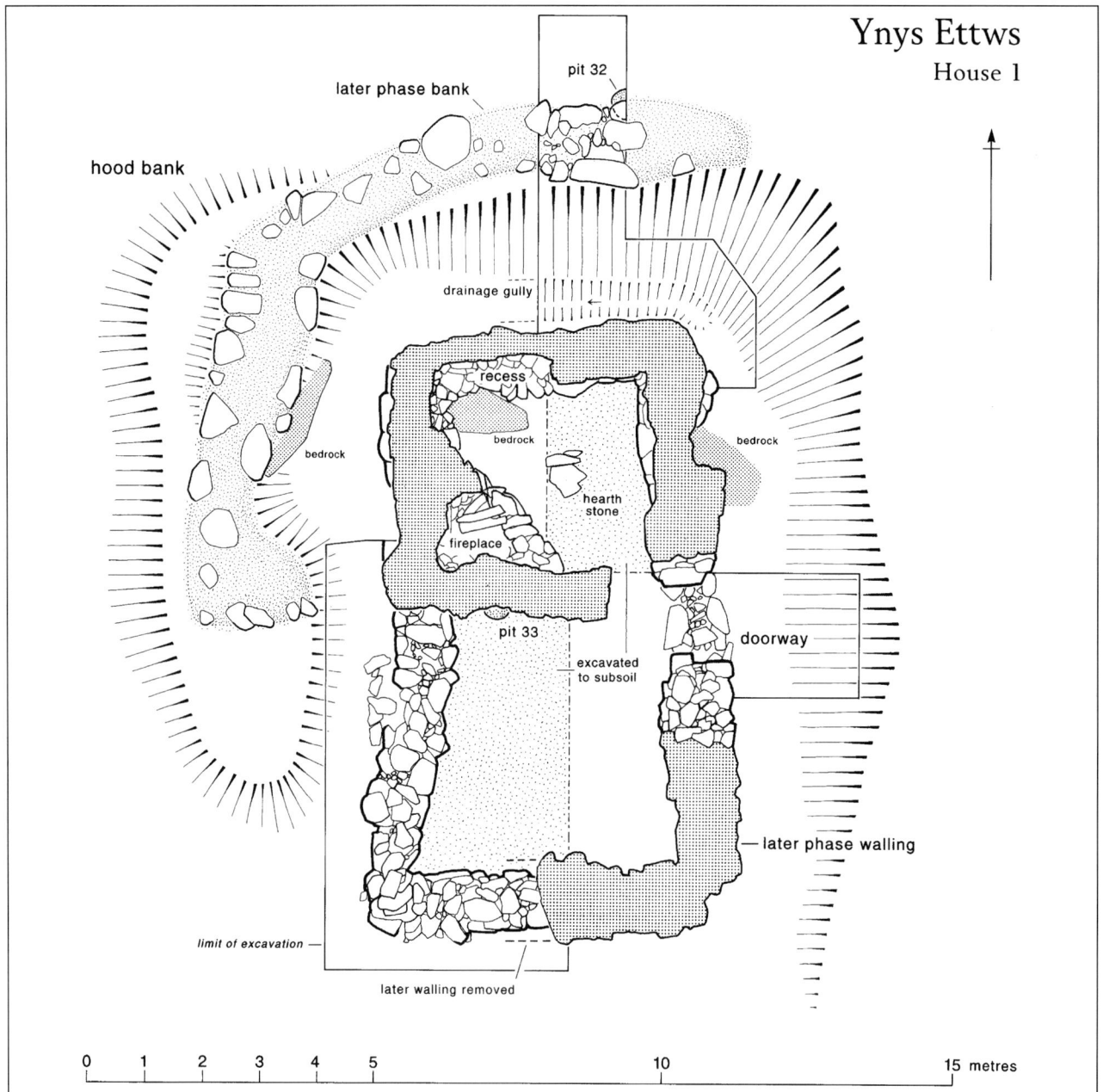

6.4 Ynys Ettws house 1 excavation plan

geophysical survey by fluxgate gradiometer was carried out over most of the site (Fig 6.6) which successfully identified all of the earthworks recorded by Gresham, as well as a series of 'negative' features and several areas considered to have archaeological potential.

6.3.2 Excavation

Three trenches were excavated. Trench 1 (Fig 6.5) investigated the putative house itself, another (trench 2) was put across a bank that formed one side of an enclosure around the house, while the third (trench 3) investigated a possible drain, downslope from the house, picked up by the geophysical survey.

Trench 1 initially covered c. 50% of the platform on which the building had stood. Part of the north-west wall of a building had been preserved below a modern shelter wall, but excavation found little other evidence of structural remains and efforts were concentrated on trying to establish the dimensions of the building. Due to lack of either footings or robber trenches it was concluded that the walls must have been built directly on the surface of the platform. A single stone-packed posthole, central to the width of the platform, was probably part of the structure, but no others were found. A culvert running parallel to (and outside) the east side of the house was interpreted as bringing a water supply to the house, probably from a spring uphill, since diverted.

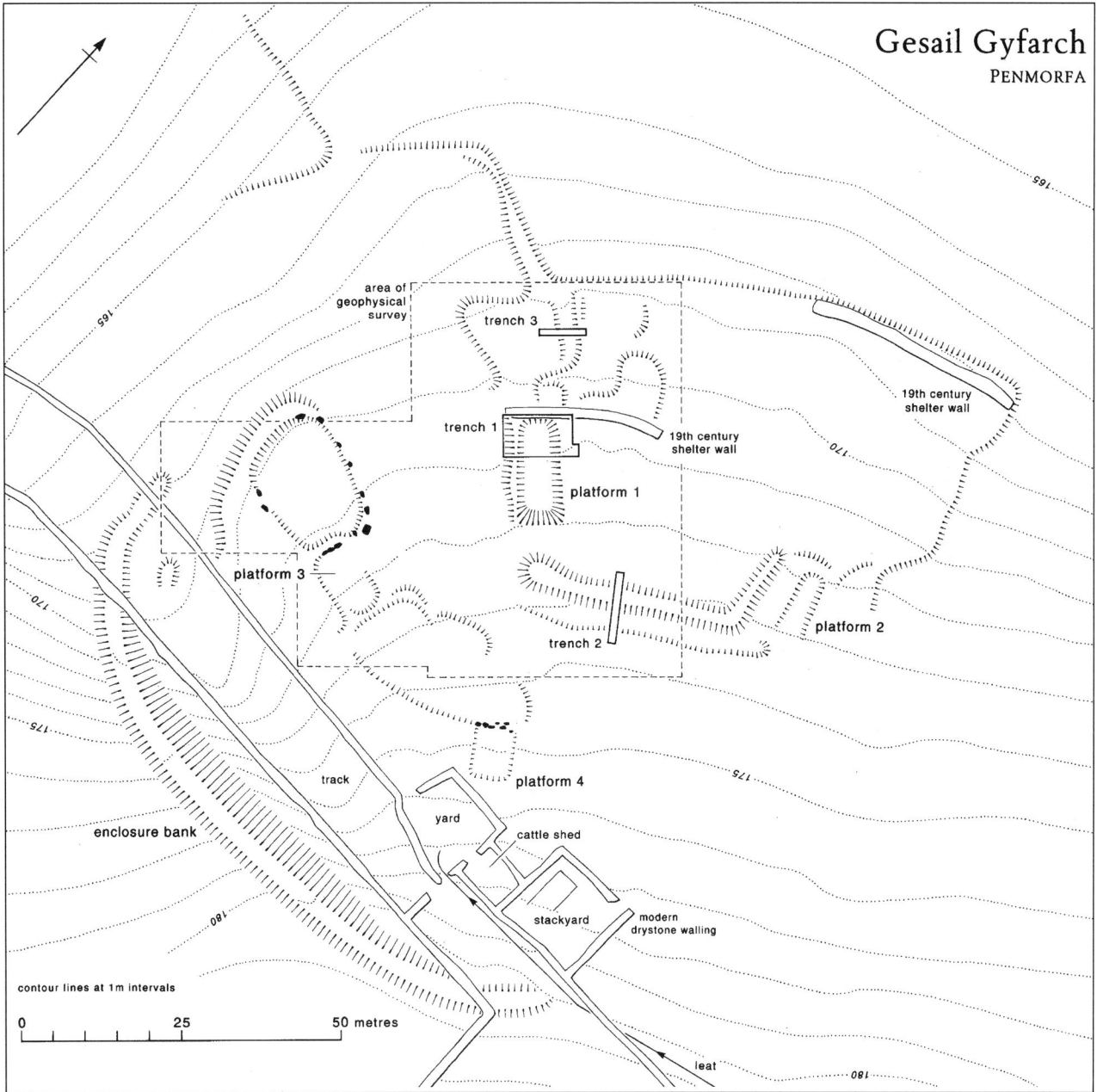

6.5 Gesail Gyfarch site plan

6.6 Geophysical survey of Gesail Gyfarch

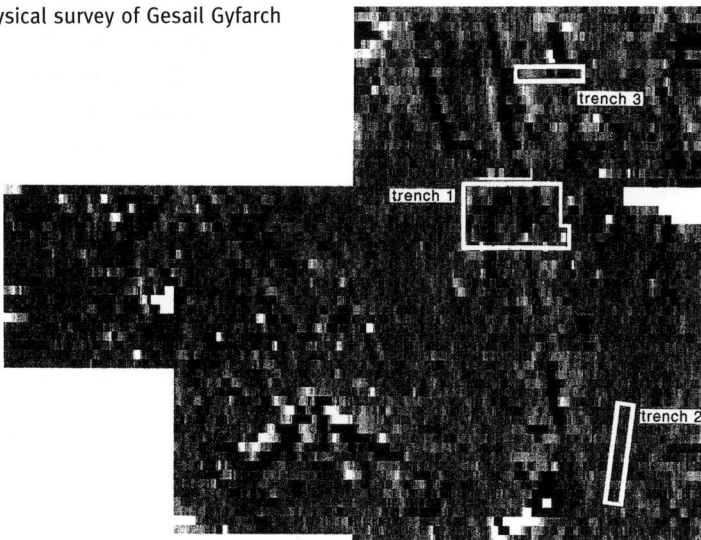

Several finds came from the topsoil, including medieval and post-medieval pottery, horseshoes, fragments of roofing slate, and several iron nails. The only sherd in context (the lower topsoil) was dated to the middle or second half of the 13th century, although five sherds (probably late 15th- or 16th-century in date) were retrieved from the stony surface spread which probably represents a demolition layer. The floor of the building contained three iron nails, while the top fill of the ditch produced one small fragment of pottery, probably intrusive. There were no other finds from earlier contexts. An absence of suitable contexts prevented any environmental samples being taken.

Trench 2 investigated the large hood or enclosure bank immediately uphill of the platform. This was found to be less substantial than had first appeared. A scatter of stones, probably eroded from the bank, contained a fragment of pottery of 14th- or 15th-century type, while the buried soil beneath the bank probably represented a thin, well-grazed turf or even ploughsoil.

The third trench investigated a linear feature identified by the geophysical survey. It proved to be a small ditch whose upper fill produced four iron objects (mainly nail heads and fragments) and one piece of medieval pottery, while the lower fill produced five iron objects, a fragment of roofing slate, and five pieces of pottery (again probably dating from the first half of the 14th century). The small part of a platform exposed in the west side of the ditch lacked any kind of stone structural evidence, suggesting that it had contained a yard rather than a building.

6.3.3 Discussion

The lack of structural evidence surviving from the building in trench 1 is surprising. This had been interpreted as a house of some status, and obviously had been of a considerable size with substantial walls (to judge by the portion surviving under the shelter wall). A contemporary account of a siege of the house c.1462–68 suggests the house was of half-timbered construction. The evidence serves to show that on sites like this, which survive as platforms in improved pasture, any buried remains are very vulnerable to damage by ploughing or tractor traffic.

The medieval origins of the building are confirmed by the pottery evidence, the earliest piece of which, in a secondary context above the building, is of mid- to late 13th-century date. The RCAHMW (1960) and Gresham (1954) both suggested that the probably 16th-century house adjoining the modern farmhouse was the direct successor to the platform house settlement. The two sherds of pottery from the demolition levels of the building would support this assumption, falling within the range of late 15th to early 17th century. It is possible that the platform building may have continued in use as an agricultural building.

Gresham's identification of this building as the principal house of the settlement because of its size might be supported by the probable presence of further rooms or wings at the north, downhill end. The present survey shows three platforms, of which at least two are probably for buildings. This is what we would expect of a high-status medieval hall, which would have had additional private and service rooms. The size of the other platforms in the settlement, by contrast, suggests single-roomed dwellings. In addition, this building occupies a central position in the settlement as a whole and the enclosure to the east of it, protected by the hood bank and ditch, seems to be associated with it. However, the hood bank seems to have functioned more as a drain than to delineate an enclosure since the bank stops abruptly at the west end (Fig 6.5).

The lack of dating and other interpretative evidence prevents satisfactory interpretation and is also surprising considering that the house may have been in use for up to three centuries. The pottery proves the medieval origins but there is no direct evidence about the function of the building and little about its construction. The ambiguities of the results at Gesail Gafarch illustrate the perils of predicating the interpretation of field survey on historical hypotheses. While Gresham saw this site as a small, loosely nucleated settlement of three or four houses, an alternative interpretation could be that the building, as the largest building of a manorial-type complex, might be a communal barn, not a house. The large enclosure could then be explained as a farmyard with another building (2) perhaps a subsidiary farm building. Platform 3, however, is detached with its own small yards, more like a typical platform house plan and could actually be the main house of the settlement.

The majority of sites that have produced medieval pottery in north Wales have royal, ecclesiastical or military connections and are close to the coast. Although the medieval assemblage from Gesail Gyfarch is small it is nevertheless noteworthy for providing evidence of rural domestic use of ceramics, albeit high status, and provides more evidence for the distribution of pottery probably made in Cheshire and north-eastern Wales.

6.4 Llystyn Ganol, Bryncir, Gwynedd

6.4.1 Description and background

The site lies on gently undulating land on a plateau at 145m OD (Fig 6.7). The surrounding area is mainly improved permanent pasture for cattle, with occasional patches of unimproved wet or stony land. The site is now an isolated building but was once possibly part of an extensive scattered settlement, now largely lost through the effects of land clearance. The settlement was considered to have particular interest for the likelihood of a continuation of occupation from a possible early medieval high-status site (Edwards and Lane 1988), built over the remains of the Roman auxiliary fort of Pen Llystyn close by. This is supported by some excavated evidence and the presence of a 6th-century memorial stone inscribed in both Latin and Ogam on the next farm to the north.

The building survived as a levelled platform (Fig 6.8), with some boulder wall-facing exposed at the downhill end, while the rest of the structure was buried under a mass of dumped field clearance stones (responsible for its survival). There were very tenuous remains of a possible platform or yard at the east end of the house which did not show up in the contour survey. The modern field also contained the remnants of an earlier field system, as well as much-disturbed and obscured remains of other rectangular structures just to the north of the house (Fig. 6.7).

6.4.2 Excavation

The area of the building available for excavation was limited by the quantity of field clearance stone covering it. The building lay at right angles to the slope and was shown by excavation to be rectangular, c. 9m by 3.5m internally. The walls were mainly of laid-slab construction with occasional orthostatic slabs. It was built on a platform cut into the natural slope, but modern ploughing had encroached on it and it was not possible to say whether there had been a hood

6.7 Llystyn Ganol site plan

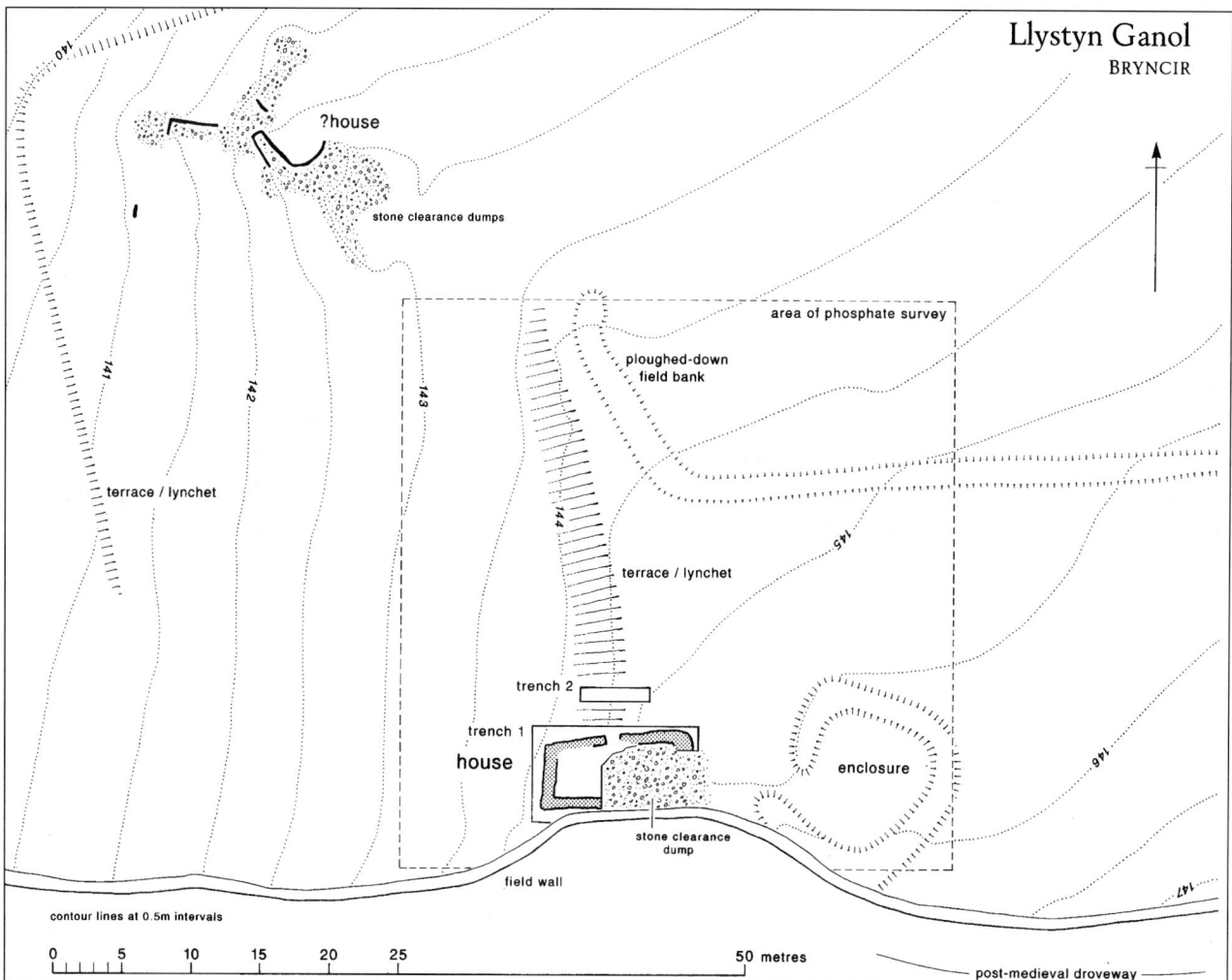

Llystyn Ganol
BRYNCIR

?house

stone clearance dumps

area of phosphate survey

ploughed-down
field bank

terrace / lynchet

terrace / lynchet

trench 2

trench 1

house

enclosure

stone clearance
dump

field wall

contour lines at 0.5m intervals

0   5   10   15   20   25   50 metres

post-medieval droveway

bank. The excavation was accompanied by a soil phosphate survey, the results of which showed some clear patterning which aided interpretation.

Below the dump of clearance rubble was a floor surface of roughly laid cobbles (Fig 6.8) which continued into a doorway (which had probably been widened later) placed roughly centrally in the (long) north side. Removal of part of the floor deposit revealed only a floor foundation of rather larger stones, suggesting that there were no earlier buried floor levels. The walls were neatly built and faced although not deeply founded, simply footed upon the glacial till, not set into it. Two small areas outside the house walls were excavated down to subsoil levels, showing no substantial depth of stratigraphy.

Trench 2 (Fig 6.7) investigated a terrace that ran up to the side wall of the house. This appeared to form part of a more extensive field system and, although excavation showed it to be a natural rocky scarp, the topographic survey suggests it nevertheless did form part of a probable early field system. The house platform was cut into the face of this scarp, rather than being built against it.

Beyond the east end of the house there were slight earthwork traces of a relatively level platform or yard area. This area was sampled for phosphates and the results identified increased levels for which the most likely explanation was that it was used for animal corralling. Phosphate samples taken from the floor in the exposed part of the house were inconclusive.

The field containing the platform house seems to have been comprehensively cleared in the early 19th century. There is no record of a building here on the OS 25 inch map of 1889. The land is permanent pasture but ploughed and reseeded from time to time,

and stone clearance takes place at every such ploughing. The rubble on the building contained 19th- to early 20th-century objects (a draft-horseshoe and cream-glazed tableware) and lay directly on the floor of the house. The only other artefacts (a piece of cream-glazed tableware, a fragment of roofing slate, a piece of horseshoe and a bead of man-made imitation jet) came from the floor of the house and were effectively unstratified. The pottery was dated to the late 18th or early 19th century. Nothing was found in the floor itself or in the sub-floor levels. No environmental or charcoal samples were taken because no suitable contexts were identified.

6.4.3 Discussion
This building is rather different to those investigated at Ynys Ettws and Gesail Gyfarch, in terms of size, construction and preservation. The small size of the doorway and lack of internal drains suggest that it was constructed as a domestic building, although the possible widening of the doorway might indicate reuse as a cattle shed. If there were a central open hearth this would, according to normal custom, have been at the uphill end and so would still be hidden below the dumped stone. The building appears to have been robbed out to near-foundation level when the dumping of fieldstones began, which suggests that it pre-dates the 19th-century improvement phase. It seems likely that the building is a house of broadly medieval date, but with no artefactual evidence this interpretation is based solely on the way in which it has been constructed. The presence of post-medieval artefacts on the floor of the house suggests that it continued in use in some form until at least the late 18th century.

6.5 Hafod Rhug Uchaf, Waunfawr, Gwynedd

6.5.1 Description and background
The site lies at an altitude of c. 175m OD on the seaward-facing slopes above Caernarfon. It is situated on a natural terrace that contains a glacial boulder field, just below which a small spring exits. The surrounding farmland consists of a small area of improved pasture amongst a larger area of semi–improved pasture and rough grazing. The site (Fig 6.9) consists of the foundations of a rectangular building, 10m by 5m internally, lying approximately north-east to south-west, parallel to the contour, around which are several other features including a terraced area to the south-west, the remains of an

earlier field system defined by 'wandering walls' and slight terraces, an area of cleared land, and a number of platforms defined by banks and scarps. At the west side of the area a small spring exits into a boggy area and this water supply probably determined the location of the settlement.

The site was obscured by dense blackthorn and scrub vegetation. The objectives of the excavation were first, to identify the function and dating of the structure, and second, to determine the long-term effects of the scrub growth on the structure and the buried stratigraphy. This was seen as having wider relevance because of changes in farming practices

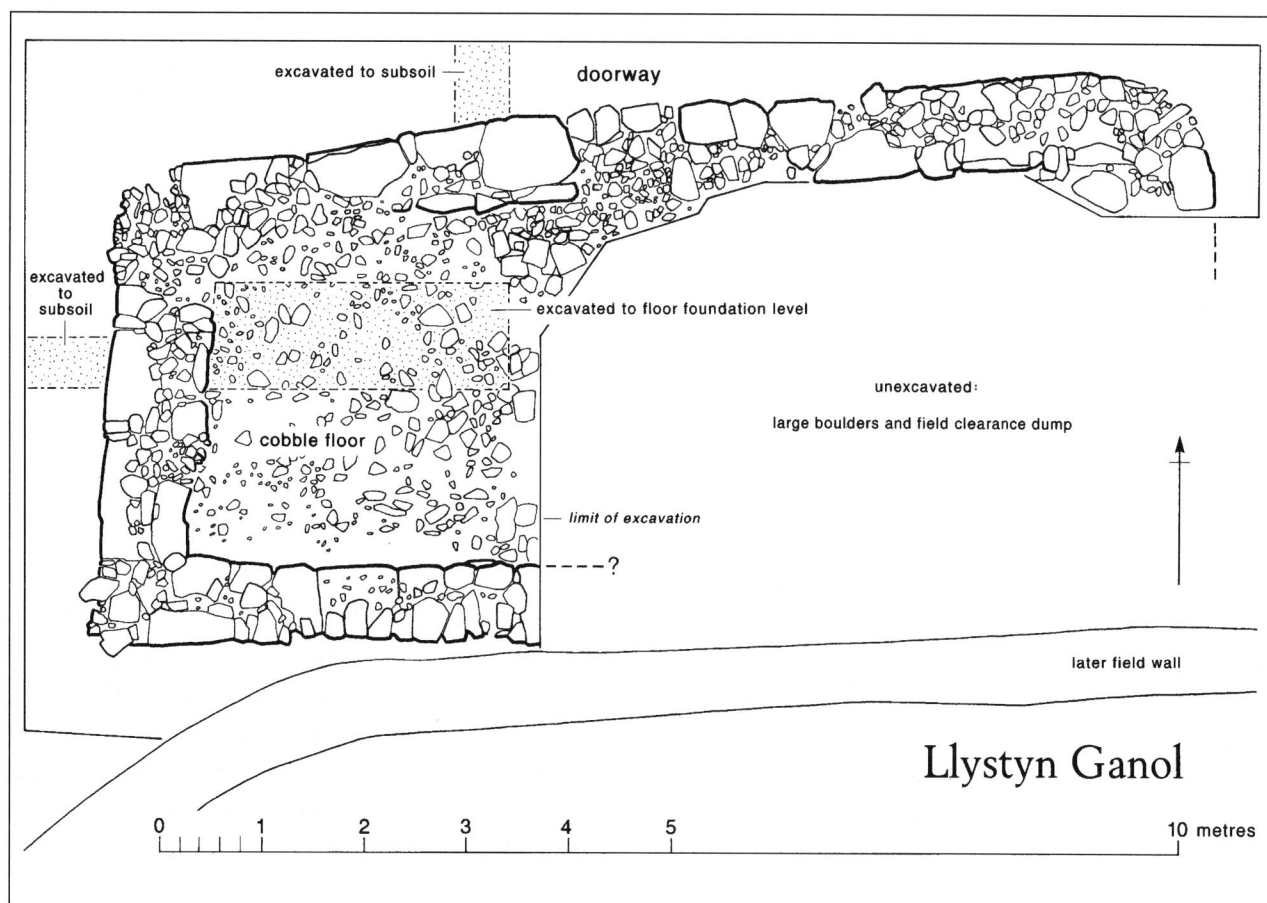

6.8 Llystyn Ganol excavation plan

resulting in lowered grazing pressure on areas of rough pasture where many monuments survive, leading to the growth of bracken, scrub, and sometimes woodland.

6.5.2 Excavation

Three trenches were excavated (Fig 6.9). Trench 1 examined the entire area of the house, defined by the low remains of three walls, all of drystone construction (with two earth-fast boulders included in the line of the east wall). Clearance of the small amount of overlying soil below the trees, bracken, and stones produced a few pieces of 19th- and 20th-century pottery and metalwork. It appeared that the building had been dismantled before it had become ruinous. A gap in the western wall was clearly an entrance, but an explanation for an apparently similar gap in the eastern wall (originally thought to represent an opposing entrance) could not be established.

The building (Fig 6.10) had a wide internal stone-built partition, with a gap at its western end containing the threshold stones of a doorway, which divided it into two rooms. The northern one was the largest and had a boulder slab floor of which the largest and best-laid stones formed that part lying across the central area in line with the doorway and along the central line of the room. Against the northern end wall was a line of large, loose boulders which was interpreted as an internal feature, such as a bench or low shelf support. There were no areas of burning or other indication to suggest that there had been a hearth of any kind in this room. A cutting was made at the south-east (up hill) side and it was established that, at this point, the building had been laid directly onto a buried soil and so must have been utilising an existing natural terrace. The buried soil was sampled for environmental information.

The only finds securely associated with this room came from the crevices between the floor slabs. These were a single piece of clay tobacco pipe stem, two pieces of pottery (dating from the late 17th or 18th centuries), and an iron fragment.

The smaller, southern, room had a floor of large flat sub-angular slabs, similar to those in the north room, which overlaid a lower but similar floor, a continuation of the one revealed in the north room. It also showed that the partition wall was built directly onto this earlier floor, so that the building must originally

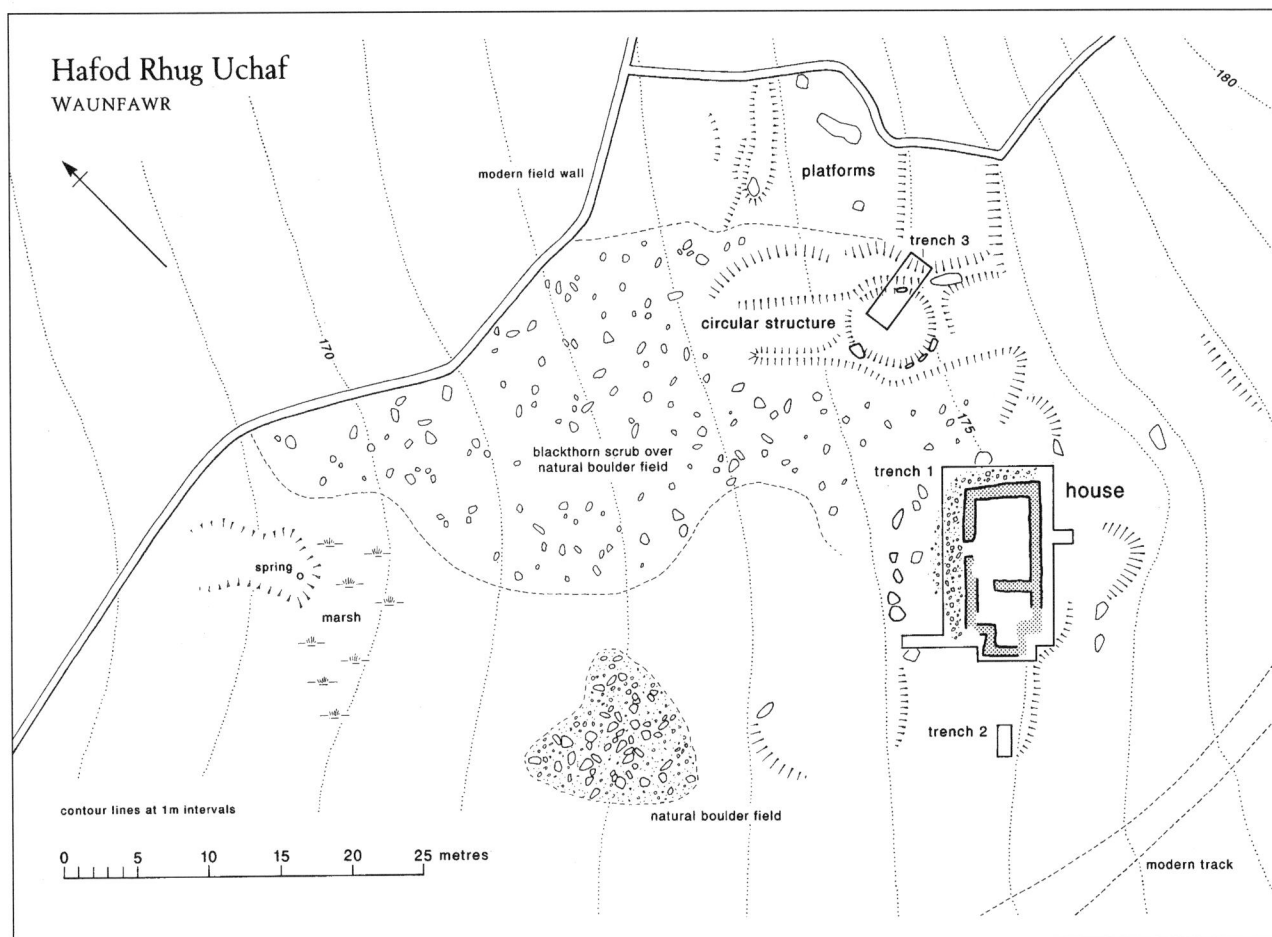

6.9 Hafod Rhug Uchaf site plan

have consisted of a single room. In the south end-wall of this room, which had been almost entirely robbed away, there had been a recessed hearth and attached end-chimney. The chimney structure lay entirely outside the line of the end wall and independent from it, providing a narrow fireplace. This kind of arrangement is relatively rare in post-medieval cottages in Gwynedd where the normal plan is of a fireplace and chimney set in a thickened end wall, or of a room-wide partitioned-off part of the room (RCAHMW 1964, clxxiv). An external chimney could easily have been added as a later feature to a building which originally had a central hearth, although there was no evidence that the end wall of the house had been removed to create the fireplace and there was also no sign of an open hearth within the floor of the original single-roomed house (although not all of this was exposed and it is possible that such a hearth could have remained hidden below the later partition wall).

Two small extensions to trench 1 were cut outside the building (Fig 6.9). The western extension exposed part of the possible small yard around the entrance to the house, defined by a line of large boulders. Its surface was very uneven, but surprisingly there was no build up of rubbish layers and there were no finds at all from this area. The north end of the house was shown to have been built into a mass of large protruding ground rocks, while outside the south side there was an approximately level terraced area which had a surface of small stones, probably deliberately laid cobbling. Trench 2, to the south, also exposed this surface and showed a low stony bank, parallel to the south end of the house, which probably formed a boundary to the yard area.

Trench 3 (Fig 6.9) was cut across a circular earthwork feature north of the building. It proved to be a structure with a wall and floor, and produced three flint flakes and numerous fragments of iron slag, mainly tap slag but including two pieces of furnace lining, which are probably associated with post-medieval activity, suggesting that the circular structure was contemporary with the building excavated in trench 1. The presence of the iron smelting material seems out of place here and it seems more likely that the material had been brought in as a soil improver, perhaps an early mineral fertiliser.

Pollen from four samples in trenches 1 and 3 are similar and suggest that both the house and circular structure were established in a predominantly open, grassland environment, probably representing rough grazing, with alder, hazel scrub, and some heathland in the area. This would support the theory that they were broadly contemporary. There was also some limited evidence for cereal cultivation represented by the occasional *Cerealia* type pollen.

6.5.3 Discussion

The building was entirely stone-built, not clay- or turf-built on stone footings, using local glacial boulders laid without mortar. An unusual feature of the construction is that the foundation stones were deliberately laid in such a way as to provide a level platform on which the upper walls could be built. This contrasts with the usual method seen in surviving local buildings where the larger foundation stones interlock with the stones of the main walls.

The house was initially a single large room built parallel to the contour, a style regarded as a post-medieval feature of construction, in contrast to the 'platform houses' of presumed medieval date that are typically aligned at right angles to the slope (RCAHMW 1964, clxxvi). The end fireplace was in use in the first identified phase, but its design suggests that it was an addition to the original plan because the projecting end fireplace plan is uncommon amongst local cottages. Smith says that, in Wales, sub-medieval houses with fireplaces began to replace hall houses from c. 1560 (1988, 172) and that in Snowdonia the type was dominant before the end of the 17th century (ibid, 174). The original house may therefore have had an open fireplace. However, this does not necessarily suggest a medieval origin for the house, since such fireplaces were recorded as still in use in the 18th century, for instance at the reused medieval houses at Aber, Caernarfonshire (Butler 1962). In its next phase the house was subdivided, with the smaller room having a raised floor, probably for drainage purposes. The smaller room contained the fireplace and must have been just the cooking area. The lack of slate debris suggests that the roof would probably have been of thatch.

The house appears to have provided the focus of a small farmstead, which may have had two barns or sheds set on platforms to the north. The house was built at some time prior to the date shown by the 17th to 18th-century pottery on its floor but its style of construction, parallel to the contours, suggests that it was post-medieval, since dated 13th-century houses like those of Ynys Ettws and Gesail Gyfarch (see above) or Graeanog (Kelly 1982) are typically perpendicular to the contours with upslope hood banks.

6.6 Tro'r Derlwyn, Black Mountain, Carmarthenshire

6.6.1 Description and background

The site lies on common land in the Nant Garw Valley, at the south-western edge of the Black Mountain, Carmarthenshire, at an altitude of 250m OD. It is one of many deserted settlement sites ascribed to the late medieval/post-medieval period in the valley. The complex consists of a core structure comprising three cells with an outer 'enclosure' or annex; a number of ancillary structures, possibly pens; and a series of putative 'field' or 'cultivation' plots. The north-western part of the core structure was under threat from river erosion (Fig 6.11). The surrounding land is now used for rough grazing of sheep, cows, and horses.

Sites in the Garw Valley were first mapped by RCAHMW (Leighton 1998), subsequently by Morgan (1988) and Ward (1991; 1995). Ward (1995) was responsible for producing the first description of the site, which was accompanied by a sketch plan. In discussing the site, he drew attention to its complex nature, compared to other deserted settlements in the valley. He proposed a constructional sequence for the core dwelling complex and suggested that the modifications represented a seasonal outstation subsequently used for over-wintering – an incipient, but failed farmstead.

6.6.2 Excavation

The core structure (Fig 6.12) is unlike any of the sites excavated in Gwynedd, all of which had the appearance of a 'standard' rectangular building, often associated with other, related, structures. This site is irregular in plan and more difficult to interpret, and comprises three main interconnected cells (the term 'cell', rather than 'room', is used throughout, as there is no evidence that all elements were roofed or always inhabited), of varying shapes and sizes, with an annex to the south, located on the edge of a stream. The north-west part of the site had already been eroded away by the stream.

The three main cells were excavated to uppermost occupation level with partial investigation below this. Part of the interior of the adjoining annex on the southern side was excavated down to the subsoil and

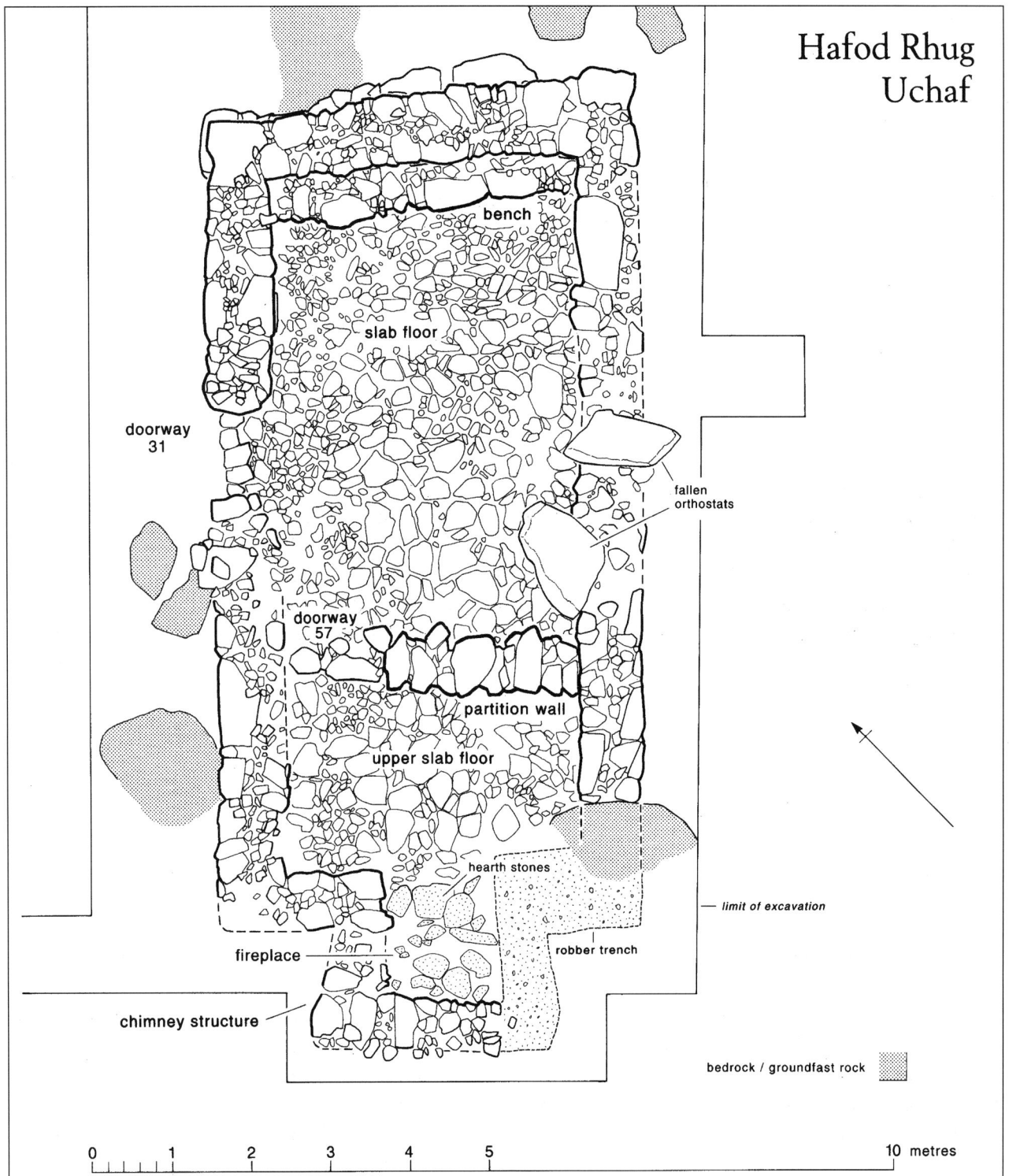

Hafod Rhug Uchaf

bench

slab floor

doorway 31

fallen orthostats

doorway 57

partition wall

upper slab floor

hearth stones

— limit of excavation

fireplace

robber trench

chimney structure

bedrock / groundfast rock

0   1   2   3   4   5   10 metres

6.10 Hafod Rhug Uchaf excavation plan

a trial trench was excavated into a boggy area at its western end for environmental sampling. Environmental samples were taken from key deposits during and after the excavation.

The north cell was rectangular, measuring 4.6 x 2m internally. The lower part of the walls was apparently soil or turf-bonded and the upper parts of the walls appeared to have been rebuilt with crude drystone walling. The cell was floored with rough flagstones, except at the northern end. The interior had been disturbed by later activity down to floor level. Towards the southern end of the eastern wall there was a possible blocked doorway or low window and in the south-east corner there were some indications of a hearth. A whetstone (simple in form and not diagnostic) was found lodged on the interior face of the eastern wall, probably having been placed there rather than being built into the wall. A small test trench, excavated externally on the east side of the cell, confirmed that the east wall was partially a retaining wall.

The south cell was not fully excavated. The interior was a maximum of 7m long by 3.2m wide, with a curved south-western corner. It had three openings, one into the southern enclosure and two others into the other cells. The low walls appeared to be constructed upon an artificial deposit. The earthen floor surface sloped quite steeply up from the southern entrance for roughly half the length of the cell, before levelling out. A number of flat stones appeared to have been deliberately placed on the surface to form a stepping-stone path. A deposit of charcoal was taken from below one of these, and a small fragment of clay pipe was recovered from just below the surface of this layer (see below).

Most of the interior of the east cell which measured 9.6 by 6.4m internally, had been cut into the hillside. The low walls were clay-bonded. The only possible entrance was from the south cell. There was no evidence of any internal activity or occupation build-up. The interior surface of the cell sloped slightly from the east down to the west. A single object, in poor condition and comprised mostly of very thin copper alloy with two conical and pierced knobs, one of which had a surviving pin, was found here and interpreted as a reflector for a lamp or candle.

Immediately to the south of the southern cell was an enclosed area, very roughly triangular in shape, with sides approximately 13m long. The northern boundary of this annex was formed by the south cell and probably, originally, by the stream. A small excavation here produced no useful information.

Environmental samples were taken from the walls, and the occupation and lower layers of the building complex. A monolith sample was taken for pollen analysis from the peat and silt deposits at the west end of the enclosure wall and a further augured sample was taken from a nearby bog. In addition, eight locations around the complex were sampled for phosphates.

Beyond the central complex, two trenches and a test pit were dug in an area containing a complex of linear features and cleared areas, 40m to the south-east of the main structure (Fig 6.11). The trenches were cut across field banks which were revealed as linear piles of stone (clearance or consumption walls). The test pit indicated very shallow and poor soil. There were no surface indications of cultivation beds and ploughing would have

been very difficult, given the stony nature of the soil. Aerial photography may have identified a building in the south-east corner of this complex, but nothing is visible on the ground. Two further trial trenches were excavated across the apparent boundaries of a further enclosure just to the north-east, and these were again interpreted as having been created from clearance.

Two groups of structures were recorded on the hillside 25m to the north-east of the core structure and just beyond the terrace. The southernmost of these consisted of a cluster of five sub-circular cells, each roughly 3m in diameter. None of these was investigated.

6.6.3 Discussion

The site of the core structure was obviously chosen to be as close to the stream as possible, presumably due to the need to water stock, and also possibly for dairy production. Although no doorways survive from the building on the streamside it is probable that one existed, as most of the similar but simpler structures elsewhere in the valley have access on their streamside.

Considerable effort had been expended in creating an artificial terrace on which the north cell was built. The southern cell appeared to have been constructed over a hollow area which had been levelled up before the walls were built. The hollow may have been the result of stock being held in an enclosure pre-dating the southern cell, and possibly contemporary with the northern cell. Calibrated dates from the charcoal sample taken from beneath the stepping stone path were cal AD 1475–1685, cal AD 1740–1810 and cal AD 1930–50 (Baa –122921) at 95% probability. The presence of the clay pipe fragment suggests that the middle date of 1740–1810 is the best match. Unfortunately, the relationship of the eastern cell to the northern and southern cells was not clearly established.

The evidence from the excavation, although sparse, would suggest that the cells fulfilled different functions. The northern one was probably a dwelling. The upper stone floor in the northern cell was apparently an original feature (the other cells apparently had only dirt floors) and covered only the southern part of the cell. The absence of stone flooring at the northern end of the cell may indicate the location of a bed, which would not necessarily have required flooring beneath it. The reddened stones and charcoal deposit in the south-east corner of the cell may represent a hearth, and the adjacent flat stone could have functioned as a work surface associated with food preparation. There may have been a window or entrance in the east wall which could have given natural light to the possible hearth in the south-east corner of the cell. Although the entrance in the south wall may have been rebuilt, the stone flooring suggests this could have been an original opening.

Although the extreme north-west corner of the south cell wall has been lost, one very large raised stone could possibly be the remains of a door sill. This, together with the area of rough stone across the northern end, may indicate the existence of a cross passage or feeding platform, supporting Ward's original suggestion that the southern cell might have functioned as a byre. The entrance into the eastern cell, opposite the possible outer doorway to the west, was narrow and apparently the only access to this cell, perhaps suggesting its use as a storage area, possibly for animal fodder.

The walls of all of the cells were very low (those of the north cell may have been higher) but this does not preclude all three cells being roofed. No evidence for roof supports or roof covering was found, although thatch or, more probably, turf would be likely.

Beyond the core structure to the east, the cleared areas and boundaries are obviously the result of deliberate actions. The poor topsoil and absence of any surface signs of cultivation possibly suggest that these areas could have been cleared to improve or increase grazing pasture or for hay. The boundaries do not appear to have been high enough to be stock proof and there was no evidence for additional fencing or hedging within the two small trial trenches, also suggesting that these plots were not intended for growing crops.

6.7 Discussion of results

6.7.1 Variety of structural types

Gesail Gyfarch, Llystyn Ganol, and Hafod Rhug Uchaf are all relatively low-lying settlements and, it has been suggested, acted as permanent centres of settlement. The building at Llystyn Ganol was built with its long axis at right angles to the slope (in the classic tradition as described by Gresham 1954), and is of laid-slab construction with occasional orthostats. It is neatly built and the walls are faced, and these factors, along with the small, original door, proper stone floor, and lack of internal drainage, suggest that it was domestic in character although there was nothing to suggest a date for its occupation. The building at Hafod Rhug Uchaf is also rectangular in plan and of a similar size. However, it was built with its long axis parallel to the (slight) hillslope. It was of drystone construction, of local, glacial boulders and was unusually laid out (although excavated examples are few) so that the foundation courses provided a level building platform for the upper walls. This might explain why it was laid out with its long side along the contour, to minimise the need for levelling up. It also had one or more laid stone floors. It is likely that this building also was domestic and, together with other buildings in the vicinity, formed a small farm, probably pre-17th century but later than the 13th century in origin. It is likely that both houses were originally thatched.

Both of these buildings are smaller than those apparently indicated by the platforms at Gesail Gyfarch (the excavated example being c. 15m by 6.2m). This is comparable to the platforms excavated at Dinas Noddfa, Gelligaer Common, Glamorgan, which varied in size from 9.4m by 4.3m to 18.2m by 5.5m (Fox 1939). What distinguished these structures is evidence for timber uprights in the construction, both in the walls and as central supports for the roof. The excavated building at Gesail Gyfarch, which is presumed to have been entirely or largely timber-built, also had a central post, but provided little further structural evidence. It might be suggested that a width of c. 3m was the maximum that could easily be spanned with a simple truss. Recorded examples of small post-medieval cottages have a typical width of about 4m, spanned by crude trusses of split branches (Wiliam 1988). A high-status medieval hall could have had a width of 5 to 7m, unsupported, but if there were an upper storey, this would be supported by central pillars or posts.

The presence of the central support at Gesail Gyfarch may suggest that there was a second storey or perhaps half-loft over the lower end of the hall, with the main part open to the roof. This corresponds to the documentary evidence that mentions the 'upper chambers in the lower end of the hall' (Gwynfor Jones 1990, 41–2). Very little evidence for the function of the building was recovered, perhaps surprising considering that pottery evidence from other areas of the site implies an occupation of more than 300 years. This, together with the lack of evidence for burning, might lead one to prefer an interpretation of a communal barn, with the actual domestic buildings on the surrounding platforms.

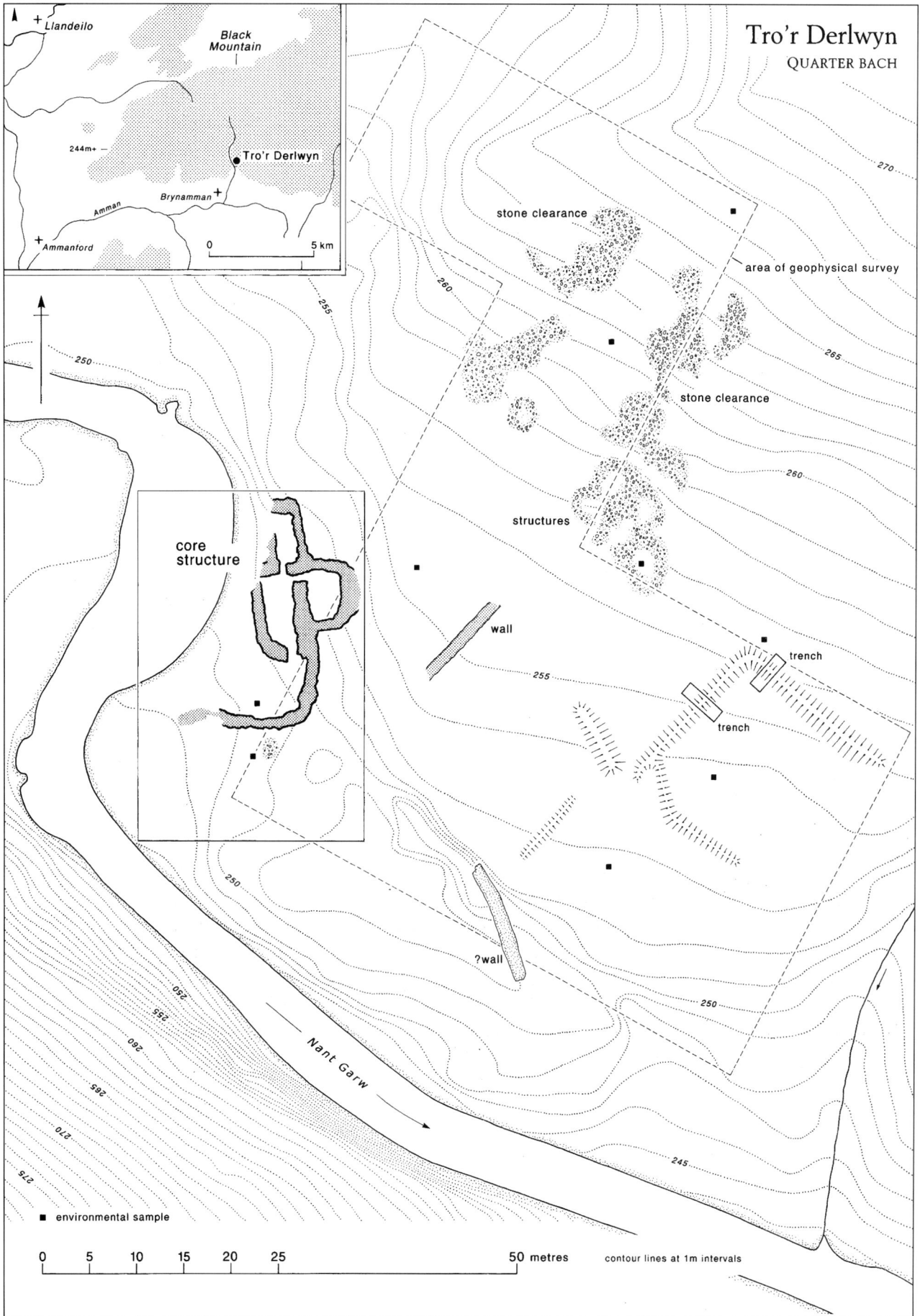

Tro'r Derlwyn
QUARTER BACH

Llandeilo

Black Mountain

244m+

Tro'r Derlwyn

Amman

Brynamman

Ammanford

0   5 km

stone clearance

area of geophysical survey

stone clearance

structures

core structure

wall

trench

trench

?wall

Nant Garw

■ environmental sample

0   5   10   15   20   25   50 metres   contour lines at 1m intervals

6.11 Tro'r Derlwyn site plan

Tro'r Derlwyn
The core structure

Nant Garw

north cell

flagstones

eroded slope

blocked opening

hearth

east cell

south cell

flood channel

enclosed
area

limit of excavation

boggy

trial trench

boggy

contour lines at 0.50m intervals

0 1 2 3 4 5   10   15 metres

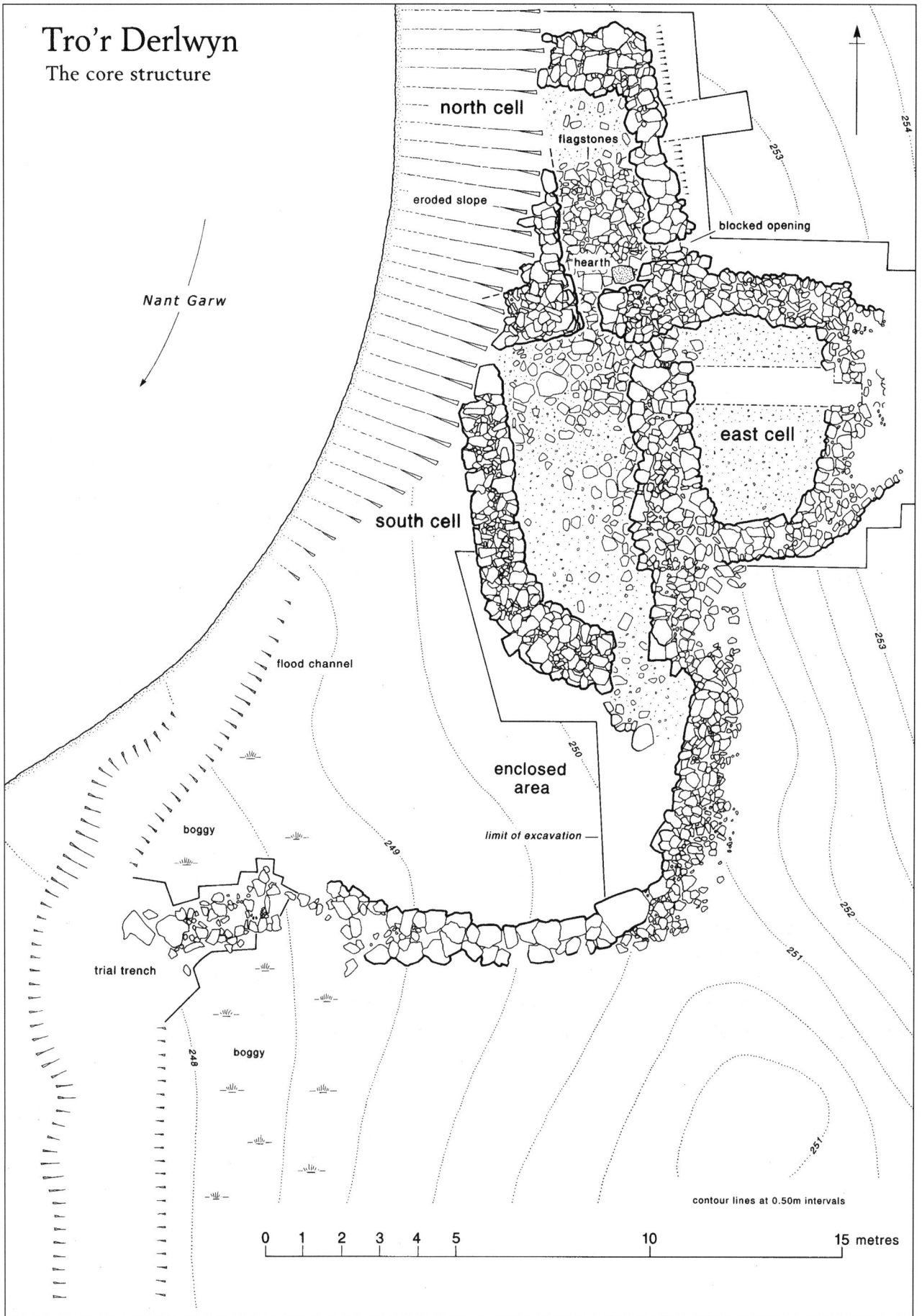

6.12 Tro'r Derlwyn excavation plan

Ynys Ettws and Tro'r Derlwyn, although quite different from each other, both belong to a different, upland, tradition. The two buildings at Ynys Ettws are comparable in size (internally) to those at Llystyn Ganol and Hafod Rhug, although somewhat larger, for instance, than those excavated at Hafod Nant y Griafolen (Allen 1993). The excavated building was of stone construction and the original building was neatly laid out. In the later period of occupation, the long room had been reduced in size and become square in shape, with an external annexe at one end. There is no complex of associated structures or any evidence of enclosures or fields which would imply permanent, year-round settlement, so its identification as a *hafod* or seasonally occupied settlement would seem reasonable (although it would be unwise to assume permanency solely on the presence of such features).

By contrast Tro'r Derlwyn is irregular in plan and construction and, as such, is actually fairly typical of a vast range of settlements that are to be found across the uplands of Wales, very few of which have been adequately investigated. Interpretation of sequence and function needs to be qualified by the uncertainty consequent upon limited excavation below the uppermost layer and inconclusive results of environmental sampling. There is some suggestion that the building cells fulfilled different purposes, and that the southern end could have served as a byre, which would imply cattle husbandry (although not necessarily exclusively). The irregular form could be explained as local adaptation to local conditions, and does not belong to any recognised tradition of vernacular architecture. There is some evidence for clearance and organisation of surrounding land, but no certain indication for cultivation. The small area of the living quarters could suggest occupation by a single person. However, it should be noted that the excavated site is only one element in a complex of proximate (unexcavated) structures within the valley which, if contemporary, may have had a functional and/or social connection.

6.7.2 Levels of survival of buried archaeological remains
The sites investigated generally demonstrate that, although survival of walls and floor levels in particular was good, they did not have a detailed stratigraphy or a complex range of internal features. Most of the archaeological evidence was found just below the current ground level.

Ynys Ettws had relatively few archaeological contexts (floors, walls, external hood, and external deposits).

Nevertheless, the information they yielded was highly significant, in particular two important radiocarbon dates and environmental data (see Caseldine, Chapter 7). By contrast, Gesail Gyfarch had more archaeological contexts, as might be expected on a complex, lowland site comprising several elements. The building itself had relatively few structural remains beyond a central posthole and a demolition level. However, when features identified by magnetometry survey outside the main building were investigated, including pits and drainage channels, a number of important finds were recovered including sherds of 13th-century pottery. The extensive land improvement which had taken place around Llystyn Ganol had effectively isolated the preserved long hut from any associated contemporary features. Investigation of the walls and the floor suggests that the building had only one period of construction and the only finds recovered were 19th- and 20th-century objects which lay directly on the floor of the building. The lack of finds and the evidence for the widening of the doorway suggest that latterly the building had an agricultural use probably as a cow house. At Hafod Rhug Uchaf the few *in situ* finds indicated the latest occupation as the 17th- to 18th-century.

The excavations demonstrated that it is important to look beyond the principal structures to subsidiary features such as hoods, banks, platforms, pits, and ditches where rubbish may have accumulated, in order to retrieve stratigraphical information, artefacts, and environmental evidence which will help in the interpretation of the settlement history. At Hafod Nant y Griafolen, Brenig, the majority of the finds came from middens located close to the houses, and thought to represent hearth sweepings and other rubbish (Allen 1993, 175).

The socio-economic function of many of the sites investigated during the project (remote dwellings, probably occupied seasonally, sometimes by a single person) means that they are unlikely to produce the range of broken or discarded artefacts that are associated with permanent, long-established lowland sites. In fact, *hafodydd* can probably be defined, at least partly, by this very absence of discarded material culture. Dating of sites will therefore always be problematic, although radiocarbon dating (where suitable samples can be obtained) has proved effective (see Caseldine, Chapter 7).

6.7.3 Assessment of the vulnerability of sites
Small, isolated sites in the countryside such as deserted

rural settlements are always going to be vulnerable to accidental or deliberate damage. Most sites survive because they are in areas which have been marginal in agricultural terms in the post-medieval (and particularly post-Second World War) period, and because they were built of stone and/or a substantial platform. The excavation at Gesail Gyfarch demonstrates the probable fate of sites which were (possibly) of wooden construction and situated on better, low-lying agricultural land.

The evidence from the project excavations suggests that most of these dwellings were built without resort to foundation trenches. The same technique was noted at nearby Cefn-y-fan, Dolbenmaen (Hogg 1954, 5), and Hafod Nant y Griafolen, Denbighshire (Allen 1993, 169). This lack of deep stratigraphy means that such structures are highly vulnerable to damage and loss of archaeological information, particularly as a result of agricultural clearance or cultivation, such as at Gesail Gyfarch and Llystyn Ganol. Once the above-ground structure is removed there will be few subsoil features or layers remaining.

Tree growth on archaeological sites is unwelcome. Trees which colonise sites (usually oak, sycamore or hazel) develop large roots which are very damaging to buried and above-ground archaeology. The growth of blackthorn, and other members of the plum family, is a particular problem, as witnessed at Hafod Rhug. These grow by spreading a huge underground network of woody roots which can be very extensive (particularly in windy areas) and can cause substantial damage to buried archaeological deposits. Other species such as hawthorn, bilberry, and heather may be less damaging. Gorse produces large root systems if it is allowed to grow, but if kept small by cutting or grazing tends to concentrate efforts into growing its above-ground canopy. The rhizomes of bracken and creeping thistle can damage archaeological deposits if the soil is shallow, although those of brambles and soft growth (such as nettles, docks etc.) are generally found to be relatively restricted.

Other threats to sites include damage caused by vehicles (as at Gesail Gyfarch), overgrazing (reduction of sward leads to erosion of underlying deposits), cattle trampling (particularly where deposits lie close to the surface), water erosion (as at Tro'r Derlwyn), and natural erosion (see Roberts, Chapter 9). Deliberate removal or reuse of stone (as at Ynys Ettws) is less damaging as it usually affects only the upper parts of the standing structure which contain the least-useful archaeological information (upper wall levels often

tend to have been remodelled in recent years for use as animal pens). Stone dumped on sites (such as at Llystyn Ganol) may serve to preserve buried deposits, but can adversely affect above-ground features and details and, perhaps more significantly, obscure sites so that their location is lost, leaving them vulnerable to future land improvement operations. The means by which such threats can be countered and managed are discussed by Roberts (Chapter 10).

Acknowledgements
North-west Wales
The excavations at Ynys Ettws, Gesail Gyfarch, Hafod Rhug Uchaf, and Llystynm Ganol were directed by George Smith of GAT. David Hopewell of GAT carried out the geophysical survey. The excavation work at Ynys Ettws, Gesail Gyfarch, and Llystyn Ganol was supervised by Susan Jones and Danny Dutton of GAT and carried out by students of Cardiff University, schoolwork experience students, and local volunteers. The work at Hafod Rhug Uchaf was supervised by Sue Jones and thanks go to the excavators, J Burman, M Foxwell, W Jones, A Lawson, R Mattinson, J Roberts, L Welbourne, and E Williams. Thanks also go to Dr Nancy Edwards for helpful comments on the inscribed stone and to David Chapman for comments on the slags. The soil phosphate study was carried out by Andrew Owen as part of a BA dissertation at the University of Wales, Bangor, under the supervision of Dr David Jenkins. The metal detection was carried out by Ian Stenson. The radiocarbon determinations were carried out by Beta Analytic of Miami, Florida. The publication illustrations are by Danny Dutton and Andrew Smith. Thanks must go to the farmers for permission to excavate and for their interest and assistance – Mr W Mostyn Jones of Ynys Ettws; John and Gwyndaf Williams of Gesail Gyfarch; Cledwyn Roberts of Llystyn Ganol; and Mr and Mrs A Jones of Hafod Rhug Uchaf.

South-west Wales
The site was excavated and the report written by Peter Crane. Don Benson was co-director of the excavation. Hubert Wilson acted as draughtsperson and assistant supervisor. The site workers were Eleanor Breen, Michael Hickling, Maugan Trethowen and students from Trinity College, Carmarthen. The aerial photography was by Toby Driver of RCAHMW.

7 THE ENVIRONMENT AND DESERTED RURAL SETTLEMENTS IN WALES: POTENTIAL AND POSSIBILITIES FOR PALAEOENVIRONMENTAL STUDIES

By Astrid Caseldine

Fundamental to an understanding of deserted rural settlements is an understanding of the landscape and environment in which they existed. In Wales, medieval and post-medieval landscapes have tended to be the Cinderella of palaeoenvironmental studies. Although in general terms there is frequent reference to the land use changes in the pollen records for these periods, it is seldom that they are the main focus of research. Environmental evidence, specifically from rural archaeological sites, is poorly represented and the contribution that it can make to deserted rural settlement studies has often been overlooked. One of the significant outcomes of the Deserted Rural Settlement Project has been the analysis of environ-mental material taken during archaeological excavations at Ynys Ettws, Hafod Rhug, and Tro'r Derlwyn which clearly demonstrates the possibilities of such work. Furthermore, as a result of the survey a much better database now exists for combined palaeoenvironmental and archaeological studies in the future.

This paper considers the potential for palaeoenvironmental work in Wales for this period and the techniques available; the environmental issues relating to deserted rural settlements and the environmental evidence that currently exists; and, in particular, the results of the recent investigations at Ynys Ettws. It also includes some recommendations for future research.

7.1 Environmental potential, techniques, and dating

Many of the sites lie in the uplands where the peaty soils offer the greatest potential for landscape reconstruction (Fig 7.1) through pollen analysis. Local survival conditions are significant since it is the upper-most levels which cover this time period and these are most likely to be susceptible to erosion, drainage, and drying out and hence the record will be lost. Unfortunately, the good potential for pollen preservation is rarely matched by survival of macrofaunal remains, for the acidic nature of the soils on many sites results in poor bone preservation. Figure 7.2 illustrates the sites in Wales where environmental information has been recovered.

Where waterlogged deposits exist close to a site there is the possibility of the survival of waterlogged plant remains and insects, as well as organic artefactual material, and even on dry sites charcoal, charred grain, and weed seeds may provide useful information about the surrounding environment or activities taking place at the settlement. Similarly, soil studies (soil micromorphology, phosphate, magnetic susceptibility) can indicate the nature of the use of structures and type of land use in adjacent areas, while phosphate survey, along with geophysics, can be used to detect archaeological remains where there is no obvious surface evidence. Supplementing pollen analysis, geochemical analyses, notably of silicon (Si) and titanium (Ti), have been identified as good indicators of erosion from forest clearance and farming activities (Görres and Frenzel 1993; Kempter et al 1997; Hölzer and Hölzer 1998), and geochemical analyses of heavy metals, for example copper, lead and zinc, may indicate trends in past industrial activity through atmospheric deposition (Battarbee et al 1988; Stevenson and Patrick 1989; Clymo et al 1990; Fritz et al 1990; Jones et al 1991; Rosen and Dumayne-Peaty 2001) and

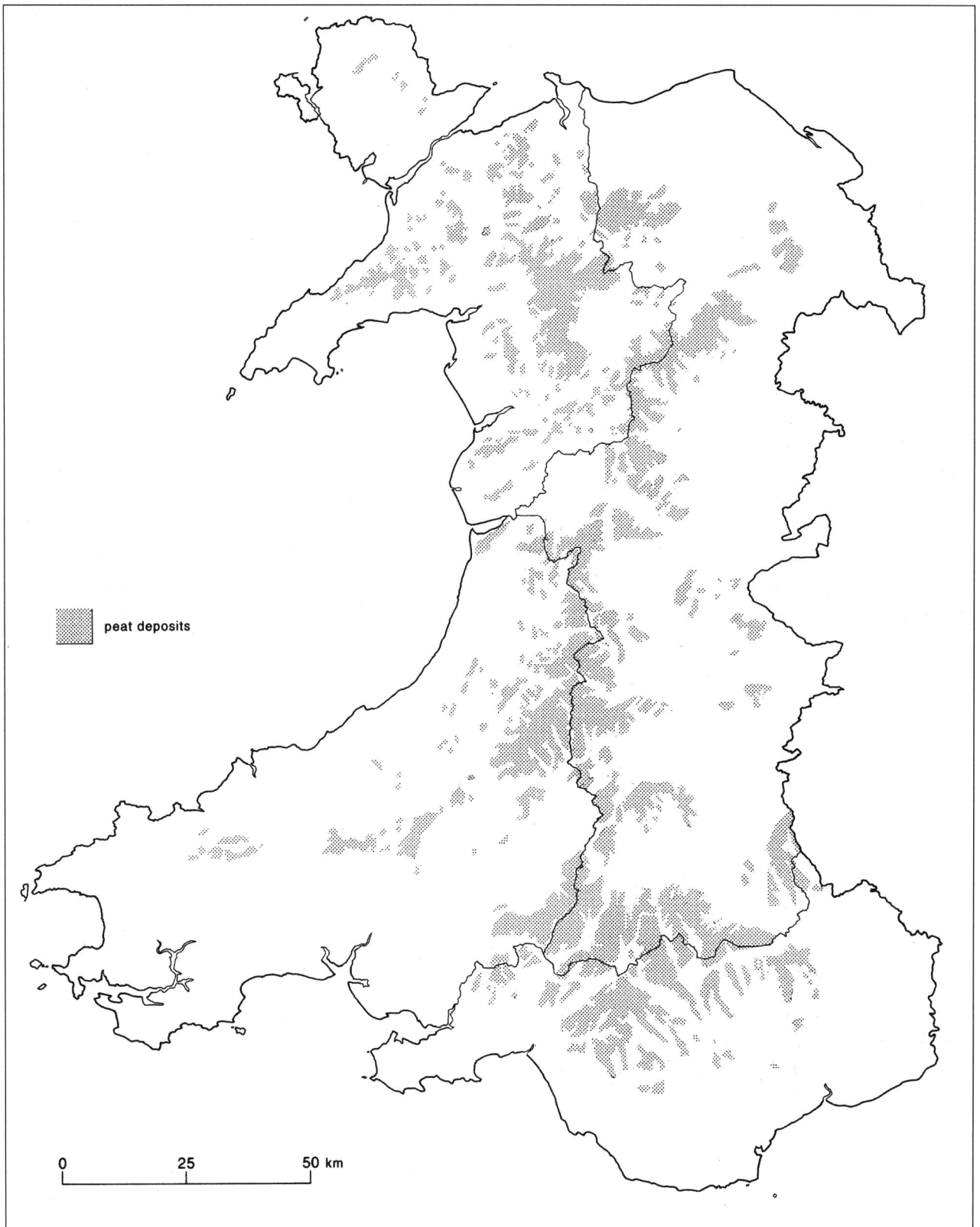

7.1 Peat deposits in Wales

fluvial deposition (Macklin *et al* 1991; Macklin *et al* 1992). Not all deserted rural settlements were necessarily involved in agriculture and some may have been associated with other activities such as mining or peat cutting.

One reason why palaeoenvironmental studies may have played a lesser role in the historic period is because of the problems of radiocarbon dating. The limitations of this technique are even more apparent for the historic period, when attempts have been made to relate changes in the pollen record to known historical events (Dumayne *et al* 1995). Baillie (1991) has identified two problems when attempting to relate calibrated radiocarbon chronologies, which, of necessity, have a range of possible calendrical dates, to calendar-dated events. One difficulty is the 'suck-in' effect whereby radiocarbon-dated events are assigned to known historical events which happen to fall within the age range of the radiocarbon date, and the second is that wide age ranges can result in synchronous events being 'smeared' over a longer period of radiocarbon time. Additionally, radiocarbon dates younger than the last 300–400 years have a calibrated age range covering the whole of that period. However, in recent years there has been an improvement in the precision of radiocarbon measurements, particularly from AMS laboratories (Bayliss 1998) and small sample, high-precision dating (Wilson *et al* 1996) has also become available. The application of mathematical modelling techniques may also provide a gain in precision of 25–35%, although not in all circumstances (Bayliss 1998). These improvements in precision are likely to increase the usefulness of radiocarbon dating for the historic period.

Additional techniques that can be employed in dating the recent past include other radiometric methods such as 'lead 210' (^{210}Pb) dating or Caesium 137 (^{137}Cs) dating (Oldfield *et al* 1994; Oldfield *et al* 1995). Another approach is to use independently dated horizons, such as the presence of 'soot' particles from the burning of fossil-fuels (Rose *et al* 1995), the first appearance of known-age exotic tree types in the pollen record (Birks 1972; Tipping *et al* 1997), or the occurrence of historic age tephras as marker horizons (Dugmore *et al* 1995; Langdon and Barber 2002). Unfortunately, whereas historic age tephras have been recorded from Scotland (Dugmore *et al* 1995) and Ireland (Hall *et al* 1993; Pilcher *et al* 1995), there has

not been the same success in Wales where only tephras of prehistoric date (Buckley 2000; Buckley and Walker 2002) have been identified.

In Wales pollen diagrams are frequently inadequately dated for the historic period, particularly those which pre-date 1980 when radiocarbon dates were less widely available, resulting in environmental changes being attributed to historical events without any independent dating control. For example, the record from Pont-Scethin, western Rhinogau (Walker and Taylor 1976), and a series of pollen diagrams from sites in west-central Wales (Moore 1968; Moore and Chater 1969) lack radiocarbon dates, resulting in all chronologies being inferred from palynological/historical correlations. In contrast, at Carneddau in upland mid-Wales (Walker 1993), although the pollen resolution permits only generalised comments for deposits dating to the historic period, radiocarbon dates provide a dating control. At Llanllwch Bog, Carmarthenshire (Thomas 1965), originally only Bronze Age radiocarbon dates were obtained and later changes in the pollen record were therefore only tentatively assigned to various periods. More recent work at Llanllwch Bog, and also at Kenfig Pool and Crymlyn Bog, enabled environmental changes, particularly in relation to industrial developments during the last 400 years, to be reconstructed in greater detail, and these were supported by both ^{210}Pb dating and radiocarbon dating (Rosen 1998; Rosen and Dumayne-Peaty 2001). ^{210}Pb dating has also been used to date increased erosion in the catchment at Llangorse during the last c. 140 years (Jones *et al* 1985; 1991), and also to date changes in both the relative importance of heathland and grassland in lake catchments and in the intensification of grazing pressure in the uplands of Wales (Battarbee *et al* 1988; Stevenson and Thompson 1993).

7.2 Environmental issues and the palaeoenvironmental record

There are a number of ways in which palaeoenvironmental studies can contribute to an understanding of deserted rural settlements and the landscapes in which they lie. Environmental evidence has tended to receive less attention, not only because of the problems of dating, but also because of the availability of documentary records. However, this in itself provides an opportunity for palaeoenvironmentalists to test their interpretations against the historical record (Bell and Dark 1998). Palaeoenvironmental evidence may also

detect processes and events unrecognised in the contemporaneous written record (Tipping 2000, 131) and, in fact, may be the only line of evidence where there is no written record. A number of issues can be identified, many of which are inter-related, and these are considered below with summaries of work done to date. Pollen evidence independent of excavations dominates and environmental evidence from archaeological sites is scarce, demonstrating the need to recover such information in the future to aid interpretation.

7.3 Marginality

Many of the deserted rural settlements occur in upland areas which are considered to be 'marginal' for agriculture and for settlement. Marginality is a complex issue and no single explanation is likely to be satisfactory; rather it is likely to involve a combination of environmental, economic, social and political factors. More important than the inherent qualities of the land itself may be the way in which the landscape is both perceived and exploited (Coles and Mills 1998, 10), and palaeoenvironmental studies can play a part in deciphering both the way in which exploitation has occurred and also the influence of contemporary environmental conditions. Encompassed within the issue of marginality are questions such as the effect of climate, changes in settlement, and cultivation limits. These are discussed in more detail below but evidence interpreted as indicative of marginality includes the abandonment of the medieval settlement and preservation of late or post-medieval ridge and furrow at at Erw-wen, Ardudwy, where an integrated archaeological and environmental study was undertaken (Chambers *et al* 1988). Similarly, a distinct cereal pollen horizon identified in many pollen diagrams from Cardiganshire has been attributed to cereal growing on marginal land during the Napoleonic Wars (Moore 1968; Moore and Chater 1969), as also has increased erosion in the catchment at Llangorse (Jones *et al* 1985; 1991). At Cefn Hirgoed some limited evidence for an expansion in arable farming is considered as possibly relating to medieval marginal settlement on adjacent hillslopes (Walker *et al* 1997).

7.4 Climatic change

The extent to which climatic change may have influenced settlement and land use during the medieval and post-medieval periods has been a frequent subject of debate. Much of the archaeological evidence for deserted rural settlements in Wales lies in the uplands, a 'marginal' area where successful settlement and farming are likely to be more strongly influenced by the vagaries of the weather than in the lowlands. But human responses are frequently multi-causal, reflecting economic and social stimuli as well as climatic (Mayes and Wheeler 1997, 290), and abandonment of settlement and cereal cultivation may be as much to do with changes in the social and economic system as environmental factors. Also, adaptive strategies may be developed to cope with deteriorating conditions (Coles and Mills 1998, 10), making direct links between settlement, land use and climate difficult to establish.

Prior to systematic meteorological observations the evidence for climate change must be based on indirect, ie 'proxy' climate data. Much of the evidence during the medieval period in the British Isles is based on documentary evidence, largely from England rather than the more peripheral areas such as Wales, Scotland, and Ireland for which there is little written evidence (Ogilvie and Farmer 1997). Furthermore, interpreting such evidence is not always straightforward. Alternatively, there are various environmental techniques such as plant macrofossil and rhizopod analyses of peat deposits or chemical and isotope analyses of ice cores which can be used to produce 'proxy' climate records, but these too are not without problems and limitations although they are independent of the social and cultural complications of documentary evidence.

The traditional view is of a warmer period termed the 'Little Climatic Optimum' or 'Medieval Warm Period' followed by a period of cooler climatic conditions known as the 'Little Ice Age'. However, it has become increasingly apparent that while broad generalisations can be made, the evidence varies in detail, both in degree and timing and depending on the geographical area (Hughes and Diaz 1994). On a global scale it is considered that a well-defined warm interval is much less likely, although a period of relatively warm temperatures probably occurred in parts of the northern hemisphere (eg Europe and neighbouring regions) during approximately the 11th–14th centuries (Houghton *et al* 2001). Temperatures around 1°C higher than today are suggested by ice-core data from Greenland (Dahl-Jensen *et al* 1998), and dendrochronological and glacier records from Sweden, while documentary sources in Britain indicate extensive agriculture in the 12th and 13th centuries which suggests an increase in both summer and winter warmth (Lamb 1995). Mean temperature estimates for the northern hemisphere are around 0.2°C warmer for the 11th to 14th centuries than for the 15th to 19th centuries (Jones *et al* 1998; Mann *et al* 1999; Crowley and Lowery 2000; Houghton *et al* 2001).

The exact beginning and end of the 'Little Ice Age' is uncertain. Analysis of documentary data from

Pollen Sites

1 Brecon Beacons
2 Bryn Cysegrfan
3 Bryn y Castell
4 Bryniau Pica
5 Carneddau
6 Carningli
7 Cefn Graeanog
8 Cefn Gwernffrwd
9 Cefn Hirgoed
10 Coed Taf
11 Corn Du
12 Crawcwellt
13 Crymlyn Bog
14 Dolaeron
15 Dolfrwynog
16 Erw-wen
17 Foel Ddu
18 Gwbert-on-sea
19 Hafod Rhug Uchaf
20 Kenfig Pool
21 Llangorse
22 Llanllwch
23 Llannerch

24 Llyn Cororion
25 Llyn Llagi
26 Llyn Morwynion
27 Llyn Padarn
28 Llyn Peris
29 St Harmon
30 Migneint
31 Mynedd Llanbedr
32 Pen Rhiw-wen
33 Pont Scethin
34 Talley Lakes
35 Tregaron
36 Tro-r Derlwyn
37 Ty Rhyg
38 Waun-Fignen-Felen
39 Ynys Ettws

Other environmental evidence

40 Cefn Drum
41 Gelligaer
42 Hafod y Nant Criafolen
43 Llystan Ganol

• pollen site

⊙ other environmental evidence

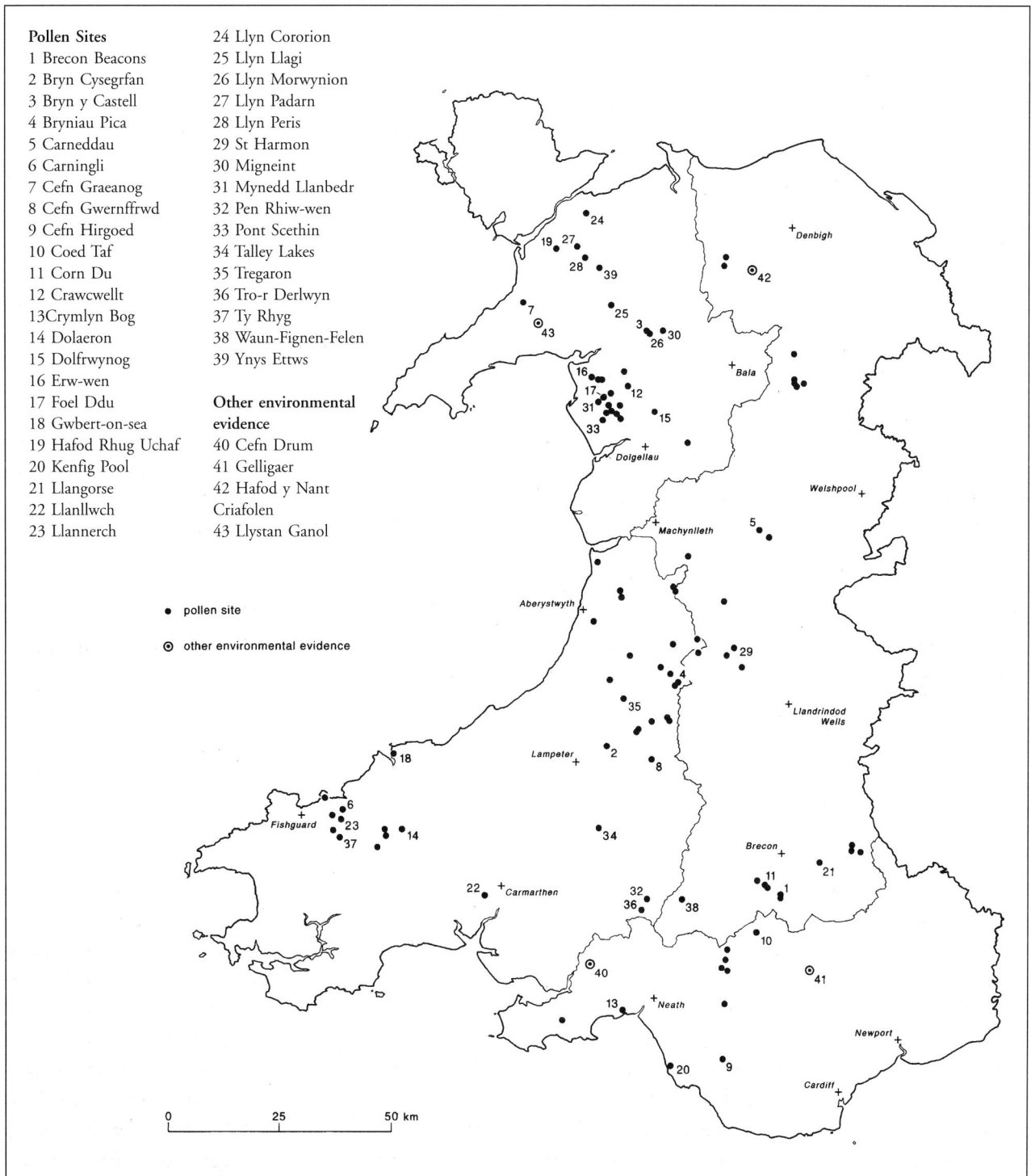

7.2 Map of sites with environmental evidence

England suggests a long time-scale cooling c. 1240 to c. 1340, warming c. 1510, and thereafter cooling (Ogilvie and Farmer 1997, 130). A date of roughly the 17th to 19th centuries for the Little Ice Age in Europe and neighbouring regions has been proposed (Houghton *et al* 2001), while for the northern hemisphere as a whole there is evidence (Mann *et al* 1999; Jones *et al* 1998) to suggest the 15th to the 19th centuries were the coldest of the millennium, but that

hemispherically only a modest cooling of less than 1°C relative to late 20th-century levels occurred (Houghton *et al* 2001). A significantly colder period has been recognised in the 17th century (Crowley 2000) with a second cold period during the 19th century but this was more severe over North America (Jones *et al* 1998). Although the reconstructed northern hemisphere record suggests a temperature range of no more than ~ 0.5°C, it has been found (eg Hughen *et al*

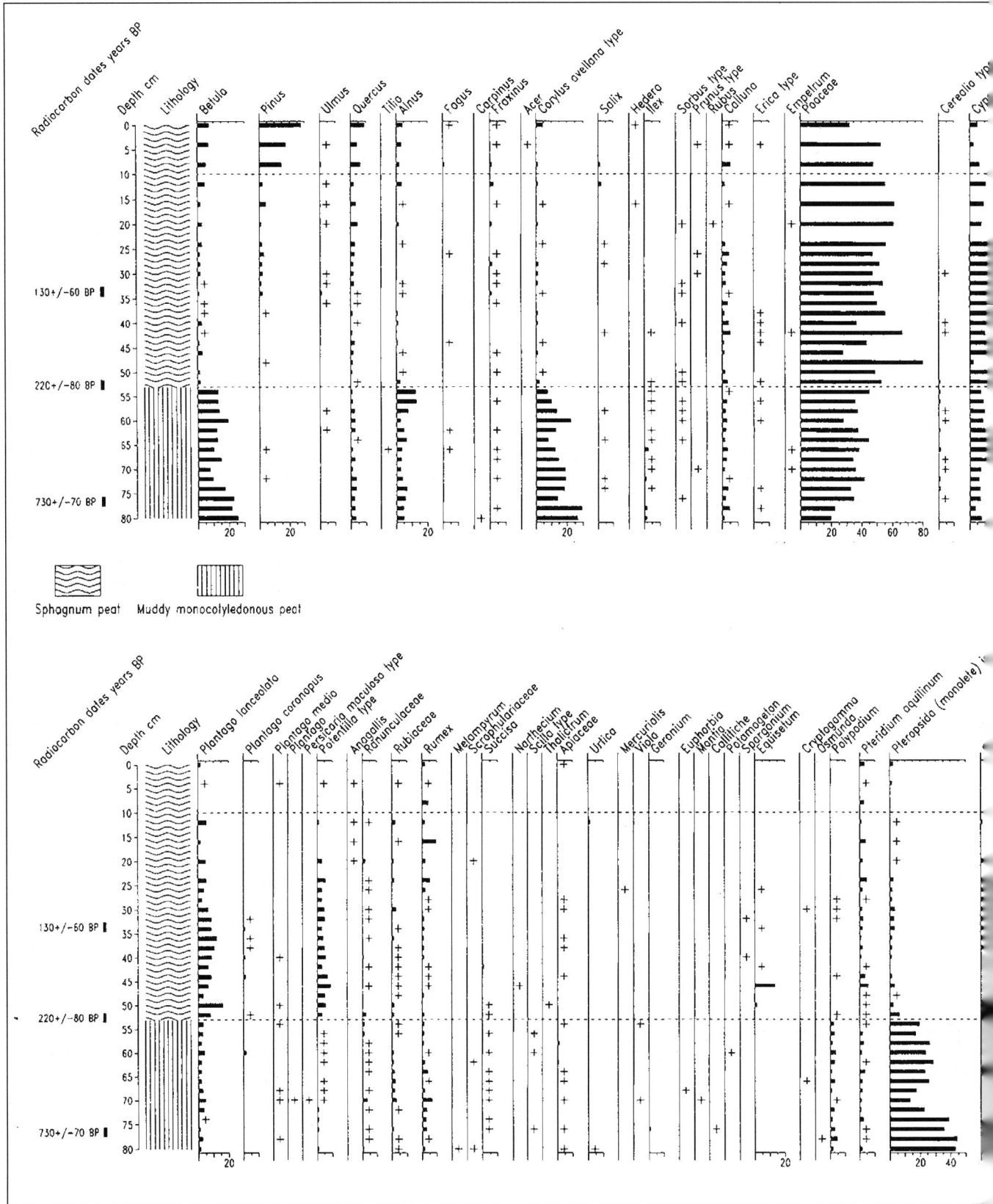

7.3 Ynys Ettws pollen diagram

2000) that in marginal situations variations may have been of the order of 1–2°C during the period of the Medieval Warm Period and Little Ice Age, which would have had implications for settlement and agri-culture. In addition, the Little Ice Age was typified by highly variable weather patterns, and more important than long-term change may have been short-term 'risk' periods when bad weather over several years may have settlement and land use in the uplands of Wales during the historic period has yet to be fully explored using palaeoenvironmental evidence. Although changes in the pollen record, for example at Carneddau (Walker 1993) in mid-Wales and in the Preselis (Seymour 1985), have been considered to reflect possible climate change, there have been relatively few studies specifically involving the investigation of proxy climatic data. Peat sequences, particularly in upland areas, contain abundant evidence for past climate change. This includes data on temporal variations in mire-surface wetness, an approach which has been most widely applied in northern England and the Scottish borders (Barber *et al* 1994a; Barber *et al* 1994b; Barber *et al* 1998; Mauquoy and Barber 1999; Hughes *et al* 2000; Hendon *et al* 2001). An area in Wales where such data have been collected is the Migneint where there is clear evidence for a Dark Age (1400 BP) climatic deterioration (Blackford 1990; Blackford and Chambers 1991). This is also widely recognised elsewhere, although possibly beginning slightly earlier, around the end of the 4th century cal AD and lasting for 300–400 years (Hendon *et al* 2001). More recently a wetness horizon of Dark Age date has been recognised at Brynau Pica in upland Ceredigion (Buckley 2000; Buckley and Walker 2001). Peat initiation at Coed Taf, in the uplands above Merthyr Tydfil, is dated to c. 1400 BP (Chambers 1983a), supporting Crampton's (1966b) view that a major expansion in peat growth in south Wales occurred at this time and may also be at least partially attributable to climatic deterioration. There is also evidence of a climatic deterioration, indicated by peat erosion, from the Brecon Beacons c. 490 cal BP (Chambers 1982a; Blackford and Chambers 1991) which broadly corresponds with the so-called Little Ice Age and, similarly, several 'wet-shifts', ie shifts to wetter surface conditions, recognised in peat sequences from the Migneint during the last 600 years which broadly correlate with climatic deterioration during the 14th century and the Little Ice Age (Blackford 1990).

The influence of climate on land use is most likely to be reflected in the viability of crops to grow at altitude. One palaeoenvironmental study designed specifically to test the influence of the Little Ice Age on cereal cultivation has been undertaken in the Cheviot Hills (Tipping 1998), challenging Parry's (1975; 1978) thesis that later historic agricultural change in the adjacent Lammermuir Hills was climatically driven. Tipping (1998) has argued that for the Cheviot Hills viable cereal cultivation continued throughout

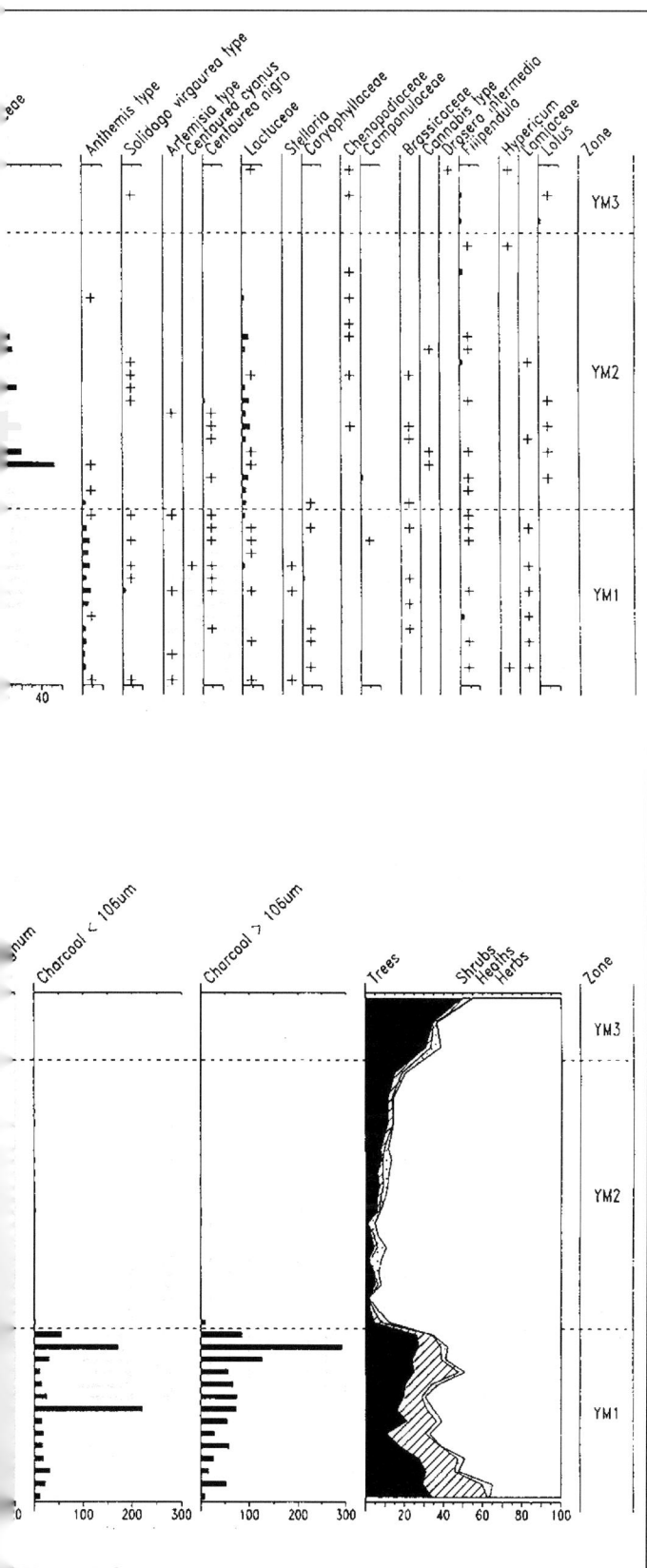

resulted in contiguous crop failures leading to abandonment of land.

The extent to which climate change, either in the long-term or the short-term, may have influenced the Little Ice Age and this could equally be applicable to the Lammermuirs, where the abandonment of cereal growing could simply reflect the fact that it was no longer needed with the development of agricultural specialisation. However, he acknowledges that in the former there are not the extensive cultivation ridges evident in the Lammermuirs and the two areas may have been regarded differently by their respective farmers. As yet, no comparable investigation has been undertaken in Wales and further work is required to determine if the Little Ice Age had any discernible effect on agriculture and settlement. The evidence for upland arable agriculture in Wales during the medieval period and later will be returned to below.

As well as influencing agricultural activity in the uplands, climate may also have exerted an influence on farming in coastal areas through dune building. Short-term climate shifts during the Little Ice Age seem to have led to conditions conducive to dune development on both the North Sea (Orford *et al* 2000; Wilson *et al* 2001) and Irish Sea (Pye and Neal 1993; Wilson and Braley 1997; Gilbertson *et al* 1999) coasts of the British Isles at different times. However, there are few records from the Irish Sea coasts of Wales and south-west Scotland (Wilson *et al* 2001), although the abandonment of settlements in Wales through be-sanding is well established (Davidson 2002). Pollen results from below blown sands at Gwbert in south Ceredigion have been interpreted as reflecting a mixed medieval and immediately post-medieval economy (Taylor 1987) but evidence is limited and the dune systems of Wales warrant further detailed palaeoenvironmental investigation to complement archaeological studies.

7.5 Woodland

Some indication of the nature and extent of woodland during medieval times in Wales is provided by documentary records, such as the Book of Llandaff, the Welsh Laws and the Domesday Book (see Linnard 2000). Similarly, Giraldus Cambrensis in his *Itinerae Kambria* (1188) and *Descriptio Kambriae* (1194) and Leland in his travels through Wales in 1536–39 include descriptions of the existing woodland. Place-names also frequently suggest the existence of woodland (Hooke 1997; Linnard 2000) and even the *ffridd* name, usually interpreted as mountain pasture, could indicate woodland or forest. Palaeoenvironmental studies provide an independent record, complementing these other lines of evidence and allowing assumptions drawn from them to be tested. They can help to clarify the extent of any upland woodland prior to medieval settlement as well as indicating or confirming the existence, clearance or regeneration of woodland in later centuries. It is assumed that the structures associated with platform sites were made of wood and that wood would frequently have been used as fuel. Pollen and macrofossil evidence can help determine the availability of woodland resources in the vicinity of deserted rural settlement sites.

Woodland clearance is clearly detectable in the palaeoenvironmental record, although the mechanism involved is less certain and the extent to which clearance episodes can be dated depends on the availability of independent dating controls. There is evidence that in some areas of Wales woodland regenerated after the Roman period before further clearance in medieval times, whereas in others, once cleared, the landscape remained open. Woodland clearance is indicated c. 1200 ^{14}C years BP in lowland Gwynedd, at Llyn Cororion (Watkins 1990), but there are signs that birch re-invaded the edge of cleared areas. A major decline in tree and shrub taxa at c. 780±60 ^{14}C years BP is considered to be associated with *Cannabis* cultivation. In contrast, less detailed records from Llyn Padarn and Llyn Peris, at the lower end of the Llanberis Pass (Elner and Happey-Wood 1980), have been interpreted as indicating the surrounding catchment area was dominated largely by open heath and grassland community, from c. 1900 ^{14}C years BP (but see Ynys Ettws discussed below). Further south in Snowdonia, at Bryn y Castell (Mighall and Chambers 1995) and Llyn Morwynion (Caseldine *et al* 2001), the records also suggest a largely open landscape in post-Roman times as does the evidence from the Hiraethog Moors, Clwyd, where an increase in heather occurs around 2060 ^{14}C years BP (Lascelles 1996). However, at Crawcwellt, Trawsfynydd (Chambers and Lageard 1993), there are indications for a recovery in woodland during the early historic period, while in upland Ardudwy a short-lived recovery in woodland may have occurred c. 800 AD followed by a decline from about the mid-12th century (Chambers and Price 1988). This suggests that for the early medieval period there might have been more woodland resources available than at present. To the east, in the Berwyn Mountains, there is also evidence for post-Roman woodland regeneration followed by a phase of increased agricultural activity during the

7.6 Seasonal or permanent settlement

A major issue for the study of deserted rural settlements is the question of the extent to which the upland settlements represent seasonal or permanent occupation. The inconsistencies in the criteria used to distinguish the seasonal dwelling from the permanent farmstead for excavated sites in Wales have been discussed by Ward (1997). The question has also been considered by several of the authors in this volume (Locock, Silvester and Sambrook). To date, it is perhaps only at Cefn Graeanog (Kelly 1981–82), a lowland site in Gwynedd, that there is sufficiently strong evidence, including economic data, to allow a positive identification of the site, in this case, as a permanently occupied medieval settlement. Much of this is based on palaeoenvironmental investigation, in particular the pollen and plant macrofossil evidence which indicated cereal cultivation (Chambers 1982c, 1983b; Hillman 1982).

Pastoralism and the role of transhumance are central to the issue of seasonal settlement and the *hafod/hendre* system, although it has been claimed that the role of transhumance in upland agriculture in Wales has been over-emphasised and that daily movement was a more practical and common occurrence (Kelly 1981–82, 885–7). However, the latter is perhaps dependent on the proximity of the grazing land to the main farm and the desirability of making daily journeys from the point of view of time and animal welfare. It is generally accepted that in the spring the cattle, sheep, and goats were driven to the upland pastures where they were herded and milked for the preparation of butter and cheese, returning to the main farmstead for the winter. It was also common practice to collect moorland hay (*Molinia*), providing a welcome additional contribution to the store of winter fodder (Roberts 1959; Crampton 1966b; Davies 1984–5). The abandonment of

hafodydd and the establishment of *lluest* or shepherding stations, as well as a change in the relative importance of cattle and sheep may be reflected in the palaeoenvironmental record. Sambrook (this volume) suggests by the 18th century sheep were often kept on the hills throughout the winter months and *lluest*, rather than a seasonally occupied settlement, became permanent.

Ward (1991) has argued that the sharp division between permanent settlement and settlements used exclusively for summer occupation may be an over-simplification and that seasonal occupation and periods of longer use are not necessarily mutually exclusive through time. It has been suggested, on the basis of the archaeological evidence, that Tro'r Derlwyn (Ward 1995; Thompson, this volume) in the Black Mountain area, may represent a transitional phase in settlement, its role extending beyond being purely seasonal but involving over-wintering of animals and cereal production, probably for fodder. Limited palynological work at the site (Caseldine and Barrow 2000), in association with excavations undertaken as part of the Deserted Rural Settlement Project (Chapter 6), supported the view that that the settlement was principally concerned with pastoralism. The occasional pollen grain of cereal and weed of cultivation was recorded but could reflect arable activity in the lowlands rather than in the immediate area, although this possibility cannot be ruled out.

Resolution is poor for the historic period in the pollen record from Erw-wen, Ardudwy, but the presence of large grass pollen grains comparable to cereal are noted and it has been debated whether the medieval settlement represents a *hafod* or, given the presence of arable fields, a year-round dwelling (Chambers *et al* 1988).

7.7 Pastoralism

Whether secular or ecclesiastical, exploitation of the uplands during the medieval period and later is considered to have been largely based on pastoralism. Both cattle and sheep were pastured in the uplands, although there has been some debate as to their relative importance (Roberts 1959; Hughes *et al* 1973). The status of goats is less certain, but they too would have had a noticeable effect in browsing down any young trees (Crampton 1968). The effects of grazing

have been reviewed in detail by Hobbs and Gimingham (1987) and most closely studied in relation to sheep. Grasses are preferred to *Calluna* and other ericaceous species but the latter are an important food, especially in winter (Martin 1964; Grant *et al* 1976). In contrast to sheep, hill cattle are not strongly selective and can be maintained throughout the year on areas which are largely heath covered (Gimingham 1972). Trampling by adult cattle will also help to check the spread of bracken and maintain a balance between *Agrostis Festuca* heath swards and the less favoured moorland types of grazing such as *Nardus* and *Molinia* (Roberts 1959).

Charcoal in the palaeoenviromental record may be an indicator of deliberate management practices. Fire can be used effectively to improve grazing for sheep on dry heath where it does not seem to harm the heathland system and maintains the heathland plant community (Hobbs *et al* 1984). A reduction in burning will result in the establishment of scrub and woodland unless prevented by grazing pressure (Miles *et al* 1978). Variations in the presence of grass and heather pollen and other pastoral indicators, along with the presence or absence of charcoal, where this has been recorded, suggest variations in management practices and grazing intensities. Much of the uplands was cleared of woodland in prehistoric times with further clearance, as previously outlined, during the historic period. Following clearance activity, changes in the palaeoenvironmental record in Wales have been widely attributed to grazing, and some indication of the grazing intensity and management practices in upland pastoral areas can be discerned. Frequently the changes have been ascribed to the influence of monastic houses; for example, renewed agricultural activity has been linked to the establishment of Strata Florida Abbey near Tregaron and the abundance of grazing indicators to intensive grazing by sheep (Moore 1968; Moore and Chater 1969), while at Dolfrwynog in the Vale of Trawsfynydd (Ernst 1969) the pollen record also indicates pastoral activity, probably associated with the Cistercians at Cymer Abbey. Similarly, the influence of the abbey at Talley may be represented in an undated pollen diagram (Butler 1984). It was suggested that sheep grazing was associated with the hill granges linked to the abbey and that both pastoralism and arable farming occurred in the valleys.

At Bryn y Castell (Mighall and Chambers 1995) and Llyn Morwynion (Caseldine *et al* 2001) in north Wales the records suggest a largely open landscape in post-Roman times. At the former site an increase in values for grass, *Plantago lanceolata* (ribwort plantain) and *Rumex* (docks) pollen was interpreted as reflecting an intensification of pastoral activity and a transhumance type of farming, while at the latter, fluctuations in heather, grass, sedge, and other taxa, along with variations in charcoal concentrations, suggest burning activity and variations in grazing pressure. Again, it is likely that a transhumance type of farming system was

operating. Further south, peaks in pastoral weeds in soil pollen records from Mynydd Llanbedr (Walker and Taylor 1976) have been attributed to post-medieval increases in sheep and cattle populations and to 16th-century encroachment.

Evidence from archaeological sites in west and mid-Wales is limited but investigations below a pillow mound dated to 575±60 ^{14}C years BP at Bryn Cysegrfan in Ceredigion indicated a largely grassland environment (Walker 1988), while the pollen sequence from beneath a medieval platform in Radnorshire indicated heathland giving way to grassland at the time of platform construction (Crampton and Webley 1964). At Carneddau, where the pollen evidence also indicated pastoralism dominated during the medieval period, a burnt horizon was interpreted as possibly reflecting a deliberate management strategy (Walker 1993).

An increase in heather pollen was dated to the medieval period at Cefn Gwernffrwd in mid-Wales (Chambers 1983b), with a change to grass and sedge vegetation communities, suggesting a change in grazing activity, to post-medieval times. A more open environment and a change from heather to grassland communities has also frequently been recorded at sites in the uplands of south Wales (Chambers 1982a, 1983a; Chambers and Lageard 1993; Smith and Green 1995; Lawler *et al* 1997; Walker *et al* 1997; Rosen 1998; Caseldine and Barrow 2000), and the vegetation changes have been interpreted as indicating changing moorland practices, including increased sheep populations and burning, as well as manuring and fertilising practices.

Differences in heather and grass pollen values from buried soils beneath cross-ridge dykes in Glamorgan have been interpreted as indicating different dates for their construction (Crampton 1966b). The date of a major decline in *Calluna*, interpreted as reflecting an intensification of grazing pressure, recorded at a number of sites investigated as part of a study of lake acidification in the United Kingdom (Battarbee *et al* 1988), has been shown to vary from 200 to 400–500 years ago, using ^{210}Pb dating (Stevenson and Thompson 1993).

Finally, although pollen evidence demonstrates the importance of pastoralism and rich faunal assemblages have been recovered from towns and castles, very little faunal evidence is available from deserted rural settlement sites. For example, only a few herbivore teeth, including a cow molar, were recovered from Hafod Nant y Griafolen (Allen 1979; 1993) in Powys.

7.8 Cereal cultivation

The interpretation of sites as *hafodydd* is based on the absence of any evidence for cultivation which, it is argued, would be necessary if stock, notably cattle, were being over-wintered in the uplands (Davies 1984; Ward 1997). In addition, Silvester (2000, 47) has argued that, although the significance of pastoralism in the Welsh economy is not in dispute, the importance of cereal cultivation, particularly in the uplands, has often been understated. Even though documented examples of upland cultivation in mid- and north Wales (Jones 1965; 1973) exist, Jack (1988, 442–3) described land in Wales over 500 or 600 feet as being largely unsuitable for grain production. More recently Silvester (2000; this volume) has drawn attention to upland cultivation in the Berwyn mountains, while recent investigations as part of the Deserted Rural Settlement Project have identified a number of examples elsewhere in Wales. Although there is no direct dating evidence for the field systems in the Berwyns, it has been argued they are of medieval date (Silvester 2000, 57; this volume). Cereal type pollen has been recorded from pollen sites (Bostock 1980) in the Berwyns during the medieval period and later, but these sites lie some distance away from the field systems and at a higher altitude. An integrated programme of work closer to the field systems would be of considerable value in helping to resolve the nature and date of land use changes in the area.

Elsewhere the presence of cereal type pollen and weed taxa associated with cultivation at some sites also hints at upland cultivation, although possible transport by wind from lower altitudes can present interpretative problems. As well as giving some indication of cultivation limits, pollen records can help to confirm the presumed land use associated with cultivation ridges and terraced fields, and their date. In the uplands of southern Scotland, for example, a multi-disciplinary approach has been used to demonstrate that ploughing presumed to be associated with cereal cultivation in the medieval and post-medieval periods was 19th century in date, and represented a form of pasture improvement for sheep grazing (Carter *et al* 1997).

Cereal pollen is recorded from a number of sites in Wales including Cefn Graeanog (Chambers 1983c), while at Erw-wen, Ardudwy (Chambers *et al* 1988), large grass pollen grains comparable to cereal have been reported. At Llyn Morwynion (Caseldine *et al* 2001), also in north Wales, occasional cereal type pollen and pollen of weeds of cultivation may suggest

an increase in marginal arable agriculture prior to the climatic deterioration of the Little Ice Age, although cereal type pollen continues to be recorded throughout this period. This may be attributable to cereal growing in the region as a whole or may, however, indicate the Little Ice Age had little effect on upland crop growing in this area (cf. Tipping 1998). In other areas such as the Berwyns it has been proposed that decreased arable activity may be due to the effects of the Little Ice Age (Bostock 1980).

Further south a peak in cereal pollen, and arable and pastoral weeds at Pont Scethin, western Rhinogau (Walker and Taylor 1976) has been assigned to the medieval period by correlation with evidence from Bwlch-y-Figyn (Taylor 1973), which was dated by shoe remains to 1400–50, while soil pollen records from Mynydd Llanbedr (Walker and Taylor 1976) suggest cereal cultivation occurred as high as 305m during the historic period. Smith and Taylor (1969), on the basis of soil pollen evidence in north Cardiganshire, suggest that a cereal phase may relate to cultivation at the time of the Napoleonic wars, but, as at sites in west-central Wales (Moore 1968; Moore and Chater 1969), dates need to be confirmed. At Tregaron, cereal cultivation has been ascribed to the Cistercian community at Strata Florida (Turner 1964; Hughes *et al* 2001; Morriss 2001) and possibly to the Premonstratensians at Talley (Butler 1984).

At a number of other sites, although pastoralism dominates, there is some evidence for arable activity, for example, at Bryn Cysegrfan, Ceredigion (Walker 1988), Carneddau (Walker 1993), and Cefn Hirgoed (Walker *et al* 1997). At Penrhiwen on the Black Mountain (Cloutman 1983) results suggest that from around 1200 BP extensive clearance occurred in the valleys and lower slopes, with farming activity involving both cereal cultivation and pastoralism, while in the uplands pastoralism dominated. Similar conclusions were reached at the post-medieval settlement at Tro'r Derlwyn (Caseldine and Barrow 2000), also on the Black Mountain.

In lowland Carmarthenshire at Llanllwch Bog (Thomas 1965), on the basis of palynological/historical correlation, a period of more intensive and continuous agriculture was assigned to the Norman occupation c. 1100, and high cereal pollen frequencies to an expansion of cereal planting at the time of the Napoleonic wars. The latter has been confirmed in a recent, dated, pollen investigation (Rosen 1998).

Further east at Llangorse, cereal pollen and an increase in erosion has similarly been attributed to increased cultivation resulting from the Napoleonic Wars (Jones *et al* 1985; 1991). An increase in grass pollen as the 19th century progressed has been related possibly to a depression in agriculture or decline in proportion of arable land in the catchment and a shift to pastoralism (Chambers 1999).

7.9 Enclosure and settlement change

It is generally accepted that enclosure did not affect the uplands significantly until the 16th century and typically later changes in the pollen record have been attributed to post-medieval increases in sheep and cattle populations, and 16th century encroachment (Walker and Taylor 1976; Moore and Chater 1969). It has also been argued that rather than the decline of the *hafod* system being consequent upon the spread of sheep farming, it was the spread of parent farms into upland areas that could not adequately supply crops to maintain the animals through the winter that resulted in the obsolescence of the *hafod* economy and led to sheep farming becoming characteristic of the pastures (Davies 1984–5, 87). Palaeoenvironmental records could help to confirm the sequential development of settlement and land use in an area where it has been suggested that seasonal pasturing in the 12th and 13th centuries eventually led to small holdings in the 16th century, and finally to their abandonment in the 18th and 19th centuries. Recent analysis of soil pollen samples from a homestead at Hafod Rhug Uchaf, Snowdonia, investigated as part of the Deserted Rural Settlement Project (see Chapter 6), supported the view that the house, which was probably entirely post-medieval in date, was established within a fresh intake of rough grazing (Caseldine 2001).

There are also examples of changes from permanently farmed land to seasonal usage which should also be detectable in the pollen record, for example at Cwm Pennant (Silvester this volume) where it has been proposed that platform settlements and associated fields were followed by *hafodydd* in the late medieval period. However, not only the sequence of land use but also the timing of changes appears to have varied. Transhumance seems to have declined earlier in eastern Radnorshire than in the west and north-west of Wales (Silvester this volume). Certainly there is some evidence to suggest differences in date for the widespread change from heather moorland to grassland, which has been interpreted as an increase in grazing intensity by sheep, with *Calluna* declining for at least 200 years in some areas, for example around Llyn Conwy, Llyn Llagi, and Llyn Dulyn; in others, for example around Llyn Clyd, from as early as c. 1300; and in others, for example Llyn Gynon, Llyn y Bi, and Llyn Irddyn, much more recently, within the last 150 years (Stevenson and Thompson 1993).

Agricultural activity may also have affected valley alluviation and in the Ilston valley the onset of one episode of valley alluviation has been tentatively dated to around 1440–1600, and attributed to enclosure and increased agricultural activity in the catchment (Saunders *et al* 1989).

7.10 Settlement activity

It is not only the nature of the farming in the surrounding landscape but the activities taking place within the settlement itself that are of interest. Here palaeoenvironmental studies can make a contribution, for example, by indicating whether cereals were being processed on site, whether there is evidence for animal fodder as well as food for human consumption, what type of wood was being collected for fuel or structural purposes, whether peat was being used for fuel, and whether there is evidence for the use of particular structures, for example as byres.

However, there are relatively few deserted rural settlement sites in Wales where these types of study have been carried out. At Cefn Graeanog, Gwynedd,

the charred assemblage (Hillman 1982) indicated plants were being collected for weaving, bedding, fodder, and fuel, and provided evidence for the tillage methods employed, while at Erw-wen, Ardudwy (Conway 1988), high phosphate values associated with a rectangular structure were considered to indicate its use as a byre or sty. A difference in phosphate values within buildings at Bryn Cysegrfan, Ceredigion (Gerrard 1988), and Cefn Drum, Gower (Kissock 2000), has been interpreted as possibly reflecting the typical longhouse division into living accommodation and byre. Phosphate enrichment of the soils at Tro'r Derlwyn, Carmarthenshire, has been interpreted as indicating the ancillary structure was used for livestock and that either the enclosures were used for the penning of livestock or had received manure for cereal production (Crowther 1999). Increased phosphate levels at Llystan Ganol, Gwynedd, have also indicated that a platform or yard area was possibly used for animal coralling (Owen 1999).

7.11 Recent palaeoenvironmental investigations: the evidence from Ynys Ettws

As part of the Deserted Rural Settlement Project a limited amount of excavation was undertaken, providing an opportunity for environmental sampling (see Chapter 6). Brief reference has already been made to the results from Tro'r Derlwyn and Hafod Rhug. Here the results from Ynys Ettws, Nant Peris (Fig 6.3), will be discussed in more detail.

Ynys Ettws was selected for investigation because it had been considered to be a classic example of a *hafod* (summer dwelling) (Lynch 1995). The purpose of the palaeobotanical investigations at Ynys Ettws was to ascertain the environmental setting of the settlement and to recover any evidence which would indicate the nature of the agricultural activity associated with it. The study included pollen (Fig 7.3) and plant macrofossil analyses (Tables 7.1 and 7.2), charcoal and wood identification (Table 7.3 and 7.4), and radiocarbon dating (Table 7.5). Samples were recovered from two environmental pits excavated in a small boggy area to the south of the house where a spring emerged, from a buried soil beneath the surrounding hood bank and from various contexts exposed during the excavation of the house itself (details, including laboratory methods, in site archive). Three pollen zones, reflecting changes in pollen frequency, have been recognised in the pollen diagram from the environmental pit (Fig 7.3).

Radiocarbon determinations from charcoal from the old land surface (880±70 ^{14}C years BP: Beta–127671), from a small pit taken to represent the first phase of occupation (780±70 ^{14}C years BP: Beta–127670), and an extrapolated date for the base of the organic deposits (c. 800 ^{14}C years BP) are broadly in agreement. A second phase of occupation possibly dates to the 17th or 18th century.

The earliest evidence suggests that some birch and hazel woodland or scrub still persisted in the area when the settlement was first established, contrasting with the pollen record from c. 5–6km away at the lower end of Llanberis Pass which was interpreted as reflecting a largely open catchment (Elner and Happey-Wood 1980). Oak, alder, and ash were probably growing in the valley below. Confirmation of the presence of these taxa is provided by the charcoal identifications (Table 7.3). A range of seeds indicative of shallow water and

muddy places reflects the conditions around the spring at that time, and waterlogged seeds of birch and alder and hazelnut fragments in the deposits also support the pollen evidence for contemporary local woodland. However, although variations in the arboreal pollen record during zone YM1 may indicate periods of clearance and regeneration they could also reflect deposition of the woody material either naturally or deliberately, redeposited pollen, or possibly sediment disturbance by stock trampling around the spring. Nevertheless, local hazel may have been cleared first, followed by birch, with later minor fluctuations perhaps reflecting recolonisation and renewed clearance associated with differences in activity in the area. Clearance could have been deliberate or could relate to grazing pressures, while some woodland may have been retained both for fuel and to provide shelter in inclement weather. Around 390 ^{14}C years BP (interpolated date) there may have been a brief period when land was abandoned and birch and hazel woodland expanded, before almost total clearance of woodland in the area by c. 220±80 ^{14}C years BP (Beta–136985). Immediately prior to this an increase in *Alnus* values suggests a limited expansion in alder woodland, perhaps in the valley below. The limited archaeological evidence for activity is considered to indicate a relatively short period of occupation, although if it was a *hafod* little evidence might be expected (Peate 1946), and the record during zone YM1 could largely represent changes following abandonment.

One tree which is surprisingly well represented in zone YM1 and in the soil pollen record is holly (*Ilex aquifolium*). Although holly is a common constituent of oakwoods in Wales, *Ilex* pollen is generally rare in peat deposits because of poor dispersal characteristics. It is likely to be abundant in more minerogenic deposits where forest clearance has resulted in soil erosion (Moore *et al* 1986). Its relatively high values in this zone suggest either the close proximity of contemporary holly to the site, which is supported by the presence of seeds, or the possibility that some of the pollen is redeposited. It is regarded as a grazing-resistant shrub, although intensive grazing does limit the survival of holly seedlings (Moore *et al* 1986). Throughout the zone both microscopic and macro-

8th–10th centuries, before further woodland clearance in the 13th and 15th centuries accompanied by major agricultural expansion (Bostock 1980).

Further to the south a marked phase of woodland clearance and intensification of grazing in an undated diagram from Pont-Scethin, western Rhinogau (Walker and Taylor 1976), has been assigned to the medieval period, while the disappearance of woodland on the upland margins in north Ceredigion, identified in soil pollen records, has been assigned largely to the post-medieval period (Smith and Taylor 1969). Dates of changes in the pollen record from a series of sites in west-central Wales (Moore 1968; Moore and Chater 1969) have been based on palynological/historical correlations rather than radiocarbon dates. It was suggested that following a period of regeneration, which was interpreted as post-dating the Roman withdrawal, renewed activity was linked to the establishment of Strata Florida Abbey and organised pastoral farming, and instructions from Edward I in 1280 for the clearance of woodland. A pause in woodland destruction was tentatively ascribed to the Black Death and Owain Glyndwr's rebellion. Renewed woodland clearance was attributed to the growth of the cattle rearing industry and enclosure of the uplands. Finally, it was suggested the abandonment of upland holdings led to some recovery in woodland during the 19th and 20th centuries, initially aided by deliberate afforestation by individuals and later the Forestry Commission.

Recent work at Tregaron in lowland west Wales (Hughes *et al* 2001; Morriss 2001) has confirmed earlier findings (Turner 1964) in suggesting a period of scrubby woodland regeneration during the Dark Ages followed by removal of the woodland. At Carneddau in upland mid-Wales, extensive clearance occurred in the Romano-British period (Walker 1993). However, some scrub woodland regeneration in the post-medieval period may indicate abandonment of the area during the so-called Little Ice Age before a return to upland agriculture in the 18th century onwards led to the final clearance of remaining woodland and scrub and the development of the present, open landscape. Further south at Cefn Gwernffrwd, near Rhandirmwyn, it has been suggested that the plateau woodland had largely disappeared in Romano-British times and an open landscape predominated thereafter (Chambers 1983b).

At Coed Taf in the Brecon Beacons vestigial hazel scrub was finally removed by c. 1155 ^{14}C years BP (Chambers 1983a). In contrast at the nearby site of Corn Du a decline in hazel possibly occurred c. 2000 ^{14}C years BP (Chambers and Lageard 1993), while at

Llangorse a largely open landscape, but with more shrub (mainly hazel), developed during the post-Roman period (Jones *et al* 1985; 1991). Both to the east in the Black Mountains (Price and Moore 1984) and to the west at Waun-Fignen-Felen (Smith and Cloutman 1988) on the Black Mountain, there is some evidence for woodland regeneration at the end of the Romano-British period, while at Penrhiwen (Cloutman 1983), also on the Black Mountain, some woodland in the upper valleys may have persisted before widespread clearance c. 1200[14]C years BP. At Cefn Hirgoed, Glamorgan (Walker *et al* 1997), the onset of peat accumulation during the medieval period appears to coincide with a major landscape change from woodland to a more open environment.

In the Preselis, in south-west Wales, an intensification of clearance activity has been dated to c. 950 ^{14}C years BP at Ty Rhyg, which post-dates c. 1100 ^{14}C years BP at Dolaeron (Seymour 1985). A decline in woodland has also been recorded at Carn Ingli during the 12th and 13th centuries (Pearson *et al* 1997). A period of woodland recovery and reduced activity has been dated to c. 500 BP at Llannerch and attributed to factors including the dissolution of the monasteries, the Black Death and climatic change before renewed activity in the late 17th and 18th centuries (Seymour 1985).

At Llanllwch Bog near Carmarthen a reduction in tree pollen was ascribed to the demand for oak and elm in the 18th-century changes and the appearance of *Pinus* pollen to planting in the early 19th century (Thomas 1965). A more detailed and accurately dated account of woodland and clearance activity from the 14th century onwards at Llanllwch is given by Rosen (1998). At Crymlyn Bog near Swansea (Rosen 1998; Rosen and Dumayne-Peaty 2001) substantial woodland clearance did not occur until c. 1885; prior to this there was only some small-scale woodland disturbance, and arable and pastoral agriculture near the site.

Whilst changes in the availability of woodland during the medieval period and later are apparent from the pollen record, very little charcoal and wood has been recovered from deserted rural settlement sites. At Gelligaer in the Glamorgan uplands hazel, hawthorn, oak, possible alder, field maple, pine, and *Prunus* (cherry, blackthorn) were recorded (Mabey 1939; Hyde 1939) but, apart from indicating their possible presence in the area and use as a resource, the extent of woodland is unknown. Charcoal from Hafod y Nant Criafolen in the Brenig Valley, Clwyd, was interpreted as representing open woodland and heath (Morgan and Keepax 1979).

scopic charcoal is present, reflecting occupation and activity at the site. Higher charcoal values towards the end of the zone coincide with an increase in minerogenic material and a decline in arboreal pollen suggesting renewed local clearance and/or soil erosion. The beginning of zone YM2 is dated to 220±80 ^{14}C years BP (Beta–136985) and marks a lithostratigraphic change to a *Sphagnum* peat, while a radiocarbon determination of 240±70 ^{14}C years BP (Beta–12670) from beneath the slab floor is taken to represent the second phase of occupation and the construction of a small hut. Charcoal is not recorded and changes in the pollen record suggest a different level of activity at the site. By this time the bare, open mountainsides of today were established, although an increase in *Pinus* pollen and other arboreal taxa in zone YM3 indicates renewed afforestation in the 18th and 19th centuries and the establishment of conifer plantations.

Throughout the period covered by the pollen diagram, abundant grass (*Poaceae*) pollen, and pollen and seeds of weed taxa indicative of grassland predominate, although small amounts of *Calluna* pollen perhaps indicate some heather communities at higher altitudes, suggesting that the settlement was primarily associated with pastoralism. However, there is evidence to suggest some cultivation locally or that cereal was being brought onto the site during the first phase of occupation. If cultivation was not taking place in the immediate area it was possibly occurring not too far away, perhaps at Ynys Ettws Cottage 200m below in the valley. Cereal type pollen is relatively well represented in zone YM1, although some of the grains could be derived from wild grasses (Dickson 1988). Confirmation that cereals were present at the site is provided in the macrofossil record. Even though no cereal was recovered from the house itself, charred oat (*Avena* sp.) grains were found in the samples from the marshy area as well as waterlogged oat remains, including one grain and a number of floret bases. The floret bases demonstrate that the oat was cultivated rather than wild, and suggest that both common oat (*Avena sativa*) and bristle/black oat (*Avena strigosa*) were present. A rachis node of wheat (*Triticum* sp.) was also recovered. Pollen of weeds of cultivation includes *Anthemis* type pollen, which is frequent, and occasional grains of mugwort (*Artemisia* type) and cornflower (*Centaurea cyanus*). Corn marigold (*Chrysanthemum segetum*), a common weed of cultivation, is included in the *Anthemis* type pollen group, and waterlogged seeds of corn marigold are frequent in the plant macrofossil record, as well as a few charred

seeds. Similar evidence for corn marigold was also recorded at the medieval farmstead of Cefn Graeanog (Chambers 1982c, 1983c; Hillman 1982). *Rumex* pollen values are also relatively high and dock and sheep's sorrel seeds are frequent. These could reflect cultivation, but docks occur in a variety of habitats including grassland and damp places. One or two charred dock and sheep's sorrel seeds occur in sample 18 from a pit associated with the first building, but their presence may simply reflect plant remains used as tinder or accidentally burnt rather than waste from crop processing deliberately burnt as there is an absence of any cereal remains. Although the occurrence of heath grass is indicative of mountain and moorland habitats it has been recorded with cereals in a number of charred seed assemblages from archaeological sites, leading to the suggestion that formerly it was an arable weed (Hillman 1982). Its inability to survive ploughing if a mould board plough is used has also led to the suggestion that its presence indicates the use of an ard (Hillman 1982).

The presence of waterlogged cornfield weeds and chaff suggests that grain was being brought to the site unprocessed, or only partially processed, or that cultivation was taking place close to the site and the remains became incorporated naturally or accidentally in the deposits rather than deliberately. Oat is a spring-sown crop and it might have been feasible for there to have been some small-scale cultivation during the summer months, but there is no archaeological evidence to support this, or that the settlement was permanent rather than a *hafod*. Oat could have been used for human consumption in the form of oatcakes or porridge, or used as a supplementary feed for cattle, and certainly the crop processing waste could have been used as fodder.

Other plants which could have been used for fodder include holly, which in the past has been used for sheep and other stock, particularly in the winter, and trees were often pollarded for this purpose (Nicholson and Clapham 1975). Gorse was also valued as a fodder crop, while heather and bracken were formerly used as flooring or bedding. Two circular features just above the hut might have been stack stands for ricks of fodder or bedding, and again the botanical evidence would support this. Finally, apart from the botanical evidence suggesting that the site was primarily used for pastoralism, two probable sheep droppings were recovered from the environmental pit.

Apart from the cereal remains found in the samples from the environmental pit, charred bramble fruit stones and hazelnut fragments were found in the pit associated with the first phase. These could represent wild resources collected for food, although they could simply reflect woody material used as fuel. Burnt bone was frequent in the sample from the pit and, together with the charred plant remains, appears to represent waste material. Waterlogged remains of bramble and hazelnut taxa, as well as a seed of wild strawberry, also occur in the samples from the environmental pit and similarly could indicate deliberate collection.

Artefactual evidence from the site was scarce but there was one slender piece of wood, identified as yew (*Taxus baccata*), which showed clear toolmarks made by a metal tool. This was the only piece of wood recovered from the spring area which showed evidence of woodworking, the remaining pieces consisting of small pieces of roundwood, ie twigs, of birch, alder, and hazel, chips of oak and one small chip of rowan/hawthorn type (*Pomoideae* type). Apart from the yew and rowan/hawthorn, the same species occur in the charcoal record, with the addition of ash.

By c. 220±80 ^{14}C years BP there are clear changes in the palaeoenvironmental record which probably relate to the second phase of occupation, the establishment of a small hut probably used as an occasional shepherd's or cowherd's shelter. Grassland predominates and *Plantago* and *Potentilla* type pollen values increase, possibly suggesting an increase in grazing

pressure. There is no cereal pollen evidence. The occasional *Cannabis* type grain probably reflects hemp growing in the lowlands, as evidenced at Llyn Cororion (Watkins 1990), rather than local activity. Charcoal is also absent, confirming the lack of woodland in the area by this time and perhaps indicating that peat was being burned in the later house. The evidence tends to suggest that any activity at the site was more limited than during the first phase. This period broadly relates to a period of climatic deterioration indicated by proxy climatic records as being a period of cooler and wetter decades from c. 1680–1850, corresponding with the later phase of the Little Ice Age (Barber *et al* 1999).

To summarise, some woodland may have survived in the area when the first settlement was established, providing shelter and a fuel resource. It seems most likely that the settlement during the initial phase of occupation was a *hafod*, although there is some evidence to suggest that the seasonal habitation may have been longer than just summer. The evidence does support the view that the second phase of settlement was impermanent and probably consisted of a hut for a shepherd or cowherd. The absence of cereal in the later record and the change in settlement character may reflect climatic change but social and economic factors may have been more important and further work would be necessary to resolve this.

7.12 Future investigations

The extensive peat deposits in Wales mean there are many possible areas where palaeoenvironmental investigations could be carried out, although this does not necessarily mean the record for the historic period survives. Although the presence of peat deposits in the vicinity of deserted rural settlement sites was not consistently recorded during the survey, such evidence was frequently observed. In north Wales, for example, peat deposits close to two platform houses at Ysbyty and a long hut at Llechwedd Erwent were noted as well as peat cutting near Pen y Gadair. There are also a number of deserted rural settlement sites associated with ridge and furrow where peat deposits occur within the vicinity, for example, near the platform houses Craig-y-Gesail, Beudy'r Garth, and Gesail Gyfarch but at the last named there is evidence of peat cutting. Another area where there may be suitable deposits for analysis not far from cultivation ridges with platforms associated is Cwm Pennant, Llandrillo (Silvester this volume). Similarly, in the

hills above Tregaron and Llandewi Brefi, examples of platforms, long huts, and ridge and furrow occur with possible peat sites not far away. Further south on Fforest Fawr and Mynydd Du there are traces of arable activity (Leighton 1997, Fig 55). At Craig Cerrig-gleisiad platforms, cultivation terraces, enclosures, and lynchets occur at 460m OD and although there is a pollen diagram (Walker 1982) from the area it provides only an early and mid-Holocene record, serving as a reminder that the historic record is not always present. Clearance features are associated with platform groups on Pant y Gadair and Coetgae, and peat deposits occur within these areas but at a much higher altitude. In the Mynydd Myddfai area there are examples of cultivation ridges in the vicinity of rectangular buildings which may be contemporary, and a single platform which may be associated with arable activity. The existence of peat deposits in the general area may offer a means of confirming this. Deserted rural settlements are frequently located next to streams or springs and the example of Ynys Ettws demonstrates the possibility of the survival of environmental and economic evidence where a spring exists close to such a site. Not only this, but the possibility of organic artefactual remains surviving in waterlogged contexts suggests that such deposits should be investigated during any excavation, if they occur.

7.13 Conclusions

Although there is a considerable body of palaeoenvironmental evidence for the historic period much of it has been obtained independent of archaeological investigations. Whilst a number of general trends can be identified, it is equally apparent that there are local differences and generalisations might be misleading, particularly if applied to areas where there is little or no palaeoenvironmental evidence. Integrated studies are required in the future to help determine the function of deserted rural settlements and their environmental context, for example, whether they represent permanent settlement or seasonal settlement associated with transhumance and a *hafod/hendre* system, although this division may be too simplistic. Palaeoenvironmental data can be used to test assumptions derived from other lines of evidence and, where possible, a multidisciplinary approach combining documentary and place-name evidence, as well as archaeological survey and excavation, with palaeoenvironmental evidence, supported by dating techniques, should be adopted to advance and refine our understanding of the settlements and their contemporary environment.

Table 7.1 Waterlogged and charred plant remains from the environmental pit at Ynys Ettws
Montia fontana includes all four subspecies, ie ssp. *fontana*, ssp. *variabilis*, ssp. *amporitana*, and ssp. *minor*.

Sample	A	B
Ranunculus repens type (Creeping buttercup)	2	36
Ranunculus flammula type (Lesser spearwort)	6	3
Charred *Ranunculus flammula* type	1	-
Ranunculus sp. (Buttercups)	-	3
Urtica dioica L. (Common nettle)	6	4
Betula sp. (Birch)	237	336
Betula sp. – catkin bracts	41	55
Betula sp. – catkins	1	9
Alnus glutinosa (L.) Gaertner (Alder)	15	55
Alnus glutinosa (L.) Gaertner – cone	1	-
Alnus glutinosa (L.) Gaertner – cone-scales	-	4
Corylus avellana L. frags. (Hazel)	5	28
Charred *Corylus avellana* L. frags.	-	3
Montia fontana L. * (Blinks)	14	1000+
Stellaria media (L.) Villars (Common chickweed)	-	1
Stellaria uliginosa Murray (Bog stitchwort)	8	29

Persicaria hydropiper (L.) Spach (Water-pepper)	16	14
Persicaria hydropiper (L.) Spach – perianth	1	-
Rumex acetosella L. – and perianth (Sheep's sorrel)	-	6
Rumex acetosella L.	2	11
Rumex sp. – and perianth (Docks)	7	28
Rumex sp.	18	84
Immature *Rumex* sp.	-	13
Rumex perianth	-	6
Rumex tubercle	1	-
Viola sp. (Violets)	-	11
Cardamine type (Bitter-cresses)	-	20
Calluna vulgaris (L.) Hull (Heather)	4	3
Calluna vulgaris (L.) Hull – shoots	4	8
Lysimachia sp. (Loosestrifes)	1	1
Rubus fruticosus L. agg. (Brambles)	2	2
Potentilla erecta (L.) Raeusch (Tormentil)	2	14
Potentilla sp. (Cinquefoils)	-	2
Fragaria vesca L. (Wild strawberry)	-	1
Ulex sp. – spines (Gorses)	5	-
Ilex aquifolium L. (Holly)	2	1
Linum catharticum L. (Fairy flax)	1	-
Oxalis acetosella L. (Wood-sorrel)	-	1
Prunella vulgaris L. (Selfheal)	1	-
Callitriche sp. (Water-starworts)	-	1
Galium uliginosum L./ *G.saxatile* L.(Fen/heath bedstraw)	-	1
Lapsana communis L. (Nipplewort)	-	3
Chrysanthemum segetum L. (Corn marigold)	29	107
Charred *Chrysanthemum segetum* L.	1	4
Juncus sp. (Rushes)	100s	100s

Luzula sp. (Wood-rushes)	5	3
Isolepis setacea (L.) R. Br. (Bristle club-rush)	-	1
Carex spp. – biconvex with utricle (Sedges)	4	100
Carex spp. – biconvex	5	63
Carex spp. – trigonous	10	30
Carex sp. – utricle	-	1
Avena cf. *strigosa* type – floret bases(Bristle oat)	3	1
Avena strigosa/sativa – floret bases	23	3
Avena cf. *sativa* – floret bases (Oat)	-	2
Avena sp.	1	-
Charred *Avena* sp. – grain (Oats)	-	2.5 + 2 frags
Avena/ Large Poaceae – floret bases	24	12
*Avena/*Large Poaceae – pedicels	-	1
Bromus sp. (Brome)	1	1
Triticum sp. – rachis node (Wheat)	1	-
Charred Cerealia indet. frags.	-	2
Danthonia decumbens (L.) DC. (Heath grass)	1	4
Poaceae > 2mm (Large grasses)	6	19
Large Poaceae – pedicel	1	-
Poaceae < 2mm (Small grasses)	9	8
Poaceae – lemmas	8	1
charred node	-	1
straw frags.	3	-
Buds	10	9
Bud scales	5	-
Thorns	4	1
Pteridium aquilinum (L.) Kuhn – leaf frags. (Bracken)	52	60
Charred *Pteridium aquilinum* (L.) Kuhn – leaf frags.	3	-
Fungal sclerotia	-	1

Table 7.2 Charred plant remains from Ynys Ettws

Sample	11	12	13	16	18	19
Context	9	18	41	34	34	35
Corylus avellana L. frags (Hazel)	-	1	-	-	18	-
Rumex acetosella L.(Sheep's sorrel)	-	-	-	-	2	-
Rumex sp. (Docks)	-	-	-	-	1	-
Rubus fruticosus L. agg. (Brambles)	-	-	-	-	1	-
Avena sp. (Oats)	-	-	1	-	-	-
Burnt bone frags.	34	-	-	12	407	-
Bone frags.	-	-	-	-	3	-

Table 7.3 Charcoal identification from Ynys Ettws

Sample	11	12	13	16	A	B
Context	9	18	14	34		
Quercus sp. (Oak)	3	1	3	2	-	4
Betula sp. (Birch)	7	19	4	16	5	-
Alnus glutinosa (L.) Gaertner (Alder)	4	-	3	1	-	2
Corylus avellana L. (Hazel)	2	-	4	-	1	5
Fraxinus excelsior L. (Ash)	2	-	5	-	2	1

Table 7.4 Wood identification from Ynys Ettws

Sample	Basal deposit	A	B
Quercus sp. (Oak)	-	2	2
Betula sp. (Birch)	-	2	-
Alnus glutinosa (L.) Gaertner (Alder)	2	-	-
Corylus avellana L. (Hazel)	1	-	1
Pomoideae type (Rowan, hawthorn etc)	-	1	-

Table 7.5 Calibrated radiocarbon dates from the pollen monolith from Ynys Ettws

Laboratory code	Sample depth (cm)	Conventional radiocarbon age	2 Sigma calibrated result (95% probability)*
Beta–136984	32.5–34.5	130±60 BP	Cal AD 1650–1955 (Cal BP 300–5)
Beta–136985	51.5–53.5	220±80 BP	Cal AD 1480–1955 (Cal BP 470–5)
Beta–136986	75.5–77.5	730±70 BP	Cal AD 1185–1395 (Cal BP 765–555)

*Stuiver, M. *et al* 1998 INTCAL 98 Radiocarbon Age Calibration. *Radiocarbon* 40 (3), 1041–1083.

8 DESERTED RURAL SETTLEMENT: THE ARCHITECTURAL EVIDENCE

By Judith Alfrey

8.1 Introduction

Many of the abandoned dwellings, disused farms and farm buildings which are still scattered across the rural landscape retain substantial architectural fabric and are derelict rather than completely ruinous. These 'architectural ruins' are – alongside archaeological sites – an important class of evidence for the study of deserted rural settlement, and of rural building. Virtually all of them are post-medieval, and many may be no older than the 19th century. They encompass a surprising range of building types. Some are whole farmsteads, others small cottages, or isolated field-barns, some even substantial gentry houses (Fig 8.1). Some had quite specific historical contexts, as for example the development of remote quarrying communities, or the encroachment or enclosure of upland wastes in the expansion of rural settlement in the late 18th and early 19th centuries (Fig 8.2). Many of these turned out to have been short-lived, abandoned on the closure of quarries, or deserted in a shift of settlement into the nucleated villages which grew up during the 19th century (Fig 8.3). Others lie within settlement patterns which have otherwise remained substantially viable. Occasionally, for example, an old house lies derelict alongside its replacement, direct testimony to a process of renewal and change long characteristic in the history of buildings (Fig 8.4). Wherever they are, these buildings are often not very different in kind from those which elsewhere have continued in occupation. Many of the smallest cottages can be matched with surviving examples. However, removed at some time from the sequences of change which characterise most inhabited buildings, these ruins may store valuable information about what rural buildings were once like.

Derelict buildings introduce several important themes in deserted rural settlement studies. These *standing ruins* are largely post-medieval, witness to the fact that desertion has afflicted settlement in all period,

and indeed continues to do so, and not only for the marginal settlement or the poor building. Desertion may be about change in either a major or a minor key in the organisation of settlement and the development of building types – that is, it may be the result either of radical change in the organisation of settlement (wholesale abandonment) or of relatively minor adjustment (farm consolidation, for example) (Fig 8.5). These ruins also show that desertion was not always the result of structural change in settlement patterns, but could simply be the effect of change in building traditions, or in social aspiration expressed through building – as witnessed by rebuilding in more permanent materials, or on a bigger scale, for instance. In addition, the distribution of derelict buildings in the landscape begins to modify the map of settlement provided by buildings in use, revealing a greater density of habitation, especially at higher altitudes and on marginal land. These are all themes which can be paralleled in the deserted settlements considered elsewhere in this volume.

In addition to those buildings which retain recognisable architectural character, there are other sites where built remnants are more fragmentary. There is, for example, a tide-mark of ruins beyond the upper limits of contemporary settlement in almost any upland landscape. Settlement sites where there are now only scant remains could simply be the relics of properties similar to those which still stand, but abandoned long enough ago to have arrived at a more advanced state of decay. If so, surviving buildings may hold the key to their detailed interpretation through a comparative process. But it is also possible that some of these fragmentary remains are quite different types of site, with no equivalent in the stock of surviving buildings. In such a case, these sites may add qualitatively as well as quantitatively to the picture of rural settlement

8.1 Penrhos, Caerleon, Monmouthshire. An abandoned multi-period gentry house, a reconstruction dated 1718 of an earlier 17th-century house, itself perhaps with medieval origins. (Crown copyright: RCAHMW)

which more intact standing buildings can provide. After all, the corpus of standing buildings has many gaps in it, which perhaps archaeological evidence could fill. The chronological range of surviving buildings is in some areas short, with few early structures; the typological range is often also restricted, weighted in favour of higher-status houses, especially for earlier periods. Historical research yields evidence for building types which have long gone, and whose traces are rare or non-existent: there are numerous documentary references to hovels and *tai unnos*; there are also references to seasonally occupied dwellings. All of these are site types with no significant extant counterpart, for which the best evidence will therefore be archaeological.

Buildings are a rich historical archive, which at its best gives detailed information about land use, economic organisation, and social fabric. All of this is encoded in the distribution of buildings in the landscape, and in the details of their construction and design. By extending the chronologies and typologies of standing buildings, archaeological study has the potential to enhance considerably our understanding of past rural society. At the same time, the study of standing buildings suggests tools for the interpretation of this archaeological record, not least by elucidating the ways in which buildings are cultural constructs.

This chapter seeks to identify the types of site which may have been abandoned, and the types of building which may have been lost. It does this by taking as a point of departure the evidence offered by standing buildings for the physical settlement pattern and the social and economic structure of rural society in the past. It identifies where there are gaps in the information they provide – missing pieces in the jigsaw of rural settlement – and asks to what extent these gaps can be filled by archaeological evidence. It also considers the extent to which standing buildings can be used as a guide to interpreting the archaeological record.

8.2 Patterns of settlement

The picture of rural settlement which can be assembled from the evidence of standing buildings is partial. The map which they offer is distinctive, but incomplete. The defining character of rural settlement across much of Wales is one of dispersed farmsteads, with

dispersion at varying densities. But this surviving pattern represents a certain rationalisation of settlement. Less-favoured land was colonised at times of population pressure, with the establishment of upland farms and smallholdings, *hafotai* and remote quarry settlements. These were all abandoned in shifting patterns of agriculture and industry; even in the lowlands, farmsteads fell victim to consolidation, and as villages grew up, so the scatter of cottages across farmland was lost.

Witnesses to the Royal Commission on Land frequently referred to the depopulation of the rural landscape. Richard Roberts of Trawsfynydd, for example, described farms 'running out of cultivation and becoming one with the mountain', and said that around Trawsfynydd 'during the last forty years fifty-one labourers' cottages were lost. There are also twelve or thirteen farmhouses less than forty years ago' (Royal Commission on Land Vol 1, 1895, 389). There were similar reports from Carmarthenshire: at Cilycwm 'within a radius of four miles, fifty cottages have disappeared, and twenty-three farms have been consolidated'. Another witness reported 'I know of about fifty small farms which have been added to others in the parishes of Llanybyther, Llansawel, Cayo and Talley, and one hundred and twenty one labourers cottages and labourers houses in the above which have been allowed to fall into ruin in the last thirty to forty years' (Royal Commission on Land Vol. 3, 1895, p160 and 182). Similar examples could be cited from almost anywhere in rural Wales.

These stories of abandonment are relatively recent and there are others which would be more recent still, but historians have also identified similar processes which operated much longer ago: the girdle settlements associated with the ramifying communities of kindred groups fell victim to consolidation even before the 16th century as the process of fragmentation associated with partible inheritance became unsustainable. Most of the early hamlets associated with bond communities shrank over the course of time to single farmsteads (Thomas and Carter 1957, p121–81).

This ebb and flow of settlement continues: many of those rural buildings which are now derelict were inhabited within living memory. But these cycles of change contain different processes. One of these is a shifting pattern of adjustment, of movement away from the margins – the smallholders' cottages which lie empty on the quarried margins of Snowdonia are akin to examples which survive less remotely, and the upland farms established on poor land at times of population pressure may conform to the same traditions as their better-favoured neighbours. The buildings on these abandoned outlying holdings were not necessarily different in kind from examples which survived elsewhere. Change was sometimes even more haphazard. Whether a particular farmstead survived or was lost to consolidation may have been an accident of its condition and occupancy at a time of changing land management. The importance of ownership histories in determining the history of individual buildings is also clear, and is demonstrated for earlier periods elsewhere in this volume (Locock, Chapter 3).

There were also more radical qualitative changes, in which some forms of settlement were lost altogether.

8.2 Ruined quarry cottages above Waunfawr, Gwynedd, clearly illustrating local traditions of stone working (Crown copyright: RCAHMW)

Of these, it is the seasonal settlements which have commanded particular interest: 'Their produce is cattle and sheep, which during summer keep very high in the mountains, followed by their owners with their families, who reside during that season in hafod-dai or summer dwellings, or dairy houses ... During summer the men pass their time either in harvest work in tending their herds, the women in milking or making butter and cheese ... towards the winter, they descend to their hen dref' (Jones n. d., 53). *Hafotai* which survived the complete abandonment of transhumance did so only by adaptation and reconstruction as new farmsteads – there are no known structures surviving intact which match Pennant's famous description: 'these houses consist of a long low room with a hole at one end, to let out the smoke from the fire' (Kirk 1998, 1784, 169–70). This description was repeated in other early 19th-century accounts of Merioneth and Caernarvonshire. One of these perhaps implies that the buildings were built anew each year: '. . . leave their winter habitations and take up residence amidst the hills, where they erect what are termed havodtai ... which are merely huts ...' (Evans 1802, 206).

It is not suprising that buildings which were 'merely huts' have not survived in recognisable form. Archaeological investigation, however, can begin to identify such sites and enable their organisation to be better understood. Central to the organisation and use of land in upland regions, the pattern of *hafod* and *hendre* changed with alterations in tenurial arrangement – these changes are considered in the chapter by David Longley. Elsewhere in this volume, physical evidence for a possible typology of seasonal settlements is assembled. The suggestion that there may also have been deliberately short-term settlements (Locock) cautions against oversimplifying our models of earlier settlement organisation and building traditions, by introducing the possibility that abandonment was not only intentional, but foreseen. Intentionally temporary structures have probably always formed part of the building stock – a part about which little is so far known.

8.3 Chronologies

In the course of change, many early standing structures have been erased from the landscape. There simply are not enough surviving medieval buildings to permit interpretation of former settlements from standing buildings alone.

The idea of a 'great rebuilding' – a major period of building activity before which little has survived and which defined the architectural character of an area – was first identified by W G Hoskins (Hoskins 1965, 131–48). The phenomenon is now widely recognised, but it is acknowledged that this activity took place at different times and at different rates in different areas and for different social groups. In some areas of Wales, notably, for example, Ceredigion and parts of Carmarthenshire and Pembrokeshire, pre-19th century buildings are conspicuous only by their absence (see for example Smith 1998). In areas like these, any account of earlier settlement patterns and architectural traditions must draw heavily on archaeological evidence. In more prosperous counties such as Monmouthshire and Montgomeryshire, and areas with better access to good building materials, such as Merioneth and Caernarvonshire, a continuous architectural development sequence can be assembled from the later 16th century with some evidence for even earlier periods (Smith 2001). But these early buildings are virtually always the homes of a prosperous class – it is only from the late 18th century that there is any consistent survival of buildings with more humble origins (for example, Wiliam 1982a).

Nearly everywhere, a far-reaching rebuilding programme associated in part with changes to the structure of landed society and to the nature of land-holding, has resulted in a historic buildings' stock dominated by houses and farms of the 19th century. The earliest buildings to survive in any region (whether they are late 16th-century or late 18th- are clearly heirs to more-or-less sophisticated traditions of building about which we often know little. For example, in areas dominated by stone, such as Merioneth and Caernarvonshire, there is evidence for a prior tradition of timber-framing: a number of cruck-framed buildings have been identified in these upland areas (Fig 8.6), and the quality of carpentry in late 16th-century stone-built houses suggests that a highly developed tradition lay behind these early survivals (Smith 2001). Although reconstruction on the same site was presumably common, contraction or relocation of settlements should also mean that evidence of earlier buildings has survived archaeologically. Although the present study has focused its attention mainly on upland landscapes, some consideration has also been given to lowland sites (Sylvester, Chapter 2; Sambrook, Chapter 5). From these areas, material is

8.3 A ruined landscape of interspersed quarrying and farming, Nantlle Valley, Gwynedd (Crown copyright: RCAHMW)

emerging which enables extension of the typologies yielded by standing buildings by providing evidence for earlier modes of building. More detailed archaeological work would clearly be of value in this area.

Evidence from the deserted upland settlements – and many of those which formed the basis for this study are presumed to be medieval – could also deepen our knowledge about the development of building traditions: these settlement sites may represent a valuable pool of evidence for earlier periods. Interpretation of this evidence, however, will need to be securely based on an understanding of the social, economic, and cultural context of these settlements: the evolution of building design and construction is a social process.

8.4 Social histories

A detailed social hierarchy of buildings can be reconstructed in some areas for the more recent past, ranging from the substantial gentry house to the labourer's cottage. Similar reconstruction is much more difficult for the sub-medieval period and earlier, because survival is weighted in favour of higher-status buildings. Most surviving sub-medieval houses are the dwellings of a small upper class which was wealthy enough to employ tradesmen building in recognisable architectural traditions (Smith 2001). Although it has been estimated that by the late 17th century between a quarter and a third of the population belonged to the labouring classes (Howells 1975, 263), we know almost nothing about how they were housed. It is only from the late 18th century that there is any systematic survival of labourers' dwellings. These lost small dwellings could be recovered archaeologically. But, less substantially built than the larger contemporary farmhouses, they will perhaps have left little visible trace.

What the evidence of surviving buildings also reveals is the contemporary use of different building traditions (of setting out as well as of construction) depending on social context. This has important implications for interpretation of the archaeological record. Whilst it is possible to identify a clear typological progression of constructional techniques and plan forms, it is less easy to apply a firm chronology to this development. The downhill siting which gives the characteristic platform site and is often taken as evidence of medieval settlement, was used well into the post-medieval period. Rounded corners (again sometimes thought to evidence medieval building) have

8.4 Pwll-ffein, an 18th-century farmhouse at Rhydowen, Ceredigion, abandoned in favour of a newer house close by
(Crown copyright: RCAHMW)

been found on some post-medieval buildings in Ceredigion, for example. Nineteenth-century cottages may in some cases have a similar ground-plan to sub-medieval farmhouses, albeit at a different scale. Lower-status buildings continued to use constructional methods (such as timber-framing) after wealthier builders had adopted other materials. Even within a single material, techniques varied with the resources available: the difference between fine masonry work and coarser rubble is as likely to be one of social and economic status as it is one of dating.

Detailed economic structure is also recorded in the buildings of the recent past. Whole farmsteads survive in significant numbers from the 19th century, and the geographical distribution of farm types can be mapped, with the longhouse and its derivatives (with house and byre in-line) occurring mainly in the less-favoured uplands associated with small-scale stock-raising farms, and the larger, formally planned farmstead more common in the more prosperous lowlands. Relatively little is known about earlier farm types and their distribution, but documentary evidence suggests that 19th-century building campaigns in the name of 'agricultural improvement' brought about radical change in the types of farm

building and the layout of farmsteads. The earlier, haphazard arrangements were condemned by surveyors – in Caernarvonshire, for example, 'the farmers are not only in want of houses, sheds and farmyards, but even those they have are frequently detached from each other. Small miserable huts are built on different parts of the farms, each sufficient only to contain a cow or two' (Kay, 1796). If the loss of *hafotai* was one significant change to the spatial organisation of the farmstead, a reduction in the numbers of dispersed animal shelters which had been a characteristic of farming in Snowdonia, at least, may well have been another.

There are tantalising glimpses of possible earlier modes of organisation in sites which show clear patterns in the arrangement of their several buildings. It is only through more detailed investigation, however, that clear evidence for the use of individual buildings (whether domestic or agricultural) can be established. Meanwhile, however, the interpretation of buildings is inextricably linked to an understanding of the patterns of land use with which they were associated. This is an area which falls comfortably within the scope of archaeological investigation, and has been a central feature of the present study.

8.5 Architecture and building traditions

Thanks to the work of Peter Smith and others, the general developmental outlines of building traditions have become clear (Smith 1967; 1985). The progression of plan forms, as the hall-house and its derivatives gave place to storeyed, and then more centrally planned house types, and the distribution and development of regionally distinctive types are now reasonably well known. The regional distribution of materials and techniques for their use, and the succession of materials (stone replacing timber-framing, for example), can also be traced. Inflections of this progressive account to allow for the somewhat different traditions embodied in smaller houses and cottages have also been acknowledged. But 'great rebuildings' have often made this sequencing fragmentary. Successive replacements of buildings on the same site will also have removed archaeological evidence for the precursors of surviving buildings, though evidence of earlier forms may have been retained in abandoned sites.

Once again, what surviving standing buildings represent is an edited sequence. More-or-less radical changes in the spatial conception and organisation of the house have left only scant trace, as most buildings have gone through cycles of alteration. In particular, there is evidence to suggest that up to the sub-medieval period the household may sometimes have taken a more dispersed form than was the case thereafter. Detached kitchens are now rare, for example, and the surviving distribution of 'unit system' sites of several linked households may not accurately reflect the true incidence of the practice (Hemp and Gresham 1942–3, 98–134; Smith 1967).

Perhaps the most notable example of this process of change concerns the changing relationship of house to farm buildings exemplified by the longhouse tradition. The true longhouse is a building in which house and byre are in line, with the house entered via the feeding-passage of the byre. Few examples survive intact, as later fashion has divided or successively rebuilt the component parts, and interpretation of the evidence has often been contentious (Peate 1946, 59–67; Jones

8.5 Old Llanerch, Snead, Montgomeryshire. A timber-framed house of c.1700: a victim of farm consolidation
(Crown copyright: RCAHMW)

8.6 Relics of a cruck tradition, encapsulated in an upland farm, Llanaber, Gwynedd (Crown copyright: RCAHMW)

and Smith 1963, 1964, 1965 and 1966; Smith 1988, 710–12). The distribution of known longhouses in Wales corresponds closely with those areas where a gable-end lobby entry plan form is most common – especially Gwent, Glamorgan, Breconshire, Carmarthenshire, and Ceredigion. In these areas, there are recorded examples in which house and cow-house form a single build, others where there is clear evidence for the alternate development of the two parts, and some where the cow-house is either lost or replaced. Far more widespread in its distribution is the superficially similar linear farmstead in which house and farm buildings formed a single range, but without direct internal interconnection. This layout remains common in upland areas and on small farms, but was probably far more widespread before 19th-century agricultural improvement.

Some building traditions have left only a fragmentary legacy. There are sufficient surviving earth-built houses in Ceredigion and Lleyn to ascertain that this was a genuine building tradition based on a coherent body of craft technique and conventions of setting out or planning. This tradition was especially associated with the home-made homes of the rural poor, but was also used for durable cottages and even for small farms. It was not necessarily primitive; it was time-consuming to construct, and was sometimes associated with elements of traditional carpentry techniques (such as scarfed crucks). But the distribution of surviving examples does not do justice to the probable one-time spread of earth-building. There is a detailed documentary record of cottages built out of mud and thatched with straw, in Ceredigion, Pembrokeshire, and Carmarthenshire especially. It has been suggested that in Ceredigion, at least, the reason why so few early buildings survive may be that many more were of earth construction and were only replaced when stone and brick became more widely available during the 19th century. Elsewhere, good stone construction from an early date produced durable buildings which did not need to be replaced (Smith 1998 and 2001).

Even in areas with an established stone-building tradition, earth remained the common material for the dwellings of the rural poor, who were unable to afford the more durable local materials, until the early 19th century at least. The village of Dinas Mawddwy, rebuilt as part of the estate of Edmund Buckley in the later 19th century, had previously consisted of 'mud cottages one storey high with rush-clad roofs' (Evans 1802, 75). The report on agricultural labour noted the 'ink bottle houses' of the squatter districts of Merioneth and Montgomeryshire with their mud or earth walls, straw-thatched circular – presumably hipped – roofs (Royal Commission on Agricultural Labour 1893). Surviving examples of mud-built houses are often carefully planned and set out, and were

constructed according to coherent traditions of craft. The same is true of the stone cottages of north Wales. Others, though, may have been more rudimentary: the homes of the rural poor were notoriously mean before a rebuilding process that got under way from the later 18th century. They appear to have been characterised by flimsy construction in timber, mud or turf, or by drystone walling, improvised techniques which differ in more than just degree from those of their more affluent neighbours (Wiliam 1988; Lowe 1985).

In north Wales, in 1802, for example, 'The cottages of Caernarvon appeared worse than those of Merioneth, and this was generally the case, as we proceeded in a westerly or north-westerly direction toward the sea. Here, turf and clay with chopped rushes supplies the place of stone, except towards the mountains, where they are constructed of pebbles placed upon each other ... the walls are about six feet high, over which are raised maiden poles not even stripped of their bark for rafters ... over these is placed heather or rushes, kept down by ropes of the latter' (Evans 1802, 160).

8.7 Cwmdwrgi, Uwchygarreg, Machynlleth: exterior. A sub-medieval house, based on earlier principles of planning, and even retaining an open hall. Deeds revealed that the 18th-century wing was a dower house, reserved for farmers' widows. (Crown copyright: RCAHMW)

8.8 Cwmdwrgi, Uwchygarreg, Machynlleth: interior (Crown copyright: RCAHMW)

And in the Towy Valley c. 1800, 'the mud houses in these parts are of a most wretched construction. The walls do not consist of lath and plaister … but are entirely of earth, and that not of straw wrought up with it … and the chimnies, scarcely rising above the roofs, are of conical wickerwork, barely plaistered over'

8.9 Cottage at Abercych, Ceredigion: exterior (Crown copyright: RCAHMW)

(Vaughan 1927, 49). The physical traces of such flimsy constructions will inevitably be slight.

The most celebrated example of a 'primitive' building tradition comes in the custom of the *ty unnos*. 'Many dwellings of various pretensions date their origins to these insignificant clod houses ... whose owners have no better right of tenure than that given by the now obsolete custom of possession through the right of a caban un nos ... the intending proprietor and his friends proceeded there at nightfall and with great activity cut clods or square pieces of the green sward ... The company commenced building up the walls with the clods, the previously prepared roof was put on and thatched with straw rushes' (Bygones 1875, 142). Surviving small dwellings are virtually all built within a mainstream of architectural tradition and although some may have originated as 'morning surprises', there are no known intact examples of unambiguously 'home-made', unskilled houses.

Most of our architectural knowledge is derived from a coherent tradition with a relatively limited chronology and a definite body of practice. There is much that could be recovered concerning the lost generations of buildings at every social level, and also prior traditions of building. There is some scope for archaeology to fill gaps in the building profile, but this is limited by the nature of survey. It is not always possible to make reliable inferences about building use or construction methods without excavation. Anything other than stone construction will yield little information to field survey, and it may not be possible to determine the detailed use of buildings on a site (whether domestic or agricultural) without more detailed investigation.

Architecture is an art in three dimensions, and the detail of a superstructure does not have an exact correspondence in the archaeological footprint that once supported it: buildings of significantly different form could be created from the same ground-plan (for example, a hall with upper-storeyed gables to cross

8.10 Abercych, Ceredigion: interior. A simple Ceredigion dwelling recorded in 1997. The underthatch, fixed by rope to rough rafters, provides an example of the type of fragile detail often lost in buildings which remain in use (Crown copyright: RCAHMW)

wings; a hall with ornate open roof or full second storey). Subtle distinctions in the handling of materials – the manner of timber framing, or the techniques of masonry construction – which are potentially important sources of historical information, will not be identifiable in any other than standing remains. The use of different materials for footings and super-structure (the common use of stone in earth and timber-framed farnstruction) may also not be readily apparent archaeologically. Interpretation is further complicated by the survival of similar plans, layouts and even constructional techniques in buildings of more humble status, even when there had been innovation in higher ranking buildings (Figs 8.7 and 8.8). There are, for example, recognisable similarities between the plan of the later medieval small open-hall house, and the 19th-century croglofft cottage. Many plan-forms introduced in the sub-medieval period endured over several centuries – for example the end-chimney, direct entry houses of Merionethshire (Smith 2001, 432). In addition, the timing of change and the introduction of new plans or constructional systems varied from region to region and from social group to social group.

8.6 Architecture and archaeology: problems and prospects

Combining social and economic purpose in a deliberate creative process, buildings are a uniquely detailed source for understanding the nature of past rural culture and society. Their value as evidence rises in direct proportion to the survival of architectural detail. We can therefore recover much of the fine grain of rural society for the more recent past, which is relatively rich in surviving buildings, but suffer from progressive lack of definition for remoter periods. The evidence also becomes narrower in its range as different social groups and patterns of activity are lost from direct view. Archaeological evidence becomes invaluable where architectural material is missing, above all for its ability to restore detail to the cultural geography of settlement. Other chapters of this book have considered the archaeological potential of lowland areas, and set out the evidence for both medieval and post-medieval upland settlement and its abandonment. The patterns of transhumance that sustained *hafotai* and *lluestau* have also been discussed. Many of these themes are virtually invisible from the perspective of architectural history.

For some periods and some building types archaeology represents the only available tool for accessing the material. Interpretation will benefit from recognition of the architecture implicit in the archaeological record. Even this restricted archaeological evidence begins to suggest that many of these abandoned sites had been built according to quite definite traditions: conformities in siting, orientation, setting out and size are sometimes apparent, and suggest the existence of specific conventions (Longley, Locock). There is also limited evidence for earlier methods of construction. There is here a valuable chance to see a vernacular beyond the visible range of standing buildings.

Not all archaeological sites are different in kind from those occupied by standing structures: the presence of so many ruinous buildings is a reminder that even historically recent, high-status and well-crafted houses have been prone to abandonment. Some archaeological sites may therefore lie within established regional building traditions, and their interpretation may be informed by examples which have survived intact.

8.11 Rhiwson Uchaf, Ceredigion: exterior. A longhouse-derived plan, in which the house is entered from a through-passage in the adjoining farm range (Crown copyright: RCAHMW)

8.12 Rhiwson Uchaf, Ceredigion: interior. This retained a traditional roof construction, in which branches form rough rafters under the thatch (Crown copyright: RCAHMW)

For the future, there is also considerable scope for the more detailed archaeological investigation of derelict or ruined structures which potentially carry information of a kind lost in buildings with a continuous history of use. Ruined structures sometimes exhibit techniques of construction which have either fallen out of use, or been radically changed in buildings that have remained in use. With occupied buildings and archaeological sites, these ruins are part of a continuum of evidence for past rural society and worthy of attention (Figs 8.9–8.12).

Section Three: Conclusions and future developments

9 THE DESERTED RURAL SETTLEMENT PROJECT: A SUMMING UP

by Kathryn Roberts

The Deserted Rural Settlement Project was essentially an extensive recording and management exercise carried out by the four individual Welsh Archaeological Trusts in order to improve the quality and reliability of the regional SMR databases. Consequently, the work was undertaken on a regional basis with each Trust collating and reporting its own individual results; this has dictated the structure of this volume. It must be appreciated, however, that the geographic boundaries of each of the Trusts are to a large extent arbitrary (albeit related to county boundaries) and, taken in isolation, the results may give a misleading picture. The purpose of this chapter, therefore, is to draw upon some of the regional findings in order to assess their contribution to our overall understanding of Welsh rural settlement and to present an overview of the results of the site condition surveys.

9.1 A consideration of the contribution which the project has made to the study of medieval and later rural settlement in Wales

The background, objectives and methodology have already been outlined in Chapter 1, and in the individual regional reports (Chapters 2–5). During the early stages of the project it became apparent that difficulties were experienced due to the inherent variable quality of records and inconsistent terminology applied both within and between regions. A working group was set up, therefore, to develop a glossary of terms (Appendix I), and standardised forms were introduced in order to enable descriptive information to be recorded in a more systematic manner. However, achieving the desired level of consistency proved to be a more difficult task than anticipated due to the very subjective nature of the survey process.

In order to maintain the project within manageable proportions it was necessary to introduce a chronological cut-off point when determining the criteria for site selection. In view of the acknowledged limited extent of previous field-based research of medieval and early post-medieval settlement, three of the Trusts (Gwynedd, Clwyd-Powys and Glamorgan-Gwent) concentrated specifically upon that period, thereby excluding any sites that could be shown to have originated in the 18th century or later. Had this restriction not been imposed, the number of potential sites would considerably have exceeded available resources. Obviously there are inherent dangers when applying any selection process, in this case in no small part due to the inability accurately to date individual sites. Consequently, it is probable that Gwynedd, Clwyd-Powys and Glamorgan-Gwent Trusts did include within their datasets some 18th-century and later sites. Also, since currently occupied buildings were (in general) not investigated, potentially relevant sites which had remained in occupation into the 19th–21st centuries were excluded, except in a few instances (see Locock, Chapter 3).

The Dyfed Trust argued a case for adopting a broader chronological spread and extended its selection parameters in order to include sites known to post-date 1800, in the belief that this might open up additional avenues of research leading ultimately to better overall understanding. Since this decision inevitably would substantially increase the number of potentially relevant sites, Dyfed's sampling technique entailed restricting the study to eighteen selected areas (Sambrook, Chapter 5). As the project progressed, it became increasingly apparent that benefits would have been gained had a uniform level of survey been carried out across all four regions. Between 2001 and 2004, therefore, Dyfed extended its survey exercise to include sites in those areas which had not previously been investigated, this time applying the same selection criteria as those adopted by the other three regions. An initial desk-top appraisal of these sites was completed in 2002, the results of which are incorporated within Chapter 5; this work was subsequently followed up by field visits carried out between 2002 and 2004, some of the results being incorporated in this chapter.

When all sites known to be of 19th-century or later date had been excluded, the potential number of relevant sites identified across the four regions was of the order of 4300+. Ultimately the total number of confirmed sites was substantially fewer (Table 9.1) since the original figure included vague, inaccurate or duplicated references, together with sites which upon inspection were found not to fall within the project criteria – all of which were, however, documented for general record purposes. New records were created in respect of all previously unrecorded sites which were identified during the course of the project. The precise number of newly identified sites has not been quanti-

fied and in any event is arguably less relevant than the clear evidence that, in the majority of areas, traces of deserted rural settlement were encountered wherever field survey was conducted.

Distribution maps are provided in each of the individual regional chapters; these have now been combined in Fig 9.1 to provide a national overview. This is restricted to the three basic field monument types which, on the balance of evidence, are believed to represent the dwelling elements of settlements: platforms, long huts and longhouses. These are also presented individually in Figs 9.2a–c and Table 9.1. Ancillary features such as enclosures, animal pens, and stores are not included. Attributing site types is a mechanism primarily intended to facilitate an initial sort of the database. This crude indication of distribution is based purely on current morphological characteristics and in itself tells us very little about the nature, development, and chronology of deserted rural settlement in any part of Wales. It is also heavily influenced by external factors such as fieldwork bias and overall site survival. It is unfortunate that there is so little specific dating evidence for all but a handful of the numerous sites. However, the collation of such a considerable quantity of new survey data offers an opportunity not previously available to consider emerging patterns in the nature and form of medieval and later rural settlement, although any conclusions drawn must still be viewed as speculative.

Table 9.1 Distribution of site types by region

	Platform	Long hut	Longhouse	Total
Glamorgan-Gwent	113	92	5	210
Clwyd-Powys	583	556	-	1139
Dyfed	260	419	74	753
Gwynedd	126	498	-	624
	1082	**1565**	**79**	**2726**

Possibly the most striking aspect is the apparent marked regional bias in respect of longhouses (Fig 9.2c). Whereas both Robert Silvester (Clwyd-Powys) and David Longley (Gwynedd) remark on their inability positively to identify structures bearing the true hallmarks of longhouses (a divided and stepped interior with a cross-passage division), 74 such sites

were identified in Dyfed and five in Glamorgan-Gwent. However, it would be unwise to attempt to read too much into these figures since it may well be that they are heavily influenced by two factors: variable selection criteria and site condition. As previously noted, the four Trusts applied different selection criteria when producing their initial datasets – specifically the

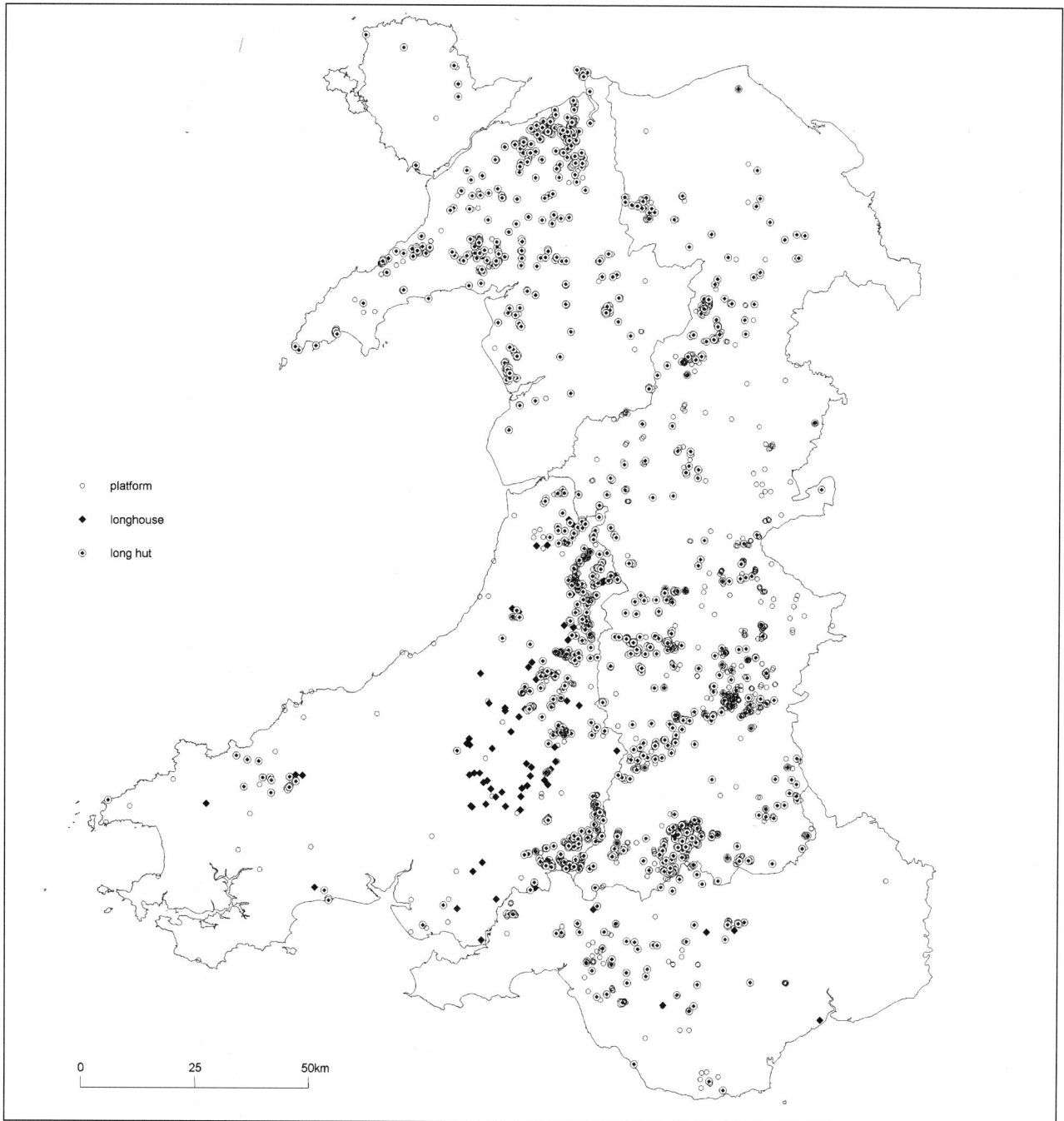

9.1 Deserted rural settlement site distribution

chronological range examined. All of the sites identified as longhouses by Dyfed (which investigated the broadest chronological range) were well-preserved stone-built structures which demonstrated the appropriate characteristics. By way of contrast, Clwyd-Powys reported that designation of the term longhouse was not applied in their area since the level of site preservation was generally not considered sufficiently good to be able to distinguish these features with any degree of accuracy from field inspection alone. Obviously better preserved buildings or shells enable a reasonably firm architectural characterisation. All five longhouses located in Glam-

organ-Gwent were previously known to the Trust and were incorporated within standing buildings (for example, Hafod Fach which had recently been the subject of detailed survey prior to demolition). Similar examples almost certainly exist elsewhere in Wales but fell outside the applied selection criteria. However, it is interesting to note that the overall distribution spread is more or less compatible with later evidence which suggests that longhouses were most commonly built in those marginal areas which adopted the gable-end lobby entry form, ie south and west Wales (Judith Alfrey, Chapter 8). In Chapter 11 David Austin presents a critique of the study of the longhouse in Wales with particular attention to the ongoing debate on its origins and significance.

Platforms and long huts are the two most frequently encountered basic types of rural settlement sites. These are not in themselves exclusive forms, since a platform may often display the foundations of a long hut upon it. The two descriptive terms merely indicate a coarse division emerging from morphological characteristics reflecting two elements: the building itself and the levelled ground on which the building was erected. This distinction is determined by several practical factors, including: location (since platforms are only necessary on sloping ground); building material (whether constructed of stone which leaves a physical trace or timber/clom which does not); subsequent land use; and relative site visibility (since stone foundations are more readily located). To these we should add chronology and function, although often these cannot be deduced from field evidence alone. In general earth platforms are more commonly found in areas where stone was less readily available. Hence, whereas 48% of sites in east and south-east Wales bear structural remains, this figure rises to 65% in west Wales and 78% in Gwynedd where plentiful quantities of stone constituted a convenient source of building material. The absence of structural remains above ground on platforms does not, in itself, conclusively indicate that the original building form was constructed solely of degradable materials, particularly in those areas which have been subjected to substantial agricultural improvement. However, it merits mention that those areas in which bare platforms are most numerous (the south and east) generally tend to correspond with those regions which subsequently established a tradition of timber-framed vernacular buildings.

It can be seen that the distribution maps indicate particular concentrations of deserted rural settlement sites within upland regions where better survival is a well-known phenomenon. This upland bias also strongly reflects the intensity of previous fieldwork in those areas. Since the early 1980s, field survey of the upland areas of Wales has been a primary concern of many organisations (including Cadw, the RCAHMW, and the National Trust), as a consequence of which the number of identified deserted rural settlement sites has increased substantially. This emphasis on upland survey has caused the SMR records to be heavily skewed in favour of upland sites; this is illustrated in Clwyd-Powys where over 85% of all recorded sites lie above 244m OD. Many site clusters clearly mirror

fieldwork campaigns, including those in Brecknock and the Berwyn (Powys), Trawscoed and Moel Bronmiod (Gwynedd), and Cefn Drum (Glamorgan).

Since the local Sites and Monuments records formed the initial project database, the overall direction of field survey work was effectively dictated by the distribution of known sites. Although the aim of the Deserted Rural Settlement Project was to produce as comprehensive a record as possible of all known sites within Wales, it did not actively seek to identify new sites other than in the limited number of areas selected for rapid identification survey (see Chapter 1, section 1.5.2). The purpose of the rapid identification survey programme, therefore, was to extend upland surveys into adjacent agricultural areas which otherwise would not have been investigated (in particular, enclosed farmland with few or no previously recorded sites), in order to ascertain whether additional sites existed and, if so, their type and condition. These include studies at Castell Rowen, Cwm Pennant, Anglesey, Ystumgwern and Castell (Gwynedd); Aberedw and the lands covered by the Badminton Manorial Estate (Powys); and Gelligaer Common, Carn-y-wiwer, and Cwm Cadlan (Glamorgan).

Except in Anglesey, where the effects of long-term intensive agriculture were found to have had a seriously detrimental impact upon site survival, the rapid identification surveys resulted in a substantial increase in the number of recorded sites. A wide range of site types was identified in this way, with newly recorded sites ranging from simple bare earthworks, shelters, and folds to ruined buildings. Survey of enclosed agricultural fields surrounding Aberedw common (where previously only eleven known sites had been recorded) identified a further 38 sites including 24 platforms, a long hut and fourteen farmsteads. Some of these newly recorded sites have been interpreted as the result of 17th-century commons intakes, details of which are recorded in a series of contemporary lease documents (Fig 9.3).

Survey at Ystumgwern, Gwynedd (where the extent of land clearance ranges from minimal to intensive), also revealed evidence for previously unrecorded sites. There, in addition to the five known sites, ten new settlements were identified (concentrated in two areas on each side of the occupied Bron-y-foel-uchaf farm), which have tentatively been identified from 13th-century charter documents as medieval free hamlets. The fact that all of the newly recorded sites at Ystumgwern are located in fields which had been subjected to only minimal land clearance raises the question whether similar sites may also have existed in the more

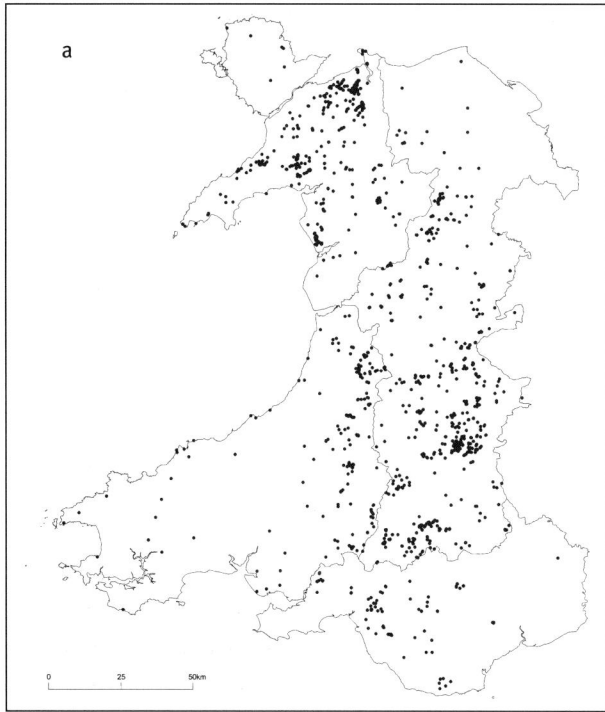

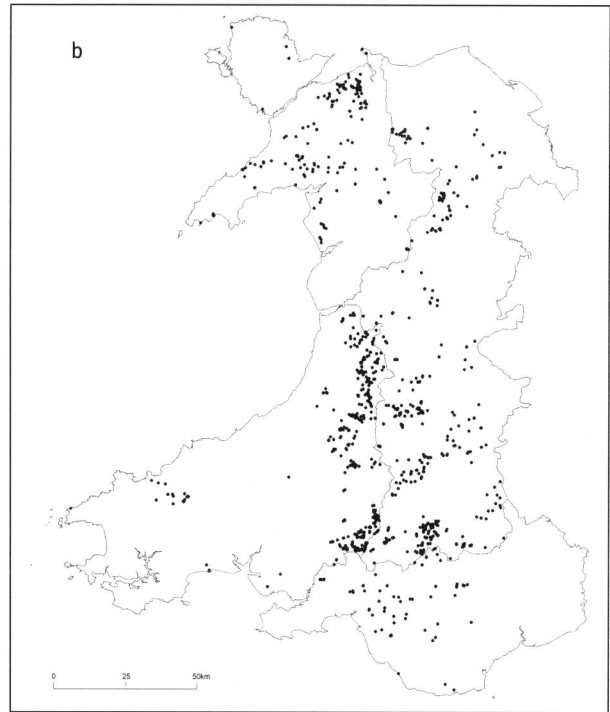

9.2 (a–c) Individual distributions of (a) platforms, (b) long huts and (c) longhouses

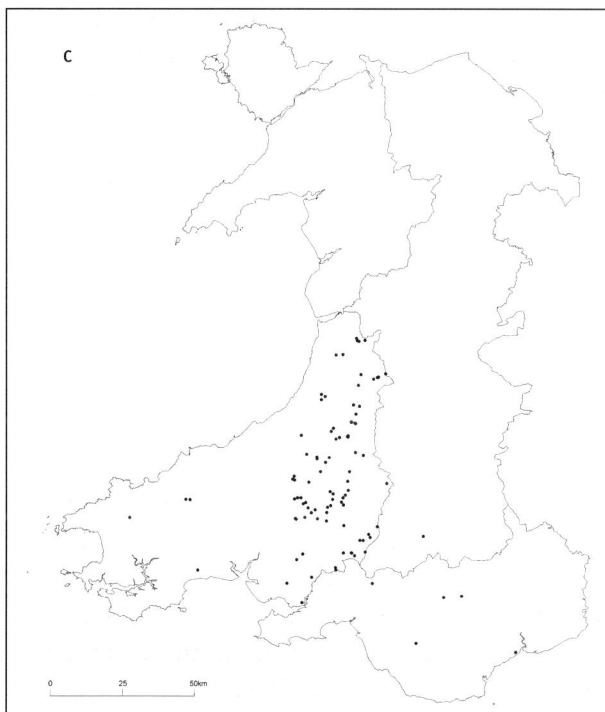

intensively improved areas. What is clear, however, is that by prudent application of rapid identification surveys it is possible to detect evidence of deserted rural settlements even within agriculturally improved land. The increase in site numbers demonstrated by the rapid identification surveys is an indication of the incomplete nature of the recorded dataset and hence the need to apply caution when attempting to draw conclusions from site distributions.

There are some areas where very few identified sites are recorded, such as Anglesey, Flint, and Wrexham

(Tables 9.2 and 9.3), and much of lowland south-east Wales. Intensive agriculture is thought to have played a significant role in eliminating evidence for sites in Anglesey. Silvester (Chapter 2) puts forward a number of possible explanations for the lack of sites in north-east Wales including topography and level of fieldwork intensity, although he ponders whether due to unspecified 'cultural considerations' such sites ever existed in this area.

The distribution maps as presented relate only to those sites investigated during the project and do not include potentially contemporary settlement site types (such as villages) or currently occupied farmsteads, which did not form a part of the investigation and yet play an important role in creating an overall picture of rural settlement. Several contributors to this volume have attempted to explore this relationship, most notably David Longley (Chapter 4). The interpretation of deserted rural settlement in Gwynedd benefits greatly from the body of earlier studies of medieval commotal centres throughout the region, which Longley builds upon to propose an apparent complementary relationship between the platforms, long huts and medieval core settlements. He suggests that the relative distributions of sites indicate a mutually exclusive relationship, illustrated by clusters of rural settlement sites set along commote boundaries (as at Arlechwedd Uchaf and Isaf

near Conwy), with a general fanning out of settlements away from commotal centres possibly in order to exploit seasonal resources. The recognition of these patterns is assisted by documentary and place-name evidence, for example, on the Llyn Peninsula where it is possible that two clusters of long hut sites identified during the project may represent the surviving remnants of documented 13th- and 14th-century *hafodydd*. It is interesting that these two clusters are located on either side of a recognised commotal boundary, possibly suggesting two separate communities. Austin (Chapter 11) expresses the view that the relationship between dispersed rural sites (which formed the focus of the project) and larger settlement sites (which did not) is a subject which has suffered from lack of investigation and merits further consideration.

Table 9.2 Distribution of site types within Gwynedd

	Anglesey	Snowdonia	Llyn	Meirionnydd	Total
Platform	3	69	32	22	126
Long hut on platform	3	207	34	69	313
Long hut	5	129	21	30	185
Other/not identified*	-	7	5	-	12*
	11	412	92	121	636

* Sites not subject to field investigation – exact site type not established.

Table 9.3 Distribution of site types within Clwyd-Powys

	Brecknock	Montgomery	Radnor	Denbigh	Flint	Wrexham	Total
Platform	162	108	275	33	1	4	583
Long hut on platform	53	22	48	10	1	2	136
Long hut	267	51	42	56	-	4	420
Other/not identified*	30	15	39	14	1	2	101*
	512	196	404	113	3	12	1240

* Sites not subject to field investigation – exact site type not established.

Clearly what is lacking from the distribution maps (Figs 9.1 and 9.2) is any indication of chronology or function, and morphological characteristics alone are unlikely to be significantly informative in this respect. Robert Silvester (Chapter 2) expresses the view that a platform which is apparent only as an earthwork is intrinsically undatable, although he speculates that the absence of structures on many platforms may indicate widespread use of timber for building at a time when this material was readily available. Historical and environmental sources suggest that by the late medieval period supplies of timber were becoming increasingly scarce, prompting greater use of stone for construction purposes. It is possible, therefore, that in some cases bare platform sites precede those where stone was used as the sole building material. However, this crude rule of thumb cannot be applied in areas where only one or other building tradition is encountered, for example, in Gwynedd where 80% of all sites have some visible surviving building foundations, or many areas of eastern Wales where bare platforms predominate. A further difficulty when applying this interpretation is the limited number of palaeoenvironmental studies which have been carried out to determine the extent of woodland in medieval/post-medieval Wales (Caseldine, Chapter 7).

The proportion of sites which bear structural evidence varies considerably: 15% in Radnor; 25% in Brecknock; over 75% in Snowdonia and Meirionnydd. In those instances when both platforms and structural remains were encountered together, they were measured and recorded separately. In general the visible foundations were found to occupy most of the level platform area although it cannot be ascertained from field survey alone whether platform and visible structural remains are contemporary. It is noted that some excavations have demonstrated more than one phase of occupation at sites. For example, investigative work carried out on a platform site at Ynys Ettws in Gwynedd (Chapter 6) identified that at least two separate periods of activity had taken place between the 11th and 18th centuries, during which time the size and form of the building changed. Excavation demonstrated that the initial building (which saw its main period of use between the 11th and 17th centuries) was well constructed and almost twice the size of the simple rough shelter which, following a period of abandonment, marked the final phase of occupancy in the 18th century.

From field evidence we can describe a typical relict rural settlement building as being of simple rectangular form (8–15m in length x 4–9m wide), defined by grassy banks or low rubble/stone walls, and with a door/doors set halfway along the longer side. Little, if any, regional variation in size was apparent although an identifiable trend noted in Gwynedd was that at higher altitudes the length of the structure increased in proportion to width. However, as Judith Alfrey comments, the same outline can accommodate buildings of significantly different form, and subtle distinctions in the handling of materials are generally absent from the archaeological record (Chapter 8). Since the project was primarily based on field observation, available evidence was restricted to that which was identifiable without recourse to excavation. The extent of our knowledge of building superstructure and internal arrangements remains limited. We have little direct evidence for the type of roofing used, although sketches of peasant dwellings from the post-medieval period suggest a turf roof supported by thin poles. There are few examples which indicate a chimney or hearth; although a number of long huts in Gwynedd have indications of defined areas at one end, or contain large flat stones which could have served as a hearthstone, such examples account for only 16% of Gwynedd's total. The indications are that most dwellings in rural Wales did not have a constructed fireplace, and the writings of later travellers suggest that this situation continued until as late as the 18th–early 19th century (Chapter 8). The same documentary sources indicate widespread use of earth/mud (or clom) as a building material both for the self-built homes of the rural poor and for more durable cottages and even small farms. Although we can speculate that many of the sites investigated during the study may have been of clom construction, since such structures would have been particularly prone to rapid weathering leaving little trace, it is unlikely that the distribution of surviving examples accurately reflects the true extent of earth-building (Fig 9.4).

The use of platforms to support buildings is not restricted to any single period of history. Certainly platforms were utilised in the medieval period (Cefn Graenog, Gwynedd; Gelligaer, Glamorgan), but their presence beneath surviving 16th- and 17th-century houses in Radnorshire demonstrates their continued use in later periods. There is some evidence to suggest that from an earlier orientation perpendicular to the contour, subsequent platforms came to be rotated 90° to lie along it. In some areas in Radnorshire this variation may have begun as early as the second half of the 16th century, while at the same time the earlier

9.3 Aberedw Hill, Radnorshire. The substantial enclosure with central building is the most obvious sign of settlement and probably represents 17th-century encroachment on to common land. Yet it is not the only sign of occupation – further downslope on the left of the photo are three simple earth platforms and two long huts set within small embanked enclosures. (photo: Paul Sambrook)

design was still being utilised. At Plas Berw, Llanidan, in Anglesey, a 15th-century hall, built with its main axis set across the contour, was replaced in the 17th century by a new mansion which was aligned along the contour. However, it is probable that houses lying perpendicular to the ground contour continued to be built well into the 18th century. In the absence of other evidence, therefore, a platform cutting across a slope cannot be dated, although a platform running along the contours of a slope is likely to date to the 17th century or later.

While the majority of platforms demonstrate a basic width:length ratio of 1:1.6 or 1:1.8, the survey identified some exceptionally long platform sites where the length much exceeds the width. Robert Silvester (Chapter 2) draws parallels between sites at Drysygsol and Hen Ddinbych, Radnor, and a group of similar sites in England previously identified and interpreted by Christopher Dyer as the remains of medieval covered sheepcotes (Dyer 1995). Another example is at Hafod Eidos, Cwmystwyth (Ceredigion), where a platform measuring over 20m provides structural evidence in the form of low foundation walls (today overlaid by a later field wall and recent drystone-walled sheepfold). The location of this site within the upland estate of Strata Florida Abbey supports its interpretation as the site of a medieval monastic grange (Fig 9.5). However, no such structures are identified by Locock in his study of the upland estate of Margam Abbey, although he does report clusters of more standard-sized platforms which he interprets as representing eleven recorded Abbey granges.

Deserted rural settlement structures investigated during the survey were most frequently found in isolation (70–80% of sites), occasionally in pairs, and less commonly in groups – in all cases with or without a range of ancillary structures. It was noted (particularly in east and south Wales) that pairs of platforms are often situated so that one platform lies to the side and downslope, possibly to facilitate access to entrances located approximately centrally in the long sides. Silvester comments on a number of cases of paired structures in east Wales where one platform shows evidence for a building while the other remains bare, which he suggests may indicate a house and ancillary barn or byre, but cautions against making assumptions on the basis of field evidence alone. The absence of recognisable internal features within long huts, and particularly in respect of bare platforms, prevents interpretation of the nature or function of those settlements which display more than one potential dwelling

structure. This frustrates attempts to identify those sites where byres may have been constructed to enable animals to be over-wintered, suggesting a degree of permanent occupancy.

Since we have discounted morphology of the platform or long hut alone as a reliable indicator of chronology or function, we must consider the contribution provided by field evidence of ancillary features and associated structures, such as the presence of upland tracts of ridge and furrow cultivation which can be indicative of medieval occupation. The use of aerial photography proved to be a useful means of identifying ridge and furrow cultivation at sites at Llandrillo, Lake Vyrnwy, and Cwm Pennant in east Wales, all of which Silvester describes as indicating 12th- or 13th-century occupation at a period of climatic optimum. However, only a small percentage of sites provide evidence of such associations (for example, 10% in Gwynedd, 5% in Clwyd-Powys). In south-east Wales, Martin Locock did not find any conclusive evidence for medieval arable farming associated with rural settlement sites, although spade-cut ridges at some sites (Tirlan, Mynydd Marchywel) suggest limited arable farming, possibly root crops.

The value of documentary and cartographic sources to assist the investigation and dating of rural settlement sites proved to be varied; contemporary written evidence from the 11th–13th centuries is sparse and does not readily lend itself to confirmation by fieldwork. Gwynedd is fortunate in both the quantity of available medieval documentation and the extent to which it has been researched, which in several instances has enabled Longley (Chapter 4) positively to identify named medieval *hafodydd*. Contemporary documentation is more readily available in respect of post-medieval and later periods, although not necessarily relating to rural settlement. Several authors in this volume call upon such contemporary references, including Silvester's study of the Earl of Worcester's Crickhowell and Tretower Estates, which employed survey information compiled in the Badminton Estate Maps of 1587. Fieldwork demonstrated that although none of the buildings outside the villages referred to the documents had survived, their location could generally be identified except in the case of upland dwellings. In roughly half of the cases the lowland sites continued to be occupied although present buildings are of later construction (Chapter 2/Appendix III).

Another successful complementary application of documentary and field research is Sambrook's investigation of the *lluestau* of the Cambrian Mountains in

Ceredigion (Chapter 5). Surviving deeds which refer by name to individual upland shepherding settlements (the oldest document dating from the early 17th century) have enabled some sites to be identified, at least tentatively, in the field. These documents highlight the close relationship between the *lluest* and its parent *tyddyn* (permanent farmstead), the former often serving as an upland dairy station, probably predominantly for sheep. The field evidence for *lluestau* is characteristic in the form of a dwelling, generally set alongside or close to a river, with a number of ancillary structures including enclosures, pens, and underground stores, and occasionally supplemented by lazy beds. Sambrook suggests that use of the place-name *lluest* was in the main restricted to a relatively small geographical area within the Cambrian Mountains although the type of site which it defines is widely found within Dyfed (including the Black Mountain and Cwmystwyth areas), which suggests similar patterns of upland exploitation. The majority of *lluestau* are likely to have originated as seasonally occupied dwellings; contemporary documents suggest that by the mid-18th century many had developed into permanent upland holdings. However, caution must be exercised when attributing function since direct evidence for actual usage and date is often absent; in some cases sites may have had no agricultural basis but were associated with mining, quarrying, peat digging, and other extractive processes. This latter aspect may well benefit from further investigation.

The transhumance system is a feature of Welsh social history that is inextricably linked with rural settlement. It is probable that a substantial number of the sites investigated were associated with the summer seasonal pasturing of animals. A variety of *hafod/hendref* systems is believed to have existed throughout much of rural Wales from at least the early medieval period until the onset of industrialisation, embracing a broad range in terms of numbers of participating people, scale of activities and distances involved. It has been suggested that, with the passage of time, the scale of social dislocation associated with transhumance in Wales evolved from mass migration of entire communities to summer pastures (as discussed by David Longley, Chapter 4), to movement on a smaller scale by individual shepherds, with or without their families, as illustrated by the west Wales *lluestau* (Chapter 5).

The varied topography of Wales which played such an important role in the practice and nature of transhumance is reflected in the physical characteristics of the sites investigated. The *lluestau* of Ceredigion were remotely sited some distance from their associated *tyddyn* and therefore needed provision for storage facilities, which in some cases took the form of built 'sunken' shelters that were possibly used as cool stores for dairy products. This is contrasted by sites in Radnorshire, where upland pastures were seldom further than a few miles from the lowland settlements which potentially allowed daily movement of stock and shepherds.

The use of place-names has often proved to be a useful consideration when applied to the study of seasonal settlement; to date perhaps the most comprehensive piece of research is that produced by Davies (1980). Obviously a degree of caution is necessary – as Paul Sambrook comments, in Wales the term *hafod* is associated with a wide variety of situations including existing farmsteads, sites of deserted settlements, and extensive blocks of upland pasture. In west Wales many currently occupied farms which bear the name *hafod* are found at the edge of marginal land or on upland fringes, possibly indicating earlier seasonal use which may have subsequently developed into permanent occupation following the enclosure and improvement of surrounding land. Locock found that only rarely in Glamorgan were *hafod* place-names found to be associated with physical remains as opposed to fields. It is probable that, with the passage of time, the word *hafod* lost its original seasonal connotation, so that by the 18th century this term was also used by writers to describe remotely sited and/or upland farms that were permanently occupied, as would appear to be the case with the 19th-century descriptions of upland Ceredigion provided by the Reverend John Evans (Sambrook, Chapter 5).

David Longley, in his review of medieval transhumance in Gwynedd, makes extensive use of both place-name and documentary evidence, focusing particularly on land owned by the Welsh Princes of Gwynedd both before and after the conquest of 1283. With the assistance of contemporary documents he traces the changing use of upland areas of Gwynedd, from the pre-conquest communal model of seasonal pasturage to subsequent individual land use (initially for large-scale pasturage, then individual enclosure and settlement). The lease or purchase by wealthy individuals of communal, Crown and in particular monastic upland *friddoedd* often caused the land to be subdivided between tenants, each of whom would build a house or farmstead, as occurred in Meirionnydd during the 16th and 17th centuries. Several sites which displayed

9.4 Clom cottage, Carmarthenshire. An example of an abandoned and rapidly deteriorating clom cottage, once a familiar site throughout rural Wales (photo: Mick Sharp for Cadw)

these characteristics were identified during project fieldwork, not only in Gwynedd but elsewhere (for example, the Radnorshire Commons).

An important aspect in the study of rural settlement is the impact of enclosure and encroachment onto common land throughout Wales from the 17th century onwards. Eighteenth-century documentary sources for the Crown land at Cantref Maelienydd (northern Radnorshire) list over 784 encroachments of which 421 involved the erection of a house, which practice continued into the 19th century. The subsequent abandonment of these holdings left a pattern of ruined buildings which survive in varying states of completeness. In some areas encroachment reached its peak during the 19th century. Sambrook discusses the archaeology of squatter settlements (such as in the Preseli Mountains, Eglwyswen) and draws attention to the extensive rural population of 19th-century Dyfed, particularly the landless labouring classes who inhabited simple cottages built on the edges of fields and beside roads. However, even when the location of such sites is marked on available maps, there is often little remaining field evidence. At present, documentary evidence is the only source of information of the existence of the 'one-night houses' (*tai un nos*) of Welsh folk tradition and it is likely that, if these buildings were constructed as hastily as tradition implies, no significant archaeological traces remain.

9.2 Results of the site condition survey

Although prior to the instigation of the Deserted Rural Settlement Project it was generally acknowledged that these sites are vulnerable to loss and/or damage, it was not possible to quantify either the nature or extent of the associated threat. A basic requirement of the project, therefore, was to gather accurate information on the condition of monuments in this class, which would enable sound advice to be given and informed decisions to be made as part of the planning process and overall heritage/countryside management strategy. Since original form and subsequent land use history are the major factors which determine the degree of site survival, details of current land use, site condition and perceived threats were recorded in respect of each site.

Each Trust already had in place (and continued to use) its own system and terminology when assessing the condition of archaeological sites, but there was no single integrated system for condition reporting across all four regions. The results are presented by region, since variations in individual Trust policies determining the extent of information transferred onto computer and incompatible computer software make it difficult at this stage to produce pan-Wales statistics;

this is reflected in discrepancies which may be apparent in some tables presented in this chapter.

9.2.1 Current land use

Tables 9.4–9.7 indicate current land use of recorded sites throughout Wales. Overall, it was found that approximately 67% of sites are located in areas of rough grazing and moorland, which figure corresponds with the perceived upland bias previously discussed, and 25% lie within improved pasture. Very few sites are recorded in forested areas, which is perhaps surprising in view of the substantial number of ruined 18th- to 20th-century farmsteads and settlements which exist in such areas. However, it is usually the case that our knowledge of the location of deserted rural settlement sites in forested areas is derived from maps which pre-date afforestation; little exploratory field survey has taken place and it is probable that the number of sites in forested areas is substantially under-estimated. Although an archaeological assessment of all lands managed by Forest Enterprise in Wales has recently been carried out, this was principally an SMR-based survey of known sites and did not specifically set out to identify new sites.

Table 9.4 Current land use: Clwyd-Powys

Current land use	Platform	Long hut on platform	Long hut	Shelter	Other	Total
Moorland	71	18	100	11	7	207
Rough grazing	195	54	204	14	22	489
Improved pasture	198	38	25	1	23	285
Forestry	2	-	4	-	2	8
Woodland/scrub	16	3	4	-	5	28
Other/not established					223	223
	482	113	337	26	282	1240

Table 9.5 Current land use: Glamorgan-Gwent

Current land use	Platform	Long hut	Longhouse	Other	Total
Moorland	48	51	-	2	101
Pasture	26	16	-	4	46
Arable	9	3	1	1	14
Forestry	21	7	-	1	29
Other	9	15	4	22	50
	113	92	5	30	240

Table 9.6 Current land use : Gwynedd

Current land use	Platform	Long hut on platform	Long hut	Total
Moorland	3	26	23	52
Rough grazing	63	171	113	347
Improved pasture	53	103	38	194
Forestry	-	2	4	6
Woodland/scrub	1	2	4	7
Peat bog	1	2	-	3
Other	5	6	4	15
	126	312	186	624

Table 9.7 Current land use: Dyfed*

Current land use	Platform	Long hut	Longhouse	Total
Moorland	1	2	1	4
Rough grazing	81	198	17	296
Improved pasture	16	12	-	28
Forestry	-	3	-	3
Woodland/scrub	-	1	-	1
Peat bog	-	3	1	4
Other	2	-	6	8
	100	219	25	344

* These data refer only to the 18 selected study areas

9.2.2   Current site condition

It must be remembered that assessment of site condition is a subjective exercise, which in this case is further confused by the application of inconsistent terminology between Trust regions. Gwynedd Archaeological Trust assesses the condition of 69% of all sites as 'very good/good/fair' compared with only 31% considered to be 'poor/bad'. Glamorgan-Gwent reports similar results, with the condition of 63% of sites assessed as 'intact/nearly intact', compared with 9% as 'damaged' and 28% as 'nearly destroyed/destroyed'. However, the results from the other two Trusts show a marked contrast. Clywd-Powys assesses only 14% of its sites as being 'intact/near intact', 77% 'damaged' and 9% 'near-destroyed/destroyed'. Dyfed reports 14% 'substantially intact', 79% 'in a state of advanced ruination but main characteristics still discernible' and 7% 'near destroyed/destroyed'. As can be seen, there is little at this stage which can be read into these results; however, they form a useful baseline against which individual site condition can be monitored in the future.

9.2.3   Threats

In view of the predominantly upland rural setting of the majority of the sites investigated, it is perhaps not surprising that a substantial proportion are not considered to be subject to any immediate specific threat. This is illustrated by the statistics provided by the Gwynedd and Dyfed Archaeological Trusts (Tables 9.8 and 9.9). Gwynedd reports no specific threats in respect of 294 out of a total 624 recorded sites, ie 47%. Similarly, Dyfed reports no specific threats in respect of 316 out of a total 753 recorded sites, ie 42%. Similar statistics are not yet available for Clwyd-Powys and Glamorgan-Gwent.

Table 9.8 Perceived threats by site type: Gwynedd

Perceived threat	Platform	Long hut on platform	Long hut	Total
Afforestation	-	7	6	13
Animal burrowing	11	18	18	47
Bracken/scrub	3	5	12	20
Building	-	4	-	4
Coastal erosion	-	3	-	3
Land improvement/ ploughing	29	83	19	131
Pylons	-	-	3	3
Quarrying	2	3	1	6
Stone dumping	1	1	1	3
Stone robbing	-	5	1	6
Stream/water erosion	4	11	13	28
Vehicle erosion	7	11	8	26
Visitor erosion	-	13	4	17
Weathering	6	6	11	23
Total	63	170	97	330
No specific threat				294
				624

Table 9.9 Perceived threats by site type: Dyfed

Perceived threat	Platform	Long hut	Longhouse	Total
Afforestation	3	15	1	19
Animal burrowing	-	1	-	1
Building	2	10	3	15
Erosion	11	78	14	103
Land improvement/ ploughing	89	69	12	170
Stock trampling	1	1	1	3
Other	22	7	6	35
Not assessed	33	43	15	91
No specific threat	99	195	22	316
	260	419	74	753

Fieldworkers in all four Trust areas identified the most damaging factors as agricultural improvement (in particular stone clearance, subsequent ploughing and reseeding) and, to a lesser extent, erosion (natural and vehicle). During the survey of Cwm Pennant, Gwynedd, it was noted in several instances that sites previously described by Colin Gresham in the 1950s as 'stone defined features' are now completely devoid of stone and visible only as slight platforms. The fact that a greater number of earth platforms have survived in Clwyd-Powys, compared with the corresponding lesser number of sites with structural remains, may in part be due to similar improvement activity, such as occurred at Beili Bedw, Radnorshire. However, land improvement does not necessarily result in complete destruction of sites; for example, several cases are recorded in Gwynedd where stones removed from fields during land clearance have been piled within the walls of long huts, thereby effectively preserving the structure although no longer within any recognisable context.

Whereas the main thrust of the condition survey exercise was visual field inspection, only excavation can reveal the true extent of survival of buried archaeological remains. Due to resource constraints, however, the excavation programme was restricted to five locations, each of which was deemed representative of a range of sites undergoing typical active damage: Gesail Gyfarch, Llystyn Ganol, and Ynys Ettws (agricultural activity); Hafod Rhug Uchaf (scrub encroachment); and Tro'r Derlwyn (water erosion). The latter type of damage demonstrates the vulnerability of sites which lie close to water courses, in particular those which are subjected to additional human interference to modify water flow, such as damming. The excavation results are fully discussed by George Smith and David Thompson in Chapter 6.

Overall, no foundation trenches were found under any of the excavated buildings and in most cases vulnerable archaeological evidence was close to the surface. Physical disturbance was seen to have had a seriously detrimental effect, as at Gesail Gefarch where it was found that all archaeological evidence has been lost along the length of a tractor track which crosses the main platform. However, despite the poor condition of the platform, the excavation was still considered justified. It is worth noting that the recovered fragments of 13th-century pottery were located in cut features close to the platform. These finds endorse the importance of investigating not only main structures but also ancillary features including pits, middens, enclosures, and secondary platforms. Unfortunately, ancillary features (such as those which proved so productive at Gesail Gyfarch) are

9.5 Hafod Eidos, Cwmystwyth, Ceredigion. The long earthwork platform is overlain by later walls and shelters

particularly vulnerable to the impact of land improvement. Although the site of a long hut at Llystyn Ganol had been preserved (due to its use as a collection point for stones removed during general land clearance), excavation of the long hut itself was not productive and, since the entire immediate surrounding area had been subjected to agricultural improvement, there was no opportunity to investigate subsidiary features (if any).

By means of contrast, a site at Hafod Rhug Uchaf had become heavily overgrown with blackthorn and scrub as a result of reduced grazing. Despite this, excavation proved to be most successful, revealing many internal features including stone slab floors, partitions, and a fireplace. Although only a limited range and number of artefacts were recovered during excavation, recent analysis of soil pollen samples was productive (Caseldine, Chapter 7). It is probable that the robust nature of the predominantly stone-built long hut at Hafod Rhug Uchaf contributed greatly to its relatively good state of preservation beneath such dense vegetation.

9.3 Conclusion

Although the Deserted Rural Settlement Project is now concluded, interpretation and application of the accumulated information by those engaged in heritage management is ongoing. Thanks to the expertise of all those involved in this ambitious undertaking, our understanding of rural settlement in Wales is much enhanced. We are now better informed, not only in respect of site numbers and location, but also site condition and the impact of changing land use. Already one of the most immediate outcomes is the increased level of protection which can be afforded through the process of scheduling. In addition, management programmes continue to benefit from improved SMR records (Chapter 10).

However, the project has generated as many questions as answers. The importance of tracing the ebb and flow of human settlement in Wales is clear; the improved field data present the opportunity to reassess and increase the contribution which these sites can make to the overall understanding of rural settlement in Wales (Chapter 11). There remains considerable scope for ongoing study and it is the hope of all those who have contributed to this volume that it will serve to stimulate further interest and inspire continued research into this most fascinating of subjects.

10 MANAGEMENT ISSUES

by Kathryn Roberts

10.1 Introduction

This chapter discusses some of the means by which protection can be afforded to deserted rural settlement sites, including the roles of statutory designation and agrienvironmental schemes. It also offers some insight into how Cadw and the Welsh Archaeological Trusts provide advice and support to a wide range of individuals and organisations involved with rural land management.

It can be argued that survival of the majority of recorded deserted rural settlement sites in Wales can be attributed to their location within relatively remote marginal areas which have experienced little agricultural improvement or development – in other words, survival by default. Although during the Deserted Rural Settlement Project some attempt was made to identify the extent to which other sites may have existed at some time within more intensively farmed lands, it is not possible to determine how many such sites have been irretrievably lost. Several authors in this volume remark that sites of cottages and farms, the existence of which is identified on historic maps, have now vanished without trace – largely as a consequence of intensive land improvement (see Sambrook, Chapter 5; Silvester, Chapter 2). This clearly illustrates the potential vulnerability of these historic sites and highlights the importance of ensuring that an appropriate level of recording and protection is afforded to surviving examples.

The upland and marginal areas of Wales have in general been spared the destructive impact of intensive arable agricultural activity, which represents the single greatest threat to archaeological monument preservation. However, sites remain vulnerable to intensification of other traditional land use practices including land improvement, grazing, mineral exploitation, and military use, together with associated erosion (natural/stock/vehicles/visitors) (Roberts and Sambrook, 2003). In addition, there are the potentially damaging effects of forestry and large-scale alternative energy development.

Approximately 14% of Wales is currently under woodland cover, two-thirds of which comprises non-native conifers (National Assembly for Wales 2001). As pointed out in Chapter 9, a surprisingly small number of recorded deserted rural settlement sites are located in forested areas, although this figure is probably under-estimated. Many of the forests planted in the early post-war years are now reaching maturity, being felled and replanted, as a consequence of which there is great potential for sites to be lost without having been properly recorded.

Since the introduction of the Electricity Act 1989, the drive to meet the Non-Fossil Fuel Obligation (NFFO) has led to the construction of fourteen wind power stations in Wales, mostly in upland areas (approximately 49% of the UK total); more are in the planning stage (Countryside Council for Wales 1999). Fortunately, the potentially damaging impact of large-scale developments such as wind-farms, water-power schemes and extractive industries can be controlled to some extent through the planning process (Welsh Assembly Government 2002). However, condition surveys carried out during the project indicate that the most serious current threats are agricultural land improvement (which does not require planning permission) and erosion (both natural and man-made).

If we are to preserve our heritage and encourage future research, it is evident that a broad range of management techniques must be applied. These include: statutory protection for both individual sites and more extensive landscapes; 'hands-on' management to limit site deterioration; and adequate recording and investigation of those sites for which no practical means of preservation exists. It is important that regular and constructive communication is maintained between archaeologists, heritage managers and those people responsible for actual day-to-day management of the rural environment – in particular, landowners. In Wales this valuable link is provided by the four regional Archaeological Trusts which offer advice to a large number of organisations and individuals, including the Countryside Council for Wales (Tir Gofal initiative), National Park Authorities, National Trust, Forest Enterprise, Local Authorities, and (most importantly) to landowners.

10.2 The role of Cadw

Cadw is the Welsh Assembly Government's historic environment service. It is responsible for advising the Assembly on the scheduling of ancient monuments under the Ancient Monuments and Archaeological Areas Act 1979, and the listing of historic buildings under the Planning (Listed Buildings and Conservation Areas) Act 1990. It also plays a major role in the protection, preservation, and presentation of the built heritage of Wales, largely through the provision of grants for practical conservation and archaeological investigation.

10.2.1 The scheduling process

Perhaps the most direct way that protection can be ensured is through the process of scheduling. Scheduled monument sites are protected by law from damage or destruction, therefore no activity that would materially affect a site may be carried out without prior consent. Wardens employed by Cadw carry out regular site inspections, providing early identification of potential problems which may threaten continued survival in order that appropriate action can be taken, including proactive repair work.

When the project was set up in 1997 it was generally acknowledged that deserted rural settlement sites were under-represented on the Welsh Schedule. At that time only fifteen medieval or later deserted rural settlement sites were scheduled in their own right as ancient monuments of national importance, nine of which were in Glamorgan. However, a number of additional long huts and platforms were included as secondary items within other scheduled areas, many located within areas granted scheduled status following the Gwynedd Hut Group Project (1993–7), during which archaeologists investigating prehistoric and Romano-British hut groups identified a number of rectangular buildings situated near or overlying prehistoric settlement sites. The true total number of scheduled deserted rural settlement structures was therefore greater than fifteen – probably in the region of 80 – but this still accounted for less than 2% of the 4000+ sites at that time recorded on the Sites and Monuments Record. Moreover, the majority had been scheduled primarily on the basis of their proximity to other sites rather than on their own merit, and were not necessarily the most representative or best-preserved examples of their type. With the benefit of information gained during the Deserted Rural Settlement Project, we now know that only 7% of deserted rural settlement sites within Gwynedd are located in close proximity to hut circles, although previous scheduling was heavily biased in this way.

In order for a site to merit scheduled status it must be deemed to be of 'national importance'. During the course of the project each of the Trusts was invited to submit to Cadw details of any site potentially considered suitable for scheduling. Eight basic criteria were employed: survival and condition, period, rarity, fragility or vulnerability, diversity, documentation, group value and potential (Welsh Office Circular: 60/1996). Some degree of professional judgement must also be applied in order to take into account any regional and structural diversity.

In addition to the original fifteen scheduled sites, at the time of writing a further 90 sites have been awarded scheduled monument protection, including examples of all of the different types of structures encountered during the project. These range from simple earth platforms to complete settlements, and include examples of houses, barns, animal pens, and storage features. Scheduled areas range in size from isolated platforms/long huts to (in one case) an area in excess of 18 hectares surrounding the scattered settlement at Pentre Jack, Llanstephan, Radnorshire.

The scheduling process is not always the most effective way of dealing with landscapes which incorporate field systems or widely spread features. By their very nature, individual sites are part of a wider settlement pattern, and it is perhaps as elements of the broader landscape that their full potential is best realised. In some instances where a number of separate structures are spread over a broad landscape, these have been scheduled individually (as at Cefn Wylfre, Radnorshire, or Cymystwyth, Ceredigion) although it was not possible to include the areas between. Ideally, however, we should think beyond single sites and explore ways of extending protection to entire deserted rural settlement landscapes.

10.2.2   Register of Landscapes of Historic Interest
The Register of Landscapes of Historic Interest in Wales is produced as a joint exercise by Cadw, the Countryside Council for Wales (CCW) and the International Council on Monuments and Sites (ICOMOS, UK). It comprises two parts: Landscapes of Outstanding Historic Interest (Cadw 1998c) and Landscapes of Special Historic Interest (Cadw 2001). The 58 landscapes identified to date (Fig 10.1) include several outstanding examples of surviving rural settlement patterns, for example, upland Ceredigion, Ardudwy, the Elan Valley, and Newport and Carn Ingli. Although the Register does not have statutory status, it provides a useful source of information for many organisations at both local and national level, in particular when Unitary Development Plans (UDPs) are being drawn up and the potential environmental impact of large-scale development schemes is being considered.

10.3 Developing long-term management strategies through partnership

The management of the rural historic environment is intrinsically linked with the rural economy and communities. Since, in the main, the major threats to deserted rural settlements lie outside the planning process, survival of these sites lies in the hands of the people who own, manage, and control the use of land. These include: landowners (both corporate and individual); Unitary Authorities and National Parks (development plans, countryside strategies, warden services, economic development strategies, biodiversity action plans, access and leisure strategies); local communities; conservation groups and organisations; the Forestry Commission (Woodland Grant Schemes and Forest Design Strategies); the Countryside Council for Wales (SSSIs, SACs, SPAs); and the Environment Agency (adapted from Thompson and Yates 1999).

In order successfully to develop and operate protection strategies there are three basic requisites: firstly, the provision of accessible and accurate information (readily available from the regional SMRs); secondly, sympathetic landowners who are willing to adapt their methods in order to mitigate damage; and thirdly, a reliable means of combining the two. In the past possibly the greatest challenge which archaeologists faced was failure properly to communicate with those best placed to provide practical assistance. It is encouraging that current opportunities for contact are good and improving; this is in no small part due to the activities of the four Welsh Archaeological Trusts, which play an active role in achieving wider recognition of the historic environment.

Agri-environment schemes, such as Tir Cymen and more recently Tir Gofal (Countryside Commission for Wales 1998), provide practical opportunities and mechanisms for heritage management. Although such schemes do not enable geographic areas to be specifically targeted (since they are demand-led), they open up valuable lines of communication between archaeologists and landowners, for example, through the provision of advice for incorporation within farm management plans. Unfortunately similar contact between archaeologists and farmers is still somewhat limited. Although a desktop survey of heritage assets is carried out in respect of all farms entered under the Tir Gofal scheme, only 20% are subjected to archaeological inspection, and farm plans are developed by Tir Gofal case-workers, few of whom are professionally trained heritage managers. However, the results of the condition reports produced during the Deserted Rural Settlement Project are put to good use by Tir Gofal at both site level when providing heritage management advice, and in the training programme provided for its case-workers.

10.4 Communication and outreach

Sometimes the simple expedient of drawing attention to an archaeological site can contribute significantly to its conservation, or at least cause it to be spared from accidental destruction as a result of ignorance (Thompson and Yates 1999). Wherever possible, therefore, the opportunity was taken during project fieldwork to engage with local landowners and communities in order to explain the purpose of the project and communicate information about the site under investigation. Fieldworkers were often greatly encouraged to discover the extent of local interest engendered in this way, and it was not uncommon that a landowner was able to point out additional, previously unrecorded, sites.

An important consideration throughout the project was that information would be disseminated as widely as possible. The four Welsh Archaeological Trust websites were regularly updated to include details of regional survey work and fieldworkers presented talks to local community groups. The regional SMRs,

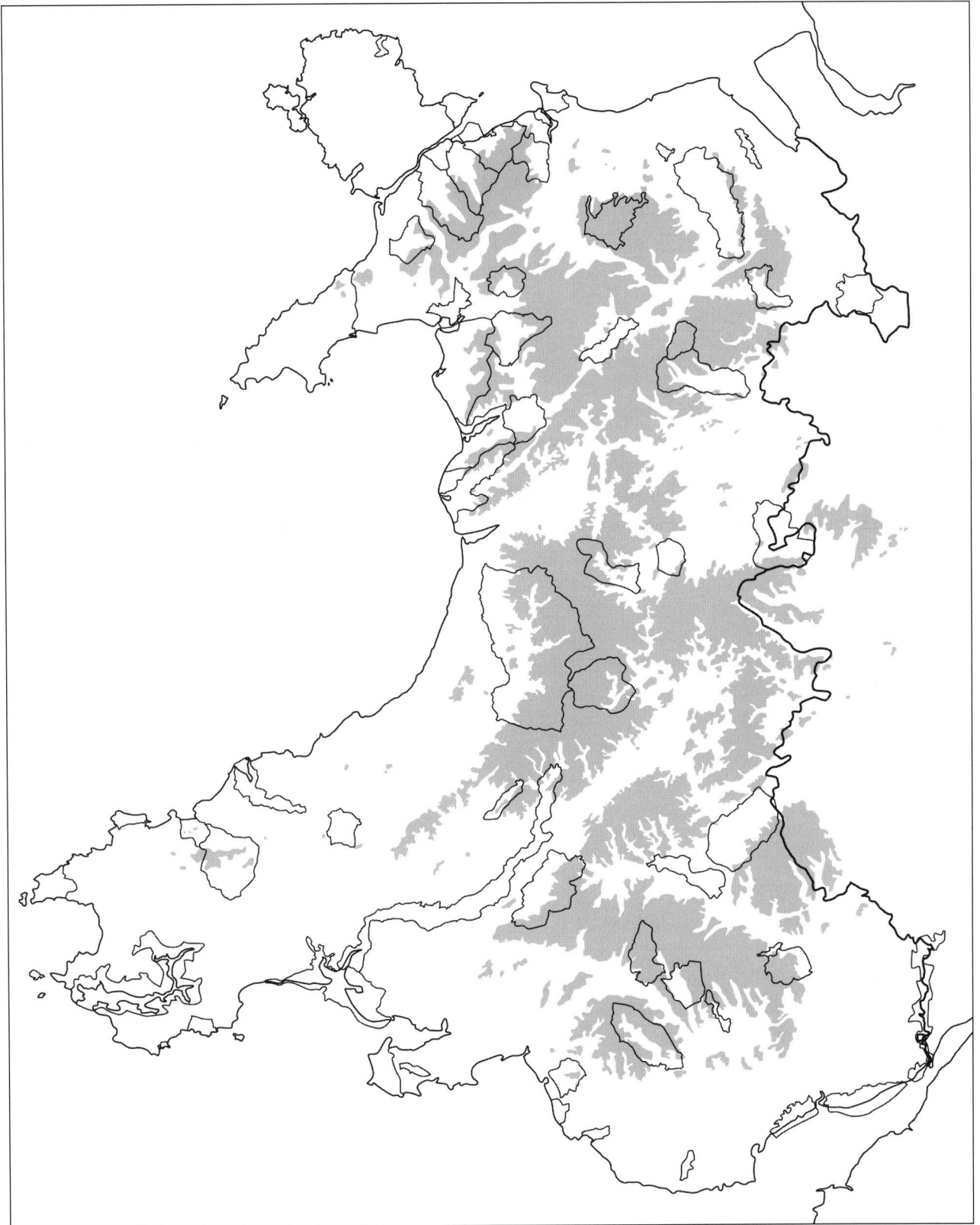

10.1 Historic landscapes in Wales

updated as work progressed, form the basis of heritage management advice and are readily available to the general public. In recent years the number of requests for access to this information has risen considerably. Upon completion of the project, Cadw financed the publication of a booklet 'Caring for Lost Farmsteads' which provides an overview of the project and offers advice on how sites can be identified and protected. This booklet, which is aimed at a broad readership and distributed to a wide range of individuals and organisations engaged in planning and land management, is complemented by a mobile exhibition for display at local and national agricultural shows, and in museums and libraries across Wales.

One possible means of communication which has yet seriously to be explored in Wales is through public presentation of selected sites, for example, the use of on-site information/interpretation panels. Although many deserted rural settlement sites are in relatively remote locations, there are a number of accessible sites which potentially offer presentation opportunities, either individually or as part of walking trails, especially in areas which already enjoy some degree of managed access (for example, land owned by the National Trust or the Forestry Commission).

10.5 Conclusion

From the outset of the Deserted Rural Settlement Project it was proposed that its findings would create a sound knowledge base upon which to build future protection strategies. Although interpretation and application of the information gained during the project are still ongoing, heritage management already benefits from enhanced site records, increased understanding and improved communication. The archaeologists of today are more directly engaged than ever before in providing advice to farmers, corporate landowners, local authorities, and other agencies involved in the management of the rural landscape. This excellent work must continue. Above all, we must strive to generate and increase public awareness of our national heritage, which in turn will stimulate appreciation and much-needed support for its conservation.

11 THE FUTURE: DISCOURSE, OBJECTIVES AND DIRECTIONS

David Austin

11.1 Introduction

As expressed elsewhere in this volume, the programme of study was begun for a clear purpose: that of management. As such it is necessarily limited by these aims and by the constraints placed on the scholars in terms of intention, methodology and resource. It is no part of this essay, therefore, to offer criticism of that process nor indeed to offer a detailed summary or commentary on the contents: this has been done in the previous chapter by Kathryn Roberts. I was asked rather to step back a little from the exercise and offer some thoughts on what, in general terms, we are trying to achieve in Wales in our research on rural settlement. Again I am not offering an overview of work under- taken or in progress; that would be to repeat much of what has been said before in this volume and, indeed, in the recent exercise to provide a research agenda for Wales (http://www. cpat. org. uk/research). Despite the restrictions of the brief, this publication gives a clear view of our current knowledge based on the collective experience of practising archaeologists both past and present. As such it is an important contribu- tion at a particularly interesting time.

It is important because it raises the profile of a problematical and undemonstrative class of monument in the Welsh landscape. The problematical aspects lie in assigning these sites to specific points in time, in agreeing a common descriptive and taxonomic language, in identifying them with documented places, and in finding resources for their proper understanding. They are undemonstrative because they are out of the way, very common in the landscape, and related to the lives of ordinary working people. In addition, as individual places, they largely relate to local, rather than national history. Yet the time is interesting because there are changes afoot in the body politic – in its aspirations and challenges – that make these places potentially significant for both

the nation and the communities which should have intellectual and emotional ownership of them. The stories they represent as a collection of monuments, it is possible to argue, are essential to the identity and well-being of Wales. This will be one purpose of my argument.

I want to consider the discourse in which the studies in this volume exist and the contexts informing that discourse. Their basis is essentially empirical, designed principally to explain the structures of society, usually in terms of adaptive and evolutionary systems, within which human beings act, not so much as agents but as depersonalised elements of the systems themselves. In this pattern of explanation, humanity is either ignored – being seen as largely controlled by the systems – or it is limited to the creators and controllers. This kind of structural explanation is drawn not principally from archaeology itself but rather from allied and cognate disciplines based on primary documentary sources. In empirical terms, agency in these sources (that is identifiable individuals) does indeed seem to be limited to those who are powerful within the systems. However, I want to argue that archaeology, as a discipline, is fundamentally based on seeing and understanding the results, as material depositions, of individual action – whether these are surveyed sites or excavated features. Archae- ology thus has the primary responsibility to analyse and explain those acts in themselves. It is also my strong feeling that archaeology, working in traditional agrarian societies, is best at identifying the action of people not as named individuals but as members of small groups – families within specific locations, whether a house, a farm or small settlement. In terms of narrative, we might call this 'biography of place'. This, incidentally, is the form of narrative probably best suited to an audience predominant in rural Wales, that is, the largely dispersed communities themselves and the individuals constituting them.

I feel that we still have work to do in creating such narratives in the case of deserted rural settlements, partly because we have not yet done enough to reconstruct the local contexts of these human groups in a rigorous fashion. Even more significantly, we have not excavated them and, when we have, our small-scale methodologies have either limited our capacity to interpret them or, more likely, we have felt inadequate in the face of the chronological precision and the scope of the systems made so apparent by documentary study. An example of this is that we have tended to explain upland house sites automatically in terms of *hafod*/*hendre* or temporary transhumance systems, rather than look at the physical variables of visibility, contextual associations in the landscape or presence/absence of certain kinds of material. In our anxiety to inject our places into existing systems of explanation we give more emphasis to the things we think are the same (which tend to permit structural explanation) as opposed to other things, however small, which are different (which tend towards agency). Thus we create distribution maps based on sameness of characteristics or try to fix relationships to documented locations, but usually this strategy allows us simply to insert the material culture into the already established systems and their processes, forcing us into patterns of explanation which should, perhaps, be secondary to the contribution our discipline can make to the debates. What, in fact, we tend to finish with is, at best, a descriptive affirmation of the analyses or, at worst, mute adjuncts to the debates which others have generated and seek to resolve.

This is not intended to deny the value of working in an inter-disciplinary way, but after 30 years of such collaboration with history I have to say that unless archaeology brings its own contribution to the table, with confidence, our colleagues in other disciplines are unlikely to take us seriously. Inter-disciplinary results too often actually mean two or more parallel, but largely unrelated narratives, which may share common terms, but actually derive different meanings from them. In surveying the literature of both architectural historians and social and economic historians working on Welsh material there is, for example, scarcely a mention of archaeological findings. A clear example of the former is Peter Smith's magisterial *Houses of the Welsh Countryside*, of which more anon, and of the latter is Professor Beverley Smith's 'Lord of Snowdon', chapter five in his powerful study of *Llewelyn ap*

Gruffudd. This has much to interest archaeologists and is of direct relevance because it enunciates the social and economic system within Llywelyn's patrimony and questions some of the conclusions drawn by predecessors. Not least do I find an implicit challenge to Peate's notion that a *ty hir* in the documents is what we archaeologists, borrowing from vernacular architectural historians, tend to call a 'longhouse', a basic peasant dwelling. Rather it is a lord's hall, which suggests that we should drop the term 'longhouse' completely in the peasant rural context, certainly in Wales (Smith J Beverley 1998, 234). I also find a challenge to the notion that the medieval *hafod* of the Gwynedd documents had anything to do with the kind of house-sites we are examining throughout this volume, since these relate to the royal vaccaries, rather than peasant exploitation (Smith J Beverley 1998, 232–4 and 240–1; see also Sambrook, *infra*, typescript 13–15). This shows is how difficult it is for archaeologists to be truly analytical historians and how we tend to accept the basic simplicities of the systems and impose them on our sites in a reductionist fashion (ironically, a good example is Austin 1988). The fact that in chapter five of *Llewelyn ap Gruffudd* the archaeology is limited to the footnotes is no fault of Professor Beverley Smith's; it simply serves to show how little archaeologists actually have to offer this kind of structural view of the world. We should also reflect that the most significant contribution, to judge from the footnotes, was the only site to have received extensive and thorough excavation in the modern era, Cefn Graeanog (Kelly 1982b).

Within these external patterns of explanation there are also narratives, or even metanarratives, such as *hendre*/*hafod*, which are essentially analytical descriptions of how the systems and structures change and vary over space and time. Sometimes these descriptions engage us also in attempts to 'theorise' the innate laws and processes of change, mostly evolutionary theory of one kind or another, which we believe drive or motivate the systems to change or to remain in stasis. This provides the narrative framework within which we attempt to interpret our essentially difficult material. It is not, however, the only way of explaining and interpreting, but I do not say this in opposition to what has been achieved by this programme of work, but rather as a means of enriching and complementing the discussion from a wider palette of possibilities.

In many ways this has been, in recent years, familiar territory for historical archaeology (eg Austin 1990; Johnson 2000; and Tarlow and West 1999) and many other disciplines (see Tosh 1999 for history; Rose 1993 for geography), but it needs to be articulated here in the specific context of this study before we can consider the future directions for the subject area. The construction of an agenda, however contested it might be, whether theoretically or empirically, is an essential prerequisite not just for the kinds of history we seek to write, but also for the landscapes we are seeking to conserve and manage, and for the multiplicity of audiences we seek to reach and influence.

11.2 Socio-economic systems

In the study of medieval and later settlements, there is no doubt that the primary discourse is economic history and that the principal system identified is agrarian production and the social institutions that enabled it. This has been so since the dawn of medieval rural archaeology in its study of English deserted villages and farms (Austin 1990). The main motivation was the attempt to derive evidence for the chronology, living standards, and economies of medieval peasants who were, at that time, being highlighted and described in terms of a class dialectic by certain scholars (eg Hilton 1985). This dialectic was based both on Marxist ethnographic descriptions of 'peasantry' as a European under-class (Wolf 1966; Shanin 1971) and on various critiques and explanations of the fundamental historical transitions from the antique modes of production to the feudal and then to the capitalist (Weber 1968; Bloch 1949) sometimes expressed as 'grand theory' or master systems (eg Mann 1986; Wallerstein 1974). There was also, however, an older and more extensive tradition of empiricist scholars whose analyses were embedded in a broadly 'Whig Theory of British History' (Kumar 2003, 202–07), and focused more on the institutions and categories of social organisation, their productive outputs and markets in terms of classical economics, and their gradual evolution and progress into modernity (Seebohm 1882; Maitland 1897; Vinogradoff 1892; and the contributions to the main modern authority, the *Cambridge Agrarian History of England And Wales*). For most practising archaeologists, our work developed in a symbiotic relationship with both lines of analysis, especially those which took the form of specific, localised studies of parishes, manors, and communities (eg Razi 1980; Howell 1983) or estates (eg Finberg 1969; King 1973). At the local level the tradition was deeply laid in a topographic, spatially territorial and map-based understanding of the British landscape best represented by the hundred/wapentake and parish-based volumes of the *Victoria County History*, especially the more recent ones such as Shropshire. The main objective in these studies was a mapped reconstruction of a local past landscape, a methodology now so ingrained that we lose sight of the fact that this is also a system-based view of history cast in modern Enlightenment terms within the tradition of 'topography' (see Cosgrove 1984 for a general critique).

All of this is a very 'English' pattern of study, and it is a hard truth that most archaeologists looking at historic rural settlement in Wales, including myself, came from this tradition and inevitably imported its basic assumptions. These views are detectable in this volume. In a sense this was also part of the tradition of British scholars looking to Wales explicitly for an understanding of 'pre-Germanic' institutions and their later suppression or adaptation (eg Seebohm 1897; Jolliffe 1926, Faith 1997, 9–14). Amongst Welsh scholars this tradition is also evident, but cast as an expression of Welsh distinctiveness. There is, for example, a focus on the laws and patterns of social responsibility laid out in the landscapes of Wales for the pre-1284 era (eg Jones-Pierce 1961; Davies 1978). Glanville Jones in particular goes on to focus on the articulation from these patterns of a specific and universalising 'multiple estate' model for demonstrably 'Celtic/British' territories of land use and lordship (eg G R J Jones 1971; for a recent critique and alternative, R A Jones 1998).

This tendency is heightened by a comparative dearth of surviving documents for the economic and social history of the 11th, 12th, and 13th centuries of the kind that enables the detailed topographic studies which underpin English scholarship. Often we have to rely on the evidence of post-1284 Crown surveys or much later estate material to identify the patterns of social and economic ordering of the landscape for this period (eg Thomas 1968; Longley, *infra*). We also do not have, in Wales, sufficient evidence for the close examination of the estate management of the great monasteries and sees which is such a basic staple of English medieval economic history and, indeed, landscape and land use reconstruction. There are many very good overviews which project the European understanding of Cistercian economies onto specific Welsh foundations and landscapes (Williams 1990);

these are sustained by some fundamental, but largely untested, assumptions about how such houses actually operated in the Welsh context. Overview, whether at county (eg Howells 1987), or national (eg Emery 1967) level, is also how we understand the later medieval agrarian economies and the transitions to modernity, and it is only from the later 17th or 18th centuries that we begin to have the data and the analyses for specific estates and their management of the agrarian landscape (eg Morgan 1997, 181; Thomas 1979).

Despite all of this difference in source and resultant analyses, some clear models of land use and agrarian systems have emerged in the literature for Wales. The two most dominant for the Middle Ages are the 'colonial' village and open field systems of the Vale of Glamorgan and South Pembrokeshire, and the dispersed upland farm and hamlet landscapes of the rest of Wales. This distinction may appear to sit comfortably within the prevailing metanarrative generated in England as proposed by a consensus of scholars (eg Rackham 1986; Williamson 1988; Taylor 1995) in which the dispersed patterns are suggestive of deeply ancient forms of social and economic organisation (Uhlig 1961) unless they are demonstrably the result of either assart or enclosure, and the nucleated patterns are redolent of 'new' or champion organisation specific to manorial and 'feudal' systems. In Wales this is fitted into a chronology of the Anglo-Norman colonisation in the 11th and 12th centuries for the 'new' and into the resistance of *Pura Wallia* for the 'ancient'. This is a gross over-simplification and is currently under debate (eg Kissock 1997; Thomas 1992), but it does underlie a great deal of the economic and social system analyses and interpretations which are at present on offer.

The primary assumptions and arguments of these forms of structural analysis almost exclusively underpin the empirical work in this volume. I am not proposing here that those assumptions are necessarily wrong, but it should be remembered that they are system frameworks that archaeologists have imported from elsewhere, however circumstantial the evidence on which they may be based in other disciplines. We must revisit the original sources to determine how reliable the proposed models are – and some are quite insecure – notably the transhumance and related *hendre/hafod* systems. At best all these system models must be regarded as hypotheses and not substitutes for archaeological material evidence.

In the case of transhumance and *hendre/hafod*, for example, we have, in order to suit the systemic argu-

ments, locked our descriptive discussion of building morphologies into terminologies such as 'temporary' and 'permanent', notions given us not by the archaeology itself, but by the socio-economic systems within which we seek to interpret them. Such notions from an archaeological perspective have been challenged by, for example, Wrathmell's brilliant reinterpretation of excavated house-plans from Wharram Percy and elsewhere (Wrathmell 1989). Prior to this the excavated remains of medieval peasant houses were interpreted as temporary, being constantly rebuilt. They are now interpreted as permanent buildings with strong timber frames. The notion of temporary was, it can be argued, actually derived from the preconceptions instilled in archaeologists from the Marxist structural and generic image of the medieval peasant as an under-class living in wretched conditions. In other words the historical perception drove the archaeological. Wrathmell's work has exposed both the weakness of our interpretative procedures and the fact that the concepts of 'temporary' and 'permanent' are actually modern and related to our own living experiences in an industrial city-based and capitalist society. We must, as archaeologists, face the bitter truth that we have almost no evidence at all of our own to support the notion that the farms and hamlets on the valley floor in upland Wales had any more or less 'permanency' than the building and enclosure complexes on the *ffriddoedd*. Elsewhere in Britain building complexes on the upland are direct copies of those on the valley floor and just as permanent. Why not in Wales?

Another case in point is the very fine work in this volume by Longley, mapping the systems of north Wales and contemplating the visible archaeology in relation to the documented pattern of settlement and agriculture known from surveys and place-names (Longley, *infra*). This is a valuable starting point, but even so, the map of *dref* centres is a projection of an idealised system, based on top-down views expressed in administrative documents rather than evidence drawn from the material world. It may progress our understanding of the documented structural system, and make the best use of present knowledge, but the work does challenge archaeologists to go further in establishing what exactly was happening in the material world of the Middle Ages. In essence the maps are the spatial logging of documented place-names through their correlation with modern place-names. We still have little idea, in the vast majority of instances, what these places looked like in the past or even precisely where they were: and this should be the primary responsibility and contribution of the archaeologist. This is doubly underlined by the realisation that so many of the sites in the upland that we can identify physically on the ground cannot actually be traced in the documents. Why is this? In dealing with these issues we have again to consider agency as opposed to structure.

Before we do this, however, it is important to reflect on at least one other aspect of the economic structural models that lay beyond the framework of this study. This is the nature of the market and the processes of production and distribution. We may be reasonably clear in this modelling that the identifiable and documented urban locations of the Middle Ages were, in many ways, part of the 'new' and colonial, even if implemented by the Welsh themselves. The deliberate and planned introduction of a money economy and regulated markets is part of the shock of the European, courtesy of colonialism. Physically, within the urban centres and among the nucleated villages of the south, there is extensive evidence for the importation of English royal coinage. There has also been some speculation about the extent of money circulation in *Pura Wallia* before the 14th century, based in part on documentary sources and in part on a few hoards (Boon 1986; Besly 1995), but beyond the high-status sites and the boroughs there is no archaeological evidence for the circulation of coinage in the rural heartlands, in apparent contrast to the tariffs of exactions made by Welsh princes such as Llewelyn (Smith J Beverley 1998, 255–7). We need to look also at the products of an embedded coinage, that is the material culture created for commercial markets, such as pottery. Again we can find it in abundance in the Anglicised areas of the south and in the elite sites (Johnstone 1995) and boroughs of the north, but elsewhere in the ancient dispersed locations it is not so evident (Papazian and Campbell 1992). There are clearly issues of physical survival, particularly in the upland acidic soils, but material will actually survive in such conditions if delivered in the quantities, which an embedded economy would deliver. If we compare upland acidic locations in England, such as Dartmoor or the Pennines, the material culture is there in abundance from the 12th century onwards. The fact that, at most of the sites in Wales where excavation has been carried out, there is very little evidence up to the 16th and 17th centuries, actually needs explaining. We should also keep an open mind and not simply accept that the absence is an indication of temporary occupation in a transhumance system. There are other systems of power and meaningful distribution that should be considered, alongside issues of agency and deposition (see Wickham 1985).

11.3 Environmental systems

There is one other major source of models we must consider: the environmental. I would argue that there are two main relevant aspects to this: concepts of marginality and wilderness or waste which include the upland/lowland dichotomy; and physical and topographical regionality which includes the issue of the vernacular and its material locality. Determinist arguments lie at the heart of all these. Such determinism has long been an issue for archaeologists and is still a contemporary concern, even if only due to our engagement in current debates about the future of agriculture and the impact of climate change. Long gone are the days, however, when we would overtly or consciously concede that the environment was the prime cause of settlement, land use or social phenomena. We tend to look for more complex explanations for the processes we think we see through our interpretation of the landscape evidence. Indeed this is why we borrowed the systems approach from ecologists and behaviourists in the first place. However, such causalities and determinisms have become subconscious, surfacing either in our graphic representations of the past (eg on maps dominated by contour lines) or as expressions of self-evident facts. That they are neither representative nor self-evident in relation to their role in human history, cultural behaviour, and individual action seems not to be accepted. We should at least admit the presence of an argument which identifies the problems as lying as much in our own mind-sets as in the intractability of the evidence. I want to argue, with others, that the relationship of people to their locations and environments is mediated by the cultural and that this needs to be understood. So the archaeological questions about sites and places ought, for example, to be considering what people can see from these places and how they themselves can be seen in the landscape – asking what these sites might signify in localised cultural terms and in relation to the histories and identities of both observer and observed. In Wales we need less emphasis on environmental systems and more on detailed historical ecology so that the results can contribute to the evocation and narrative of specific places in the past human experience of Wales. This, and the relationship to the natural not as contoured altitude, but as hills and rock outcrops, is now a commonplace of prehistory (Bradley 2000), but not something archaeologists are yet prepared to consider in terms of the more recent past – largely because we feel that documents or architectural history tell us most of what we want to know about the people of these historic periods and their relationship to the environment. This belief is questionable.

11.4 Marginality

There are three strands to the environmental consideration of marginality: altitude, climate, and soil. Their capacity to affect agrarian productivity is undoubted, but the main issue is how much they impact on human action and culture? This is not just a matter of yield, growth, and agricultural technology, but one also of perception and interpretation by the people who had an interest in the spaces we designate as marginal. In Wales this is largely the land above the *penclawdd* (head-dyke), that is the *ffridd* (hill pastures) and *mynydd* (mountain waste), but we must remember also marsh (*cors*), moorland (*rhos*), and wooded slope (*allt*). However, this implies that the land below the *penclawdd* is, or has been, not marginal and is thus fertile and cultivable. In strictly empirical terms it is all relative, of course: using absolute UK land use criteria, for example, most of the land of Wales can be categorised as marginal. In complete contrast to this view, there have been arguments to suggest that traditional farming societies, past and present, do not have this sense of marginality: everything is exploitable and in survival and risk-defraying strategies everything is used in some form or other (Fleming 1988, 107; Withers 1995, 44–5; Ward 1997, 104–05). Difference in use and place may be signified by words which distinguish, such as *ffridd* and *tir gwelyog*, but these are as much cultural words of hierarchy, rights of access, kin relationship, and render as they are indicators of the topography. To translate *mynydd*, for example, simply as 'mountain' is to do a grave injustice to the complexities of Welsh cultural history. To view these terms as absolutes fixed by the environment is also a problem: the relative volatility is apparent through the richness of the archaeological record displayed in this volume. The land may be hard to plough, but if you need the grain enough and the organisation of power permits it, you can plough it. The graphic air photographs of the Berwyns clearly demonstrate this (Silvester 2000).

In spite of all this, the concept of marginality **did** exist in medieval and post-medieval Wales; it is embedded in words such as 'waste' (*terra vastata*), or 'unimproved' and, to bring us right up to date, 'wilderness' and 'marginal' itself. These are words to be found in charters and monastic accounts of the Middle Ages, estate maps and terriers of the 17th and 18th centuries, improvement manuals and 'views' of the 18th and 19th centuries, government studies and analyses of agriculture in the 19th and 20th centuries, and environmentalist tracts in the 20th and 21st centuries. In all of these the concept is one to be associated with top-down applications of authority, sometimes masquerading as high-minded morality, and very specifically that kind of authority which either comes in from the outside or adopts the rhetoric of outsiders. The notion was, and still is, that unused (actually 'uncultivated'), marginal space exists to be exploited as a resource with the potential to be converted either into revenue, for example Cistercian sheep-farming or modern forestry, or into playground, for example medieval hunting forests or National Parks. The archaeology which survives is as much about the tension and conflict between these two different mind-sets as it is about the differences between the physically marginal and core lands. It is remarkable, therefore, that tensions such as these, so apparent in our modern countryside, should be so absent from the narratives we create about landscapes in the recent past. Again it is because we tend to see landscapes as single, simplified and harmonious systems when in reality they operate in many different ways with many different, often conflicting, human attitudes engaged. This is a similar argument to Ward's in his work on the Black Mountain, although his is based on economic factors (Ward 1999, 337).

It is possible that some of the archaeology on the upland reviewed in this volume results from conflict, maybe not physical, but certainly cultural and conceptual. What of the existence, side-by-side on the same piece of the *ffridd*, of long-hut sites and monastic buildings? What of the thousands of *bwthyn* (cottages) and their small fields, built by the Welsh poor on hard land in the 18th century? These are known from Welsh oral custom, but find no mention in English written law and were deliberately excluded from tithe maps and terriers often created by the managers and agents of the great estates. The marginalised elements of society, even in the Middle Ages, were the dispossessed, the outcast and were, in Geremek's terms, 'invisible' in the documents (Geremek 1990). The archaeology makes them visible and certainly reveals agency working against the structures.

Another aspect of determinism is the so-called *hafod/hendre* system (Sayce 1956; Sayce 1957; Richards 1959; Richards 1960) devised within the twin discourses of anthropological geography and place-name studies. This accepts, as a base proposition, the determinism of the lowland/upland dichotomy and expresses it in terms of a long-term agrarian and social inter-relationship between valley floor and mountain, based essentially on short-distance transhumance. Locked into the theory is the sense that the pattern of human living required permanent settlement and residence on the valley floor, while on the mountain it was all much more temporary and seasonal. Less explicitly expressed is the assumption that this was a uniquely Welsh pattern of life rooted in the environmental limitations of the land and in the social and economic structures identifiable in the Welsh law codes and the later English surveys of appropriated royal demesnes. So the key concepts of the *hafod/hendre* system are: its long-term persistence, its embeddedness in the landscape, its reflection of environmental realities, its complete integration into the social order and power structures, and its Welshness. Very few scholars now accept this uncritically and indeed there is good reason to believe that the originators of the idea themselves did not seek to be absolute about the system. Sayce, for example, saw the phenomenon as at least pan-European and an aspect of politically marginalised upland societies (Sayce 1956, 117–19), although others contest this generalising (Smith J Beverley 1998, 241).

Today historians are sceptical that medieval and later administrators saw the world in these terms: Longley, in this volume, finds it difficult to relate the upland sites to anything he finds in the post-1284 English extents and Ward makes the same point for the later records (Ward 1999, 335). The majority of the place-names, we now recognise, are late and problematical and other terms, such as *lluest*, might be more meaningful (Sambrook this volume), especially when we know little about the processes of naming places and, indeed, about the mobility and persistence of place-names. I would add to this the fundamental doubt about whether seeing the past and its spaces in simple reductive relationships, such as the *hendre/hafod* system, is at all helpful. The need for mixed-farming traditional societies, for example, to move cattle around their resource, **wherever** it is situated, cuts across topographies and is both the same and very different as we move from culture to culture and even from community to community. The practices differ because of the variable dynamics of access rights, fixed and altered by genealogy and social position. We must even contemplate that some of the potentially medieval structural remains we find on the upland pastures today are the result of activity whose only relationship to the system was illegal violation of it and so totally unrecorded or invisible. We know that the mountain was an important place for such illegitimacy and resistance and was indeed part of its cultural identity: think of Twm Sion Catti.

11.5 Identity and the Vernacular

Right at the core of the ideas being addressed in this volume is the issue of vernacular architecture and its role in the historical debate on Welsh identity and regionality. The essays in this volume display some different positions on this issue, which usually surface as definitional problems, rather than being related to their ideological roots. It seems that at the heart of these contrasting approaches is an unresolved debate about the nature, meaning and causes of Welsh vernacular culture.

In a seminal set of essays published in 1963 to honour Sir Cyril Fox, Lord Raglan proposed that both architectural design, even in the vernacular, and the major principles of construction were disseminated on a class basis: spatially they were thus widespread, national, and even supra-national in their nature. In other words, in the historic periods where we can see surviving buildings, the *mentalité* of shape and ways of living were not culturally and ethnically embedded, but determined first by status and aspiration to status (Raglan 1963, 384–5). He even denied that there was a distinct sub-stratum of 'folk' or 'peasant' architecture made by the lower classes of farmer and based on localised traditions of craft (Raglan 1963, 386). The vernacular was, he argued, the result of lesser men building in universal styles, but executing them in local materials and making minor adaptations as required by the nature of those materials. In other words class and the individual drove the fundamentals of style and the patterns of living, rather than the ethnic culture or the environment. Furthermore, Raglan concluded that what we see – either as surviving buildings or excavated and surveyed remains – are not the relics of some ancient cultural tradition existing before the elite built in their new fashions – but the ragged remnants of the later trickle-down of these new fashions to the lower echelons.

Although Raglan did not say it, this defies the idea of innate, long-term, environmentally determined regional cultures and folk style, the exact opposite of Jope's argument in his famous article on medieval regional cultures published in the same volume of essays (Jope 1963). In a sense this is what the archaeology of buildings described in this volume seems to tell us: it all looks much the same whatever fine tuning we want to introduce by way of problematical taxonomic distinctions between, say, long-huts and long-houses, wherever we are looking at them. In Raglan's terms, the building type is actually not a lot different from what we find in contemporary Devon, Dartmoor or Galloway. If this is so, then what is 'Welsh' about it, and what of the existence of regions within Wales? We know that there were political regions or territories, such as princedoms, *cantrefau* and shires, but did these have any but the most insignificant impact on material culture and the way of life? More worryingly, what does this tell us of the historical distinction between Welsh and English, and the processes of colonisation? Was there as much cultural resistance in the architecture as there was in the oral and ideological sphere?

Raglan's position was radically different from the view of Iorwerth Peate who, in the *Welsh House*, spoke of the vernacular architecture in terms of it being 'original material', 'traditional' which 'outcrops only here and there from beneath a deep stratum of a later, overlying culture' (Peate 1946, 3). In his view, community in Wales 'has always been essentially peasant in character' (Peate 1946, 3–4). Its poverty and its subjugation are represented by its vernacular architecture and by its craft, and these are political:

A nation bereft of its sovereignty cannot promote the growth of the fine arts, except by indirect and generally innocuous means. In such a country, incorporated moreover since 1536 in a neighbouring virile state, the only national architecture is peasant architecture. (Peate 1946, 4)

The peasant forms which do survive are also unremittingly moulded by the environment and, as the peas-

ants throw up their rough shelters for protection, 'there are no architects' (Peate 1946, 5, quoting Ling 1936, 845). The craft is stratigraphically embedded, therefore, in Peate's mind, as the firm foundation of a culture such as Wales. It is primitive, basic, unified, strong and enduring, rooted in rock and shaped by rain:

The Welsh house ... is therefore an expression of Welsh life – indeed a facet of it, for the peasant house is always indivisible ... In the same way true peasant architecture knows no time: it represents the past, the present and the future. (Peate 1946, 5)

For Peate this timelessness was coming to an end in modernity. Here, as elsewhere, he betrayed his intellectual forebears as Morris and the Romantic socialists of the Arts and Crafts Movement, as well as Iolo Morgannwg and the Romantic nationalists: the golden age was **always** the past and that past had never changed until its brutal destruction by a contemporary tyrant. Peate perceived 'the tyrant' as the English way and not, as for Morris, modernity itself and the class-based capitalism of the world system.

To sum this up then, Raglan was an evolutionary progressive and Peate a stoical fundamentalist. However, Raglan was also a member of the Anglo-Welsh Establishment, which had sold out to England, whereas Peate was a true patriot.

That this represented a fundamental difference of view surfaced in what at first sight seems a somewhat obscure debate in another part of the volume for which Raglan wrote in 1963. The argument centred on the definitions of the 'longhouse' and its cultural significance. The point is raised again later in the volume, only for it to remain still unresolved. The protagonists then were Peate himself, who had invented the term out of the Welsh *ty hir* found in the law codes, J T Smith, and Peter Smith (Peate 1936; 1946; 1963; J T Smith 1963; P Smith 1963). Peter Smith had triggered the debate in 1958 by challenging Peate's work on the *ty hir* (Smith and Owen 1958), a point he expanded at an unpublished lecture in 1960. His thoughts were later underlined in a study by Lloyd, Vernon and Bevan-Evans in 1963 (Lloyd *et al* 1963). Peter Smith argued, in support of Raglan and *contra* Peate, that the longhouse was the result of cultural diffusion from England and, indeed, that all surviving examples had been conversions of earlier buildings into longhouses at a later, post-medieval date. Thus he denied that the Welsh longhouse had ever been a single unitary design and that it had ethnic origins in a timeless Welsh past.

Peate argued vehemently that this viewpoint was 'both misleading and untrue' – on the grounds that the longhouses were fundamental lived-in spaces experienced by Welsh people over a long period of time and were thus present as a cultural constant (Peate 1963, 442). The tone was clear and the argument consistent with the earlier work. Peate drew deep on his own authority: he restated the long cultural tradition; he appealed to a Welsh cultural context; and he reiterated the environment as the prime cause and determinant. Peate (1963) sniped again, but the issue was never resolved and the other protagonists never re-engaged, perhaps because of growing ethnic sensitivity. In a telling footnote in his masterwork on the *Houses of the Welsh Countryside* Peter Smith dropped a dead bat on the debate, but he too remained quietly steadfast (Smith 1988, 170, n. 4).

This debate, one of cultural identity, was never again brought into the open in the context of vernacular architecture. Peate's successors have taken for granted the force of the cultural and environmental argument, even elaborating on various Welsh sub-regions, not just north and south, but also east and west (eg Wiliam 1982; Jenkins 1976). For them Wales is defined by its raw materials and its long socio-cultural traditions and has a unique appearance or even a number of unique appearances. Their work finds echoes, even down to the present day, in the arguments for an enduring instinct for resistance and survival in Welsh culture, sometimes, even if metaphorically, expressed in terms of genetic ethnicity (Aaron 2003).

Peter Smith, on the other hand, along with other vernacular historians such as Brunskill and Alcock, still saw Wales in the context of British regional style (not Welsh houses, but period houses **in** the Welsh countryside) and continued the study by applying the neutralising terminology of detailed classification. Smith's basic position is rationalist and evolutionary, exploring the evidence in an empirical manner in the tradition, and with the rhetoric, of Raglan himself. He essentially holds fast to his position in terms of both culture and process. He does this by ignoring almost all archaeological evidence, especially for the humbler peasant house which is the subject of this volume. Instead, he reserves his focus for the class of buildings which emerge as a 'sub-medieval type' in the late 15th and 16th centuries, the storeyed houses with cross-passages belonging to the lesser gentry and substantial farmers. 'They illustrate a society living under the rule of law [by this Smith means English law, post 1536] ...' (Smith 1988, 169).

What is striking is that, for this period, Smith argues, the Welsh house is the extant building of the rural middle class represented as an integrated part of English society, an adjunct of its rising 'middling sort'. There is neither reference to the houses of the rural poor and the lesser tenantry, nor any acknowledgement that this middle and lesser gentry class represented itself in truly Welsh ways, not least in its genealogies, poetry, antiquarianism and its other expressions of identity (Williams 1985, 121–31). The Welsh gentry at this time had signed up to 'Project England' in the belief that the Tudors had made it 'Project Britain' (Roberts 1998). In other words, I would argue, Smith's buildings are as de-contextualised from the totality of their societies as they are from the landscapes they once inhabited.

More important than any of this, however, is the issue Peate half gets hold of. The house is an organisation of space which is culturally familiar and is understood by its occupants as patterns of time-honoured action and relationship, interpreted and experienced in the context of movement and encounter within the constructed space (Glassie 1990, 279): what is called the lived-in experience, the *habitus*. That encounter includes the exterior as well as the interior, something that has concerned historians, architects and environmentalists in a much wider discourse on the house and its meaning (eg Glassie 1975; Rapoport 1990; Samson 1990; Johnson 1993). In terms of entering the longhouse, for example, the fundamental human concern in reading its space was who was encountered and under what physical and semiotic circumstances. Entry into a single long building divided between beast and human, with the entrance then leading into the main communal living room with private spaces beyond was a daily experience full of subconscious meaning as well as function (Austin and Thomas 1990). In this case, in terms of the human experience, the excavated 13th-century longhouse in Devon or Wales is much the same as Smith's 'sub-medieval storeyed houses'. So, although Smith is right in saying that the longhouse is not simply Welsh, he is wrong in implying that it is not even Welsh. For the Welsh it was Welsh and had its own particular cultural and social context in the Welsh mind. It comes down to this: the Welsh house, is it the house **in** Wales or the house **of** Wales? The unexpressed consensus is probably that it is a bit of both: stylistically a period house **in** Wales and materially and socially a house **of** Wales and the Welsh land. It is thus, culturally, a hybrid.

The real question, then, is one of agency: through which people, in what minds, and by what processes did design as the template of living get transferred throughout the social structures? Peate was clear: there were two processes, at times set in dialectical opposition to each other whether as class or *gens*: the peasant, arising by long-term gradual evolution from basic principles of living determined by custom, environment and locality; and the elite, more volatile and determined by the whim of power and fashion. Raglan was equally clear about this: style change happened suddenly as the result of architect-centred, self-conscious innovation, then by rapid transmission ('diffusion') among mobile European elites and then trickled down through the social order. Currently the balance of opinion and analysis outside of Wales is on Raglan's side (eg Grenville 1997, 130–2 for peasant houses with halls). Thus, in a social sense, it is possible to argue that the longhouse is merely the peasant form of the 'feudal spatial geography' of the in-line hall, solar and services of the emergent manor-house of the 11th and 12th centuries, just as the town-house is the vertical expression of the same. Both the longhouse and the town-house appear at more or less the same time in the archaeological and architectural record as the manor-house. Indeed, *prima facie*, there is sufficient synchronicity to suggest that there was not enough time for either outward or downward diffusion. It is as if a total design formula was being delivered for all in the later 11th and 12th centuries.

However, in the post-Peate and post-Raglan Welsh literature on historic buildings, we have shied away from the questions of style transmission. There are simply re-statements of the positions set out in 1963. Style and its design are not analysed in these sorts of ways. What we are given as a first step towards this,

perhaps, are empirically rigorous distribution maps, based on the developed classifications, showing the location of different distinctive and visible features of style. The location of a building on the map, however, cannot be a representation of the human experience, and at best it is a poor substitute. Smith, for example, in his *magnum opus*, simply states that there are regional styles because material differences are visible from region to region. He indicates that there are various opinions about how such differences might be explained, and he identifies three main bodies of thought: environmental determinism; ethnic explanation; and 'social' explanation (citing Eric Mercer from unpublished manuscripts) as 'reflection of social, political and economic circumstance' (Smith 1988, 3–4). He is not explicit about his view, but throughout the book and, indeed, in his other work, Smith appears to accept that the environment and the social circumstances (as defined in relation to Mercer's work) play an equal role. He denies the ethnic in any genetic sense, whether English or Welsh, preferring Raglan's diffusionist view that architectural ideas moved from the Court downwards (Smith 1988, 10). What Smith also ignores is that ethnicity, in an anthropological sense, is socially located and not merely genetic: it is a continual process of human self-identification with a series of defining principles, emotions and practices. So, to attempt to distance himself from the problems and rhetoric of the national debate by hiding behind an abstraction like 'the Court', he ignores that it was (and still is) the English court in the mind, sentiment and behaviour of most Welsh people whether born to be Welsh (genetic identity) or Welsh by adoption (fictive identity).

11.6 Region and the vernacular

What is also ignored by Smith is what the distributions of material culture, especially building typologies within Wales, actually mean in historical terms. A major contribution springing from this present volume would be the production of integrated national maps, which could, for example, be put alongside Smith's or indeed those in the National Atlas of Wales especially those showing linguistic isoglosses (Carter 1981). The comparison would begin to lend greater depth to the consideration of cultural region. We should also aim to complete those rural settlement maps which have been deployed to identify empirically both major and minor embedded cultural regions in the adjacent parts of England (Roberts and Wrathmell 2000). One of our abiding

problems, however, is that definitions and criteria for a systematic and uniform national typology of cultural forms within Wales cannot yet be agreed. This is compounded when regions are based not on empirical or any other form of analysis, but on the assumption of historic political and administrative divisions which are, in the end, unjustified and unjustifiable as ways of identifying the regional cultures of Wales. It may be an irritant to this problem that the Archaeological Trusts are themselves locked into these structures and charged with the assembly and analysis of material each within their own domains. Ironically all of this in itself is a demonstration of the inherent instability of the region: it is constantly being renegotiated in complex socio-political circumstances. Of themselves these unresolved differences suggest that there is no fixed and ancient substratum of regional identity. We are still left then with two ways of looking at the issue, neither of which is derived from archaeological analysis: the geographical determinist and the socio-political. We are back to the same kinds of debate as we have seen already in this essay and again we find ourselves locked into a pragmatic and 'safe' ambivalence.

Safety is often found in the 'natural'. There is still a tendency to rely on an out-dated regional geography of Wales (e.g. Bowen 1965) which emphasises solid geology, altitude, soil and rainfall mapping as the foundation determinants of variation in regional culture. In a very well argued paper in this volume Longley goes a little further and divides Gwynedd into a number of micro-regions based on these kinds of criteria (fig. 4.3), used essentially, however, as descriptive background. This is nonetheless an important step forward and this will help us to ask how precisely the cultural interacted with the natural, but until we do this we are going to be left with very incomplete statements of how Wales in the past functioned spatially. In Longley's piece, the more telling map, in terms of historical space, plots commotes together with documented medieval locations and some 'selected' archaeological sites on a background not of altitude, but the 'extent of historical enclosure'. The correlations are clearly important for issues of archaeological survival and visibility and for an indication of 'lowland' *hendre*-type farming and by this means we gain some insight into how the totality of the social and economic systems might have functioned. Such a map is in a strong tradition which can be traced in Wales back though William Rees, Jones Pierce, Glanville Jones and others. In this tradition, however, the natural is absent or subdued, since it emphasises largely the cultural, and in this case indeed literally the cultivated. The mapped commotes, discrete estates or manors are territories and can never be defined as regions, and so spatial variations in culture actually become harder to identify or explain. Indeed one effect of such mapping is to create the impression that the cultural phenomena being examined, for example upland buildings and settlements, are more or less uniform and indistinguishable. This rather promotes the feeling that there is no micro-regional culture and history in Wales at least in the Middle Ages and the Early Modern period, leaving aside the issue of whether there are macro-regional cultures in Wales. This rather goes against the notion that the landscape

of Gwynedd, and of Wales as a whole, 'is one of considerable contrasts' (Longley *infra*, typescript p. 1) This is not to be critical of Longley whose paper takes us much further in understanding how the social systems worked as settled landscapes in Wales. Rather I use it to demonstrate where we archaeologists currently stand in relation to the issue of region in Wales. We are ambivalent and leave much to assumption and common sense. We are all still creating a somewhat incomplete statement of how Wales in the past worked spatially.

Compare, for example, the same strategy followed both in Peter Smith's *magnum opus* (Smith 1988) and in the classic study by Eurwyn Wiliam of the farm buildings of north-east Wales (Wiliam 1982). Wiliam begins his map sequence with the natural micro-regions of the north-east, but never deploys them in his analysis, except as descriptive locators of specific examples, and not consistently. Smith, on the other hand, is more careful and strictly empirical, but in his text the regional exists and indeed it lies both at the beginning of his analysis and in a chapter which is headed the 'Architectural Personality of Wales', consciously echoing Fox's famous determinist title, *The Personality of Britain* (Fox 1932). His regional narrative is presented as a given and is then not explored or analysed any further. Smith's distribution maps, not cited in this overview chapter, but based on stylistic typology, then stand on their own. However, his proposition is clear and entirely consistent with his 1963 position: in challenging Fox's simple division which puts Wales entirely in the Highland zone, Smith is clear that there were, and are, contrasts and differences in style capable of being mapped for Wales, but that they are plastic and variable:

In rather simplified terms the types of regional contrast which emerge fall into a number of different categories whose overlapping yields a fascinating variety of stylistic blends. The first contrasts are between those one would on general grounds most expect, the contrasts between east and west, between those districts looking towards the riches of the English plain and those facing the storms of the Irish Sea. Wales stands both literally and figuratively between England and Ireland. In the east substantial storeyed houses predominate, as they predominate in England; in the west, single-storeyed cottages are more numerous, as they are in Ireland ... (Smith 1988, 13)

It is important that this primary assertion is not supported by a single distribution map and if we look at the maps which use the word 'region' or 'regional' in the title, this assertion does not stand scrutiny, except for Fig 26b which shows two north–south lines demarcating the relatively larger survival of early farmhouses in the east. This is to be contrasted with the previous map 'Regional House-types – summary diagram' (fig 26a, actually based on sub-medieval house-types) which identifies four major regional blocks, one in each corner of Wales. To be fair to Smith, he does proceed to define two other essential divides that emerge from the mapping (Smith 1988, 16). In neither case, however, does he cite any of his maps and the reader is left to make his own analysis. Smith is, in effect, saying that although there were and are regions in Wales, they are plastic, variable, and 'overlapping', as they are plotted both through time and by specific taxonomic characteristics (Smith 1988, 17).

What is implicit, therefore, in Smith's argument, is that, since the human geographical definition of cultural regions depends on conjunctions of many variables, there actually were no regions in Wales, except in the sub-medieval period when multiple variables can be plotted together, although almost uniquely in his analysis not by the use of spot distributions, but rather by mapped assertions (Smith 1988, Fig 26a). So there is an essential contradiction in the work as a whole. Smith appears to be a regionalist and adopts the regional rhetoric of vernacular historians asserting the meaning of region, without actually ever demonstrating it empirically. What he fails to understand is that culture and the spatial identity, known as region (or even 'tribe'), which is derived from culture, is a formulation of socially contested constructs drawn from the total experience of human beings. Thus, region, and the emotion of belonging which goes with it, is often defined by what one is **not** rather than what one is. Without these considerations the plotting of individual characteristics drawn from one kind of material can at best only be a contribution. The rest is rhetoric. For Smith, the over-riding view of Wales and its regions identifies its culture as dependent on environment and England as the conduit of the westwards and northwards diffusion of ideas and styles. This is supported by detached objectivity and sanctioned by an idea of culture which is largely devoid of people, their minds and emotions. This fundamentally misunderstands what culture is and denies the primacy of the truly social, as a recursive mechanism of memory and experience, centred on personal and group identity. What is needed is serious thought about what we are trying to achieve here: we need some intellectual clarity and debate about fundamentals. We cannot be driven by an unthinking acceptance of methodologies and assumptions created in the theoretical Dark Ages of our discipline. The problem for archaeologists working in this same domain is that they have been drawn into this pattern of thought, because of the overwhelming authority of the discipline of architectural history. Archaeology does not have to make the same mistakes and there are other ways of looking at buildings and their settlements.

This is not a matter of obscure interest for a few. It lies at the heart of our enterprise in the heritage of Wales. The establishment and representation of identity through material culture must be the first objective of our endeavour and we must recognise that it is not to be established simply by objective criteria. Identities and the articulation of difference lie at the heart of spatial culture. So, for example, the Yorkshire Dales and their identity are defined, amongst other things, by the natural glacial limestone valleys, by the types of field barn and stone wall which fill the landscape, and by the accent and attitude of the inhabitants. These collectively give a unified sense of space which is then used to give power to local communities, to promote tourism through distinctive imagery, and to permit the National Park to conserve the most important elements of the landscape whether cultural or natural. The truth is that cultural identity is bestowed on objects and buildings both in the act of making and in the act of preserving; it does not derive inherently from the objects, sites or landscapes themselves.

I would argue then that a knowledge of the regions of Wales and their identity is essential for Wales, but there are clearly some big questions here for us. Do we honestly believe that regional cultures exist in Wales? If they do, how important are they for our understanding of Welsh culture? Alternatively, should we take more account of vertical distinctions of class, wealth, political or religious affiliation which might transcend the horizontal significance of regions and their rivalries? What, in any case, **are** the cultural and economic regions of Wales? Are they in some sense immutable, timeless and determined by the environment? Or are they flexible, complex, and volatile, at the mercy of shifts in power and wealth? In the end are these questions unanswerable and should we not instead look only at the local where we might stand a better chance of understanding how some people in Wales lived and built their identities through time?

11.7 Conclusion: the future

I have adopted a mode of critique in this essay not to belittle the great achievements of the last 40 years or so, but to understand these achievements and how far we have got. As Roberts says in this volume, we have in some ways actually achieved very little as archaeologists, especially when we compare ourselves with architectural historians and more recent historians looking at Welsh identity and culture (eg Davies 1984; Lord 2000). The judgement may be that we have done a lot, but not actually achieved as much. The problem may lie in our methodology as much as in our epistemology. We have developed our methods perhaps only to enable ourselves to do more of the same thing to meet the needs of our limited ways of managing the archaeology of Wales rather than to innovate to meet the needs of historical understanding and cultural identity. We have also failed perhaps to develop our critical analysis of the discourse and merely accepted a kind of neutralised intellectual *status quo* centred on objective typologies and unpeopled distributions. However, we must recognise the contribution of this volume. We have quite properly paused to review what we have done. Only because we have paused to find out how much we know have we been able to reveal how we know it. The issue now is how to proceed from here without going round in circles and merely repeating ourselves. There are several fairly obvious needs.

My belief is that the priority now is for work which focuses on what earlier I called the biography of place. We need to take specific locations and study them in depth with extensive excavation and deep analysis of context and meaning whether of environment, social institutions, individual agency, cultural process, territory, gender or class. It is really insupportable that we allow ourselves to be driven by categories and taxonomies which are entirely of our own making and with little or no demonstrable relationship to the past mind whether collective or individual. So, for example,

isolating study to particular types of settlement, whether peasant farms, castles, gentry houses or monasteries, detaches one from another – this was never how people experienced their landscapes in the past. The worlds in which people moved and worked were dominated by the totality of what was around them in the landscape from small tools to whole mountain areas. The clear deficit, archaeologically, in Wales is in the local and in the particulars of past place and individual experience. Wales needs, at one scale of resolution, national maps to set alongside those of England and Ireland. We need to be even more ambitious, as in Ireland (Aalen *et al* 1997), aiming to produce a comprehensive overview of our landscapes in Wales. On the other scale we need at least one or two in-depth projects for Wales – like Shapwick (Aston and Gerrard 1999), Wharram Percy (Beresford and Hurst 1990) or Hanbury (Dyer 1991).

Of all these, I think extensive excavation on a number of sites in the same locality is the most urgent requirement to give us our biographies of place. Archaeologists bear a terrible responsibility, and Peate, even if only for vernacular architecture, laid it on the line:

> Can the origins of this house-type (the long-house) be traced further? Much more excavation of medieval, Dark Age and prehistoric sites is required before any coherent story emerges ...
> (Peate 1963, 443)

Well, in one way we have had more excavation, but we have not really progressed much beyond the position we were in when Peate wrote those words in 1963; we have failed also to widen the interpretative agenda. Because of the work done for this volume, we do now know much better where the potential for such excavation might be, but in reality we can leave it no longer. We are simply depriving ourselves of the main method we have for contributing to the very large issues which a resurgent Wales needs us to address.

Acknowledgements

I want to thank Anthony Ward for his very useful comments on an earlier draft of this text.

APPENDIX I:
GLOSSARY

Deserted rural settlement: Overall description of a group of settlement-related features, ie a dwelling or dwellings with ancillary structures or features.

Fold: An unroofed structure used for penning animals. Range from single-cell structures to large multi-cell arrangements associated with sorting animals returning from mountain pasture.

Longhouse: Single, long, low, rectangular building which houses both the family and its cattle. The dwelling is at the upper end (*pen uchaf*), and the byre at the lower (*pen isaf*). Between the two is the door and cross passage.

Long hut: A rectilinear structure (stone built or earthwork) which may have one or more compartments, not necessarily always a dwelling.

Platform: Any bare platform, regardless of relationship to slope (cross-contour or parallel to contour) and size.

Shelter: A structure which protects an area of ground from the weather. A minor structure, either rectilinear or sub-circular in form which would once have been roofed.

Storage clamps: Elongated earthwork cuts designed for burying root vegetables for storage.

Sunken shelter: An elongated, narrow cut into a slope, often with a drystone revetment along the sides of the cut. Believed to be a storage structure associated with dairy products.

Appendix II:
Names and addresses of
relevant organisations

Cadw: Welsh Historic Monuments
Plas Carew
Unit 5/7 Cefn Coed
Parc Nantgarw
Cardiff CF15 7QQ

Clwyd-Powys Archaeological Trust
7a Church Street
Welshpool
Powys SY21 7DL

Dyfed Archaeological Trust (now Cambria Archaeology)
The Shire Hall
Carmarthen Street
Llandeilo
Carmarthenshire SA19 6AF

Glamorgan-Gwent Archaeological Trust
Heathfield House
Heathfield Road
Swansea SA1 6EL

Gwynedd Archaeological Trust
Craig Beuno
Garth Road
Bangor
Gwynedd LL57 2RT

Royal Commission on the Ancient and Historical Monuments of Wales
Crown Building
Plas Crug
Aberystwyth
Ceredigion SY23 1NJ

Appendix III:
The Badminton Manorial Survey

By Robert Silvester

What is normally referred to as the Badminton Manorial Survey, but is known more correctly as the survey of the Crickhowell and Tretower estates of the Earl of Worcester, whose heirs were to become the Dukes of Beaufort, was compiled by Richard Johnson, the Earl's steward, in 1587 (*NLW Manuscripts and Maps: Badminton Vol 3*). It comprises the earliest surviving collection of Welsh estate maps (and possibly indeed the earliest from the British Isles as a whole) that were drawn to a common scale (Henderson n. d.). It is also one of the very few cartographic surveys of large estates in Wales that pre-dates the later 18th century. The series of 45 maps covers lands within and close to the valley of the Usk in Breconshire and depicts nearly 100 buildings (see pl 00), and though some lie within the nucleated settlements of Tretower (in the parish of Cwmdu), Llangynidr, and Llangattock, and are thus outside the remit of the study, many are in rural locations. This permits an assessment of a significant sample of dwellings that were occupied at a specific time in the early post-medieval era, establishing the survival and loss of houses in different topographical zones over the past 400 years. Quantifying building loss is generally an impossible exercise where conditions are not conducive to the identification of debris scatters through fieldwalking, but because of the early date of the maps, the Badminton Survey usefully contributes to the discussion.

The tenanted holdings of the earl did not form a single coherent tract of land but were broken into blocks of varying size spread across six parishes, and included both enclosed upland and lowland, and also took in several commons. They can be rationalised into four groups, two of which are considered in detail here: the low-lying valley lands adjacent to the Usk and its tributaries, and Dyffryn Crawnon (the Crawnon Valley); the other two are the Black Mountains fringes, and the villages (see Table 1).

Table 1 Rural buildings in the Badminton Manorial Survey

Area	Number of rural sites	Number assessed	Original building	Later building	Ruin	Foundations/earthworks	No trace
Usk Valley	56	37	1	17	-	6	13
Black Mountains	16	7	-	-	1	2	4
Dyffryn Crawnon	26	25	-	7	9	2	7
Total	98	69	1	24	10	10	24

The Usk Valley lowlands

The buildings in the Usk Valley fall broadly into two classes: those where a building remains on the site, almost without exception the successors of those structures shown on the maps, and those that have completely disappeared. The latter constitute more than a third of the total. This high rate of disappearance apart, it is the occupation of the commons in the late 16th century that is perhaps the most interesting feature.

There were several commons and wastes attached to the Usk Valley manors on which encroachment was already under way. Coed-yr-Ynys common, lying beside the river near the village of Llangynidr had fourteen cottages or other buildings around its edge and two more established on the common itself. The open area was largely enclosed by the time of a later survey in 1760 and settlement within it had expanded. Only two cottages showing in 1587 can be satisfactorily linked to farmsteads that have remained to the present day, but there is some uncertainty with several of the cottages around the edge of the common whose positions cannot be pinpointed with any accuracy. Similar problems beset one of the 'forests', those areas which from medieval times were reserved for the lord's hunting. The 'forest of Fawstock', colonised now by the village of Ffawyddog, a short distance to the north-west of Llangattock, was largely open with about thirteen encroachments around or within its boundary, three or four of which seem to have been set within their own enclosures. The common has shrunk considerably since that date and only one relatively small patch of open ground remains. Correlating the cottages depicted on the 1587 map with their modern counterparts is feasible only in a few instances, and there are several sites that cannot be located. All of the original dwellings have been replaced, many probably in the second half of the 19th century when the Glanusk Estate acquired the land. It is only on the west side of the common where the sites of three cottages can be discerned clearly, two as faint relict earthworks and the third as an occupied house seemingly of no great antiquity, though with a converted barn or outbuilding supported by massive buttresses and clearly much older. The survival of amorphous earthworks may herald one further site within the common.

That so little remains is of no surprise. These small tracts of common and forest held by the Beaufort estate, continued as magnets for encroachment and settlement after the 16th century. The cottages that had sprung up on them by 1587 were undoubtedly small, flimsy and often poorly built, little better than the 'hovels' which were so named on 18th-century estate maps in the region. Where the owners and their descendants thrived, these cottages were subsequently replaced by more substantial buildings; where the family died out or moved on the cottage disintegrated quickly.

There are exceptions. The earthwork remains of a large complex beside what was Bell Fountain Park to the east of Crickhowell were shown in 1587 as a group of at least six buildings, the main house with double chimneys appearing as a substantial residence, part of a complex that included what could be an H-shaped building, presumably a hall-house. While the main residence was set along the contour there was another dwelling house (assuming the presence of a chimney is a guide) within the group and this was set down the slope. The remaining three structures must have been ancillary buildings. The whole group had disappeared from contemporary maps by 1839 and now there is neither a name for the house, nor a local tradition of its existence. However, the mutilated earthworks of several platforms together with some stone walling remain in improved pasture, although it is not possible to equate the ground remains with the buildings shown on the map. Nevertheless, the cartographic evidence allied to the physical remains reveal a large farming establishment to match those still visible on the far side of the Grwyne Fawr valley to the east.

This pattern of several grouped dwellings is repeated at the farm of Tre Graig in Llanfihangel Cwmdu. On the map there were no less than five chimneyed buildings around what must have been a large yard: from the map three were of simple plan but two others were of more complex designs. The emergence of several houses in a group appears to relate to the Welsh system of partible heritance (*cyfran*) whereby all male heirs had a right to an equal share of their father's estate, though by 1587 this was in decline, having been abolished as an obligatory requirement in 1542. Its architectural signature has been suggested elsewhere in Cwmdu for the farms at Cilfaenor, Llwynau Mawr, and Llanddegman (Cadw 1998a, 11), while more than 30 years ago Jones and Smith (1966/67) noted the gradual accumulation of evidence for the practice in Wales.

Dyffryn Crawnon

The Earl's lands in Dyffryn Crawnon were amongst the most extensive in his Breconshire manors, and contained a larger number of dwellings than elsewhere. The valley, about 7km in length, cuts down from one of the limestone plateaux in the eastern Brecon Beacons north-eastwards to its confluence with the Usk, just to the west of Llangynidr. It is steep-sided with average gradients on the south side of the valley of 1:3 and on the north side only slightly less pronounced. The tenanted holdings were broken up into five discrete land blocks, all of them on the southern side of the valley: three at the eastern end where the valley begins to open out, two others, more widely spaced, higher up the valley. Together these blocks, extending over about 112ha or little more than 1km², constitute just under half of the enclosed land on the southern slopes of the valley.

While the southern side appears less attractive to settlement because of its aspect and steepness, and the majority of active farms today are on the opposite slopes, Ordnance Survey maps reveal that the number of named farms and cottages on either side of the valley was almost precisely equal at the end of the 19th century. Certainly, the adverse elements were not sufficiently serious to inhibit settlement on the southern face in the historic period.

The Badminton Survey depicts twenty buildings or groups of buildings in the five tracts of land. One of these is atypical – a mill on the valley floor close to the Crawnon. The status of the remaining buildings (together with three cottages that were constructed after 1587) is summarised in Table 2, together with their names where these can be established. The condition, whether inhabited, ruined or lost, is also indicated from field observations.

Settlement in the valley

The story of the building stock in Dyffryn Crawnon is one of gradual decline. Apart from the mill, 6 other buildings, one probably a barn, had disappeared by the time of the 1760 survey, two centuries later. The position of only one can be discerned, the others having disappeared leaving virtually no trace above ground. Virtually no new buildings were established between 1587 and the later 18th century, except for three new cottages that emerged as roadside encroachments. Only one is known by name and all had disappeared by the close of the 19th century. Between the later 18th century and the Tithe Assessment in 1840 one

or two farmsteads had been abandoned. The real decline came during the 20th century, with the abandonment of five of the eighteen buildings, representing a significant proportion of the total stock. This figure might have been higher but for the refurbishments leading to a number of house conversions and second homes along the valley. Of twenty buildings shown on the set of 1587 maps only six of the sites are now in use.

Typology of settlement

Where there is surviving evidence of a building on the site shown in 1587, it is normally in the form of a ruin or foundations, rather than an earthwork. As to whether a surviving house is the actual building depicted in 1587 cannot be determined, but generally this seems most unlikely. All of the ruined buildings are either of stone or set on stone foundation walls, and in almost all cases there is nothing in the external architectural detail to signal a date. Where ruins survive, they appear to be typical of the simple stone constructional methods adopted in the 18th and 19th centuries. Rebuilding during the early modern era must have been common. This, however, is not to say that the basic styles could not have been employed at an earlier date. Of the standing buildings none has been examined internally, but Pant-y-paerau is possibly the best candidate for an early date, and has been attributed to the 17th century on the basis of external observations (Cadw 1998b, 33). Half of those farmsteads where a building plan can be discerned are terraced into the hillside at right angles to the contours. This cannot be taken as a sure indication that these originated in the medieval period, but it is at least a possibility (see below).

Some of these sites, were the houses to be completely demolished, would undoubtedly leave residual platforms, yet only one earthwork platform of traditional form was identified during the survey. Others of course might have been recognised if systematic fieldwork had been undertaken. Much larger platforms are present for three or perhaps four steadings, the ground being extensively levelled, presumably to provide a basis collectively for the farmhouse, its outbuildings, and a yard.

Table 2 Buildings in Dyffryn Crawnon: survival and names

1587	1760	1840	1888	2000	Modern Conversion
● Tere Griffith Dee	● Blaen Crannant	●	● ?	○	
●	● Tir-y-Tyley	● Tille Bach	● Tyle-bach	● Tyle-bach	●
● Tere Ienn Meredite	● Tir-yr-arglwydd	● Ty yr Arlwdd	● Pen-y-garn	● Pen-y-garn	
●				✺	
●	●	● Ty Gwillim Grotter	● Cae-hen	○	
●	■ ? Scybor (= barn)	■ ?	■ ?	□	
●	●	■	■	■	
● Cae Llin	● Pen-yr-wrlod	○ Peny Wrlod	○	○	
■ ?				✺	
●	● Glog Fawr	● Glog Fawr	● Clog-fawr	● Clog-fawr	
● Ter y Glog Fawr				✺	
* (mill)				✺	
●	■ (barn)				
●	●	●	■ ?	●	●
●	● Tir-y-Tyley	● Tille	● Tyle	○ Tyle	
●	● Pant-y-pyrey	● Pany y Piry	● Pant-y-paerau	● Pant-y-paerau	●
●				○ ?	
●	● Nant-y-llaethdy Ucha	○ ?	○ Tyle-uchaf	●	
●	● Nant-y-llaethdy Issa	● Nant-y-llaithdy	● Tir Hywel Sais	□ Pen-y-waen	
●				✺	
	●	● ?		✺	
	●			✺	
	● Tir-cae-gronon	○ ?			

● = inhabited dwelling. ○ = abandoned dwelling ■ = barn in use □ = abandoned barn. ✺ = no surviving traces

The settlement pattern in the valley

The topography of Dyffryn Crawnon exerted a fundamental influence on the pattern of settlement in the Tudor period as it may well have done in the preceding medieval era. The valley floor has always been avoided, except in its upper reaches where farms of uncertain date such as Wern were set close to the fledgling stream. The lane running up the south side of the valley, initially 20m or 30m above the river, but in the higher reaches immediately beside it, was an important line of communications in earlier times, yet the number of dwellings beside that lane is small. Pant-y-paerau, together with the cottages that had been established by the end of the 18th century, and other farms in different ownerships, such as Tir Alsome and Wern, constitute only a small proportion of the settlement total. An artery for access it may have been, but it did not attract settlement. Rather it was a natural shelf at a higher level on the hillside that attracted the settlement. Pen-y-waen, Pen-y-garn, Cae-hen, Pen Wrlod and Clog-fawr, together with other unnamed sites, all lie 200m or more away from the road on gently shelving ground that in places corresponded with the base of the steepest slopes tipping down from Mynydd Llangynidr. These farmsteads represent an early phase of settlement in the valley but how early remains uncertain. It may be of significance that sites such as Clog-fawr and Pen Wrlod would be the type of locations favoured for medieval platform sites. They were linked to the road below by tracks often running straight uphill though occasionally traversing the slope. But there is a possibility that an earlier track ran along the contours at this higher altitude, hints of such a feature remaining in the vicinity of Pen-y-waen. In at least one instance there is a degree of chronological depth to the settlement pattern, for the house below Pen-y-waen was approached by a track from the latter, indicating a secondary development.

Even higher up the slope towards the open common on the plateau were farms such as Tyle-uchaf and several unnamed habitations. Others such as Cwrt-yr-icos, 500m beyond and 130m higher than Pen-y-garn, certainly came into existence after 1587, and the same may be true of Cae-Rees, at the same altitude and 250m to the south-west of Cwrt-yr-icos. The expansion of settlement in the 18th century higher up what are exceedingly steep slopes is hardly unexpected, the appearance of Tyle-uchaf and the others only slightly lower down, even less so. All these have now been abandoned, but the fact is that in 1587 Dyffryn Crawnon was a well-populated valley with agricultural settlements located high up the hillslopes. The distribution of settlement visible in the first half of the 19th century was not the result of much recent expansion; it was a pattern largely established by the end of the 16th century.

Conclusions

The main points to emerge from this study centre on the survival and loss of buildings in the four centuries since 1587. In those rural areas owned by the Earl of Worcester virtually no building outside the villages appears to have survived to the present, and on current evidence only Heoldrew in the hinterland of the Usk retains a feature from the building that was depicted in the Manorial Survey. But if virtually every building of 1587 has been swept away, the continuity of many of the sites is clearly evident. More than a third of the sites have an occupied building still on them, and if ruins are included, the proportion rises to one half.

Nevertheless, over one-third of the buildings shown in 1587 have disappeared without leaving any surface trace (see Table 2). In somewhere like the heavily agriculturalised Usk Valley, the processes of dereliction and demolition after abandonment is of little surprise, particularly if it is assumed that a significant number of those buildings, probably cottages, were predominantly of timber or other perishable materials. But elsewhere, in upland landscape settings, where remains might have been anticipated, there is nothing to see. A small group of buildings beside Cwm Nant-yr-ychain on the edge of the Black Mountains, conceivably all barns but more likely to be a farmstead, has completely disappeared; likewise, in a nearby valley all but the largely imperceptible traces of a house and associated ancillary structure beside Cwm Charles have gone. Both lie on ground that has been improved though probably infrequently. A comparable picture is presented by Dyffryn Crawnon where the steepness of the valley sides might lead to the assumption that some trace of a building's location would remain even if the building had gone. Several of the 1587 buildings belie that assumption.

REFERENCES

Primary sources

Roberts, Rev. H, 1976, *Excavation at Cwrt, Myddfai, Carmarthenshire* (MS letter)

GGAT   South-East Vale Survey project archive, St Andrew's parish, St A 6:2:84 Jem, Field 339

NLW   MS, Llanstephan 179b

NLW   Tithe map, Cadoxton-juxta-Neath, 1840

NLW   Tithe map, Glyncorrwg, 1840

NLW   Tithe map, Llangwynyd, 1840

NLW, RM A118 Morris, L, 1744, '*A plan of the Mannor of Perveth*'

WGRO D/D BF E/1   Briton Ferry estate, map book, c. 1798

WGRO D/D D E/157   Neath Abbey estate, map book, 1770–1

Printed sources

Aalen, F H A, Whelan, K, & Stout, M 1997 *Atlas of the Irish Rural Landscape.* Cork: Cork University Press

Aaron, J, 2003 *The Welsh Survival Gene: the 'despite culture' in the two language communities of Wales, the National Eisteddfod Lecture 2003.* Cardiff: Institute of Welsh Affairs

Adams, L, 1973 Report on excavations at Hendai, Newborough Warren. RCAHM(W) files (unpublished)

Aitkin, A, 1797 *Journal of A Tour Through North Wales.* London

Alcock, N W, 1994 Physical space and social space: the interpretation of vernacular architecture, in Locock, M (ed.) *Meaningful Architecture: social interpretations of buildings,* Worldwide Archaeol Ser, **9**. Aldershot: Avebury Press, 207–30

Alcock, N W, & Smith, P, 1972 The long-house: a plea for clarity, *Medieval Archaeol,* **16**, 145–6

Alfrey, J, 2000 Carmarthenshire farm buildings: a source for socio-economic history, *Carmarthenshire Antiq,* **36**, 126–37

Allen, D W H, 1979 Excavations at Hafod y Nant Criafolen, Brenig Valley, Clwyd, 1973–4, *Post-Medieval Archaeol,* **13**, 1–59

Allen, D W H, 1993 Excavations at Hafod y Nant Griafolen, in F Lynch *Excavations in the Brenig Valley,* Cambrian Archaeol Assoc, Monograph **5**

Allen, D, 1993 Later History of the valley, in F Lynch *Excavations in the Brenig Valley,* Cambrian Archaeol Assoc, Monograph **5**, 169–82

Astill, G, & Grant, A, 1988 The medieval countryside: efficiency, progress and change, in G Astill & A Grant (eds) *The countryside of medieval England.* Oxford: Blackwell Publishers

Aston, M, & Gerrard, C, 1999 'Unique, traditional and charming' the Shapwick Project, Somerset, *Antiq J,* **79**, 1–58

Aston, M, Austin, D, & Dyer, C (eds), 1989 *The Rural Settlements of Medieval England.* Oxford: Blackwell Publishers

Atkinson, J A, Banks, I, & MacGregor, G (eds), 2000 *Townships to Farmsteads: rural settlement studies in Scotland, England and Wales,* BAR Brit Ser **293**. Oxford

Austin, D A, 1988 Excavations and survey on Bryn Cysegrfan, Llanfair Clydogau, Dyfed, 1979, *Medieval Archaeol,* **32**, 130–65

Austin, D, 1989 The excavation of dispersed settlement in medieval Britain, in Aston *et al* (eds) 1989

Austin, D, & Alcock, L (eds), 1990 *From the Baltic to the Black Sea: Studies in Medieval Archaeol.* London: Unwin Hyman

Austin, D, 1990 The proper study of medieval archaeology, chapter 1 in Austin & Alcock (eds) 1990

Austin, D, & Thomas, J, 1990 The 'proper' study of medieval archaeology: a case study, chapter 2 in Austin & Alcock (eds) 1990

Baillie, M G L, 1991 Suck-in and smear: two related chronological problems for the 1990s, *J Theoretical Archaeol,* **2**, 12–16

Baker, D, 1999 *An Assessment of English Sites and Monuments Records,* Historic Environment Conservation Report 97/20. Chelmsford: Association of Local Government Archaeological Officers

Barber, K E, Chambers, F M, Dumayne, L, Haslam, C J, Maddy, D, & Stoneman, R E, 1994a Climate change and human impact in north Cumbria: peat stratigraphic and pollen evidence from Bolton Fell Moss, in J Boardman, & J Walden (eds) *The Quaternary of Cumbria: field guide.* Oxford: Quaternary Research Assoc, 20–54

Barber, K E, Chambers, F M, Maddy, D, Stoneman, R, & Brew, J S, 1994b A sensitive high-resolution record of late-Holocene climatic change from a raised bog in northern England, *The Holocene,* **4**, 198–205

Barber, K E, Dumayne-Peaty, L, Hughes, P, Mauquoy, D, & Scaife, R, 1998 Replicability and variability of the recent macrofossil and proxy-climate record from raised bogs: field stratigraphy and macrofossil data from Bolton Fell Moss and Walton Moss, Cumbria, England, *J Quaternary Science*, **13**, 515–28

Barber, K E, Battarbee, R W, Brooks, S J, *et al*, 1999 Proxy records of climate change in the UK over the last two millennia: documented change and sedimentary records from lakes and bogs, *J Geol Soc*, **156**. London, 369–80

Battarbee, R W, Anderson, N J, Appleby, P G, Flower, R J, Fritz, S C, Haworth, E Y, Higgitt, S, Jones, V J, Kreiser, A, Munro, M A R, Natkanski, J, Oldfield, F, Patrick, S T, Richardson, N G, Rippey, B, & Stevenson, A C, 1988 *Lake Acidification in the United Kingdom 1800–1986: evidence from analysis of lake sediments*. London: Ensis Publishing

Bayliss, A, 1998 Some thoughts on using scientific dating in English archaeology and buildings analysis for the next decade, in J Bayley *Science in Archaeol*. London: English Heritage, 95–108

BBC: J. Gwenogvryn Evans (reproduced & ed.), *The Black Book of Carmarthen*, Pwllheli, 1906

Bell, M, & Dark, P, 1998 Continuity and change: environmental archaeology in historic periods, in J Bayley *Science in Archaeol*. London: English Heritage, 179–93

Beresford, M W, & Hurst, J G, 1990 *Wharram Percy, Deserted Medieval Village*. London: Batsford

Besly, E, 1995 Short-cross and other medieval coins from Llanfaes, Anglesey, *British Numismatic Journal*, **65**, 46–82

Bick, D, & Davies, P W, 1994 *Lewis Morris and the Cardiganshire Mines*. Aberystwyth: National Library of Wales

Bil, A, 1990 *The Shieling 1600–1840*. Edinburgh: John Donald

Birks, H H, 1972 Studies in the vegetational history of Scotland, II. Two pollen diagrams from the Galloway Hills, Kikcudbrightshire, *J Ecology*, **60**, 183–217

Blackford, J J, 1990 Blanket mires and climatic change; a palaeoecological study based on peat humification and microfossil analyses. Unpubl PhD thesis, University of Keele

Blackford, J J, & Chambers, F M, 1991 Proxy-records of climate from blanket mires: evidence for a Dark Age (1400 BP) climatic deterioration in the British Isles, *The Holocene*, **1**, 63–7

Bloch, M, 1949 *La Société Féodale*. Paris

Boon, G C, 1986 *Welsh Hoards*. Cardiff: National Museum of Wales

Bostock, J L, 1980 The history of the vegetation of the Berwyn Mountains, North Wales, with emphasis on the development of the blanket mire. Unpubl PhD thesis, University of Manchester

Bowen, E G (ed), 1965 *Wales, a Physical, Historical and Regional Geography*. London: Methuen

Bradley, R, 2000 *An Archaeology of Natural Place*. London: Routledge

Bradney, J A, 1993 The Hundred of Newport, in M Gray (ed) *A history of Monmouthshire from the coming of the Normans into Wales down to the present time*. Cardiff: South Wales Record Soc

Briggs, C S, 1985 Problems of the early agricultural landscape in upland Wales, as illustrated by an example from the Brecon Beacons, in D Spratt, & C Burgess (eds) *Upland settlement in Britain. The second millennium BC and after*. Oxford: BAR Brit Ser **143**, 285–316

Britnell, W J, & Dixon, P, 2001 Archaeological excavations at Ty-mawr, Castle Caereinion, *Montgomeryshire Collections*, **89**, 55–86

Britnell, W J, & Suggett, R, 2002 A sixteenth-century peasant hallhouse in Powys: survey and excavation of Tyddyn Llwydion, Pennant Melangell, Montgomeryshire, *Archaeol J*, **159**, 142–69

Browne, D, and Hughes, S (eds), 2003 *The Archaeology of the Welsh Uplands*. RCAHMW: Aberystwyth

Buckley, S L, 2000 Palaeoecological investigations of blanket peats in upland Mid-Wales. Unpubl PhD thesis, University of Wales

Buckley, S L, & Walker, M J C, 2001 The Flandrian vegetation history of upland mid-Wales: Bryniau Pica, in M J C Walker, & D McCarroll (eds) *The Quaternary of West Wales Field Guide*, Quaternary Research Association, 93–102

Buckley, S L, & Walker, M J C, 2002 A mid-Flandrian tephra horizon, Cambrian Mountains, west Wales, *Quaternary Newsletter*, **96**, 5–11

Butler, L A S, 1962 A long hut group in the Aber valley, *Trans Caernarvonshire Hist Soc*, **23**, 25–36

Butler, L A S, 1963 'The excavation of the long hut at Bwlch-yr-Hendre', *Ceredigion*, **4**, 400–7

Butler, L A S, 1971 The study of deserted medieval settlements in Wales (to 1968), in M Beresford, & J G Hurst (eds) *Deserted medieval villages*. London, 249–69

Butler, L A S, 1991 Rural building in Wales, in E Miller (ed) *The agrarian history of England and Wales, vol. 3, 1348–1500*. Cambridge: Cambridge University Press

Butler, S, 1984 Preliminary investigation of the pollen record from Talley Lakes, *Carmarthenshire Antiq Soc*, **20**, 3–14

Bygones, 1875 *Bygones relating to Wales and the Border Counties*. Oswestry

Cadw, 1998a *List of buildings of special architectural or historic interest: county of Powys, community of Llanfihangel Cwmdu with Bwlch and Cathedine*. Cardiff

Cadw, 1998b *List of buildings of special architectural or historic interest: county of Powys, community of Llangynidr.* Cardiff

Cadw, 1998c *Register of Historic Parks, Gardens and Landscapes of Historic Importance in Wales. Part 2.1 Landscapes of Outstanding Historic Interest in Wales.* Cardiff: Cadw, Welsh Historic Monuments/ICOMOS

Cadw, 2001 *Register of Historic Parks, Gardens and Landscapes of Historic Importance in Wales. Part 2.1 Landscapes of Special Historic Interest in Wales.* Cardiff: Cadw, Welsh Historic Monuments/ICOMOS

CAP, 1999a *Forest Enterprise Welsh Heritage Assets project, archaeological survey phase 3: contract 10 (Rheola/Margam/Cymer)*, Cambrian Archaeol Projects report 77

CAP, 1999b *Forest Enterprise Welsh Heritage Assets project, archaeological survey phase 4: contract 14 (Rhondda/St Gwynno)*, Cambrian Archaeol Projects report **89**

CAP, 1999c *Forest Enterprise Welsh Heritage Assets project, archaeological survey phase 4: contract 15 (Ebbw/Wentwood/Tintern)*, Cambrian Archaeol Projects report **90**

Carr, A D, 1971–2 The extent of Anglesey 1352, *Trans Anglesey Antiq Soc*, 150–72

Carr, A J, 2001 The First Extent of Merioneth, in Beverley Smith & Beverley Smith 2001, 702–16

Carter, H (ed), 1981 *National Atlas of Wales.* Cardiff: University of Wales Press

Carter, S, Tipping, R, Davidson, D, Long, D, & Tyler, A, 1997 A multiproxy approach to the function of postmedieval ridge-and-furrow cultivation in upland northern Britain, *The Holocene*, 7, 447–56

Caseldine, A E, 1990 *Environmental Archaeology in Wales.* Lampeter: St David's University College

Caseldine, A E, 2001 The palaeoenvironmental evidence from Hafod Rhug Uchaf. Unpubl report for Gwynedd Archaeological Trust

Caseldine, A E, and Barrow, K, 2000 The environmental evidence from Tro'r Derlwyn. Unpubl report for Dyfed Archaeological Trust

Caseldine, A E, Smith G, & Griffiths, C J, 2001 Vegetation history and upland settlement at Llyn Morwynion, Ffestiniog, Meirionnydd, *Archaeol in Wales*, 41, 21–33

Chambers, F M, 1982a Two radiocarbon-dated pollen diagrams from high altitude peat in South Wales, *J Ecology*, **70**, 445–59

Chambers, F M, 1982b Environmental history of Cefn Gwernffrwd, near Rhandirmwyn, Mid-Wales, *New Phytologist*, **92**, 607–15

Chambers, F M, 1982c Appendix 3. Palynological studies, in R S Kelly The excavations of a medieval farmstead at Cefn Graeanog, Clynnog, Gwynedd, *Bull Board Celtic Stud*, **29**, 898–900

Chambers, F M, 1983a Three radiocarbon-dated pollen diagrams from upland peats north-west of Merthyr Tydfil, South Wales, *J Ecology*, 71, 475–87

Chambers, F M, 1983b The palaeoecological setting of Cefn Gwernffrwd – a prehistoric complex in Mid-Wales. *Proc Prehist Soc*, 49, 303–16

Chambers, F M, 1983c New applications of palaeoecological techniques. Integrating evidence of arable activity in pollen, peat and soil stratigraphies, Cefn Graeanog, North Wales, in M Jones (ed) *Integrating the Subsistence Economy*, BAR Internat Ser **181**, 107–22

Chambers, F M, 1999 The Quaternary history of Llangorse Lake: implications for conservation, *Aquatic Conservation: Marine and Freshwater Ecosystems*, **9**, 343–59

Chambers, F M, & Lageard, J, 1993 Vegetational history and environmental setting of Crawcwellt, Gwynedd, *Archaeol in Wales*, **33**, 23–5

Chambers, F M, & Lageard, J, 1997 Palaeoenvironmental analyses of peat samples from Pen-y-fan, Corn Du and Tomy Jones's Pillar, Brecon Beacons, in A Gibson Survey, Excavation and palaeoenvironmental investigations on Pen-y-fan and Corn-du, Brecon Beacons, Powys, 1990–1992, *Studia Celtica*, **31**, 1–81

Chambers, F M, & Price, S-M, 1988 The environmental setting of Erw-wen and Moel y Gerddi: prehistoric enclosures in upland Ardudwy, north Wales, *Proc Prehist Soc*, **54**, 93–100

Chambers, F M, Kelly, R S, & Price, S-M, 1988 Development of the Late-Prehistoric Cultural Landscape in upland Ardudwy, north-west Wales, in H H Birks, H J B Birks, P E Kaland, & D Moe, *The Cultural Landscape – Past, Present and Future.* Cambridge: Cambridge University Press, 333–48

Charles, B G, 1973 *George Owen of Henllys: A Welsh Elizabethan.* Aberystwyth: National Library of Wales Press

Clarke, E D, 1793 *A tour through the South of England and Wales and a part of Ireland: Made during the summer of 1791.* London

Cloutman, E, 1983 Studies of the vegetational history of the Black Mountain Range, South Wales. Unpubl PhD thesis, University of Wales

Clymo, R S, Oldfield, F, Appleby, P G, Pearson, G W, Ratneser, P, & Richardson, N, 1990 The record of atmospheric deposition on a rainwater-dependent peatland, *Philos Trans Royal Soc London*, **B327**, 105–14

Coles, G, & Mills, C, 1998 Clinging on for grim life: an introduction to marginality as an archaeological issue, in G Coles, & C Mills (eds) *Life on the Edge: Human Settlement and Marginality*, Oxbow Monograph **100**, Symposia of the Association for Environmental Archaeology **13**, vii–xii

Conway, J S, 1988 Soil phosphorus, in R S Kelly Excavations of two circular enclosure sites at Moel y Gerddi and Erw-wen, near Harlech, Gwynedd, *Proc Prehist Soc*, **54**, 113–19, 130

Cosgrove, D E, 1984, *Social Formation and Symbolic Landscape*. London: Croom Helm

Countryside Council for Wales, 1998. *Tir Gofal: a new agri-environment scheme for Wales*. Bangor

Countryside Council for Wales and Forestry Commission, 1999 *A living environment for Wales*. Bangor: Countryside Council for Wales

Courtney, P, 1991 A native-Welsh mediaeval settlement: Excavations at Beili Bedw, St Harmon, Powys, *Bull Board Celtic Stud*, **38**, 233–55

Crampton, C B, 1966a Hafotai platforms on the north front of the Brecon Beacons, *Archaeologia Cambrensis*, **105**, 99–107

Crampton, C B, 1966b An interpretation of the pollen and soils in cross-ridge dykes of Glamorgan, *Bull Board Celtic Stud*, **21**, 376–90

Crampton, C B, 1968 Hafotai platforms on the North front of Carmarthen Fan, *Archaeologia Cambrensis*, **117**, 121–6

Crampton, C B, & Webley, D P, 1964 Preliminary studies of the historic succession of plants and soils in selected archaeological sites in south Wales, *Bull Board Celtic Stud*, **20**, 440–9

Crane, P, 1995 *The Llyn Brianne Upland Survey*. Llandeilo: Cambria Archaeology

Crane, P, 1999 *Tro'r Derlwyn Upland Farmstead, Near Brynamman, Carmarthenshire, 1998*. Llandeilo: Cambria Archaeology

Crew, P, 1979 Early Christian and Medieval Caernarvonshire, No 67 Dinas Mot Llanberis, *Archaeol in Wales*, **19**, 35

Crew, P, 1984. Rectilinear settlements in Gwynedd, in *Bull Board Celtic Stud*, **31**, 320–1

Crowley, T J, 2000 Causes of climate change over the past 1000 years, *Science*, **289**, 270–7

Crowley, T J, & Lowery, T S, 2000 How warm was the medieval warm period?, *Ambio*, **29**, 51–4

Crowther, J, 1999 Tro'r Derlwyn, Carmarthenshire: Report on soil phosphate analysis. Unpubl report for Cambria Archaeology

Dahl-Jensen, D, Mosegaard, K, Gundestrup, N, Clow, G D, Johnsen, S J, Hansen, A W, & Balling, N, 1998 Past temperatures directly from the Greenland ice sheet, *Science*, **282**, 268–71

Darvill, T, 1988 *Monuments Protection Programme: Monument Evaluation Manual, Parts 1 and 2*. London: English Heritage

Darvill, T, 1998 MARS: the Monuments at Risk Survey of England, 1995. Main report. Bournemouth: School of Conservation Sciences, Bournemouth University and English Heritage

Davidson, A, 2002 Introduction, in A Davidson (ed) *The Coastal Archaeology of Wales*. CBA Res Rep, **131**, 1–6

Davidson, A, Davidson, J, Owen-John, H S, & Toft, L, 1987 Excavations at the sand-covered medieval settlement at Rhossili, West Glamorgan, *Bull Board Celtic Stud*, **34**, 244–69

Davies, E, 1929 *The Prehistoric and Roman Remains of Denbighshire*. Cardiff

Davies, E, 1973 Hendre and hafod in Merioneth, *J Merioneth Hist and Record Soc*, **7**, 13–27

Davies, E, 1977 Hendre and hafod in Denbighshire, *Trans Denbighshire Hist Soc*, **26**, 49–72

Davies, E, 1979 Hendre and hafod in Caernarvonshire, *Trans Caernarvonshire Hist Soc*, **40**, 17–46

Davies, E, 1980 Hafod, hafoty, and lluest: their distribution, features and purpose, *Ceredigion*, **9.1**, 1–41

Davies, E, 1984–5 Hafod and lluest: The summering of cattle and upland settlement in Wales, *Folk Life*, **23**, 76–96

Davies, R R, 1984 Law and national identity in thirteenth-century Wales, in R R Davies (ed) *Welsh Society and Nationhood: historical essays presented to Glanmor Williams*. Cardiff: University of Wales Press, 51–69

Davies, R R, 1995 *The revolt of Owain Glyndwr*. Oxford: Oxford University Press

Davies, W, 1978 *An Early Welsh Microcosm, Studies in the Llandaff Charters*. London

Davis, P R, 1988 Long-huts in the Rhondda valley, *Archaeol Wales*, **28**, 37–8

Davis, P R, 1989 An archaeological survey of the Hirwaun-Rhigos ridge, Mid Glamorgan, *Archaeol Wales*, **29**, 29–31

Dickson, C, 1988 Distinguishing cereal from wild grass pollen: some limitations, *Circaea*, **5**, 67–71

Drewitt, P, 1983 Mynydd Preseli 1983.1st Interim Report. Unpubl report (held by Dyfed Archaeological Trust SMR)

Drewitt, P, 1984 Mynydd Preseli 1984.2nd Interim Report. Unpubl report (held by Dyfed Archaeological Trust SMR)

Drewitt, P, 1985 Mynydd Preseli 1985.3rd Interim Report. Unpubl report (held by Dyfed Archaeological Trust SMR)

Dugmore, A J, Larsen, G, & Newton, A J, 1995 Seven tephra isochrones in Scotland, *The Holocene*, **5**, 257–66

Dumayne, L, Stoneman, R, Barber, K, & Harkness, D, 1995 Problems associated with correlating calibrated radiocarbon-dated pollen diagrams with historical events, *The Holocene*, **5**, 118–23

Dyer, C C, 1989 The retreat from marginal land: the growth and decline of medieval rural settlements, in Aston *et al* (eds) 1989

Dyer, C C, 1991 *Hanbury: settlement and society in a woodland landscape.* University of Leicester Department of English Local History, Occasional Papers, 4th series, **4**

Dyer, C C, 1995 Sheepcotes; evidence for medieval sheepfarming, *Medieval Archaeol* **39**, 136–64

Edwards, N (ed), 1997 *Landscape and Settlement in Medieval Wales,* Oxbow Monograph **81**

Edwards, N, & Lane, A (eds), 1988 *Early Medieval Settlement in North Wales, AD 400–1100*

Elner, J K, & Happey-Wood, C M, 1980 The history of two linked but contrasting lakes in north Wales from a study of pollen, diatoms and chemistry in sediment cores, *J Ecology,* **68**, 95–121

Emery, F, 1967 The farming regions of Wales, in J Thirsk (ed), *The Agrarian History of England and Wales, vol. 4, 1500–1640.* Cambridge: Cambridge University Press

Emery, F, 1989 The landscape, in D H Owen (ed) *Settlement and Society in Wales.* Cardiff: University of Wales Press

Ernst, W, 1969 Pollen analytischer nachweis eines Schwermetallsasens in Wales, *Vegetatio,* **18**, 393–400

Evans, D S, 1977 *Historia Gruffudd vab Kenan.* Gwasg Prifysgol Cymru

Evans Revd J, 1802 *A Tour through North Wales,* London (2nd edn)

Evans, Revd J, 1804 *Letters written during a tour through South Wales in the year 1803.* London

Faith, R, 1997 *The English Peasantry and the Growth of Lordship.* London: Leicester University Press

Fenton, A, 1999 *Scottish Country Life.* East Linton, East Lothian: Tuckwell Press

Fernie, K, & Gilman, P (ed), 2000 *Informing the Future of the Past: Guidelines for SMRs.* English Heritage

Finberg, H P R, 1969 *Tavistock Abbey.* Newton Abbot: David & Charles

Finberg, H P R (ed), 1972 *The Agrarian History of England and Wales, vol 1. ii AD 43–1042.* Cambridge: Cambridge University Press

Fleming, A, 1988 *The Dartmoor Reaves.* London: Batsford

Foster, I L L, & Alcock L (eds), *Culture and Environment: Essays in Honour of Sir Cyril Fox.* London: Routledge and Kegan Paul

Fox, A, 1937 Dinas Noddfa, Gelligaer Common, Glamorgan: excavations in 1936, *Archaeologia Cambrensis,* **92**, 247–68

Fox, A, 1939 Early Welsh homesteads on Gelligaer Common, Glamorgan: excavations in 1938, *Archaeologia Cambrensis,* **94**, 163–99

Fox, A, 2000 *Aileen: A pioneering archaeologist.* Leominster: Gracewing Press

Fox, A, & Fox C, 1949 'Platform' house-sites of South Wales type in Swydd Buddugre, Malienydd,

Radnorshire, *Trans Radnor Soc,* **19**, 33–5

Fox, C, 1932 *The Personality of Britain: its influence on inhabitant and invader in prehistoric and early historic times.* Cardiff: National Museum of Wales

Fox, C, 1939a A settlement of platform houses at Dyrysgol, St Harmon, Radnorshire, *Archaeologia Cambrensis,* **94**, 220–3

Fox, C, 1939b Dinas Noddfa, Gelligaer Common, Glamorgan, *Bull Board Celtic Stud,* **9**, 295–9

Fox, C, & Fox, A, 1934 Forts and farms on Margam Mountain, Glamorgan, *Antiquity,* **8**, 395–413

Fraser, D, 1993 The British Archaeological Database, in J Hunter & I Ralston (eds) *Archaeological Resource Management in the UK. An Introduction.* Gloucester: Alan Sutton Publishing Ltd

Freeman, Revd G J, 1826 *Sketches in Wales or a Diary of three Walking Excursions in that Principality in the years 1823, 1824, 1825.* London

Fritz, S C, Kreizer, A M, Appleby P G, & Battarbee, R W, 1990 Recent acidification of upland lakes in north Wales: Palaeolimnological evidence, in R W Edwards, A S Gee, & J H Stoner (eds) *Acid Waters in Wales.* London: Kluwer Academic Publishers, 27–37

Gardiner, M, 2000 Vernacular buildings and the development of the later medieval domestic plan in England, *Medieval Archaeol,* **44**, 159–80

GAT, 1996 Medieval and Later Deserted Rural Settlements in Gwynedd: pilot study report, GAT report 200. Bangor

Gelling, M, 1984 *Place-names in the landscape.* London

Gelling, M, & Cole, A, 2000 *The Landscape of Place-Names.* Stamford

Geremek, B, 1990 The marginal man, in J Le Goff (ed) *The Medieval World* (trans. L G Cochrane). London: Collins and Brown, 347–72

Gerrard, G A M, 1988 Appendix II. Phosphate analysis of buildings 1–4, in D Austin Excavations and survey at Bryn Cysegrfan, Llanfair Clydogau, Dyfed, 1979, *Medieval Archaeol,* **32**, 153–61

Gilbertson, D D, Schwenninger, J-L, Kemp, R A, & Rhodes, E J, 1999 Sand-drift and soil formation along an exposed North Atlantic coastline: 14,000 years of diverse geomorphological, climatic and human impacts, *J Archaeol Science,* **26**, 439–69

Gimingham, C H, 1972 *Ecology of Heathlands.* London: Chapman and Hall

Glassie, H. 1975 *Folk Housing in Middle Virginia.* Tennessee: University of Tennessee Press

Glassie, H, 1990 Vernacular architecture and society, in M Turan (ed) *Vernacular Architecture: paradigms of environmental response.* Aldershot: Avebury Press, 271–84

Görres, M, & Bludau, W, 1992 Der Zusammenhang zwischen pollen-und 14C-analytisch ermittelten

Siedlungsphasen und erhohten Mineralstoffgehalten in Profilen des Weidfilzes (Starnberger See), *Telma*, **22**, 123–44

Görres, M, & Frenzel, B, 1993 The Pb, Br and Ti content in peat bogs as indicators for recent and past depositions, *Naturwissenschaften*, **80**, 333–5

Grant, S A, Lamb, W I C, Kerr, C D, & Bolton, G R, 1976 The utilisation of blanket bog vegetation by grazing sheep, *J Applied Ecology*, **13**, 857–69

Green, H S, 1954 Medieval platform sites in the Neath uplands, *Trans Cardiff Nat Soc*, **83**, 9–17

Grenville, J, 1997, *Medieval Housing*. London: Leicester University Press

Gresham, C A, 1954 Platform houses in north-west Wales *Archaeologia Cambrensis*, **103**, 18–53

Gresham, C A, 1973 *Eifionydd*

Gresham, C A, Hemp, W J, & Thompson, F H, 1959 Hen Ddinbych, *Archaeologia Cambrensis* **108**, 72–80

Griffiths, M, 1989 The emergence of the modern settlement pattern, 1450–1700, in D H Owen (ed) *Settlement and Society in Wales*. Cardiff: University of Wales Press

Griffiths, W E, 1954 Excavations on Penmaenmawr, 1950, *Archaeologia Cambrensis*, **103**, 66–84

Griffiths, W E, 1955 Excavations on Bodafon Mountain, 1854, in *Trans Anglesey Antiq Soc*, 12–24

Gwynfor Jones, J (ed), 1990 *Sir John Wynn, The History of the Gwydir family, and memoirs*. Llandysul

Gwynedd Archaeological Trust, 1996 Deserted Rural Settlement – Towards a Typology, unpubl report

Hall, V A, Pilcher, J R, & McCormac, F G, 1993 Tephra-dated lowland landscape history of the north of Ireland, AD 750–1150, *New Phytologist*, **125**, 193–202

Hallam, H E (ed), 1988 *The Agrarian History of England and Wales, Vol 2, 1042–1350*. Cambridge: Cambridge University Press

Hemp, W J, & Gresham, C, 1942–3 Park, Llanfrothen and the Unit System, *Archaeologia Cambrensis*, **97**, 98–134

Henderson, F, n. d. Robert Johnson – pioneer of estate surveying, unpublished article from 1995–7

Hendon, D, Charman, D J, & Kent, M, 2001 Palaeohydrological records derived from testate amoebae analysis from peatlands in northern England: within-site variability, between-site comparability and palaeoclimatic implications, *The Holocene*, **11**, 127–48

Hill, C, 1999 Historic Landscape Characterisation: Gelligaer Common, Caerphilly, part 1, Landscape characterisation. Swansea: GGAT report 99/069

Hillman, G C, 1982 Appendix 4. Crop husbandry at the medieval farmstead, Cefn Graeanog: reconstructions from charred remains of plants, in R S Kelly The excavation of a medieval farmstead at Cefn

Graeanog, Clynnog, Gwynedd, *Bull Board Celtic Stud*, **29**, 859–908

Hilton, R H, 1985 *Class Conflict and the Crisis of Feudalism: Essays in Medieval Social History*. London: Hambledon

Hobbs, R J, & Gimingham, C H, 1987 Vegetation, fire and herbivore interactions in heathland, *Advances in Ecological Research*, **16**, 87–173

Hobbs, R J, Mallik, A U, & Gimingham, C H, 1984 Studies on fire in Scottish heathland communities. III Vital attributes of the species, *J Ecology*, **72**, 963–76

Hogg, A H A, 1954 A 14th century house-site at Cefn-y-Fan near Dolbenmaen, Caernarvon, *Trans Caernarvonshire Hist Soc*, **15**, 1–7

Hölzer, A, & Hölzer, A, 1998 Silicon and titanium in peat profiles as indicators of human impact, *The Holocene*, **8**, 685–96

Hölzer, A, & Schloss, S, 1981 Palaookologische Studien an der Hornisgrine (Nordschwarzwald) auf der Grundlage von chemischer Analyse, Pollen- und Grossrestuntersuchung, *Telma*, **11**, 17–30

Hook, D, 1970 Cefn y Bryn, Caeo, *Carmarthenshire Antiq J*, **6**, 101–3

Hooke, D, 1997 Place-names and vegetation history as a key to understanding settlement in the Conwy Valley, in N Edwards (ed) *Medieval Settlement in Wales*. Oxford: Oxbow Monographs, 79–95

Hoskins, W G, 1965 *Provincial England*. Leicester

Houghton, J T, Ding, Y, Grigs, D J, Noguer, M, van der Linden, P J, Dai, X, Maskell, K, & Johnson, C, 2001 *Climate Change 2001: The Scientific Basis*. Cambridge

Howell, C, 1983 *Land, Family and Inheritance: Kibworth Harcourt 1280–1700*. Cambridge: Cambridge Uuniversity Press

Howell, D W, 2000 *The rural poor in eighteenth-century Wales*. Cardiff: University of Wales Press

Howells, B, 1974–5 Social and Agrarian Change in Early Modern Cardiganshire, *Ceredigion*, **3**, 256–71

Howells, B E (ed), 1987 *Pembrokeshire County History: vol 3 early modern Pembrokeshire 1536–1815*. Haverfordwest: Pembrokeshire Hist Soc

Howells, B E, & Howells, K A (eds), 1977 *The Extent of Cemaes by George Owen, 1592*, Pembrokeshire Record Soc

Howse, W H, 1955 Encroachments on the King's waste in Cantref Maelienydd as recorded in 1734, *Trans Radnor Soc*, **25**, 2727–33

Hughen, K A, Overpeck, J T, & Anderson, R F, 2000 Recent warming in a 500-year temperature record from varved sediments, Upper Soper Lake, Baffin Island, Canada, *The Holocene*, **10**, 9–20

Hughes, H, 1998 *An uprooted community. A history of Epynt*. Llandysul: Gomer Press

Hughes, H H, & North, H L, 1908 *The Old Cottages of Snowdonia*

Hughes, M K, & Diaz, H F, 1994 Was there a 'Medieval Warm Period', and if so, where and when?, *Climatic Change*, **26**, 109–42

Hughes, P D M, Mauquoy, D, Barber, K E, & Langdon, P G, 2000 Mire-development pathways and palaeo-climatic records from a full Holocene peat archive at Walton Moss, Cumbria, England, *The Holocene*, **10**, 465–79

Hughes, P D M, Morriss, S H, Schulz, J, & Barber, K E, 2001 Mire development and human impact in the Teifi Valley: evidence for the Tregaron (Cors Caron) peatlands, in M J C Walker, & D McCarroll (eds) *The Quaternary of West Wales Field Guide*, Quaternary Research Association, 76–92

Hughes, R E, Dale, J, Wiliams, I E, & Rees, D I, 1973 Studies in sheep population and environment in the mountains of north-west Wales I. The status of the sheep in the mountains of north Wales since medi-aeval times, *J Applied Ecology*, **10**, 113–32

Hurst, J G, 1971 A review of archaeological research, in M W Beresford, & J G Hurst (eds) *Deserted Medieval Villages: studies*. London: Lutterworth, 112–16

Hyde, H A, 1939 Appendix II (B) The botanical significance of the finds, together with the results of a re-examination of certain species, in A Fox 1939, 198–9

Itin. Kambr: Dimock, J F (ed), 1868 Giraldi Cambrensis Itinerarium Kambriae et Descriptio Kambriae, in J S Brewer, J F Dimock, & G F Warner (eds) Giraldi Cambrensis Opera, Rolls Series, 1861; Thorpe, L (trans.), 1978 *Gerald of Wales: The Journey through Wales and the Description of Wales*. Harmondsworth

Jack, R I, 1988 Wales and the Marches, in H E Hallam (ed) *The agrarian history of England and Wales, Vol 2, 1042–1350*. Cambridge: Cambridge University Press, 260–71

James, D B, 1988 *Myddfai: Its Land and People*. Aberystwyth: National Library of Wales Press

James, H, 1991 *Sir Gar. Studies in Carmarthenshire History*. Carmarthen: Carmarthenshire Antiq Soc

Jenkins, D, 1982 *Agricultural Co-operation in Welsh Medieval Law*. Amgueddfa Genedlaethol Cymru

Jenkins, D, 1986 *The Law of Hywel Dda*. Llandysul

Jenkins, J G, 1976 *Life and Tradition in Rural Wales*. London: Dent

Johnson, M, 1993 *Housing Culture: Traditional Architecture in an English Landscape*. London: University College London Press

Johnson, M, 2000 *Archaeological Theory: an introduction*. Oxford: Blackwell

Johnstone, N, 1995 *Llys and Maerdref: an investigation into the location of the Royal courts of the Princes of Gwynedd*. Bangor: Gwynedd Archaeological Trust, Report 167

Johnstone, N, 1999 Cae Llys, Rhosyr: A Court of the Princes of Gwynedd, *Studia Celtica*, **33**

Jolliffe, J E A, 1926 Northumbrian institutions, *English Historical Review*, **41**, 1–42

Jones, G R J, 1965 Agriculture in North-West Wales during the Later Middle Ages, in J A Taylor (ed) *Climate Change with Special Reference to Wales and its Agriculture*. Aberystwyth: University College of Wales, Symposia in Agricultural Meteorology Memorandum **8**, 47–53

Jones, G R J, 1971 The multiple estate as a model framework for tracing early stages in the evolution of rural settlement, in F Dussart (ed) *L'Habitat et les Paysages Ruraux d'Europe*. Les Congrès et Colloques de l'Université de Liège, **58**, 251–67

Jones, G R J, 1972 Post-Roman Wales in H P R Finberg (ed) *The Agrarian History of England and Wales. vol. 1(2), AD 43–1042*. Cambridge: Cambridge University Press, 281–382

Jones, G R J, 1973 Field systems of north Wales, in A R H Baker, & R A Butlin (eds) *Studies of Field Systems in the British Isles*. Cambridge, 430–79

Jones, G R J, 1985 Forms and patterns of medieval settlement in Wales, in D Hooke (ed) *Medieval Villages*. Oxford, 155–69

Jones, J G, 1995 *The Wynn family of Gwydir: origins, growth and development c. 1490–1674*. Aberystwyth

Jones, P D, Briffa, K R, Barnett, T P, & Tett, S F B, 1998 High-resolution palaeoclimatic records for the last millennium: interpretation, integration and comparison with General Circulation Model control-run temperatures, *The Holocene*, **8**, 455–71

Jones, R A, 1998 Problems with medieval Welsh local administration – the case of the *maenor* and the *maenol*, *J Hist Geog*, **24.2**, 135–46

Jones, R, Benson-Evans, K, & Chambers, F M, 1985 Human influence on sedimentation in Llangorse Lake, Wales, *Earth Surface Processes and Landforms*, **10**, 227–35

Jones, R, Chambers, F M, and Benson-Evans, K, 1991 Heavy metals (Cu and Zn) in recent sediments of Llangorse Lake, Wales: non-ferrous smelting, Napoleon and the price of wheat – a palaeoecological study, *Hydrobiologia*, **214**, 149–54

Jones, T, 1688 *Y Gymraeg yn ei disgleirdeb neu helaeth eirlyfr Cymraeg a Saesoneg*. Fascimile edition published by the Black Pig Press, Llanwrda, 1977

Jones Pierce, T, 1938 Some tendencies in the Agrarian History of Caernarfonshire during the Later Middle Ages, *Trans Caernarvonshire Hist Soc* **1**, 1–27

Jones Pierce, T, 1951 Medieval settlement in Anglesey, *Trans Anglesey Antiq Soc*, 1–33

Jones Pierce, T, 1961 Pastoral and agricultural

settlements in early Wales, *Geografiske Annaler*, **43**, 182–9

Jones Pierce, T, 1972a Agrarian aspects of the tribal system in Medieval Wales, in J Beverley Smith (ed) *Medieval Welsh Society – Selected Essays by T Jones Pierce*. Cardiff

Jones Pierce, T, 1972b Pastoral and agricultural settlements in Early Wales, in J Beverley Smith (ed) *Medieval Welsh Society – Selected Essays by T Jones Pierce*. Cardiff, 339–59

Jones, R, n. d. *An Accurate Account of Dolgelley and Caernarvon*

Jones, S R, & Smith, J T, 1963 The houses of Breconshire, Part 1, *Brycheiniog*, **9**, 1–78

Jones, S R, & Smith, J T, 1964 The Houses of Breconshire, Part 2, *Brycheiniog*, **10**, 69–184

Jones, S R, & Smith, J T, 1965 The Houses of Breconshire, Part 3, *Brycheiniog*, **11**, 1–150

Jones, S R, & Smith, J T, 1966 The Houses of Breconshire, Part 4, *Brycheiniog*, **12**, 1–92

Jones, S R, & Smith, J T, 1967 The Houses of Breconshire, Part 5, *Brycheiniog*, **13**, 1–86

Jope, E M, 1963 The regional cultures of medieval Britain, in Foster & Alcock, 327–50

Kay, G, 1796 *General View of the Agriculture of Caernarvonshire*

Kelly, R S, 1982a The Ardudwy Survey: fieldwork in Western Merioneth, 1971–81, *J Merioneth Hist and Record Soc*, **9**(1), 121–62

Kelly, R S, 1982b The excavation of a medieval farmstead at Cefn Graenog, Clynnog, Gwynedd, *Bull Board Celtic Stud*, **29**, 859–908

Kelly, R S, 1988 Two late prehistoric circular enclosures near Harlech, Gwynedd, *Proc Prehist Soc*, **54**, 101–51

Kempter, H, Görres, M, & Frenzel, B, 1997 Ti and Pb concentrations in rainwater-fed bogs in Europe as indicators of past anthropogenic activities, *Water, Air and Soil Pollution*, **100**, 367–77

King, E, 1973 *Peterborough Abbey 1086–1310: a study in the land market*. Cambridge: Cambridge University Press

Kirk, D (ed), 1998 *A tour in Wales by Thomas Pennant*. Llanrwst: Gwasg Carreg Gwalch

Kissock, J A, 1995 *Historic Settlements of South Pembrokeshire*. Llandeilo: Dyfed Archaeological Trust

Kissock, J A, 1997 God made nature and men made towns: post-conquest and pre-conquest villages in Pembrokeshire, in Edwards (ed) 1997, 123–38

Kissock, J A, 2000 Farmsteads of a presumed medieval date on Cefn Drum, Gower: an interim review, *Studia Celtica*, **34**, 223–48

Kissock, J A, & Johnston, R A S, 2000 Cefn Drum research project, *Medieval Settlement Research Group Annual Report*, **15**, 38–9

Kumar, K, 2003 *The Making of English National Identity*. Cambridge: Cambridge University Press

Lamb, H H, 1995 *Climate, history and the modern world* (2nd edition). London: Routlege

Lang, N, 1990 Sites and Monuments Records: some current issues, in M Hughes (ed) *Sites and Monuments Records: Some Current Issues*. Association of County Archaeological Officers

Langdon, P, & Barber, K, 2002 The 'AD 860' tephra in Scotland: new data from Langlands Moss, East Kilbride, Strathclyde, *Quaternary Newsletter*, **97**, 11–18

Lascelles, D B, 1995 Holocene environmental and pedogenic history of the Hiraethog Moors, Clwyd. Unpubl PhD thesis, University of Wales

Latham, J, Plunkett-Dillon, E, & Evans, N, 2001 *National Trust Annual Archaeological Review 2000–2001: Wales*. National Trust, 59

Lawler, M, Walker, M J C, & Locock, M, 1997 A Cairnfield at Cefn-yr-Esgryn, Mid Glamorgan: An Archaeological and Palaeoenvironmental Study, *Studia Celtica*, **31**, 83–105

Leighton, D K, 1997 *Mynydd Du and Fforest Fawr: The Evolution of an Upland Landscape in South Wales from the end of the last glaciation to the present day*. Aberystwyth: RCAHMW

Lewis, E A, 1927–9 The proceedings of the small hundred court of the commote of Ardudwy, 1325–1326, *Bull Board Celtic Stud*, **4**

Lewis, T, 1927 Archaeological investigations in the vicinity of Llanddewi Brefi and Llanfair Clydogau, **Trans Cardiganshire Antiq Soc**, **5**, 83–99

Lhwyd, E, 1909–11 *Parochialia being a Summary of Answers to Parochial Queries etc.*, Cambrian Archaeological Association, 3 Vols

Ling, A G, 1936, Peasant architecture in the northern provinces of Spain, *Journal Royal Institute of British Architects*, set 3, **43**, 845–63

Linnard, W, 2000 *Welsh Woods and Forests*. Llandysul: Gomer

Lloyd, F, Vernon, M P, & Bevan-Evans, M, 1963 The long-house in Wales, *Publications Flintshire Historical Society*, **20**, 98–104

Locock, M, 1995 Cosmeston to Cog Moors pumping main: archaeological watching brief, report on possible house-platform. Swansea: GGAT report 95(026)

Locock, M, 1998 Mill Farm, Lisvane, *Archaeol Wales*, **38**, 91

Locock, M, 2000a Deserted Rural Settlements in Glamorgan. Swansea: GGAT report 2000(030)

Locock, M, 2000b Deserted Rural Settlements in Glamorgan: Scheduling recommendations, 1999–2000. Swansea: GGAT report 2000/063

Locock, M, 2001a Deserted Rural Settlements in

Glamorgan and Gwent: a condition survey. Swansea: GGAT report 2001/016

Locock, M, 2001b Deserted Rural Settlements in Glamorgan and Gwent: Scheduling recommendations. Swansea: GGAT report 2001/032

Longley, D, 1991a Excavations at Plas Berw, Anglesey, 1983–4, *Archaeologia Cambrensis*, **140**, 102–19

Longley, D, 1991b The Excavation of Castell, Porth Trefadog, a Coastal Promontory Fort in North Wales, *Medieval Archaeol*, **35**, 64–85

Lord, P, 2000 *The Visual Culture of Wales: imaging the nation*. Cardiff: University of Wales Press

Lowe, J, 1985 *Welsh Country Workers Housing 1775–1875*. Cardiff

Lynch, F M, 1995 *Gwynedd, A Guide to Ancient and Historic Wales*. Cadw: HMSO

Mabey, J C, 1939 Appendix II (A) Identification of charcoals from Gelligaer Common, in A Fox 1939, 197

Macklin, M G, Passmore, D J, Stevenson, A C, Cowley, D C, Edwards, D N, & O'Brien, C F, 1991 Holocene alluviation and land use change on Callaly Moor, Northumberland, England, *J Quaternary Science*, **6**, 225–32

Macklin, M G, Passmore, D G, & Rumsby, B T, 1992 Climatic and cultural signals in Holocene alluvial sequences: The Tyne Basin, in S Needham & M Macklin (eds) *Alluvial archaeology in Britain*, Oxbow Monograph, **27**. Oxford: Oxford Press, 123–39

Maitland, F W, 1897 *Domesday Book and Beyond*. Cambridge: Cambridge University Press

Mann, M, 1986 *The Sources of Social Power. Vol 1: a History of Power from the Beginning to AD 1760*. Cambridge: Cambridge University Press

Mann, M E, Bradley, R S, & Hughes, M K, 1999 Northern hemisphere temperatures during the past millennium: inferences, uncertainties, and limitations, *Geophysical Research Letters*, **26**, 759–62

Martin, D J, 1964 Analysis of sheep diet utilising plant epidermal fragments in faeces samples, in D J Crisp (ed) *Grazing in Terrestrial and Marine Environments*. Oxford, 173–88

Mauquoy, D, & Barber, K, 1999 Evidence for climatic deteriorations associated with the decline of Sphagnum imbricatum Hrnsch. ex Russ. in six ombrotrophic mires from northern England and the Scottish Borders, *The Holocene*, **9**, 423–37

Mayes, J, & Wheeler, D, 1997 Regional perspectives on climatic variability and change, in D Wheeler & J Mayes (eds) *Regional climates of the British Isles*. London and New York: Routledge, 279–331

Meirion-Jones, G I, 1973 The long-house: a definition, *Medieval Archaeol*, **17**, 135–7

Metcalfe, D M, 1979, Cardiganshire Marginal Land Survey. Dyfed Archaeological Trust

Mighall, T M, & Chambers, F M, 1995 Holocene vegetation history and human impact at Bryn y Castell, Snowdonia, north Wales, *New Phytologist*, **130**, 299–321

Miles, D, 1995 *The Ancient Borough of Newport in Pembrokeshire*. Dyfed County Council Cultural Services Department

Miles, J, Welch, D, & Chapman, S B, 1978 Vegetation management in the uplands, in O W Heal (ed) *Upland Land Use in England and Wales*. Cheltenham: Countryside Commission

Miller, E (ed), 1991 *The Agrarian History of England and Wales, vol 3, 1350–1500*. Cambridge: Cambridge University Press

Moore, P D, 1968 Human influence upon vegetational history in north Cardiganshire, *Nature*, **217**, 1006–7

Moore, P D, & Chater, E H, 1969 The changing vegetation of west-central Wales in the light of human history, *J Ecology*, **57**, 361–79

Moore, P D, Evans, A T, & Chater, M, 1986 Palynological and stratigraphic evidence for hydrological changes in mires associated with human activity, in K-E Behre (ed) *Anthropogenic Indicators in Pollen Diagrams*. Rotterdam: Balkema, 209–20

Morgan, D E, 1988 Black Mountain/Mynydd Ddu Survey, *Archaeol in Wales*, **28**, 41–3

Morgan, G, 1991 Early Hafod tenants and the founding of the estate, *Friends of Hafod Newsletter*, 1991, 5–7

Morgan, G, 1997 *A Welsh House and its family: the Vaughans of Trawscoed*. Llandysul: Gomer Press

Morgan, G C, & Keepax, C, 1979 Charcoal, in Allen 1979, 46

Morris, B, 1954 Medieval platform sites in east Gower, *Gower* 7, 40–2

Morriss, S, 2001 Recent human impact and land use change in Britain and Ireland: a pollen analytical and geochemical study. Unpubl PhD thesis, University of Southampton

Mytum, H, 1985 Fron Haul, Newport, *Archaeol in Wales*, **25**. CBA: Wales, 52

Mytum, H, 1986 Fron Haul, Newport, *Archaeol in Wales*, **26**. CBA: Wales, 65

Mytum, H, 1988 The Clydach Valley: A 19th century landscape, *Archaeol Today*

National Assembly for Wales, 2001 *Woodlands for Wales. The National Assembly for Wales strategy for trees and woodlands*. Aberystwyth: Forestry Commission

Nicholson, B E, & Clapham, A, 1975 *The Oxford Book of Trees*. Oxford: Oxford University Press

Ogilvie, A, & Farmer, G, 1997 Documenting the Medieval Warm Period, in M Hulme, & E Barrow (eds) *Climates of the British Isles, present, past and future*. London: Routledge

Oldfield, F, Crooks, P R J, Gedye, S S, Jones, R, Nijampurkar, V D, Plater, A J, Richardson, N, & Thompson, R, 1994 Geochronology of the last millennium, in B M Funnell, & R I F Kay (eds) *Palaeoclimate of the Last Glacial/Interglacial Cycle*, Special Publication 94/2 of the NERC Earth Sciences Directorate. Swindon, 77–80

Oldfield, F, Richardson, N, & Appleby, P G, 1995 Radiometric dating (210Pb, 137Cs, 241Am) of recent ombrotrophic peat accumulation and evidence for changes in mass balance, *The Holocene*, **5**, 141–8

Orford, J D, Wilson, P, Wintle, A G, Knight, J, & Braley, S, 2000 Holocene coastal dune initiation in Northumberland and Norfolk, eastern UK: climate and sea-level changes as possible forcing agents for dune initiation, in I Shennan, & J Andrews (eds) Holocene land-ocean interaction and environmental change around the North Sea, *Geol Soc, London, Special Publications*, **166**, 197–217

Osborne, B, 1978 Glamorgan agriculture in the 17th and 18th centuries, *National Library of Wales J*, **20**

Owen, A, 1999 Phosphate survey at Llystan Gannol. Unpubl report for Gwynedd Archaeological Trust

Owen, D H, 1991 Wales and the Marches, in E Miller (ed) *The agrarian history of England and Wales. Volume 3, 1348–1500*. Cambridge: Cambridge University Press, 92–106

Papazian, C, & Campbell, E, 1992 Medieval pottery and roof tiles in Wales AD 1100–1600, *Medieval and Later Pottery in Wales,* **13**, 1–107

Parry, M L, 1975 Secular climatic change and marginal agriculture, *Trans Inst Brit Geog*, **64**, 1–17

Parry, M L, 1978 *Climate change, agriculture and settlement*. Folkestone: Dawson & Sons

Pearson, A W, Collier, P, Fry, C, Stamp, T R, Farres, P J, & White, I D, unpublished Palynological evidence of agricultural activity on Mynydd Carn Ingli, Pembrokeshire

Peate, I C, 1936 Some Welsh houses, *Antiquity*, **10**, 448–59

Peate, I C, 1946 *The Welsh house: a study in folk culture* (3rd edn). Liverpool: H Evans & Sons

Peate, I C, 1963 The Welsh long-house: a brief re-appraisal, in Foster & Alcock, 373–88

Percival, D, 1993 The boundary of the medieval grange of Dolhelfa, *Trans Radnor Soc*, **63**, 42–5

Pilcher, J R, Hall, V A, & McCormac, F G, 1995 Dates of Holocene Icelandic volcanic eruptions from tephra layers in Irish peats, *The Holocene*, **5**, 103–10

Price, M D R, & Moore, P D, 1984 Pollen dispersion in the hills of Wales: a pollen shed hypothesis, *Pollen et Spores*, **26**, 127–36

Pritchard, E M (ed), 1906 *The Taylors Cussion by George Owen, Lord of Kemeys (circa 1552–1613)*. Facsimile edition. London

Pye, K, & Neal, A, 1993 Late Holocene dune formation on the Sefton coast, northwest England, in K Pye (ed) The Dynamics and Environmental Context of Aeolian Sedimentary Systems, *Geol Soc, London, Special Publications*, **72**, 201–17

Rackham, O, 1986 *The History of the Countryside.* London: Dent

Rackham, O, 1995 *Trees and Woodland in the British Landscape*. London: Weidenfeld & Nicolson

Raglan, Lord, 1963 The origin of vernacular architecture, in Foster & Alcock, 373–88

Rapoport, A, 1990 Systems of activity and systems of settings, in S Kent (ed) *Domestic Architecture and the Use of Space: an interdisciplinary cross-cultural study.* Cambridge: Cambridge University Press, 9–20

Razi, Z, 1980 *Life, Marriage and Death in a Medieval Parish: Economy, Society and Demography in Hale-sowen, 1270–1400*. Cambridge: Cambridge University Press

RCAHMW, 1911 *An Inventory of the Ancient Monuments in Wales and Monmouthshire. Vol 1 County of Montgomery*. London: Royal Commission on the Ancient and Historical Monuments of Wales

RCAHMW, 1913 *An Inventory of the Ancient Monuments in Wales and Monmouthshire. Vol 3 County of Radnor.* London: Royal Commission on the Ancient and Historical Monuments of Wales

RCAHMW, 1914 *An Inventory of the Ancient Monuments in Wales and Monmouthshire. Vol 4 County of Denbigh*. London: Royal Commission on the Ancient and Historical Monuments of Wales

RCAHMW, 1921 *An Inventory of the Ancient Monuments in Wales and Monmouthshire. Vol 6 County of Merioneth*. London: Royal Commission on the Ancient and Historical Monuments of Wales

RCAHMW, 1956. *An Inventory of the Ancient Monuments in Caernarvonshire: Vol 1 East. The Cantref of Arllechwedd and the Commote of Creuddyn.* London: HMSO

RCAHMW, 1960 *An Inventory of the Ancient Monuments in Caernarvonshire: Vol 2 Central. The Cantref of Arfon and the Commote of Eifionydd*. London: HMSO

RCAHMW, 1964 *An Inventory of the Ancient Monuments in Caernarvonshire: Vol 3 West. The Cantref of Lleyn.* London: HMSO

RCAHMW, 1976 *An Inventory of the Ancient Monuments in Glamorgan Vol 2 part 1 The Stone and Bronze Ages.* Cardiff: HMSO

RCAHMW, 1982 *An Inventory of the Ancient Monuments in Glamorgan: Vol 3 Medieval secular monuments Part 2: non-defensive.* London: HMSO

RCAHMW, 1988 *An Inventory of the Ancient Monuments in Glamorgan: Vol 4 part 2 Domestic architecture from the Reformation to the Industrial Revolution; farmhouses and cottages.* London: HMSO

RCAHMW, 1991 *An Inventory of the Ancient Monuments in Glamorgan: Vol 3 part 1 Medieval secular* monuments: the early castles, from the Norman Conquest to 1217. London: HMSO

RCAHMW, 1997 An Inventory of the Ancient Monuments in Brecknock (Brycheiniog). The prehistoric and Roman monuments. Part 1. Later prehistoric monuments and unenclosed settlements to 1000 A. D. Stroud

RCAHMW, forthcoming Houses and history in the Welsh Marches. The late medieval and Tudor houses of Radnorshire and their transformations. Aberystwyth

Rec. Caern. Quart. Sess: Williams, W O, 1965. Calendar of the Caernarvonshire Quarter Sessions Records, vol 1 1541–1558. Aberystwyth

Rec. Caern: Registrum Vulgariter Nuncupatum 'The Record of Caernarvon', Ellis, H (ed) 1838, London

Rec. Court of Augment: Lewis E A, & Conway Davies, J (eds), 1954 Records of the Court of Augmentations relating to Wales and Monmouthshire. Cardiff

Rees, W, 1924 South Wales and the March, 1281–1487. Oxford: Oxford University Press

Rees, W, 1974 Caerphilly Castle and its place in the Annals of Glamorgan. Caerphilly Local Hist Soc

Rhys, J (ed), 1883 Tours in Wales by Thomas Pennant, with notes, preface, and copious index by the editor. Caernarvon: H Humphreys

Richards, M, 1959 'Hafod and hafoty in Welsh place-names: a semantic study', Montgomeryshire Collections, 56, 13–20

Richards, M, 1960 'Meifod, lluest, cynaeafdy and hendre in Welsh place-names', Montgomeryshire Collections, 57, 177–87

Richards, M, 1969 Welsh administrative and territorial units: medieval and modern. Cardiff

Roberts, B K, & Wrathmell, S, 2000 An Atlas of Rural Settlement in England. London: English Heritage

Roberts, K, & Sambrook, P, 2003 Site Preservation and Management, in Upland Archaeology. Aberystwyth: RCAHMW

Roberts, P, 1998 Tudor Wales, national identity and the British inheritance, in B Bradshaw, & P Roberts (eds) British Consciousness and Identity: the making of Britain, 1533–1707. Cambridge: Cambridge University Press, 8–42

Roberts, R A, 1959 Ecology of human occupation and land use in Snowdonia, J Ecology, 47, 317–23

Robinson, D M, 1982 Medieval vernacular buildings below the ground: a review and corpus for southeast Wales, GGAT Annual Report 1981–1982, 94–123

Rogers, T, 1979 Excavations at Hen Caerwys, Clwyd, 1962, Bull Board Celtic Stud, 28(3), 528–33

Rose, G, 1993 Feminism and Geography. Minneapolis: University of Minnesota Press

Rose, N L, Harlock, S, Appleby, P G, & Battarbee, R W, 1995 Dating of recent lake sediments in the United Kingdom and Ireland using spheroidal carbonaceous particle (SCP) concentration profiles, The Holocene, 5, 328–35

Rosen, D Z, 1998 Recent palaeoecology and industrial impact on the South Wales landscape. Unpubl PhD thesis, University of Wales, Swansea

Rosen, D Z, & Dumayne-Peaty, L, 2001 Human impact on the vegetation of South Wales during late historical times: palynological and palaeoenvironmental results from Crymlyn Bog NNR, West Glamorgan, Wales, UK, The Holocene, 11, 11–23

Royal Commission on Agricultural Labour, 1893 Report on Agriculture in Wales

Royal Commission on Land in Wales and Monmouthshire, 1895–6 Minutes of Evidence Vols 1–6. London: HMSO

Sambrook, P, 1997 Medieval or Later Deserted Rural Settlements Survey: 1996–7 pilot study, an interim report, Cambria Archaeology report PRN 32844. Llandeilo

Sambrook, P, 1998 Mediaeval or Later Deserted Rural Settlements in Midwest Wales: Report on the 1997–98 Survey. Llandeilo: Cambria Archaeology

Sambrook, P, 1999 Mediaeval or Later Deserted Rural Settlements in Mid and West Wales: 1998–99 Survey. Llandeilo: Cambria Archaeology

Sambrook, P, 2000 Mediaeval or Later Deserted Rural Settlements in Southwest Wales: 1999–2000 Survey. Llandeilo: Cambria Archaeology

Sambrook, P, & Page, N, 1995 Historic Settlements of Dinefwr. Llandeilo: Cambria Archaeology

Sambrook, P, & Ramsey, R, 1998 Medieval or Later Deserted Rural Settlements in mid-west Wales: report on the 1997–98 survey, ACA report PRN 35605. Llandeilo

Samson, R (ed), 1990 The Social Archaeology of Houses. Edinburgh: Edinburgh University Press

Saunders, G E, Wood, S J, & Burrin, P J, 1989 Late Glacial and Holocene environmental change in the Gower Peninsula: evidence from the alluvial valley fill of the Ilston River, Quaternary Newsletter, 57, 14–23

Sayce, R U, 1942 Popular enclosures and the one-night house, Montgomeryshire Collections, 47.2, 1–12

Sayce, R U, 1956 The old summer pastures, part 1, Montgomeryshire Collections, 54, 117–45

Sayce, R U, 1957 The old summer pastures, part 2: life at the hafodydd, Montgomeryshire Collections, 55, 37–86

Seebohm, F, 1882 The English Village Community. London: Longmans, Green & Co

Seebohm, F, 1897 The Tribal System in Wales. London: Longmans, Green & Co

Seymour, W P, 1985 The environmental history of the Preseli region of south-west Wales over the past 12000 years. Unpubl PhD thesis, University of Wales

Shanin, T, 1971 Peasants and Peasant Societies.

Harmondsworth: Penguin

Silvester, B, 1997 Deserted Medieval and Later Rural Settlements in Radnorshire: field assessment, CPAT report 227. Welshpool

Silvester, B, 1998 Deserted Medieval and Later Rural Settlements in eastern Conwy, Denbighshire and Montgomeryshire: field assessment, CPAT report 251. Welshpool

Silvester, B, 1999 Deserted Medieval and Later Rural Settlements in Radnorshire: the second report, field assessment. CPAT report 305. Welshpool

Silvester, B, 2000 Deserted Medieval and Later Rural Settlements in Brecknock: the first report. CPAT report 358. Welshpool

Silvester, B, 2001 Deserted Medieval and Later Rural Settlements in Powys and Clwyd: the final report. CPAT report 425. Welshpool

Silvester, R J, 1991 Medieval farming on the Berwyn, *Medieval Settlement Research Group Annual Report*, **6**, 12–14

Silvester, R J, 1997a Historic settlements in Clwyd and Powys, in N Edwards (ed) 1997

Silvester, R J, 1997b The Llanwddyn Hospitium, *Montgomeryshire Collections*, **85**, 63–76

Silvester, R J, 2000 Medieval upland cultivation on the Berwyns in north Wales, *Landscape Hist*, **22**, 47–60

Silvester, R J, 2001 Ty Mawr and the landscape of Trefnant township, *Montgomeryshire Collections*, **89**, 147–62

Silvester, R J, 2004 The commons and the waste: use and misuse in central Wales, in I D Whyte and A J L Winchester (eds) *Society, Landscape and Environment in Upland Britain*, Birmingham: Society for Landscape Studies, 53–66

Smith, A G, & Cloutman, E W, 1988 Reconstruction of Holocene vegetation history in three dimensions at Waun-Fignen-Felen, an upland site in South Wales, *Phil Trans Royal Soc London*, **322**, 159–219

Smith, A G, & Green, C A, 1995 Topogenous peat development and late-Flandrian vegetation history at a site in upland South Wales, *The Holocene*, **5**, 172–83

Smith, G, 1999 Gwynedd Hut Circle Settlement Survey, GAT report 358

Smith, J, Beverley, 1998 *Llywelyn ap Gruffudd, Prince of Wales*. Cardiff: University of Wales Press

Smith, J, Beverley, & Smith, Ll, Beverley (eds), 2001 *History of Merioneth, vol 2, The Middle Ages*. Cardiff

Smith, J T, 1963 The long-house in Monmouthshire: a reappraisal, in Foster & Alcock, 389–414

Smith, P, 1963 The long-house and the laithe-house: a study of the house-and-byre homestead in Wales and the West Riding, in Foster & Alcock, 415–38

Smith, P, 1967 Rural Housing in Wales, in J Thirsk (ed)

The Agrarian History of England and Wales, Vol 4, 684–814

Smith, P, 1988 *Houses of the Welsh Countryside, a study in historical geography.* London: HMSO (2nd edn)

Smith, P, 1989 Houses and building styles, in D H Owen (ed) *Settlement and society in Wales*. Cardiff: University Wales Press, 95–150

Smith, P, 1998 The Domestic Architecture of the County in G Jenkins, & I Gwynedd Jones (eds), *Cardiganshire County History Vol 3: Cardiganshire in Modern Times*

Smith, P, 2001. 'Houses c1415–1642', in Beverley Smith, & Beverley Smith 2001

Smith, P, & Owen, C E V, 1958 Traditional and Renaissance elements in some late Stuart and early Georgian half-timbered houses in Arwystli, *Montgomeryshire Collections*, **50**, 120

Smith, R T, & Taylor, J A, 1969 The post-glacial development of vegetation and soils in Northern Cardiganshire, *Trans Inst Brit Geog*, **48**, 75–95

Stevenson, A C, & Patrick, S T, 1989 Palaeoecological evaluation of the recent acidification of Welsh Lakes. I. Llyn Hir, Dyfed. Palaeoecology Research Unit Working Paper, **16**, Department of Geography, University College London

Stevenson, A C, & Thompson, D B A, 1993 Long-term changes in the extent of heather moorland in upland Britain and Ireland: palaeoecological evidence for the importance of grazing, *The Holocene*, **3**, 70–6

Suggett, R, 1996 The chronology of late-medieval timber houses in Wales, *Vernacular Architecture*, **27**, 28–37

Suggett, R, 2005 *Houses and History in the March of Wales, Radnorshire 1400–1800*. Aberystwyth: Royal Commission on the Ancient and Historical Monuments of Wales.

Tarlow, S, & West, S, 1999, *The Familiar Past*. London: Routledge

Taylor, C C, 1995 Dispersed settlement in nucleated areas, *Landscape Hist*, **17**, 27–34

Taylor, J A, 1973 Chronometers and chronicles: a study of palaeoenvironments in west central Wales, *Progress in Geography*, **5**, 247–334

Taylor, J A, 1987 *Timescales of Environmental Change*. Aberystwyth: University College of Wales

Thirsk, J (ed), 1967 *The Agrarian History of England and Wales, vol 4, 1500–1640*. Cambridge: Cambridge University Press

Thomas, C, 1964 Encroachment on to the common lands in Merioneth in the sixteenth century, *Northern Univ Geog J*, **5**, 33–8

Thomas, C, 1967 Enclosure and the rural landscape of Merioneth in the sixteenth century', *Trans Inst Brit Geog* **42**, 153–62

Thomas, C, 1968 'Thirteenth-century farm economies in North Wales', *Agric Hist Rev*, **16**, 1–14

Thomas, C, 1979 'Estates and the rural economy of north Wales 1770–1850', *Bull Board Celtic Stud*, **27**, 259–304

Thomas, C, 1992 A cultural-ecological model of agrarian colonization in north Wales, *Landscape Hist,* **14**, 37–50

Thomas, C, 2001 Rural Society, Settlement, Economy, and Landscape, in Beverley Smith & Beverley Smith 2001, 168–224

Thomas, G C G, 1997 *The charters of the abbey of Ystrad Marchell.* Aberystwyth: National Library of Wales

Thomas, H J, 1966 Uchelolau (Highlight) deserted medieval village, *Morgannwg*, **10**, 63–6

Thomas, H J, 1967 Uchelolau (Highlight) deserted medieval village, *Morgannwg*, **11**, 314–15

Thomas, H J, 1970 Uchelolau (Highlight) deserted medieval village, *Morgannwg*, **14**, 88–92

Thomas, H J, & Davies, G, 1972 A medieval house site at Barry, Glamorgan, *Trans Cardiff Nat Soc*, **46**, 4–22

Thomas, H J, & Dowdell, G, 1987 A Shrunken Medieval Village at Barry, Glamorgan, *Archaeologia Cambrensis*, **136**, 94–137

Thomas, H M, 1992 *A Catalogue of Glamorgan Estate Maps.* Cardiff: Glamorgan Record Office

Thomas, J G, & Carter, H, 1957 *Wales: A Physical Historical and Regional Geography.* London

Thomas, K W, 1965 The stratigraphy and pollen analysis of a raised peat bog at Llanllwch, near Carmarthen, *New Phytologist*, **64**, 101–17

Thompson, D, & Yates, M, 1999 Deserted rural settlement in Wales – a framework for study, a strategy for protection, in J Fridrich (ed) *Ruralia III.* Prague: Institute of Archaeology

Tipping, R, 1998 Cereal cultivation on the Anglo-Scottish Border during the 'Little Ice Age', in G Coles, & C M Mills *Life on the Edge: Human Settlement and Marginality.* Oxbow Monograph **100**, Symposia of the Association for Environmental Archaeology, **13**, 1–11

Tipping, R, 2000 Palaeoecological approaches to historical problems: a comparison of sheep-grazing intensities in the Cheviot Hills in the Medieval and later periods, in Atkinson *et al* (eds) 2000, 130–43

Tipping, R, forthcoming *Climatic variability and 'marginal' settlement in upland British landscapes: a re-evaluation*

Tipping, R, Carter, S, Davidson, D A, Long, D, & Tyler, A, 1997 Soil pollen analysis: a new approach to understanding the stratigraphic integrity of data, in A Sinclair, E Slater, & J Gowlett (eds) *Archaeological Sciences 1995.* Oxford: Oxbow Monograph 64, 221–32

Tosh, J, 1999 *The Pursuit of History* (3rd edn). Harlow: Pearson Education Limited

Toulmin Smith, L (ed), 1906 *The Itinerary in Wales of John Leland in or about the years 1536–1539.* London: George Bell & Sons

Turner, J, 1964 The anthropogenic factor in vegetation history I. Tregaron and Whixhall Mosses, *New Phytologist*, **63**, 73–90

Uhlig, H, 1961 Old hamlets with infield/outfield systems in western and central Europe, *Geografiska Annaler,* **43**, 285–307

Vaughan, E, 1966 Lluestau Blaenrheidol, in *Ceredigion,* **5**, 246–63, Cardiganshire

Antiq Soc. Llandysul: Gomerian Press

Vaughan, H M, 1927 A Synopsis of Two Tours Made in Wales in 1775 and 1811 by Sir Thomas Gery Cullum, Bart and his son the Rev. Sir Thomas Gery Cullum, Bart, *Y Cymmrodor,* **38**, 45–78

Vinogradoff, P, 1892 *Villainage in England: essays in English medieval history.* Oxford

Walker, M F, & Taylor, J A, 1976 Post-neolithic vegetation changes in the western Rhinogau, Gwynedd, North West Wales, *Trans Inst Brit Geog New Ser*, **1**, 323–45

Walker, M J C, 1982 Early and mid-Flandrian environmental history of the Brecon Beacons, S. Wales, *New Phytologist*, **91**, 147–65

Walker, M J C, 1988 Appendix 1, Pollen analysis of sample from buried turf layer (07) below mound PRN 8276, in Austin 1988, 157

Walker, M J C, 1993 Holocene (Flandrian) vegetation change and human activity in the Carneddau area of upland mid-Wales, in F Chambers *Climate Change and Human Impact on the Landscape.* London: Chapman and Hall, 169–83

Walker, M J C, Lawler, M, & Locock, M, 1997 Woodland clearance in medieval Glamorgan: pollen evidence from Cefn Hirgoed, *Archaeol in Wales*, **37**, 21–6

Wallerstein, I, 1974 *The Modern World System.* New York: Academic Press

Ward, A H, 1991 Transhumant or Permanent Settlement: Linear House Foundations along the Afon Clydach on the Black Mountain, South-east Carmarthenshire, in James (ed) 1991, 1–22

Ward, A H, 1995 An Incipient Upland Farmstead at Tro'r Derlwyn?, *Carmarthenshire Antiq*, **31**, 17–33. Carmarthen

Ward, A, 1997 Transhumance and settlement on the Welsh uplands: a view from the Black Mountain, in Edwards (ed) 1997, 97–111

Ward, A, 1999 Transhumance and place-names: an aspect of early Ordnance Survey mapping on the Black Mountain commons, Carmarthenshire, *Studia Celtica*, **33**, 335–48

Watkins, R, 1990 The post-glacial vegetational history of lowland Gwynedd – Llyn Cororion, in K Addison,

H J Edge, & R Watkins (eds) *The Quaternary of North Wales: Field Guide.* Coventry: Quaternary Research Association, 131–6

Weber, M, 1968 *Economy and Society.* New York: Bedminster Press

Weeks, R, 1998 Cillonydd, Newbridge, *Archaeol Wales,* **38,** 126–8

Welsh Assembly Government, 2002 *Planning Policy Wales*

Welsh Office Circular, 60/1996 Planning and the Historic Environment: Archaeology

Wickham, C, 1985 Pastoralism and underdevelopment in the early middle ages, *Settimane di Studio del Centro Italiano di Studi Sull' Alto Medioevo,* 31, 401–51

Wiliam, ARh, 1960 *Llyfr Iorwerth.* Board of Celtic Studies, University of Wales History and Law series, **18.** University of Wales Press

Wiliam, E, 1982a Peasant Architecture in Caernarfonshire, *Trans Caernarvonshire Hist Soc,* **43,** 83–107

Wiliam, E, 1982b *Traditional Farm Buildings in Northeast Wales, 1550–1900.* Cardiff: National Museum of Wales

Wiliam, E, 1986 *The Historical Farm Buildings of Wales.* Edinburgh: John Donald

Wiliam, E, 1988 *Home-made homes: dwellings of the rural poor in Wales.* Cardiff: National Museum of Wales

Wiliam, E, 1992 *Welsh long-houses: four centuries of farming at Cilewent.* Cardiff: University of Wales Press

Wiliam, E, 1994 *Welsh cruck barns: Stryd Lydan and Hendre-wen.* Cardiff: National Museum of Wales

Williams, D H, 1984 *The Welsh Cistercians,* Cyhoeddiadau Sistersiaidd. Tenby

Williams, D H, 1990 *The Atlas of Cistercian Lands in Wales.* Cardiff: University of Wales Press

Williams, G A, 1985 *When Was Wales? A History of the Welsh.* London: Black Raven Press

Williams, G, & Darke, I, 1997 A Rapid Survey of Mynydd Mallaen. Llandeilo: Cambria Archaeology

Williams, G & Muckle, I, 1992 An archaeological survey of the Groes Fawr Valley, Caron-is-clawdd, Cardiganshire. Unpubl, Dyfed Archaeological Trust, Carmarthen

Williams, S W, 1889 *The Cistercian Abbey of Strata Florida.* London

Williamson, T, 1988 Explaining regional landscapes: woodland and champion in southern and eastern England, *Landscape Hist,* 10, 5–14

Wilson, J E, McCormac, F G, & Hogg, A G, 1996 Small sample high-precision 14C dating: characterization of vials and counter optimisation, in G T Cook, D D Harkness, A B Mackenzie, B F Miller, & E M Scott (eds) *Liquid Scintillation Spectrometry 1994.* Arizona

Wilson, P, & Braley, S M, 1997 Development and age structure of Holocene coastal sand dunes at Horn Head, near Dunfanaghy, Co. Donegal, Ireland, *The Holocene,* 7, 187–97

Wilson, P, Orford, J D, Knight J, Braley, S M, & Wintle, A, 2001 Late-Holocene (post-4000 years BP) coastal dune development in Northumberland, northeast England, *The Holocene,* 11, 215–29

Winchester, A J L, 2000 *The harvest of the hills.* Edinburgh: Edinburgh University Press

Withers, 1995

Wolf, E R, 1966 *Peasants.* New Jersey: Prentice-Hall

Wrathmell, S, 1989 Peasant houses, farmsteads and villages in north-east England, in Aston *et al* (eds) 1989, 247–67

Yates, A M, 1999 The uplands of Blaenau Gwent: an archaeological survey, GGAT report 99/009. Swansea

Yates, M J, 2000 Medieval or Later Rural Settlement in Wales: an introduction to the present work programme funded by Cadw: Welsh Historic Monuments, in Atkinson *et al* (eds) 2000, 31–3

INDEX

Page numbers in italics refer to illustration or tables and/or their captions.